FATHER MAC

The Life and Times of
Ignatius D. McDermott,
Co-Founder of
Chicago's Famed Haymarket Center

Thomas F. Roeser

McDermott Foundation
CHICAGO

*"When you no longer burn with love,
others will die of the cold."*

— St. Vincent De Paul

FATHER MAC: The Life and Times of Ignatius D. McDermott, Co-Founder of Chicago's Famed Haymarket Center.

Published by the McDermott Foundation,
120 N. Sangamon St., Chicago, IL 60607.

First edition: 1   2   3   4   5

Library of Congress Cataloging-in-Publication Data:

Roeser, Thomas F.
    Father Mac the life and times of Ignatius D. McDermott, co-founder of Chicago's famed Haymarket Center / Thomas F. Roeser.—1st ed.
        p.   cm.
    Includes bibliographical references (p.) and index.
    ISBN 0-9719750-0-0 (hc.)
        1. McDermott, Ignatius D., 1909- 2. Church work with alcoholics.
    I. Title.

BX4705.M 163 R64 2002
282'.092—dc21
    [B]   2002070145

Copies of this book may be ordered directly from the publisher at the above address. Send check or money order for $29.95 per book plus $4.00 for first book and $1.50 for each additional book to cover shipping and handling.

Editorial production by Bookcrafters, Inc., Chicago.
Cover design by Bob Schemmel Associates, Glen Ellyn, IL.
Typesetting by Drawing Board Studios, Pittsburgh.

ACKNOWLEDGMENTS

There are many people to whom this author owes thanks. First comes my wife, Lillian Prescott Roeser, to whom I owe everything—spiritual and moral guidance especially. Our fond daughter-in-law, Candace Halby Roeser, a professional editor, did her job on this book with loving attention. Invaluable research and typing were done with great care and conscientiousness by Ceil Amato. Kenan Heise, veteran journalist and authority on Chicago history, performed great service and influenced me even when he lost some battles.

This book could not have been written without the assistance of the staff of Haymarket, beginning with its co-founder, Father Mac. We would meet regularly for five years, usually for dinner on Monday nights and for sessions and lunch on Saturdays. In between, there were scores of tape-recorded reminiscences with Father Mac, the people of Haymarket, and his numerous friends.

Finally, thanks is due to my parents, no longer with us, who instructed and nurtured me in Chicago lore of which Father Mac is so intrinsically a part.

Thomas F. Roeser
June, 2002
Chicago, Illinois

CONTENTS

FOREWORD

Little did we realize that the priest we had all to our-
selves, the one who used to kick the door open and burst into
the room for his weekly religion lesson, the tallest man we ever
saw, the one who prepared us for our First Holy Communion,
and taught us the Beatitudes, would become for us our sole
example of what a priest should be. He is one of the reasons
why we are still Catholic. We learned from his example, loy-
alty, charity, and love. Father Mac stuck around in our shad-
ows all our adult lives, consoling our sick, burying our dead,
and remembering the names of our children. Tonight, he is
with us still, and we give him thanks and praise.

—Suzanne O'Leary Fuentes
Address to the 35th Reunion
of the Class of 1945,
Our Lady of Peace

This is the story of a humanitarian with a South-Side-of-Chicago Irishman's zest for wit, story-telling, politics and sports, impatience with bureaucracy and slow evolving progress, tied together with a compassionate, yet realistic, respect for human nature—Monsignor Ignatius McDermott. Everyone, from the governor to the last wanderer who stumbles in from the street to the haven he founded, identifies him as "Father Mac."

His life, which spanned most of the 20th century, has witnessed major civic, religious and political upheavals, newspaper wars, strikes, riots and sports battles of a city that was never better described than by journalist G.W. Steevens in 1897: "Chicago, queen and guttersnipe of cities, cynosure and cesspool of the world"—adding—

Not if I had a hundred tongues, everyone shouting a different language in a different key, could I do justice to her
splendid chaos. The most beautiful and most squalid,
girdled with a twofold zone of parks and slums, where the

keen air from the lake and prairie is ever in the nostrils and
the stench of foul smoke is never out of the throat. Where in
the world can words be found for this miracle of paradox
and incongruity?

One cannot write of the many thousands of poor served by
Ignatius McDermott without referring to the popes, presidents,
governors, mayors, cardinal-archbishops, gangsters, downfield
blockers, .200 hitters, sportswriters and con artists who have influenced his era and, ultimately, his apostolate. That is why this
journalist's book takes many turns—delving into the stories of
down-and-outers, politicians, prelates, and alcoholic priests
among those he touched along the way.

Reading his story, one doesn't take long to distinguish the personal qualities of Ignatius McDermott. He has been unconcerned
about wealth or power, is hardworking and dedicated, and is re-
markably uncomplicated; he can be tough and blunt. By example
rather than words, he teaches individuals how to live: to forget self,
be totally dedicated to others, love God first and then humanity, always forgive, and to "carry the cross" each day of one's life.

Thus, without apology, this biography is a chronicle of con-
temporaneous urban and national history, representing human
beings at their deepest, where dwells the human condition that
Father Mac loves and understands.

CHAPTER 1

The Heart and Soul of the Man

*God never gives up on us until the undertaker picks up
our body. Why should we?*

—Ignatius McDermott

The boys and girls who attended Our Lady of Peace School in the
early 1940s remember their assistant pastor Ignatius McDermott
with respect and smiles. In interviews, they recalled him as a welcome savior from their dull studies—one who made catechism
classes come alive with energy, a warm and friendly athletic coach,
as well as a spiritual mentor.

But to one boy—now a taciturn, grizzled man who has fought
his way back from alcoholism—Father Mac meant far more: his
survival as a human being. Tom Grannan, the son of a chronically
depressed father and an overwrought, overworked mother,
thought he was going mad. The priest, without indicating that he
knew Grannan's problem, led him through the storm—not just as
a boy but through late adulthood, past two broken marriages and
decades of heavy drinking.

The story of their relationship is the best way this author can
find to introduce the extraordinary human being whom tens of
thousands of Chicagoans have come to know as "Father Mac" or
more formally, on occasion, as Monsignor McDermott.

"Father Mac came to Our Lady of Peace when I was in the
seventh grade," said Grannan. Born in 1929, Grannan was one of
six children. "My father had two nervous breakdowns. My mother
raised us and worked, washing pots and pans at Marshall Field's.
And I was a very insecure kid," he said. "Father Mac spotted it

1

right away. He knew damn well I was having problems. I mean, Christ, it was like having an epileptic fit. In those days there was no such thing as going to a psychiatrist or anything, and he took me under his wing. He always looked out for me. He always told me I was somebody. He just encouraged me. I mean, he said, 'Hey, you're Tom Grannan. You're somebody. You're not just anybody walking around.' He just encouraged me through life. To him it's no big deal. But to me it is. It is pretty big, very big to me."

Every so often Father Mac would call Grannan on the phone and ask if he wanted to accompany him on his rounds. There were hospital visits, football games, and dinners.

"He encouraged me—you know what I mean? I never thought I was much of anything. The man was golden. To me he was just a great guy. He helped me so much through life. You know what it is like for a kid in seventh grade to have them [*sic*] problems? I went to a few Notre Dame games with him. I went all through life with him.

"If he wasn't at this parish I wouldn't have been able to handle it. The guy was a pal to all—not just eighth graders. From first grade on, when he walked into that playground they all came. They'd all say, 'Father Mac!' and they'd all rush to him. Like I said, he was a golden eagle—that's the best way I could describe him."

In those days, the nuns felt free to administer corporal punishment—smacking bad boys around, whacking their outstretched hands with a ruler. But, Grannan said, the good sisters didn't dare strike when Father Mac was around.

"The nuns would [laughing] belt me when I was wrong. He'd help me then. He'd stop them. Then he'd say: 'Forget about it,' and they would."

Not just compassionate, Father Mac had a tough side to him. "I can remember," Grannan said, "in eighth grade that we were playing basketball over at St. Francis de Sales. The boys' fathers in the upper stands, they were throwing stuff down on us and this and that."

Father Mac strode out to the center of the basketball floor and addressed the unruly male adults. "He got out there and said," Grannan said, "'Listen, if any of you guys want to come down here, I'll take my collar off and I'll walk outside with you!'" They turned deadly quiet.

Grannan continued: "That's the type of guy he was. He was tough. He was a gentle guy, a good person, but he had a tough side, too. He didn't take no shit from nobody—oops, I shouldn't have swore like that—but he didn't."

After he left Our Lady of Peace, Father Mac stayed in touch with Tom Grannan. There was a lot of pastoral work to do for the boy. Tom didn't like studies and got into trouble at Our Lady of Peace. Father Mac placed Grannan in St. Felicita's at 84th and Blackstone.

"I was no prize student. He got me in there, but I didn't last long; I quit in the first year."

He became an apprentice plumber ("my family is plumbers") but his truancy was discovered and officials ordered him sent to South Shore public high school. There, again, he got into trouble. School authorities were threatening to send him to Montifiore, a disciplinary school for truants a step away from real trouble.

"I stopped off and I saw Father Mac," Grannan remembered, "and said, 'They're going to ship me to Montifiore!' I was crying and I was in bad shape. He said, 'Don't worry about it, Tom. You're not going to Montifiore.' That's what I mean—the toughness. I said, 'Yeah, they've got me scheduled. I got to go Monday morning!' He said, 'Listen, you're not going to Montifiore.' He called up South Shore right then and there. He said, 'Listen, Tom's not a bad kid. He doesn't belong in Montifiore.' He said, 'You let him back in South Shore.' He told them. He was mad about it, too. You see, the South Shore guy in charge of discipline was from our parish. So I got back in the school."

An unruly lad, he needed to know what would happen if he didn't shape up. One night Father Mac called him up on the telephone and asked the 16-year-old boy to accompany him on his rounds. It so happened he was going to visit inmates in Chicago-area prisons and hear their confessions. With the priest driving and talking to the teenager, they visited prisons.

"We left early in the morning," recalled Grannan. "It was dark. And we got home and it was dark. He took me with him because he knew I was screwed up. We hit about five prisons that day. He was visiting guys. We'd stop here and there. He brought them cigarettes. He left some dough for them in the commissary. We went to the county jail [Cook County], Stateville [the state prison near Joliet, Illinois], St. Charles [a reformatory for young men in suburban Kane County], and two others."

Was the purpose of the trip to show the teen what could happen unless he got his head together? Grannan thinks it was. But there was no real lecture; just the pleasure of helping Father Mac console the men behind bars.

Tom Grannan didn't graduate from high school. He went in the Army during the Korean War. He came out and borrowed his plumber uncle's "clout" to get into plumbing. The help meant this: all you were asked to do was show your hands. "That was the test. 'Let me look at your hands,' to see if they were rough." Grannan's were. He didn't like plumbing, though, so he got into the city water department where he stayed for 40 years. There were years of serious drinking. Father Mac would ask young Grannan to go with him to Skid Row, to impart an object lesson.

"Yeah," says Grannan, "it was Skid Row. All those guys were drinking real bad. Father Mac would be out there. We'd pull up there. You know how the police would pull up—they wouldn't take the guy out. We would. One guy was in bad shape. I remember Father Mac would go. A couple of times I helped them out of the wagon, and I would carry the guy, and the guy was loaded."

All this time he stayed in touch with Father Mac. Every so often, Grannan would go out to dinner with Father Mac, and then the priest would visit patients in hospitals. "We'd stop at a hospital maybe one o'clock in the morning. He'd say, 'I gotta go in here.' And he'd go in, just walk in. Oh yeah, Father Mac was tough. They all knew him anyway."

Grannan was in and out of Alcoholics Anonymous; Father Mac would help the struggling man ceaselessly. "He got me into the CATC [the Chicago Alcoholic Treatment Center]. I ended up at Lutheran General, this last time, 31 years ago. Oh yeah, Father Mac pulled me out of that. While he was helping me, I could see he was helping others. I seen a lot of guys when I walked in there. Father Mac was taking care of them. Most people wouldn't go near them. But this guy, Father Mac, he'd get in there and, man, I'm trying to put it across the right way, truthfully."

The priest's disinterest in class distinctions was impressive. "At Our Lady of Peace there was 'this kid's dad's a lawyer, this one's a doctor,' Grannan said. "He had nothing to do with that. He spoke all class of people's language. The man was amazing, do you understand? He didn't care what the hell you were. To him you were all equal."

Tom Grannan always refused any offer to be an altar boy. "I'd just screw it up," he said. But his biggest thrill, deepest honor, happened on the 50th anniversary of Ignatius McDermott's ordination—in 1986. The 77-year-old celebrant asked his spiritual son, 57-year-old Tom Grannan, to bring the unconsecrated hosts up to the altar for that Mass.

"That was the best day of my life," Grannan continued. "I tell you he got me through the storms in life, believe me. I'm not apologizing for myself by all means. I'm not an educated person. I educated myself through reading papers. I read every paper in the city of Chicago—the *Daily News*, the *Herald American*, the *Tribune, Sun-Times*—I read 'em all. Every day I read 'em all. But he got me through the storm. I'm only trying to explain it the best I can to you. Yeah, he always perked me up. He always said, 'You're somebody, Tom.' You know what I mean?"

All too soon, Father McDermott's time was up at Our Lady of Peace (1941–46). "The basketball court was taken down, and the rectory was no longer the haven for athletic gear and equipment," says former student Donald Kruse, sadly.

"The place was never quite the same after he went," he says.

*   *   *

The activity by which the man thousands call "Father Mac" would become best known was his after-hours, unannounced, unauthorized ministry to the streets of Skid Row, to the neighborhood of men, drunken, shuffling, shambling alcoholics and addicts.

By night he walked a neighborhood which was brilliantly lighted by the city, which had installed arc lights on the lampposts as if to cure alcoholism with brilliant illumination. But he did more than merely walk the streets. Attired in his priest's garb, he would go into their habitat—he can still recall the names of bars and flophouses—into saloons with names like Sid's Junction, the House of Rothschild, the Streamliner, the Union Bar, the Workingman's Palace, Libby's Famous Ten, the Elite, the Comfort, the System, and hotels with names like the Grange, the McCoy, the Major, the Legion, the Starr, the Cumberland, the Peerless, St. Ann, the Mohawk, the New Madison, the Desplaines, and the New Jackson (the latter name prompted Monsignor McDermott to muse, "If this dump is the New Jackson, what must the old Jackson have looked like?").

This was a territory that extended from Jefferson Street on the east to Morgan on the west and in depth from Madison to

Monroe. Accompanying him, on occasion, were Father Norkett, a classmate, and Abraham Lincoln Marovitz, then a state senator. "I used to go down to West Madison Street with him," said Marovitz. "I don't know of any individual who did more than he did, reaching out as he did."

Men were drinking wine. A bottle of Petri cost 35¢. The brands were Mad Dog, 50-50, and Irish Rose. The men worked at the "slave market," as day laborers. On Election Day, they sold their votes to precinct captains for $5 a vote—and often voted more than once.

There was no moralizing with Ignatius McDermott, no evangelizing. But the straight and narrow was definitely cited along with a gentle nudge to God. Under his aegis, he prodded cooperation between Catholic Charities and the city's Department of Housing to house some 50 to 60 men at the Starr Hotel, which was safe and clean. He would cruise the neighborhood at night whenever he could, convincing those who might otherwise die of the cold on the streets in winter to accept housing and sandwiches. A familiar sound in his ears late at night was the squawk of the police cars' sirens—famed as "the sound of the injured puppy"—as officers hauled in drunks, stopped vagrants from fighting, and responded to Father McDermott's frantic calls to aid victims of jack-rolling.

He made friends with those who had no friends, fearing that when they lay down to sleep in an alley they would either be killed outright or frozen in the winter. As author Bill Gleason wrote:

> In the warmth of late spring, the heat of the summer, and the glow of early autumn, some Skid Row characters deceive themselves into believing that they do have it made and they are putting one over on the squares who work for a living.
>
> When the weather is good, a place to sleep is a minor problem. The knowledgeable West Madison Street citizen can lay his alcoholic head on a pile of newspapers under Wacker Drive or on a jumble of lumber near a construction project or in a burned out house that awaits the bulldozer. But when the north wind comes rampaging into Chicago, the men of Skid Row know they're in trouble if they don't have a job or enough cash squirreled up to pay for a flop. The wind whistles a warning that a man may not survive unless he can get himself checked into a hospital or into

County Jail. Most street-smart ones would take pains to find a flop. Not all. Some, warmed by cheap wine, would drift to sleep in the winter.

It was the man all called Father Mac who frequently was called to identify their frozen bodies on slabs at the county morgue.

* * *

As Haymarket entered the year 2000, the dream of Ignatius McDermott reached full flower. Haymarket consisted of downtown Chicago's Haymarket Center, which included the reconstructed and redesigned six-floor building at 932 West Washington and the two structures adjoining it at 120 North Sangamon. In its entirety, the name "Haymarket" included, in addition to the Center:

- McDermott Annex, 933 West Washington, Chicago
- Haymarket/Maryville, 810 West Montrose Avenue, Chicago
- Grand Boulevard, 4910 South Martin Luther King Drive, Chicago
- O'Hare Outreach, Terminal 2, O'Hare International Airport, Chicago
- Haymarket West, 1900 West Algonquin Road, Schaumburg, Illinois.

Thirty programs in the six locations provide a full continuum of care for chemically dependent people, including detoxification, treatment, education, and case management. At the decade's end, Haymarket was serving more than 13,000 individuals yearly. The client population breakdown continued to be about 70 percent African-American; 20 percent Caucasian; and seven percent Latino. About 83 percent of those served had annual incomes of less than $7,400; 78 percent were unemployed; 90 percent received public assistance; and 68 percent had less education than a high school diploma.

Specialized treatment was extended to pregnant and postpartum women, drug-impacted children, homeless men and women, individuals with HIV/AIDS, mentally ill substance abusers, non-violent criminal justice offenders, and the elderly. Two programs have received national recognition from the U.S. Center for Substance Abuse Treatment.

Haymarket also became the largest addiction and substance abuse treatment facility for women in Illinois. Its services include a Maternal Addiction Center (MAC Unit), the first residential treatment program for chemically dependent women in Illinois, along with outpatient treatment, a recovery home, and three residential treatment programs for postpartum women who delivered drug-affected babies.

It provides a large range of services that include cooperation with 12-step groups, case-management services, individual counseling, safety planning and shelter for victims of domestic abuse and violence, prenatal education, health education, parenting classes, and pre- and post-test HIV counseling. The James M. West Clinic supplies on-site medical/psychiatric service for clients and their children involved with Haymarket Center.

Since opening its doors in 1975, Haymarket Center has saved Cook County millions of dollars through the provision of substance abuse treatment services to adult men and women. Any of these may have been criminally involved: mentally ill substance abusers; pregnant women; and other chemically addicted residents of Chicago and surrounding areas. Reducing the levels of criminal activity (which translates into a savings in criminal justice resources), relieving the economic burden generated by the after-effects of cocaine-impacted babies, and lowering any client engagement in illegal earnings are just some of the ways in which Haymarket continues to save money for taxpayers. Those suffering from substance abuse and its consequences receive services that they most likely would not have financial access to in the private sector.

Haymarket Center is the largest community-based substance abuse treatment provider in Cook County and the third largest in the state. It has provided substance abuse treatment services for chemically dependent Cook County residents for over 25 years.

As an innovator of substance abuse treatment in Illinois, Haymarket Center has initiated many of the services that are now commonplace in Chicago. Haymarket began the first social setting detoxification program and the first public residential treatment program for pregnant women at any time during pregnancy. It has been at the forefront of providing services for court-mandated drug treatment as a result of its involvement with three federally funded drug courts in Cook County.

Since 1990, its Maternal Addiction Center (the first in the Midwest) has helped pregnant addicted women receive treatment and, subsequently, deliver over 600 drug-free babies. These births represent potential savings of approximately $12 million to $24 million over a ten-year period, including in-hospital and aftercare costs to the county. Calculations are based on a 1997 average hospital cost for addicted babies of $20,000 to $40,000 to care for just one baby born to a drug-dependent mother (Cook County Hospital survey). Drug-impacted babies reported born in Cook County in 1999 totaled 1,331, the majority of whom would receive services via Cook County Hospital. Hospital care for all of these babies exceeds $26,620,000 (based upon previous calculations). Furthermore, long-term health costs for drug-affected babies can reach as high as $500,000 per infant (based upon research conducted by Centers for Substance Abuse Treatment, funded by Women and Children's Center of Northern Illinois Council on Alcoholism and Substance Abuse). Substance abuse treatment for women in the early stages of pregnancy can completely eliminate these costs.

* * *

As the '90s ended, Chicago's first baby of its last year was born to a crack cocaine-addicted woman. She had turned to treatment and entered the detox program at Haymarket Center in November 1999. At 12:01 a.m. on New Year's Day, Annita Butler delivered another new life: a baby daughter, weighing 7 pounds, 10 ounces, at Mount Sinai Hospital Medical Center.

"She made it here healthy," Ms. Butler told the press about her daughter, Jade. "The nurses were cheering Jade on. Haymarket has been a good experience. It allowed me to have a clean baby and for that I'm most grateful."

In 1993, Haymarket Center established the only rehabilitative confinement program (RCP) of its kind (in terms of continuous length of stay) in the country. RCP is an alternative to incarceration for both males and females who have been arrested and adjudicated for non-violent drug-related offenses. RCP was designed through the combined efforts of the Circuit Court of Cook County, the Cook County Sheriff's Department, the Illinois Secretary of State's office, and Haymarket Center.

The RCP has served over 2,700 offenders and has demonstrated significant cost savings by providing treatment in a therapeutic, community-based program rather than incarceration. Its success rate is impressive: 99 percent of the participants complete the confinement mandate; 86 percent follow through with the 6-to-12-month aftercare requirement; and 68 percent complete the aftercare component.

Between January 1, 1999 and April 17, 2000, Haymarket Center provided substance abuse treatment to 1,255 criminally-involved men and women in Cook County. The total approximate cost of services was $3.1 million. Approximately 388 of these clients were without a funding source. They represented an annualized expense of approximately $975,000, including detoxification, residential and outpatient services, as well as auxiliary services such as transportation, primary care, life skills training, and job readiness.

Perhaps the most significant need for substance abuse treatment for non-violent offenders is the impact treatment can have upon society. Many studies, including the Services Research Outcomes Study (SROS), the National Treatment Improvement Evaluation Study (NTIES), the California Drug and Alcohol Treatment Assessment (CALDATA), and the Drug Abuse Treatment Outcomes Study (DATOS), have demonstrated that treatment contributes to significant declines in criminal arrests and drug selling, along with improved health status. Both NTIES and DATOS reported dramatic improvement in employment status for clients engaged in long-term residential treatment. The CALDATA study also reported a 58 percent reduction in costs to taxpayers.

The cost savings benefits of treatment are real and can be substantial. A California study (Gerstein et al, 1994) indicated a cost savings of over $245 million in a single year in the early 1990s. Rajkumar and French (1996) found that the costs of crime dropped 40 percent per patient in the year following treatment. The drop in crime represented a savings that exceeded the cost of treatment. French and Zarkin (1992) found that a 10 percent increase in time spent in residential treatment programs increased legal earnings of the recovering addict by 2.4 percent and decreased illegal earnings 4.1 percent.

According to *Alcoholism and Drug Abuse Weekly*, states are starting to follow the research and establish policies and laws to provide treatment for non-violent drug possession offenders in lieu of incarceration. The objective is to reduce recidivism and costs by treating the substance abuse rather than holding the offender in jail—only to release him or her to continue the negative behavior. The California Campaign for New Drug Policies is attempting to pass an initiative that would provide drug treatment instead of incarceration for 35,000 to 40,000 chemically addicted Californians each year. The Legislative Analyst's Office of California has calculated a potential savings to the state of $100 million to $150 million annually. The cost savings are based on eliminating the cost of incarcerating the offender and subsequent savings in state operating costs and prison construction expenses.

A similar initiative was passed in Arizona in 1996. Non-violent first- and second-time drug offenders were provided treatment in lieu of incarceration. The Arizona Supreme Court published a report, in 1999, indicating that fewer positive drug tests were recorded among offenders, and the state has realized a cost savings of $2.5 million in a single year.

*   *   *

While the savings are significant to society, treatment still costs money. Father Mac's work often required incurring debts.

As Haymarket's facilities grew, a debt incurred in 1955 was paid in full 40 years later by a man who claimed he was saved by Monsignor McDermott and wanted to extend his gratitude in the form of service to society. In August 1955, William J. Dooner was a 23-year-old alcoholic, living on Skid Row. One night he was severely beaten by those who tried to roll him.

"It had been raining," *Chicago Sun-Times* columnist Steve Neal wrote. "He had been on another drinking binge. He was cut above one eye and an ear was also cut and badly infected. His shirt was covered with dried blood from a street fight. 'I was very discouraged and very much alone,' said Dooner.

"As Dooner left the old Pixley & Ehlers restaurant on the corner of LaSalle and Van Buren, he was down and out. He had been drinking rubbing alcohol and mixing it with Pepsi-Cola. He had been living in a 50¢-a-night flophouse and had thought more than once about jumping to the street from the ledge of his sixth floor window. He had nothing to live for. Or so he thought. But a brief encounter changed his life.

"As Dooner headed back toward his flophouse, he met a Roman Catholic priest. Dooner says, 'He came out of nowhere. He had the most wonderful smile I had ever seen. You didn't see that many smiles on Skid Row in those days. In those days people would kill you for a quarter to buy a drink. Father Mac's gentleness and his smile made me feel that I was still a human being.'"

Dooner started drinking at the age of nine and was an alcoholic by 12. Growing up in East Harlem, he worked in taverns and ran numbers for bookies, had been arrested eight times in New York and was shot at while fleeing the police. Wishing to make a fresh start in Chicago, he fell prey to taverns, drinks, fighting, and flophouses. But the meeting with the priest he identifies as "Father Mac" saved Dooner's life. After that fateful meeting, Dooner found treatment for his alcoholism, got a job as a laborer, met and married Eleanor Yordy of suburban Morton Grove, Illinois, and started his climb upward to sobriety and success.

As he worked on his recovery, Dooner discovered that he had a flair for business and entrepreneurial talent. He learned the outdoor-advertising business while working for several companies. He learned quickly and opened his own firm. Eventually, he built a small empire of 20 billboard firms. His energies extended from making money to social activism. He made many trips to Ireland and attempted to bring the two Irish warring camps together. In the United States, he founded a foundation to help minority businesses, for which he was named to presidential advisory councils by three presidents—Lyndon Johnson, Gerald Ford, and Jimmy Carter. All the while, Bill Dooner was trying to find the priest who helped him that night in 1955. When he located Monsignor McDermott he gave generous, extensive financial assistance to Haymarket, including a bronze bust of his priest-patron.

Commenting on Bill Dooner, Monsignor McDermott says, "Bill Dooner was rescued by cooperation with the mercy of Almighty God."

He pointed out that Dooner not only went from Skid Row's West Madison Street to New York City's Madison Avenue, mecca for advertising, but he traveled a far greater distance in personal rehabilitation thanks to "great faith and the support of a devoted family."

CHAPTER 2

Born in 1909 into an Age of Innocence

I'm not sure they were better men then—but they sure were different. If you performed an autopsy on 'em, you might find out.

—Ignatius McDermott

Nineteen hundred nine, the year Ignatius Daniel McDermott came into this world, seemed the dawn for a fresh era of innocence. For the United States, the 19th century was an aeon away. Memories of the last century's populists and members of old style blather mongers Bryan, McKinley, Hanna and Debs were fading. Now the new bright names were La Follette, Pinchott, Norris, and Hiram Johnson.

All these groveled before the most lustrous one, Theodore Roosevelt. A self-publicized war hero, populist but incurably undemocratic, ego-driven, on March 4th he left the presidential stage after eight years. But his voice resounded. He had been The Progressive Age, swallowing everything at a gulp: trust-busting, judicial recall, woman suffrage, direct primaries, initiative and referendum, the short ballot, Prohibition and public ownership, while touting inheritance taxes and income taxes on "the malefactors of great wealth."

Teddy had been a glorious, garrulous, show-horse president from 1901 to 1909. Progressivism radiated from this ingratiatingly phony, gaudy, impulsive (but not radical) president. Young Lieutenant Douglas MacArthur, TR's aide, asked him to what factor he attributed his extraordinary popularity with the voters. He replied: "To put into words what is in their hearts and minds but not their mouths." More aptly, putting into their heads ideas that wouldn't get there except for Teddy. Still, no other politician did it better. His enemies shouted that this consummate showman didn't believe in democracy for a minute. He believed in government. When he tackled the trusts, he was aiming at one big super-trust with TR at the head. He hated all pretense except his own.

TR was the first to link widely publicized, flamboyant policy steps to social betterment. *Look at them*: the bold antitrust prosecution of Northern Securities...creation out of whole cloth of the new joint Department of Commerce and Labor...passage of the *Pure Food and Drug Act* and *Meat Inspection Act* by the Feds (although not a scintilla of evidence showed that such governmental power had been imagined by the Constitution's framers). The voters loved it.

Above all, he was an entertainer. When he sent his Attorney General, Charles Bonaparte, a distant relative of Napoleon (this tickled TR), to humble giant corporations, he impressed what H.L. Mencken called the "booboisie." TR took over management of the inland waterways...intervened in a labor dispute, ending the anthracite coal strike and tweaking the bulbous nose of old plutocrat J.P. Morgan...fomented a bogus civil war against Colombia...set up a shadow Panamanian government and seized control of the Panama Canal's construction...threatened plutocracy in the federal courts...crusaded for conservation, proclaiming the view that private owners often exploited the land whereas government would protect it. An unabashed imperialist who thundered, "We are a conquering race!" he was also the progenitor of intrusive government, creating the Justice Department's Bureau of Investigation (later to become the FBI), with executive fiat in opposition to Congress, which had denied it appropriations.

And his great talents as showman had caused the electorate to kneel at his feet. The Rooseveltian corollary to the Monroe Doctrine (if necessary, the U.S. will intervene by force to keep the peace in this hemisphere)...his settling a dispute with Venezuela...his barging into a negotiation with the Dominican Republic...his "Open Door" policy in China...his mediation of a dispute between Russia and Japan, which won him the Nobel Peace Prize...a laudable sense of racial inclusion, novel for the times. He became the first president to widely publicize his dining at the White House with an African-American, Booker T. Washington (Grover Cleveland had done so earlier with dinner guest

Frederick Douglass)...his dispatch of the Great White Fleet of naval ships around the world to show U.S. power.

The irascible Teddy is very pertinent today with respect to our current troubles with terrorism. In his first message to Congress following the murder of President McKinley by terrorist Leon Czolgosz, the new president declared: "The wind is sowed by the men who preach such doctrines, and they cannot escape their responsibility for the whirlwind that is reaped...

"They and those like them should be kept out of the country, and if found here they should be promptly deported to the country whence they came, and far-reaching provision should be made for the punishment of those who stay." These words are keenly relevant for an America that is still responding to the attacks on 9/11/01.

People wondered why he did not run again in 1908, which would have him serving longer than any other president. But earlier, he had made one slip of the tongue which he regretted. In a grandiose gesture of mock humility, he said he would respect the two-term limit. No matter that he had come to power after McKinley's assassination and, technically, finished that term, to be elected only once to the presidency. Yes, he had blurted it. A mistake said in haste but he was stuck with it. And by 1909, on March 4th, he had to go. This Caesar had reluctantly turned things over to his hand-picked successor, William Howard Taft—who had not been elected to anything before—hoping that Taft would play the weak surrogate and beg TR's assistance. But Taft in 1908 polled slightly more votes than TR had in 1904. Taft determined—rather *his wife had determined*—he would be his own man. TR smoldered.

By inauguration day, Taft inherited a presidency that had grown immeasurably in prestige and power during the prior eight years. And he had gained the bitter enmity of his mentor. It is an anomaly that one of the best-tempered, sweetest-dispositioned presidents in U.S. history, Big Bill Taft, standing five feet 10-1/2 inches, weighing more than 300 pounds, did his best, was a successful president, was defeated because of his ex-mentor's incurable jealousy, and got no credit for his presidential deeds (an historic misappraisal that lasts even now). Indeed, by the progressive yardstick (although Taft was an instinctive conservative) he scored more accomplishments than Roosevelt. Taft brought more antitrust suits in his one term than Roosevelt had in nearly two. Telephone, telegraph, and oceanic cable companies became regulated by the Interstate Commerce Commission; a "Postal Savings" system put the post office into the banking business; "Parcel Post" set up the government in competition with private railroads. Teddy was envious. He steamed.

Compared to Roosevelt's Bismarckian blood-and-iron image, Taft's judicial persona made him appear stuffy, indecisive, weak. He didn't have Teddy's magnetism, love of pomp and towering ego. He wept when he heard the cruel jokes that TR made about him. But he went into battle with one man Teddy would never have dared to cross, powerful Illinois conservative Republican House Speaker Joseph (Uncle Joe) Cannon, to win lower tariffs, a cherished progressive goal. Yet Taft was doomed, to reelection and history: Teddy missed the limelight, wanted to come back and ultimately did, in a struggle where Chicago played a stirring role.

By 1909, that progressive-collectivism began to reach even into stand-pat Republican-run machines controlling state, municipal, and local governments. Progressives began to chalk up victories: the thrust to restructure state governments to make them more responsive, to increase the power of the voters, to begin to control big business, to turn to primaries to nominate party candidates, to fight for initiatives and referenda, to propose building codes.

* * *

The progressive mood of exultant innocence was thriving in Chicago, too. Three earlier mayors, traditional Democrats Carter Harrison I and II plus one vibrant Progressive, Edward F. Dunne (later a governor), had promised municipal ownership of its transit system; now even the German conservative, Republican Fred Busse, a coal company owner, warmed to the idea. Business was learning that cooperation with government was not only popular but lucrative. A new municipal charter to centralize government passed on a referendum of voters. But first, the prospect of a more beautiful city beckoned.

* * *

The year 1909 in Chicago was extolled by British evangelist Gipsy Smith as wallowing "in a luxuriousness never enjoyed by

Ignatius McDermott, about age four, rides a pony used by his father to pull the family's dairy wagon. *Circa* 1913.

The McDermott family, 1923. Ignatius, the youngest of eight, is in the center. At his left is Michael McDermott, father; at his right, Ellen Bradley McDermott, mother. Other family members (standing, left to right): Michael, Jr.; John; James; Francis; and Aloysius. Flanking her father is Martha (later Sister Mary Jeanette, RSM), and sitting to her mother's left is Kathleen (later Mrs. Joseph Stack). The photo was taken just before Martha left for the convent.

You think traffic's bad now? This is Randolph and Dearborn, 1909, the year Father Mac was born.
  –Chicago Historical Society

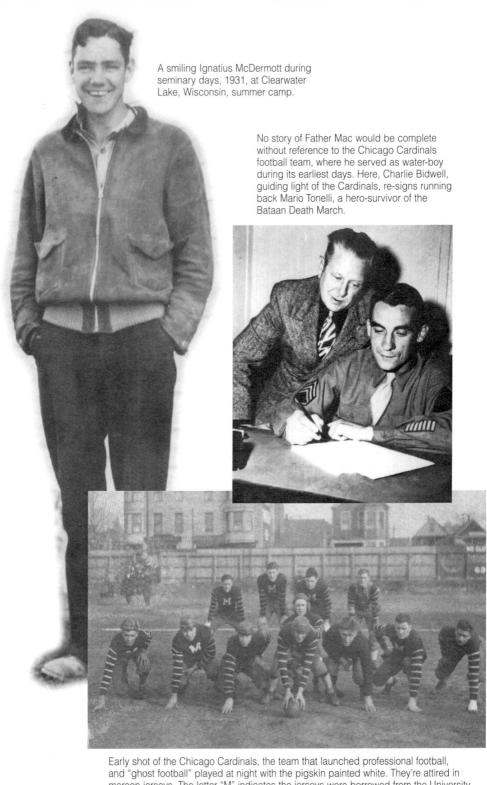

A smiling Ignatius McDermott during seminary days, 1931, at Clearwater Lake, Wisconsin, summer camp.

No story of Father Mac would be complete without reference to the Chicago Cardinals football team, where he served as water-boy during its earliest days. Here, Charlie Bidwell, guiding light of the Cardinals, re-signs running back Mario Tonelli, a hero-survivor of the Bataan Death March.

Early shot of the Chicago Cardinals, the team that launched professional football, and "ghost football" played at night with the pigskin painted white. They're attired in maroon jerseys. The letter "M" indicates the jerseys were borrowed from the University of Chicago Maroons. This scrimmage was at 61st and Racine at Normal Park.
—Chicago Cardinals photos from *When Football Was Football* by Joe Ziemba

A portrait of young priest Ignatius McDermott. He made it through Mundelein seminary despite the efforts of the rector to "tag him out at home plate." But you have to read the story to get the flavor.

Father McDermott on ordination day in 1936. Following custom among the newly ordained, he imparts a blessing to a classmate.

Chicago's former mayor Big Bill Thompson, left, with publisher William Randolph Hearst, growled to Father Mac, "Listen, I worked a full day before you saw me at noon."
–Chicago Historical Society

A variety of cardinals led Chicago's archdiocese

George Cardinal Mundelein. The "Dutch Master" had what Father Mac calls moxie, was a builder, yet concerned with spiritual well-being.

Samuel Cardinal Stritch. A cigarette chain-smoker in private, he made Father Mac a Monsignor, was less interested in details of administration than spirituality, but distrusted modern church architecture.

Albert Cardinal Meyer. Compassionate, soft-spoken, and imbued with Vatican II. He told Father Mac he had an "awful headache." It was a brain tumor that took his life.

Photos of Cardinal George and Bishop O'Connor, Catholic New World Newspaper; other Cardinals and Rt. Revs. Cooke and Molloy, Archdiocese of Chicago's Joseph Cardinal Bernardin Archives and Records Center.

Monsignor Vincent Cooke, head of Catholic Charities, played Santa Claus with a cigar. Then he doffed the beard lest it catch fire from the stogie. The kids were bewildered by this strange Santa.

Father John McLoraine, known as "Johnny Mac," was a colorful general as army chaplain and a proven entrepreneur. World War II halted in Italy when he offered Christmas Mass for Allies and Germans alike.

Three workers in the vineyard. Left to right: Timothy J. Lyne, retired auxiliary bishop of Chicago; John P. Smyth, Director of Maryville; and Haymarket chairman, Father Mac.

during Father Mac's service as priest

John Cardinal Cody. A far better leader than assumed, he helped priests afflicted with addictions, suffered greatly from criticism, had a hard time expressing deepest feelings.

Joseph Cardinal Bernardin. "You didn't have to be Aristotle to figure out you were being sacked," said Father Mac, who Bernardin removed from Charities' duties but couldn't touch Haymarket (though he wanted to).

Francis Cardinal George. A real sense of understanding for Haymarket's worth and the value of its legendary co-founder underscored this prelate's ascension.

Bishop William A. O'Connor, Catholic Charities president and TV commentator Len O'Connor's brother, was Father Mac's first boss. Mundelein ordered the bishop to New York aboard the Twentieth Century, then recalled him when his bags were still in that eastern city.

Monsignor Patrick J. Molloy. "Hey, punk!" he called Father Mac in friendly fashion. Exiled to Panama for burying Dion O'Banion with full Church honors, he later returned to Chicago in colorful style.

Classmates of Father Mac. Since he spanned two Mundelein graduating classes, he got an "extra helping" of friends.

James J. McDermott. Father Mac's oldest brother, was alderman, judge, and very nearly helped dump Richard J. Daley in his ascension to the Chicago mayoralty.

Judge John J. Sullivan, a master strategist of politics, was James McDermott's mentor. Some say he wrote the book that laid out Democratic party victories. He's not sufficiently recognized in most Chicago histories.

Father Mac and his sister, Sister Mary Jeanette, RSM (standing beside him), along with Sister Norbert Cusick and Archer Tongue of the International Council on Alcohol and Addictions.

Haymarket Center under
construction and in finished
form. It was an old piano
factory, then a casket factory.
Now it's a renowned center
of social service.

Father Mac and some residents of
Wholly Innocence Day Care Center.

John J. (Jack) Whalen, Haymarket vice
chairman, was indispensable to the founding of the Center and its current operation.
He makes the rounds of "his building"
weekly, making a list and checking it twice.

Jim Mchugh, with Father Mac. From truck driver to movie
extra with Jimmy Stewart, and now all-around helper,
Mchugh doubles as chapel sacristan. His story of Father
backing up a cortege at a funeral Mass is classic.

The two co-founders of Haymarket, Dr. James West and Monsignor Ignatius McDermott, Haymarket chairman.

Luther Phillips was the first employee of Haymarket and is today Director of Facility Service. He's the second best storyteller at Haymarket.

A gathering of leaders of Haymarket. Left to right: John J. (Jack) Whalen, board vice chairman; Mrs. Betty Whalen; Raymond Soucek, president and CEO; Anthony Cole, vice president; chairman Father Mac.

Major lineup of Haymarket all-stars: Seated: Father Mac, board chairman; Dr James West, co-founder and board member; standing: Anthony Cole, vice president; Raymond Soucek, president and CEO; John J. (Jack) Whalen, board vice chairman; John Butler, board member and secretary-treasurer.

anyone since the Roman Empire." But debauchery disturbed the preacher, who led a group of 5,000 into the notorious Levee, the red light district of the First Ward. Someone had warned the pleasure-goers of the visit and the area was quiet when the moral rescuers arrived. So they knelt and prayed at the corner of 21st and Dearborn. Shortly after they left, the Levee returned to life: a resurrection of sorts but not the kind the faithful were touting. But evidence that the Levee was not just simple rapscallion fun came with the arrest of Maurice Van Bever, a notorious "white slaver" who recruited women for Levee brothels, often by force. The police apprehended him outside the Chamber of Commerce building in the Loop.

Progressivism was also coming to Illinois labor, although by today's reckoning it doesn't look like much. In 1909, Agnes Nestor, the first woman elected president of an international union, won passage of the 10-hour work day law in the Illinois General Assembly...Chicago streets were renumbered that year with a new grid system, assigning 800 numbers to the mile, based on a zero axis point at State and Madison...47 men died when a fire broke out in a wood-lined shaft of a water crib under construction at Lake Michigan and 71st Street...nine men were convicted of spitting in public and each was fined $1 plus $1 in court costs, as the acting Chicago police chief ordered his men to go after every spitter...a new Cook County tax rate certified that a marriage license would cost $1.50, a city dog license $2. The daily fee for merry-go-rounds was $2 a day; yearly tax on a bowling alley was $5.

Baseball and sports were big in Chicago, too. Early in 1900, Charles A. Comiskey, an Irishman who owned a minor league franchise in St. Paul, brought his team to Chicago to join the newly formed American League. Initially called the White Stockings, Comiskey shortened the name to the White Sox in 1902. They played at the old Chicago Cricket Club grounds at 39th and Wentworth. The team won the league championship in its first year. In 1903 the American and National Leagues agreed that they would meet in a playoff at the end of the year to be called a "World Series." In 1906, the Sox were called the "hitless wonders" for having scored only six home runs the entire year. Nevertheless, that year they won the pennant with a record of 93-58, despite a team batting average of .230 and a slugging average of .286, both being the lowest in the league. That year the Sox met the Chicago Cubs in the World Series. The Cubs were the heavy favorite, having won 116 games and losing only 36 with the famous infield of Joe Tinker, Johnny Evers and Frank Chance.

Since then the White Sox have had their ups and downs, but on July 31, 1909, the Sox won a future, super fan with the birth of Ignatius McDermott. In that year, however, fate did not smile. The Sox lost both the pennant and—almost worse—the City Series with the Cubs. They lost, said Comiskey, known as the Old Roman, "because the team didn't fight as hard as it should have fought." Failing to lure the legendary Fielder Jones out of retirement, Comiskey enticed 41-year-old Hugh Duffy, a former National League batting champion who had been only a mildly successful manager of the Philadelphia Phillies, to pilot the Sox in 1910. To offset the Cubs, "Comiskey understood that he had to vigorously promote his product to the people he knew best, the Irish-American community on the city's South Side," writes Sox historian Richard Lindberg, "...located in Bridgeport, just three miles south of downtown, the 35th Street neighborhood was home to thousands of second- and third-generation Irish potato-famine families." Comiskey, whose father served for years as 10th ward alderman, grew up with the Irish and knew their customs and ways.

* * *

The legacy of the Irish in Chicago began on July 4, 1836, when Dr. William B. Egan, a native of County Kerry, orchestrated the groundbreaking for the Illinois-Michigan canal. It was Chicago's first great public works undertaking, establishing a link between Lake Michigan and the Illinois and Mississippi Rivers. By its completion in 1848, Chicago was destined to become the most important transportation center of the Midwest. Fleeing the potato famine, Irish immigrants came to Chicago to build the canal. From just a few canal laborers in the 1830s, the Irish population grew to 6,096 in 1850. Historian Lindberg writes, "An early community of Irish was named Bridgeport, named for a low-slung bridge over the Chicago River at Ashland and Archer in the 1860s—an area of brickyards, breweries and meat packing firms. By 1865, the animal slaughtering enterprise was transferred to the Union Stockyards immediately to the south."

As the migrants came, the Irish expanded. Bitterly discriminated against by newspapers and politicians alike, they huddled, ghetto-like, in what historian Donald L. Miller calls "a wasteboard shantytown, Chicago's first slum, on the mudflats where the canal met the south branch of the Chicago River, a place called Bridgeport." It would become home to five 20th-century mayors, including the Daleys. The Irishmen worked for whiskey and a dollar a day, moving—after completion of the canal—to jobs in the brickyards, slaughterhouses, and bleak factories on both banks of the river.

Common currency is the tale that an Irish storyteller relates: "When the Irish had no money, they lived in Bridgeport in what is now the 11th ward. When they got a few bucks they moved to what is now the 14th ward, where graying Irish mothers congregated after Sunday Mass to extol this or that priest and the Holy Father in Rome. And when they got a few bucks more, but still wanted to stay in the 14th, they moved to Garfield, known as The Boulevard."

Irish Catholicism has stirred many images in literature and politics, including fondness for description of Chicago locations by parishes, which even Protestants and Jews would so designate. "Fallen-away" Catholics and bitterly critical novelists, among them James Joyce of Dublin and James T. Farrell of Chicago, would join playwright Eugene O'Neill in describing the culture—but the fond nostalgia outlives their literary scorn.

Novelists and historians have described the imagery: the sweet smell of incense during benediction...the ringing of the heavy church bells in the neighborhoods...martinet nuns dominating the grade schools...reverence for priests as intellectual superiors (since few other neighborhood professions save lawyers and doctors had university training)...veneration of clergy as living saints...Stations of the Cross...expansive talk and much laughter of men in neighborhood saloons...love of athletic competition...wakes in private homes that lasted all night (hence the name "wakes") with whiskey poured surreptitiously in the kitchens...old spinsters telling their rosary beads...firm reliance on the Democratic party as the immigrant's vehicle to social promotion. Add to these a strict view of sexual morality—idealization of women as actual and potential mothers, stemming from veneration of the Blessed Virgin as the model for femininity.

Chicago Irish immigrants' strict sexual morality and love of Catholicism's trappings stemmed from an Old World heritage born of fervent teaching by a Dublin prelate who gave Irish

Catholicism its distinctive character, Paul Cardinal Cullen [1802–1880]. Born the son of an Irish farmer, Cullen went to Rome at age 18, was ordained as a youth, and worked his way into the church *curia*, remaining there as an influential member for 29 years. A brilliant intellectual and administrator, he taught theology at the Irish College in Rome and became its superior while in his late 20s—an unprecedented achievement. For decades he was the unofficial representative of Ireland to the popes as well as a favorite of Pius IX.

As Pius' fervent counselor, Paul Cullen (who served so long in Italy that he would lapse into Italian) returned to Ireland as Bishop of Armagh, serving as apostolic delegate to the Vatican and finally Archbishop of Dublin and Cardinal-Primate of all Ireland. His influence over a people he had found to be illiterate, superstitious, and largely fallen away from the faith can hardly be overestimated.

Finding the Irish demoralized by dregs of the Great Famine of the 1840s with only 20 percent attending regular Mass, he reinvigorated them into a nation that produced stirring demonstrations of faith and 90 percent Mass attendance. Humorless, and a rigid moralist, he stunned the country by fearlessly pronouncing that the Famine was punishment for laxity and a blessing in disguise to purify the Irish. He inveighed against concupiscence and prescribed early marriage and big families. As Pius IX was promulgating his most famous papal document, the *Syllabus of Errors*, which condemned heresy, materialism, liberalism, and atheism, Cullen was renewing an Irish Catholic faith that prompted worldwide attention. He copiously displayed pomp and ceremony, prompting awe and allegiance, inspiring among the Irish a love of Christ and His mother, winning the admiration of a later pope, Pius X.

Tribute to the influence of Cullen was paid by Monsignor George A. Kelly, Ph.D., a founder of the Fellowship of Catholic Scholars, in an address to the Franciscan University in Steubenville, Ohio, on July 13, 1997. "My parents arrived on Ellis Island in 1908, with 25,000 of their countrymen and women, already formed as practicing Catholics, thanks to the wisdom and courage of Paul Cardinal Cullen of Dublin. This prelate, within 30 years (1850–1880), transformed the impiety of the Irish church into piety, almost single-handedly. By the time Cullen Catholics appeared in New York, the American Church itself was known worldwide for what Vatican II later called its 'works of charity, piety and the apostolate.'"

Where, in an earlier era, Irishmen arriving in New York between 1847 and 1860 were "part of the pre-famine generation of non-practicing Catholics, if they were Catholics at all," said Monsignor Kelly, the contrast with Cullen Catholics who came to America was great. Monsignor Kelly pointed out that "on his deathbed in 1880, [Cullen] could take some consolation in the knowledge that 90 percent of the Irish would be praying for him at Mass the Sunday he was laid to rest." Cullen's devotional revolution "made it a bit easier for the American bishops who, between 1900 and 1920, became pastors to 900,000 of the Cullen kind of Catholic," summarized Kelly.

But Cullenism didn't dominate exclusively. While the fervent beliefs of Irish Catholics about sexual morality and the rubrics of the Church were Cullen's, there grew up among Irish immigrants an easy (perhaps too easy) toleration and understanding of the nature of sin, particularly drinking, which to Cullen had been anathema.

Wit was the key. Consider the old saying that the best stories were always reserved for the second night of the wake when the liquor flowed in kitchens out of sight of the mourners. One can still find real laughter, somewhat muffled, in the gatherings at an Irish wake, unless the deceased was a child or a mother taken from her family at a young age, or a policeman slain in the line of duty. The reason for these instances of irreverent levity: Irish Catholics venerated humor because of the brevity of life, to be preferred over the fanaticism associated with Puritan moralists and pedants.

Hatred of the Irish stemmed from their Catholic religion, with weekly gang brawls between the Irish and Protestant toughs. "The Protestants believed that these tractable but explosively volatile peasants—thought to be under rigid Roman rule—posed a threat to the Protestant republic," wrote Miller. In self-defense, the Irish organized and even lobbied Rome for bishops. (They were successful. Between 1844 and 1915 only one Chicago bishop was of non-Irish nationality.) Spreading out from the Church were closely linked Irish neighborhood organizations, parochial schools, immigrant aid societies, and patriotic organizations—many of them armed—with headquarters often in saloons and city firehouses.

By the first decade of the century, Chicago's Irish came to surging strength. WASPs, Germans, and Norwegians were dwindling. In 1870, the city's Irish population was under 40,000. At the beginning of the 20th century it was the fourth largest Irish urban center in the U.S., trailing only New York, Philadelphia, and Brooklyn.

By 1909, some 237,479 lived in Chicago, mostly on the South Side. Anti-Irish, anti-Catholic bigotry flourished. Common currency among the wealthy classes were sentiments which only the *Chicago Evening Post* had put into print years earlier: "Scratch a convict or a pauper and the chances are that you tickle the skin of an Irish Catholic at the same time—an Irish Catholic made a criminal or a pauper by the priest and politicians who have deceived him and kept him in ignorance, in a word, a savage, as he was born."

By the turn of the century, it was the White Sox that stirred a fresh flood of Irish enthusiasm. Other than as rooters of the their own baseball club, they were, by 1909, shaped by a trinity of forces: (1) Catholicism; (2) with few exceptions, Democratic politics; and (3) nationalism.

Their chief chronicler became Finley Peter Dunne, the son of Irish immigrants, reared in the shadow of St. Peter's Church at West Adams and Desplaines Streets. At age 16, he was fresh out of West Division high school where he graduated last in a class of 50. At 19 he was covering the White Sox for the *Daily News*; at 26 he was editorial chairman at the *Evening Post*. There he concocted, in a newspaper column, the character of Martin Dooley, an aging saloonkeeper and philosopher of Archer Avenue in Bridgeport. Dunne, a prodigious drinker, was a habitué of a tavern known as the Press Club (where all-night poker games reigned).

Dunne put into Dooley's mouth sentences that convey what is still Chicago's enduring skepticism about politicians: *"Trust ivirybody—but cut the cards...I care not who makes th' laws iv a nation if I can get out an injunction...Manny people'd rather be kilt at Newport thin at Bunker Hill...Th' modhren idee iv governmint is 'snub th' people, buy th' people, jaw th' people.'"* The journalist created the first completely-drawn Irish ethnic neighborhood tavern in American literature. His columns became popular, because with so many Irish and anti-Irish bigots in Chicago, they found justification for their views in what the *Evening Post* editorially called "the deplorable race."

There is no greater admirer of Dunne than the famed historian, Jacques Barzun. In his landmark book, *From Dawn to Decadence: 500 Years of Western Cultural Life—1500 to the Present* (which he completed at age 92), a book ranking with the masterworks of the historian's craft by Burchardt and Gibbon, Barzun wrote:

> The most hurried sketch of political thought in that effervescent time would be incomplete if no word was said about Mr. Dooley. His remarks in Irish brogue began to edify readers through a column of the mid-1890s in the *Chicago Post*. Mr. Dooley is a Chicago saloonkeeper who chats with his friend Hennessy and other characters on Archey Road [Archer Avenue] about every aspect of the world and a few things besides. These lifelike encounters were the creation of Finley Peter Dunne whose political understanding and gift of satirical phrasing put him on a level with all other American and English writers who make the 1890s an age of sagacity and wit. The man who noted the advent of canned goods by a passing mention of "a taste of solder in the peaches" is nothing less than a literary genius. His seven volumes of Mr. Dooley's table talk furnish the proof of this judgment and constitute a panorama of the time. There is hardly a subject—from Roosevelt's charging up San Juan Hill in the Spanish War to nationalism at the Olympics (just then revived after 1,700 years) from "Reading Books" to "The Supreme Court"—that the saloonkeeper does not enliven with pregnant observations applicable to like cases in any year. It is a disgrace to American scholarship that he is not studied and thus republished and enjoyed on a level with Mark Twain and Ambrose Bierce. The dialect in which Mr. Dooley dialogues with his crony is no more an obstacle than the several types of back-country speech in *Huckleberry Finn*. Finley Peter Dunne is only one of the names on a list of great native sons whose neglect is a reproach to the American mind.

* * *

Among these Irish in early 1909 was a South Side family with seven children, named McDermott. On July 31, 1909, on the feast of St. Ignatius Loyola, the family's eighth child was born to Michael and Ellen (called Nellie) McDermott. The baby received the name Ignatius Daniel, probably at the suggestion of his aunt, Catherine, who became Sister Mary Maurice Bradley of the Sisters of Mercy. "I'm glad it wasn't the feast of St. Polycarp," says

Monsignor McDermott. On that day, *Tribune* cartoonist John T. McCutcheon saluted President Taft for winning at long last his tariff fight against Speaker Cannon, and Orville Wright made a breathtaking 10-mile flight with his brother, Wilbur, to prove the aeroplane was not a fluke. Charlie Comiskey was pushing Irish laborers who were building a new stadium at 35th and Shields, begun in mid-February of that year, on a 600- by 600-foot lot that he had bought from the estate of early Chicago journalist and mayor, John Wentworth. The new ballpark would hold a seating capacity of 35,000—6,400 box seats, 12,600 grandstand seats, and wooden-bench bleachers to accommodate 16,000.

Years later under that stadium, young Ignatius McDermott would find a connection with none other than Babe Ruth—a near miraculous contact that would make the boy a kind of hero in this age of innocence.

CHAPTER 3

Coming of Age Back of the Yards, 1909–1923

I thought it was rather strange that my father, being a staunch Irishman and pro-Irish, was born on July 12— Orange Day—and I used to kid him about it. How did he be-come associated with William of Orange?

Ignatius traveled through the "farm system" of his par-ents. They were ever sensitive to God's presence in their daily lives. This had to rub off on their six sons and two daugh-ters. [referring to himself by avoiding the perpendicu-lar pronoun, "I," as is his style]

—Ignatius McDermott

Ignatius McDermott was to become not only a Catholic priest but a creative originator of programs for the poor of Chicago: a risk-taker, a social entrepreneur, and administrator of Catholic Chari-ties. He would develop what was at first an off-hours, free-lance ministry to helpless and homeless drunks, starting in the 1930s, picking them up off the Skid Row streets of Chicago, finding them "flops" and food in dingy hotels. Then, at an age when some of his classmate-priests would be retired, he founded a na-tionally-known public institution for treatment of addiction. How he did it, by assuming a $1.5 million personal debt at age 75, and without visible support from the Catholic archdiocese (indeed with official disapproval in some hierarchical quarters) will be the story that unfolds in the following pages.

His father, Michael, was born in Ireland's County Roscommon on July 12, 1865 (Roscommon had been the birthplace of Father Edward J. Flanagan, who founded Boys' Town). He attended school in Ireland through the sixth grade, which was a more thorough education given than that of many schools in the U.S. In 1881, at age 16, Michael immigrated to New York City.

Michael McDermott worked as a laborer in Waukesha County, Wisconsin; there he filed his declaration of intent to become a U.S. citizen (March 1890). In the early 1890s he came to Chicago to work with the McFarland Manufacturing Company, which made milk wagons. He settled in a neighborhood near the Union Stockyards—it was where most Chicago Irish then lived—called inaccurately "Back of the Yards" (actually the population lived in front of the Yards, facing Lake Michigan).

His occupation is listed in early Chicago directories as wagon-maker for McFarland, specifically one who built wagons for milk deliverymen. As a bachelor, he lived in a boardinghouse at 729 Dexter Street (now 48th Street) and attended Mass at Holy Family church, at Roosevelt Road and Racine. Across the street, at 700 Dexter, lived the Bradley family with six children. Michael met a Bradley daughter, Ellen (known as Nellie), as a neighbor. Monsignor McDermott says, "I remember my mother telling me that she would see him walking down the street." She evidently liked what she saw; they were married at Mass on February 6, 1894 at St. Gabriel's, the marriage witnessed by its popular pastor, Father Maurice J. Dorney. Michael was naturalized as a citizen the following year.

Of their eight children, all survived to adulthood—quite unusual for the time. They were James (1895); John (1896); Martha, later to become Sister Mary Jeanette of the Sisters of Mercy (1897); Kathleen (1900); Francis (1902); twins Michael and Aloysius (1906); and Ignatius (1909). They would reside initially at 45th and Lowe. As the family grew, they moved to 608 West 48th Street.

By 1916, the house at 608 West 48th Street stood in the way of a proposed Tilden high school expansion. The Board of Education condemned the land so Michael McDermott had to move. He determined not to give up his home, so he arranged that his house, a two-story, be moved. A team of horses pulled it slowly to 4847 South Union. In 1918, the McDermotts moved to 1052 West 55th Street (Garfield Boulevard), where the senior McDermotts lived throughout their lives, Nellie dying in 1937, and Michael in 1940. Their neighbor at 1048 West Garfield was Judge John J. Sullivan, who was to influence the eldest, Jim, in several ways.

Nellie McDermott was a Bradley. The Bradleys were a powerful Irish Democratic family. Patrick Bradley and his wife, Martha (Coulan), were born in County Cork. They had lived at first in Ottawa, Illinois, then moved to Chicago where Patrick was listed in an early city directory as a laborer. They had six children: Catherine (1860); Eliza (1862); John (1866); Ellen (1869); Martha (1870); and Margaret (1872).

Born in 1866, Nellie's brother John Bradley had learned the blacksmith trade in Ottawa; then at age 20 moved to Chicago to work in the Swift car-shops at the Union Stockyards. He identified early with Edward F. Dunne, who lived in the area. Dunne's political career rocketed. He served as mayor of Chicago and governor of Illinois, the only man to hold both posts. Bradley became chief clerk for the Chicago Junction Railroad, following which he became a successful realtor in the old 30th ward.

John Bradley would be role model for Ignatius' oldest brother, Jim. John became an important player in the Democratic party of the South Side. He married Julia Dunne, no relation to Edward F. Dunne. Propelled by Dunne's career, he served three terms in the city council. During Dunne's tenure as governor, Bradley was named federal marshal for the Northern District of Illinois by President Woodrow Wilson. Loss of the presidency to the Republicans caused Bradley to resign his post; he returned to real estate. News of Bradley's death at age 56 in 1922 was carried in all Chicago newspapers.

In addition to Nellie and John, another Bradley later to exert sway over the McDermotts was Catherine, who became Sister Mary Maurice of the Sisters of Mercy. She held a powerful religious influence on the family.

The neighborhood was where the Irish had settled to build a canal and work the stockyards. Back of the Yards was in the old 30th ward, now the 14th (it was an area that was economically depressed in the '30s but which pulled itself back up with the help of radical organizer Saul Alinsky, who devised strategies for the Back of the Yards Council headed by an Irishman, Joseph Meegan). When Ignatius McDermott was born, the ward extended roughly from Ashland Avenue east to State Street, 47th south to 63rd Street. As with the neighboring 11th ward (birthplace of Mayors Kelly, Kennelly, and the Daleys), political control remained with the Irish.

"The first thing anyone noticed about the neighborhood," wrote Robert A. Slayton in *Back of the Yards: The Making of a Local Democracy*, "was the stench...The odor was in the combined product of enormous slaughterhouses, miles of penned hogs, sheep and cattle, fertilizer plants, rendering vats, city garbage dumps, a fetid sewer known as Bubbly Creek, accumulated alley trash and a few tanneries."

Five years before Ignatius McDermott's birth, a young socialist author, Upton Sinclair, journeyed to Chicago where he spent seven weeks as an investigator in the area interviewing laborers, physicians, social workers, saloonkeepers, and politicians. Born in Baltimore, reared in New York, Sinclair was, writes F. Richard Ciccone, "a crank, a rabble-rouser, a reformer, a prohibitionist, a politician, a feminist, a womanizer, a dreamer, a self-promoter, a publisher, and the prolific author of more than ninety books in ninety years."

Returning to Princeton, New Jersey, Sinclair wrote fervently ("I ran wild at the end," he confessed later in his autobiography).

His book, *The Jungle*, an urban American classic published in 1906, caused eye-popping in the middle class. Revelations of the corruption of big business produced, in Sinclair's estimation, rat dung in the sausage and horrible undisclosed additives to the nation's dinner table. That same year a national outcry caused Congress to pass the *Pure Food and Drug Act* and the *Meat Inspection Act*, which President Theodore Roosevelt eagerly signed. But author Sinclair was unhappy. He had sought—by describing the squalor of the neighborhood—to impel socialism. Not so. "I aimed at the public's heart," he said, "and by accident I hit it in the stomach."

Back of the Yards began as part of the Town of Lake, so named because of the low level of its marshy land just a few feet higher than Lake Michigan. Change came slowly but resolutely; by the early 1860s, the packing industry, centered in Cincinnati, began to move westward to Chicago. Investors chose a site consisting of 320 acres from what is now Pershing Road to 47th Street and from Halsted Street to Ashland Avenue.

"Work began quickly," wrote Slayton. "By June 1, 1864, and through a wet summer, nearly a thousand men labored to build a stockyards center out of the marshes. Often dressed in their leftover Army uniforms, workmen planed the ground, dug wells and drainage ditches, and erected wooden sheds and permanent brick buildings as well as pens. On Christmas Day 1865, the Union Stockyards opened at the Halsted entrance. In 1867, Philip

Armour built his first plant, followed by Gustavus Swift in 1879. An original wood entrance was replaced that year by a sculptured bull's head in the center of the arch, designed by the architectural firm of Burnham and Root."

Author Slayton continues:

> The industrial empires of the meat packers were soon among the nation's greatest. By 1910, the complex of yards, industries, banks, and other structures—known collectively as "the Yards"—covered 500 acres, had 13,000 pens, 300 miles of railroad tracks, 25 miles of streets, 50 miles of sewers, 90 miles of pipes, and 10,000 hydrants. On a hot day, 7 million gallons of water fed the needs of cattle, machines, and humans. The site also produced its own electricity and had stations creating other forms of power as well. In 1919, a boom year, the plants processed 14,903,487 animals, including 7,936,634 hogs and 2,331,233 cattle. On one day in 1920 alone, 122,748 pigs came to the yards. In 1919, the federal census reported employment in the meat-processing plants of Chicago as 45,696 persons, 60 percent of the neighborhood's entire population. One Swift & Company factory had more than 11,000 employees. That year, the total value of meat and meat products in Illinois, an industry dominated by the area between Halsted Street and Ashland Avenue, reached $1.284 billion.
>
> To run these factories, the packers needed workers. About 1870, Philip Armour permitted 20 of his old hands to build cottages on company land at 43rd Street and Packers Avenue. Two years later, the Hutchison Packing Company erected seven houses for foremen one block north. The first of these settlements became known as Armour's Patch, the second, New Patch...
>
> The residents of these early communities were Irish and German, roughly 60 percent Celtic and 30 percent Teuton. By 1881, for example, there were at least 60 families from the Emerald Isle west of the stockyards, and St. Rose of Lima Church opened at 49th Street and Justine Avenue, one block east of Ashland Avenue, to tend to their needs. Two years later, on 8 July 1883, the church moved to Ashland Avenue at 48th Street and dedicated a new building. Shortly after, a parish school was opened and, by 1885, the Sisters of Mercy had undertaken the teaching, the church's most essential function next to the holding of religious services...
>
> The neighborhood also had its landmarks, evidence of industrialization and the packers' handiwork. The city dumps, on Damen Avenue between 47th and 43rd streets, were four great holes where clay had been removed for

nearby brickyards owned by Alderman Thomas Carey of the Twenty-ninth Ward. After the clay companies had excavated them, the city's garbage wagons refilled them. The city used one for solid waste, private carting companies filled two others, and the packers dumped their waste into the last. The meat men burned their wastes, however, so a "smoldering fire" was always going; a moat surrounded it to prevent it from spreading. Alderman Carey profited every which way from this operation. He sold the clay from the holes, charged the city for the privilege of dumping there, violated the city's sanitation regulations with impunity, and charged professional scavengers as much as $15 a week to go through the garbage. After they finished, the women and children would pick over the remains, retrieving stove wood, old mattresses, pieces of food, worn garments, furnishings and, rarely, a previously overlooked item of value such as a silver utensil. For the children, especially, it was a grand bazaar. Amidst the filth and decaying matter, all kinds of treasures could be found, including an occasional broken toy.

The dump symbolized many of the rules of existence in Back of the Yards. It typified the domination of the neighborhood by powerful forces: residents had no say about what went into or out of the pits or about how the refuse was handled. On the other hand, the piles were used as a resource by local people determined to survive.

A similar manifestation of industrial dominance was one of the best-known waterways in the urban United States. Bubbly Creek was one of the south branches of the Chicago River, and the packers who used it as their communal sewer failed to enlarge it to carry their enormous wastes. Despite dredgings by the federal government, the City of Chicago, the Sanitary District of Chicago, and private corporations that removed several hundred thousand cubic yards of material, the river-bed rose at the rate of almost half a foot a year between 1900 and 1921. In 1921, a report to the Sanitary District claimed that this was "a very sluggish stream, utterly inadequate to receive the wastes of even a young industry." At this time the daily output of "suspended matter" from the factories to the sewers of Chicago was a staggering 131,500 pounds, Swift & Company alone accounting for 52,170 pounds. All this "putrefying organic matter" released "gaseous ebullition," or bubbles, giving rise to its infamous name.

Stories about Bubbly Creek were legion. It caught fire once, and in 1915 a reporter tried to row across but turned back when a six-foot bubble enveloped his boat. Many people supposedly fell in and never came back, and even those who did were hardly welcome. One woman told how, "My uncle fell into Bubbly Creek one night and grandma wouldn't let him in the house till the next day." Residents said it looked like "a street that had been freshly tarred," "like pudding," or "a crusty old thing." If the best comment is the most succinct, however, it came from Ted P., who simply explained, "It was a filthy piece of water."

Garfield Boulevard (55th Street)—"The Boulevard"—was the area's main thoroughfare. "To have a home or own a two-flat on The Boulevard was to have arrived. And if you really came into a lot of bucks, the goal was—and *still is*—to move to the 19th ward or Beverly," wrote journalist Len O'Connor. Beverly Hills is the suburb-like, in-city neighborhood of the well-to-do, including the Irish who play important roles in the commerce, civic life, and politics of the city. The family of Michael McDermott wound up on The Boulevard—a distinct middle-class success, but still in the old 30th— now 14th—ward. The McDermotts could describe their ward—bounded by the stockyards—41st Street on the north, and on the south by the north side of 55th Street, on the east from the railroad tracks around 55th and Normal to Damen on the west.

Today, the ethnic makeup and complexion of the 14th ward has changed—but there is still Irish political leadership. A survey of the ward in the early 1990s showed Mexican stores at 47th and Ashland, a Byzantine Catholic Church at 50th and Seeley, French restaurants at 63rd and Kedzie, a Romanian Pentecostal church at 59th and California, Arab groceries and bakeries on 63rd from California to Kedzie—and a powerful Irish fixture in the city council, Edward Burke, one of the most prominent lawyers in the city.

Burke represents the old lineage that has always counted; his father, Alderman Joseph Burke, succeeded Clarence Wagner who was killed in a car wreck (about whom much more is to come in this story). Rough-hewn, ex-cop Joe Burke not only attended every council meeting (and every one of the council committees to which he was assigned), he is reported to have gone to every wedding, wake, funeral and wedding anniversary celebration in his ward. After Joe Burke died of cancer and before the last shovelful of dirt fell on his coffin in 1968, the precinct captains named 25-year-old Eddie Burke as his father's successor. And after his first race, Edward Burke, who since youth became prematurely white-haired and now is a loftily aristocratic council finance committee chairman, has remained a fixture there. Thus, has the old order of the Irish continued.

Eddie Burke has a fascination for the old days. Each election season he and the other Democratic committeemen preside over a most important function—the "slating" of candidates for the Cook County Circuit Court. All are Democrats, and with unfailing regularity Democrats slated by Burke and his colleagues get elected. Recalling his father, Joe, Burke told a slate-making group of the wondrous abilities of the old man. *Sun-Times* reporter Abdon Pallasch was allowed to hear Eddie Burke extol his father and captured the words in the magazine *Illinois Issues*.

Citing the old 14th ward office on South Halsted, Ed Burke said: "If the building were still up, I would petition the Vatican for designation as a shrine—my father used to work miracles there. A guy would go down to 54 West Hubbard and take the test for the Police Department and he'd be too short. And he'd come to see my father at 4713 South Halsted. My father would write out a little card and he'd send him back there and—believe it or not—he'd grow an inch. Someone would have a heart murmur. He'd write out a card and send 'em back to 54 West Hubbard, and suddenly they were cured. He made fat people thin. He made short people tall. It was marvelous." Reformers made efforts to institute so-called "merit selection" of judges in 1996 but failed.

* * *

In 1895, a year after he married Nellie Bradley, Michael McDermott changed his occupation. Says Monsignor McDermott: "From making the wagons, it gave him the idea of buying a wagon and going into the milk business." He started McDermott's Dairy in his basement at 608 West 48th and relocated when the house and family moved to 4847 South Union Avenue.

"My father used to go to the Pennsylvania Railroad station at 47th Street and pick up the milk cans that were coming in from Rensselaer, Indiana. In those days, it was great dairy country. He would bring [the milk] back to pasteurize it in the basement. No Board of Health problems in those days. The milk dairy was in the basement, the barn was in the backyard where my father had the wagon and the horses."

Michael McDermott would fill up the milk bottles in the basement. "In the early days," his son said, "he used to go around with a 5-gallon can of milk with a dipper in it and the people used to put a pitcher outside the door. He just filled [them] up. There wasn't any sickness in those days or anything rampant."

With the coming of glass milk bottles, Chicago customers took great satisfaction in savoring the cream that floated at the top of the bottles (although in winter, when the milk froze, the cream would pressure the bottle caps upward). Later, there were strenuous attempts waged in the city council against cardboard containers. Michael and his oldest son, Jim, who helped out at McDermott's Dairy, opposed the measure, believing "the people would be short-changed because they couldn't see the cream on the top of the bottle." Much later the dairies turned to wax cartons and the era of cream on the top of the bottles ended. By the time Ignatius McDermott went to first grade at St. Gabriel's, his father had sold the dairy business.

At Ignatius' birth, Catholics were the city's largest denomination in Chicago with 12 percent of the population and 25 percent of the churchgoers. As did many of the Irish, the McDermotts and Bradleys drew strength from their parishes—St. Gabriel's and later Visitation. St. Gabriel's was a Romanesque structure designed by famed architects Burnham & Root and dedicated by Archbishop Patrick A. Feehan in 1888. There, all the McDermott children but Ignatius completed grade school. Its first pastor, who witnessed the McDermott's marriage, Father Maurice Dorney, found work for many immigrants. He had been called "King of the Yards." At age 50, he became a lawyer in order to better represent the poor of his neighborhood. When he died, in 1914 at age 63, flags throughout the stockyards were lowered to half-mast; his funeral was said to have been one of the largest in Chicago.

By 1909, more than 740 children were enrolled at St. Gabriel's. In addition, the Sisters of Mercy operated a new St. Gabriel's high school, built in 1905, at the corner of 45th and Wallace, where no tuition was charged. Later, the McDermotts moved to Visitation parish, at Garfield Boulevard and Peoria Street, a parish formed in 1886, also with its own high school, which remained predominantly Irish for 75 years.

After attending first grade at St. Gabriel's, it was at Visitation parish that Ignatius, youngest of the family, would chiefly worship and go to school. There he found a classmate, one James O'Leary, grandson of Mrs. Patrick O'Leary, whose cow allegedly kicked over the lantern that started the Chicago Fire in 1871. Visitation had been organized in 1888 as a predominantly Irish parish (one of the largest English-speaking parishes), possessing one of the largest physical plants in the archdiocese. After offering Mass at several locations, including a public school, pastors moved the parish several times—first to Center Street (now Racine Avenue) between 50th and 51st Streets, then to 53rd and Morgan and, finally, to its Garfield Boulevard address. The cornerstone for the Gothic building was laid and blessed by Archbishop Feehan in 1888. In 1903, ground for a new school was broken at 54th Place and Peoria. By 1906, 1,206 children were enrolled in Visitation elementary school.

In first grade at St. Gabriel's, Ignatius met a chum who stayed with him in classes through Visitation, Quigley Preparatory Seminary, and three years of major seminary at St. Mary of the Lake, Mundelein. He was Joseph Carroll, who left the seminary just before he was to take the deaconate. First in his class, Joe Carroll went to Loyola law school where he graduated *summa cum laude*. He became an FBI agent, then a top assistant to J. Edgar Hoover, and, finally, moved to the Pentagon where he set up the Defense Intelligence Agency (DIA) as the youngest lieutenant general in Air Force history. General Carroll's mission during the Vietnam War was to shape the Air Force bombing pattern. A son, Father James Carroll, a Maryknoller, split with his father over Vietnam and left the priesthood to become a bitter critic of the Roman Catholic Church. When he informed his grief-stricken father he was leaving the priesthood and would desire to get married and have children, Joe Carroll said, with Irish bitterness: "Have children? Why? They'll just break your heart." James Carroll wrote of the family rupture in *An American Requiem: God, My Father, and the War That Came Between Us*, which won the National Book Award that year.

At Visitation grade school, Ignatius was deeply influenced by the daughters of St. Dominic of Sinsinawa, Wisconsin, and, particularly, by Sister Vivian, his third and fifth grade teacher, and Sister Celestine, who taught him in the seventh grade.

More than 60 years later he recalled: "They were God's talent scouts. They had the conviction that some of us would be their teammates in His vineyard of tomorrow."

From early age on, it was his eldest brother, Jim, with whom Ignatius identified.

"It was more than the big brother syndrome," recalls one who knew them both. "Jim, 14 years older than Ignatius, was every inch a kind of father figure."

Father John J. Sullivan, born in 1950 to a prominent South Side Democratic family (and whose grandfather was mentor to Jim McDermott), said Ignatius looked up to Jim throughout Jim's life because Jim McDermott was a practical man of affairs and a good Catholic.

"I knew Jim McDermott in the '50s and 1960s, when I grew up a block away on Garfield Boulevard," said Father Sullivan. "[He was a] real powerful leader, a practicing Catholic, which is of interest since so many people are not, of course, these days. I know when I was a priest in the 1980s at St. Gabriel's, which used to be part of the 14th ward, people still told me how, when they lost a parent, Jim McDermott would be the first one at the house, at 5 o'clock in the morning, loaded with food—turkeys or hams or roast beef or what have you, being there to assist people in any way possible. Especially if they were impoverished, the Democratic party of the 14th ward would help people with the burial expenses." This was the family-friendly Democratic party that Jim McDermott aspired to lead.

John Bradley, uncle of the McDermotts, served as a powerful model, especially for Jim. Jim, Monsignor McDermott says, "was inoculated" by a love of politics and, early on, aimed for a career in law and public service. Ignatius, however, became an altar boy and early developed an interest in the priesthood. He was strongly influenced by Father Walter Murphy, who started the Visitation Boys' Band in which Ignatius McDermott played coronet.

Monsignor McDermott's characterization of Murphy: "I saw him as a man who lettered in forgetting himself."

The statement illustrates Ignatius' other keen interest—sports. Ranking at the top for him was the Chicago White Sox, truly *the team* for Irish Catholics because it was South Side and Catholic-owned. The White Sox were a great cause. Michael McDermott would take his sons to the new Comiskey Park where they would sit in the bleachers, for which Michael would pay 75¢ admission (85¢ to sit in the grandstand and on special occasions $1.25 for a box seat). The kids got in free.

More than 70 years later, Monsignor McDermott recalled a day in the mid-1920s that rivaled almost any of his life, excluding attainment of the priesthood itself, when, unaccountably, the Boston Red Sox determined to trade Babe Ruth. Ignatius McDermott had followed Ruth's career avidly and hoped that he would go to the White Sox. Or, as he put it in early 20th century sportswriter-style, during a 1996 sermon delivered at Visitation Church for his 60th jubilee as a priest, the hope was that "if Babe Ruth ever changed his hose of carmine of the Boston Red Sox, it would have been for the white hose of our Sox."

"But in 1920 the owner of the Red Sox derailed our dream. Babe was traded to the New York Yankees. In the mid-'20s, Babe

Ruth and the New York Yankees were in Chicago to play our White Sox." Referring to his family impersonally—a trademark—he continues: "Our mother and dad privileged Ignatius and his two older brothers, Al and Mike, who were twins, to see Babe Ruth." Avoiding what he calls the perpendicular pronoun, "I," he refers to himself in the third person. "We boarded a streetcar fortified with two milk bottles filled with lemonade. With the multitudes, we were there, hopefully, to see the Sultan of Swat, Babe Ruth, hit a home run.

"Babe's first two at bats were futile. A grounder to the shortstop and a lazy fly to the outfield."

But later in the afternoon as Ruth was coming up in the batting order, young Ignatius—who had been imbibing freely of the lemonade—felt the need to go to the comfort station, which was located on the ground floor of Comiskey Park.

Al and Mike shouted, "You have to be crazy! Babe is coming up to bat!" But nature's call could not be denied and, rather sorrowfully, young Ignatius made his way from the bleachers to the ground floor of the stadium.

While he was on the ground floor there arose a shout as Babe Ruth had hit his eagerly anticipated homer. Ignatius groaned, distressed that he had missed the opportunity. Then, as the stands above him roared with excitement, he spotted Ruth's ball, which had dropped down through the bleachers to the floor below, right near him. He scooped up the ball and ran up the many steps to his brothers in the bleachers.

"We told you so!" they screamed. "You missed it!"

Their chortling ended when Ignatius held aloft his icon, the home-run ball that Babe Ruth had hit.

"The very next day, at Sherman Park, we baptized our 'Van Gogh of leather' with our companions," using the ball in a pickup game.

*   *   *

Equal with his love of the Sox was that of the old Chicago Cardinals football team.

Professional football in the United States appears to have begun on Chicago's South Side with the Morgan Athletic Association, a group of young men organized in 1899 by one Thomas Clancy along with two brothers, Patrick and Chris O'Brien. They played near the Union Stockyards with the team composed almost entirely of players of Irish descent.

Morgan Street was where the O'Briens lived. The Morgans shared their fans with a number of athletic clubs. These included the Garfield Athletic Club. A young player, who later would become part of the Morgans and ultimately a local politician, was Frank Ragan. The team later came to be the Chicago Cardinals, the St. Louis Cardinals, and subsequently, the Arizona Cardinals football team.

At about 1901, the O'Brien brothers and most of their teammates left the Morgan Athletic Club and formed their own team, the Cardinals Social and Athletic Club. Chris O'Brien reportedly bought some used football jerseys from Amos Alonzo Stagg, football coach of the University of Chicago. The jerseys were maroon, after their team, the Maroons. O'Brien pronounced the color "Cardinal red."

Speaking in the vivid jargon of a sportswriter (which he might well have become had he not joined the priesthood), Monsignor McDermott said in an interview recently: "The Cardinals were the city's first professional football team—even before the Bears.

"Chris O'Brien was a housepainter, with a wife and one son, Eddie. Eddie went to Visitation grammar school and De La Salle high school, starring there in football. He went on to Notre Dame, incurred a knee injury, which negated his ever becoming a football player, and wound up later as a policeman. The Cardinals played football at 61st and Racine, which is now a police station and a city court. It was called Normal Park. In the incubator days when Chris O'Brien founded them, they were called the Racine Cardinals."

Monsignor McDermott paused. It is obvious that what endeared the Cardinals to him over the Bears was that they were not the elitists.

"In the early days, the Racine Cardinals were made up of guys who didn't go to high school," he said. "They practiced at Sherman Park at 55th and Racine. We practiced . . ."

We?

"Well, I was a water boy for the team. We used to go over to practice. Those guys were working from 9 a.m. to 5 p.m. in those days, and they'd come over and practice after work. They'd practice in Sherman Park near the library because there were two lampposts there. Chris O'Brien was the author of what he called 'Ghost Football.' In order for those fellows to see the football better in the dark, he would do a Michelangelo job with the football, which he painted white. So I'm convinced that he was the father of Ghost Football."

*   *   *

One of the men Ignatius McDermott cheered for on the Chicago Cardinals was Fred M. Gillies [1895–1974]. Gillies, son of a Scottish immigrant who held down a good job at Inland Steel, had been an all-American collegiate star at Cornell, flew as a Navy pilot in World War I, and then played eight seasons as a tackle with the Cardinals. Throughout his life, he touted the career of Cardinals halfback Paddy Driscoll, whom Gillies said was "one of the great halfbacks of all time." He recalled fondly how he and Driscoll managed to mar Red Grange's professional debut in Chicago. The famed "Wheaton Iceman" (so named because he delivered huge blocks of ice to households in the suburb of Wheaton in the summer months), had starred at the University of Illinois and was expected to take pro football by storm. The Cardinals kept Grange under wraps, and the Bears to a 0 to 0 tie before a standing-room-only crowd at Wrigley Field. Gillies later helped George Halas coach his fledgling Chicago Bears.

Gillies was seriously injured in a Grant Park plane accident in which the plane owner, Edward Stinson, was killed.

"We were flying back to the field and knew we were out of gas," recalled Gillies. "It was a dual control plane and I was flying at the time. I told Stinson that we'd better put her down in the lake. Well, it was his ship and he had just brought it back from the Miami air races. He thought that maybe he could set her down. The only close place where there was an open space was the Grant Park golf course, and he headed for it. I had played on the course many times and so I began directing him to a spot near the first tee. We hit the tops of a couple of trees on the way down and, suddenly, I spotted the tall flagpole looming up before us.

"Stinson didn't see it. I shouted to him and he swerved the plane, but it was too late. We hit the pole and it sheared our wing right off. We fell like a stone. The steering wheel came back and crushed Stinson. I was thrown around like a little ball and came out of it with a broken back." The crash left Gillies nearly paralyzed from the waist down, and for the rest of his life he walked with the aid of steel braces. Yet, the disability didn't deter him. "It wasn't a very painful thing," he said, "because you lose too much sensation for that. It was a handicap, of course." After recovering, he worked at Inland Steel and became works manager at its Indiana Harbor plant. "Working at a steel mill, you have to get around a great deal," he said. "It was difficult playing golf, too. I had to learn to play all over again, this time off one foot, relying on my arms to supply all the power." After World War II, he went to West Germany to help rebuild their Ruhr Basin steel industry.

Gillies became board chairman of Acme Steel (later Interlake Steel) and spent 10 years as a volunteer fund-raiser for the United Republican Fund, becoming one of the grand old men of the Illinois GOP.

*   *   *

Ignatius would peddle newspapers at the University of Chicago stadium while the Maroons played football. He recalled the wife of the legendary coach, Amos Alonzo Stagg, would sit in the grandstand diagramming plays. He would tag around with his older brother, Jim, who in Ignatius' words "was inhaling the dynamics" of Uncle John's politics.

Like ancient Gaul, the Democratic party was divided into three parts: one, the hard-core conservative Irish faction of Roger Sullivan and George Brennan; another—more progressive—led by Tom Carey and the followers of Carter Harrison II; and the third, a liberal-radical group led by the reform-minded Edward Dunne, the mayor and governor to whom John Bradley was close.

Since years before Ignatius McDermott was born, the South Side was home to so-called athletic and social clubs, which often fostered political candidacies. Some of them were nothing less than gangs under the banners of which young toughs could wage turf wars. They were called the Hamburg Social and Athletic Club (to which Richard J. Daley belonged) or the "Hamburgers," the Aylwards, Our Flag, Standard, and Ragan's Colts. Ragan's Colts were by every account among the toughest. Frank Ragan, its founder, had long since graduated from the club and was a candidate for Cook County commissioner.

"I remember Frank Ragan when I was a little kid," says Monsignor McDermott. "He'd come home from downtown—always dressed way ahead of his time, color-wise. We'd be on The Boulevard playing and he'd tell us at election time when he was running: 'When you see me get out of the car (and cars were very scarce in those days), run across the street and form two lines.' We'd get two pennies apiece to buy candy. We'd have three or four kids on one side and three on the other. He'd get out of his car and we'd sing this song he taught us: *'What's the matter with Ragan? He's all right! What's the matter with Ragan? His hair is turning white! He's running for county commissioner. I hope he wins, he's a hustler! What's the matter with Ragan? He's all right!'"*

Ragan was a vociferous defender of the Church. Once, when an ex-priest named Crowley announced via handbills that he was going to denounce the Catholic Church in the area, Ragan mobilized not just Ragan's Colts but many volunteers to block the doors of the hall to frustrate the meeting. No one objected. The largely Irish police looked the other way and the meeting was sparsely attended.

In those days, the state senator from Back of the Yards was Bill McDermott (no relation). He owned a tavern at 51st and Ashland. Reformers grouped about his challenger, a man named Aloysius Gorman, because many local voters were incensed at the idea of being represented by a tavern-keeper. Accordingly, they designed a slogan for Gorman: "For Decency's Sake, Send Gorman to Springfield."

Those were days of the politically incorrect. In any event, at their first meeting, McDermott growled: "My opponent's slogan is 'For Decency's Sake, Send Gorman to Springfield.' I say: "For chrissake, keep McDermott in Springfield!" To his surprise, his irreverent, anti-political tirade caught on Back of the Yards and McDermott was easily returned to office.

Brawling athletic clubs may or may not have participated in Chicago's worst race riot, which began on a hot day, July 27, 1919. A black swimmer at the 27th Street beach drifted into the 29th Street beach. Whites threw stones at him causing the boy to drown. A battle summoned the police; shots were fired. It raged for four days, leaving 15 whites and 23 blacks dead, with 178 whites and 342 blacks injured. Almost 1,000 houses were set afire and 5,000 National Guard troops were called to keep order.

In his book on Richard J. Daley, *Boss*, the late Mike Royko quoted an Illinois Human Rights Commission report that placed major responsibility with the Hamburgs of Bridgeport and their rivals, Ragan's Colts. Daley, who ultimately headed the Hamburgs, was born in 1902. Seventeen years old during the riots, he later discounted that the Hamburgs brewed violence, describing the clubs as a cross between the YMCA and the Boy Scouts of America. Formal responsibility for the riots was never officially fixed, and whether or not Daley was involved was never proven.

* * *

It was a city teeming with sports, flamboyant journalism and brawling politics. William Randolph Hearst's *Chicago American* was battling Robert R. McCormick's *Tribune* for circulation...Harriet Monroe was starting the literary magazine *Poetry*...Preston Bradley was founding the interdenominational People's Church...the city supported World War I by instituting "heatless Mondays" to conserve fuel...Irwin St. John Tucker, an Episcopal priest, wrote an anti-mobilization pamphlet for which he was sentenced to 20 years in prison. He was sentenced by Federal Judge Kenesaw Mountain Landis, but the Supreme Court overturned it, citing the bias of the Judge...and in one day 381 people died in Chicago from the nation's worst influenza epidemic, which raged in 1918.

Lots of excitement. But as high school beckoned, Ignatius McDermott determined that he would forsake full-time sports, sportswriting, and politics. His goal would be the priesthood. Throughout his young life, he had been impressed with the priests, watching these dedicated men as they presided at weddings, baptisms, made "sick calls," performed the last rites, and attended numberless wakes. This ministry the Church calls the corporal and spiritual works of mercy helped focus his ambition and goal. He particularly noticed the work of young Father Thomas F. Tormey, an assistant at Visitation who organized the parish sports program. His efforts later became a model for the archdiocesan-wide Catholic Youth Organization (CYO).

The young teenager prepared to enter Quigley Preparatory Seminary. But there was something else. He had noticed vagrants, helpless alcoholics on West Madison Street, either being pushed into paddy wagons or left to danger and suffering without compassion.

CHAPTER 4

Pointed toward the Priesthood, 1923–1931

Besides being a lifelong worshipper of our eternal Head Coach, Jesus, and His mother, Mary, we have also worshipped at the shrine of Abner Doubleday, the founder of baseball.

His elevator was still going to the top at 92. [commenting on Leo XIII's intellectual acuity in advanced age]

—Ignatius McDermott

Ignatius McDermott entered the minor seminary, called Cathedral College of the Sacred Heart, at age fifteen, in 1924 in the era of George Cardinal Mundelein, Chicago's autocratic but ingeniously gifted Prince of the Church. Its central building was the former Austrian consulate. An annex, the new building at Rush and Chestnut streets, was rechristened after his first year as part of Quigley Memorial Preparatory Seminary. The origin of Quigley prep has a Visitation parish connection. Four months after Archbishop James Edward Quigley was installed, he was at confirmation exercises at Visitation. He sent for Father Francis Andrew Purcell, pastor of neighboring St. Ann's. When Father Purcell arrived, Archbishop Quigley interrupted his dinner at Visitation to direct a startled Purcell to go to Rome to receive a doctorate in divinity, which would prepare him for the rectorship of a seminary.

Purcell did so, and sailed back to America in 1905, where he assumed duties at the Cathedral College. Later Purcell became rector of the new Quigley and, finally, rector of St. Mary of the Lake Seminary. Purcell was known as a tough rector who would regularly expel students from school. After mothers would come to him to plead for the re-admittance of their sons, Purcell would

42

call the offending students in and say, "You're back in my good graces—not for anything you did, but because of the tears of your mother. Remember that!"

Quigley was (as it is now) an impressive school at Rush and Pearson Streets on Chicago's Near North Side. Mundelein had built the buildings of French Gothic style with the U-shaped building opening onto Rush Street. In the era of the Rush Street Bridge, Rush was the main thoroughfare, rather than Michigan Avenue. The chapel, dedicated to St. James, was modeled after Paris' Saint Chapelle, an 11th century structure erected by St. Louis IX. The chapel itself was a gift of Chicago's Catholic school-children, who contributed more than $200,000 during the first year of the fund-raising drive. It was dedicated on June 10, 1920.

Six hundred students were enrolled at a prep seminary designed to hold 500. All were required to wear either suits or jackets with shirt and tie. Quigley tuition was $100 per year, $50 paid by the students' parents and $50 by their respective parishes. Report cards had to be signed by at least one parent and the pastor.

At Quigley, Ignatius formed a close friendship with two other "Macs" who sat near him in classes that were arranged in alphabetical order. One was John McLoraine, later to become a highly visible pastor, gifted entrepreneur and former Brigadier General of military chaplains serving in World War II and Korea. The other was Walter McCarty, who left studies of the priesthood to become president of a large construction company. Johnny Mac, as McLoraine was known, was interviewed on March 30, 1998, shortly before his death.

Ignatius "was the sportsman. I was the student," said Father McLoraine. "However, we both managed to work our way through. He ran a sports column in the weekly Quigley newspaper [actually, the Visitation parish newspaper]. He made predictions and was known as 'Sid, the Predictor.'" However, McLoraine was no slouch himself as a vivid character in the seminary and throughout life. Monsignor McDermott remembers McLoraine sneaking time to smoke cigarettes while skulking in the shadows of nearby Fourth Presbyterian Church (smoking was forbidden at Quigley). After McLoraine went to military service as a chaplain, he became godfather by telephonic proxy to young Walter McCarty, Jr., and throughout his life remained close to the McCarty family.

"A legendary story about Johnny Mac," said the younger McCarty, in an interview on October 3, 2000, "involved an episode in World War II that has not been covered by history. He was involved in one of the bloodiest theatres of World War II—the battle for Italy by General Mark Clark. Whenever he moved from camp to camp, Johnny Mac carried a great number of chalices, liturgical vestments, and no fewer than 3,000 unconsecrated hosts [Communion wafers]. Moving them was a chore, and buck private soldiers complained about it, especially the packages of 3,000 hosts. But it all proved worth it one day in late December 1944 when, in the midst of heavy fighting in Italy, a group of German soldiers approached American lines under cover of a flag of truce.

"They asked whether a Catholic chaplain was available. When they were told that one was—Johnny Mac—they asked Father McLoraine if they could arrange a Mass at Christmas to be attended by a great number of German, as well as American, troops. Johnny received permission to do so from General Clark, and on Christmas Day 1944, the battle suddenly stopped and thousands of Germans and Americans worshipped together, with Communion distributed by Father McLoraine and other American chaplains. The 3,000 hosts came in handy!"

The stories about the priestly Johnny Mac were legion. Uncannily able to raise money through shrewd business instinct, he became pastor of a newly constructed church in suburban Mount Prospect. Not many pastors name their own church, but McLoraine did—calling it St. Emily's, after his mother. When there was some difficulty in locating a rectory, McLoraine purchased a house on his own. He disagreed with the ruling of forced retirement from active pastoral duty at age 75. The chancery office downtown—always regarded suspiciously by Father McLoraine—asked that he retire as pastor, turn all affairs over to his successor, including the keys to the rectory. Father McLoraine agreed to do so, but announced that he would retain the keys to the rectory since the house was owned by him.

"We don't know how the negotiations for control of the house went," says Walter McCarty, "but I assume Johnny Mac made out pretty well financially."

All chaplains during wartime were obliged to go to at least one meeting to coordinate their work.

"Johnny Mac was the master of one-upmanship," says his godson McCarty. "The chaplains usually tried to top each other by commandeering big planes to fly themselves to the conference.

But Johnny Mac won. He flew to one conference in a special two-seater fighter aircraft. When he approached the airport, the pilot signed 'bingo-bingo!' which meant he was low on fuel. All the other planes immediately got stacked up and Johnny Mac's plane was given an all-clear signal to land. That's how he did things."

Father McLoraine remained a close friend of Monsignor McDermott throughout his life.

* * *

Chicago's spiritual and temporal leaders were flamboyant and vastly different from those of today. Within the same year, 1915, two leaders came to command in Chicago. With a stroke of a pen by Benedict XV in Rome, an auxiliary bishop of Brooklyn, George William Mundelein [1872–1939], was made the third archbishop of Chicago. And city voters elected William Hale Thompson [1867–1944] as its last Republican mayor, ushering in the reign of a perennial boy, a rich man's son who became a city builder—presiding over an era of corruption and urban beautification.

After the Mundelein appointment, the Chicago archdiocese rose swiftly from a frontier-style suzerainty of often quarrelsome Irish, German, Polish and Slavic pastors, to become a model of near-military efficiency in a golden era of urban Catholicism led by powerful big-city bishops.

Mundelein was a German-American when that nationality had political clout. He was born in New York City and raised on the Lower East Side. He briefly considered, but turned down, a prospective appointment to the U.S. Naval Academy in 1889, choosing instead to study for the priesthood for the Brooklyn diocese.

Brooklyn's bishop, Charles McDonnell, personally ordained him in Rome, a signal honor and evidence that McDonnell had his eye on the young cleric. Two years later, when just a curate, Mundelein was named chancellor of the diocese. Elevated to monsignor at 34, he became auxiliary bishop of Brooklyn at 37. At one time, he held 10 different positions in the diocese.

Mundelein assumed full authority. He became the greatest builder that Catholic Brooklyn has seen before or since: reorganizing finances and launching St. John's preparatory seminary. As *coup de grace*, he took an unfinished Queen of All Saints cathedral, stalled for decades due to lack of funds and completed it swiftly, giving it an architectural prize-winner for a chapel. Done in French Gothic style with 14 magnificent stained glass windows, the project was completed at a cost of a then unheard-of sum of $350,000. Moreover, construction was debt-free due to Mundelein's stunningly successful fund-raising techniques. On Palm Sunday 1910, his collection raised $47,801, the largest single collection for any New York City parish. A layman announced a $25,000 challenge grant that wealthy parishioners vied to emulate.

Flourishing a brilliant entrepreneurial flair, the young auxiliary bishop told the diocese that the dearest thing to him was a statue of St. George the Dragon-Slayer given to him by the pope—but in the interest of the cathedral's completion, he would raffle it off. The statue went to a bidder who paid as if it were made of gold. Soon stories of Mundelein got around: the entire Church in the eastern U.S. marveled at his fund-raising and organizational abilities.

Even so, it was a big jump in 1915 for a Brooklyn auxiliary bishop to become archbishop of the second largest diocese in the United States. International politics played an unintentional role. Uncontradicted rumor has long held that Mundelein was destined for Buffalo, New York, while Denis Dougherty—seven years Mundelein's senior, the first bishop of the Philippines—would come to Chicago. But the government of Canada, hotly anti-German during World War I, objected to appointment of a German-American bishop serving on the border in a diocese that reached many Canadians. Rome then reportedly switched the appointments—sending Mundelein to Chicago and Dougherty to Buffalo—with a promise of finding something bigger, quickly, for Dougherty. Two years later, he became archbishop of Philadelphia.

As the youngest archbishop in the United States at age 43, Mundelein relished the opportunity to bring discipline to the Chicago archdiocese which had long been a sea of contention. Administratively incompetent ecclesiastical leadership had unwittingly promoted fierce divisiveness. One early bishop resigned after two years, another went insane and had to be removed. One notable exception was Patrick Feehan [1829–1902], who founded 140 new parishes, a record unsurpassed. But late in life, Archbishop Feehan stumbled into a feud between Irish-born pastors and Irish-American pastors. Embroiled over the appointment of

U.S.-born Patrick Muldoon as chancellor, whom he made auxiliary bishop, Feehan triggered an unheard-of revolt. It created the scandalous excommunication of a leading priest-revolutionary.

Archbishop James Edward Quigley [1855–1915] succeeded on Feehan's death—just in time to be faced with demands from the swelling Slavic population for native parishes. By Quigley's death in 1915, Chicago Catholicism was a boiling cauldron of discordant ethnic jurisdictional parishes—Irish, German, Polish, Bohemian, Slovak, Lithuanian, and Italian as well as several ethnic groups consisting of no more than one or two parishes each. With Mundelein's appointment—a German-American sent to unify the smoldering ethnic potpourri—expectations were of continued fighting, but a terrorist attempt on the life of Mundelein, by an anarchist, helped put an end to the bitter rivalries.

It happened shortly after Mundelein arrived to take command of the archdiocese. After debarking from the train on February 8, 1916, he was swept up in three days of Masses and festivities; but the climactic event came on February 10, at a banquet for 300 business, academic and political leaders. As Mundelein biographer Edward Kantowicz relates: "A kitchen employee of the University Club of Chicago...poisoned the soup with arsenic in an attempt to strike a blow for anarchism by wiping out the city's elite. Though most of the guests became ill, none died. Another cook had diluted the poisoned soup when he detected an unpleasant taste in it. Archbishop Mundelein, a veteran of formal banquets, had not touched his soup (or much else of his dinner) and was unaffected."

The anarchist, an Alsatian immigrant named Jean Crones, escaped and led police on a frenetic chase while the newspapers covered the hunt with huge front-page headlines. He was never found. Radiating unearthly calm in the midst of the furor was the new archbishop, smoothly downplaying the incident.

As virtually the only dinner attendee who did not become ill—either by the grace of God or sheer chance—Mundelein received instantaneous awe. Then he turned to management of the archdiocese in an inaugural homily, which gave a candid assessment of how it contrasted with his predecessor: "...I am different from the late archbishop [Quigley]—the Lord cast me in a different mould. Perhaps I am quicker in grasping a thing and am likely to act more quickly."

An understatement. The day after the poisoning attempt while other attendees were barely able to hold down food, Mundelein strode into the chambers of Circuit Judge John McGoorty. He took the oath of "corporation sole," which granted him title to all the diocesan assets as "the Catholic bishop of Chicago"—including $50 million worth of property.

While previous Chicago bishops had regarded the oath as symbolic, Mundelein utilized the aura that came from the frustrated poisoning attempt to apply "corporation sole" as a charter for complete legal authority. Perhaps no later archbishop could assume the authority as Mundelein had. Corporation sole was no mere power grab, but a necessity. He used it to remove what was historically known as "trusteeism," a practice which caused the Church in this country during its early years "untold sorrow and division," according to historian Father Peter M.J. Stravinskas.

Immigrants frequently came to the United States with no clergy from their homeland. As they settled into their new environment, they often wrote home to bishops or religious superiors asking for priests familiar with their language and heritage, to care for their spiritual needs. In the meantime, they bought property and even erected church buildings, which were to be in readiness when the priests arrived. When the priests did arrive, many of these were treated as employees of the laity. They were identical to some Protestant ministers who served, but were beholden to trustees.

"Thus the authority and power of the priest to preach and teach in Christ's name in an unencumbered manner was seriously threatened and compromised," writes Stravinskas. "As time went on, bishops saw the disastrous nature of such arrangements and gradually gained control of church properties by bringing them under the diocesan umbrella—referred to civilly as a 'corporation sole.' In this form of organization, the bishop is the president of every parish and other institutions under his spiritual purview, with the parish priest as the secretary/treasurer and two laypeople (nominated by the pastor and appointed by the bishop) as trustees. Bringing Catholic institutions into compliance with this procedure was not an easy task, at times being resolved only through civil litigation as parishioners sued bishops and pastors, and the clergy responded with threats of excommunication and interdict."

Mundelein utilized ownership in corporate, not personal, name to seize control of the purse strings over all parishes. Thereafter, pastors who had previously warred with the chancery had to go to the archbishop personally for approval of their budgets. Soon their parishes came under his complete control. Obedient priests were favored, rebellious ones were transferred. Thus did the newcomer archbishop swiftly impose military-style disciplinary control.

As Chicago's business and civic heads marveled, year by year he centralized all administration and spurred imaginative fundraising. He built Quigley Preparatory Seminary on Chicago's Near North Side, and unveiled a massive plan for a Catholic university of the West, St. Mary of the Lake Seminary, in a rural location 40 miles north of the city.

Ever since, the seminary has been referred to in colloquial shorthand as "Mundelein." Enthralled, the nearest town—with the nondescript name of Area, Illinois—became so admiring of the archbishop and the economic benefits the seminary was destined to bring that it took his name, and is on the map as Mundelein, Illinois.

Just as assuredly, Mundelein the builder put the Chicago archdiocese on the map. The seminary was a gigantic architectural achievement for a U.S. church that tended to use ancient buildings as seminaries. He laid out an institution on a thousand-acre tract, surrounding a small lake, that consisted of buildings of Early American design, complete with a main chapel copied from the congregational meetinghouse in Old Lyme, Connecticut. Discouraging financial aid to the Catholic University of America, Mundelein's goal was to build an internationally known seat of Catholic learning, the University of St. Mary of the Lake. He used it as a site for extension courses for all his pastors, having them take refresher seminars in theology and philosophy on a regular basis. He frequently brought industrialists to the seminary. Monsignor McDermott recalls seeing Samuel Insull, the utility magnate, with the archbishop. Plans for the university died with him, but today a glorious complex of buildings—serving only very few seminarians—is still referred to as "Mundelein."

Beyond his financial and managerial prowess, George Mundelein was an ambassador of Catholicism to U.S. politicians and governmental leaders, using his powerful reputation to allay nativist suspicion that to be Catholic was un-American and a vassal of a foreign prince. In World War I when German-Americans were suspect, due to the witch-hunting tactics of Woodrow Wilson's attorney general, A. Mitchell Palmer, Mundelein used his

German heritage to reaffirm the loyalty of Chicago's Germans to the United States.

In recognition of his talents, Pius XI named him to the College of Cardinals, in 1924, making him the first cardinal of a city west of the Appalachians, or as his devotees called him "the first Prince of the West."

Having a cardinal was important to Chicago's prestige. The position dates back to the organization of the Rome bishopric. The College of Cardinals began in the early ninth century, growing into a group of advisors to the pope, then as a kind of senate, finally an elective body with the responsibility of choosing the pope, the bishop of Rome. The Treaty of Vienna in 1815 gave cardinals the status of princes of ruling houses, which has since been altered, although the title "Prince of the Church" is still applied. Attired in full regalia, from peaked mitre to shepherd's crook of authority, George William Mundelein was every inch a Prince of the Church and one to be obeyed. In 1926, Mundelein hosted the 28th International Eucharistic Congress at Soldier Field in Chicago, which culminated in a procession of 800,000 at St. Mary of the Lake Seminary. Ignatius McDermott marched and played a coronet on the concluding day of the Congress, as part of the Visitation Boys' Band, although he had graduated from Visitation two years earlier.

Ignatius McDermott had always felt that the garishness of the cardinals' wardrobe was ill-advised, an ostentatious showing of out-of-date royalty. Princes of the Church gathered, in formal ceremony, with nine-foot-long trains of scarlet, which required footmen to trail behind holding some of the fabric in their hands. Cardinals were to wear red shoes with silver buckles. The cardinal was to wear a "tabarro," or cloak, trimmed in ermine. On elevation to cardinal, he was awarded a "galero," a wide-brimmed scarlet hat, established by Innocent IV in 1245, the color representing the cardinals' loyalty to the point of *"usque ad effusionem sanguinis,"* or the shedding of blood. But the color's origin goes back to the ancient Roman senate whose patrician members wore robes of reddish purple trim.

Latter day popes have reduced the ostentation. In 1952, Pius XII cut the royal nine-foot-long train in half. Paul VI ordered goodbye to the red shoes and silver buckles in 1969. He also updated the dress code by refusing further sanction to the "tabarro" ermine-lined cloak, although he allowed another type of cloak, the "cappa magna," to stay but without the ermine trim. Red socks were to be allowed but never worn under a plain black cassock. And Paul did away with the galero, replacing it with a red skullcap and biretta, a silk-covered square hat with no brim. The original galero was never to be worn, but treasured as a symbol of his office—a hat that would be pulled up to the top of the cardinal's cathedral after his death. There the galero was to remain, fixed by wires to the ceiling of his cathedral until passage of time would see it fade, weaken and fall. Legend had it that the red hat would fall when the cardinal had completed his time in purgatory and moved on to heaven. The galeros of Mundelein and his successors, Samuel Stritch, Albert Meyer, John Cody, and Joseph Bernardin, are still hanging in the apse of Holy Name Cathedral, Bernardin's admirers having hoisted a galero for him even though it had been forbidden in the dress code.

"There was a great mistake in making you a bishop instead of a financier," a Chicago business leader told Mundelein. "With you, J.P. Morgan would have a formidable rival on Wall Street." Business entrepreneur though he was, Mundelein was no toady to either Wall or LaSalle Streets. In sweeping fashion, he instructed the Chicago church to implement the social teachings of Leo XIII, involving responsibility of Christians to the poor and support for labor unions. He was more socially and politically liberal than most of his prelate colleagues.

His passionately progressive auxiliary Bishop Bernard J. Sheil backed labor during the sit-down strikes at Detroit's automobile plants and endorsed striking packinghouse workers' demands in Chicago. A friend and advisor to President Franklin D. Roosevelt, Mundelein capitalized on his standing as a prominent German-American to criticize Adolf Hitler in the 1930s (he called Hitler "that paperhanger") and hosted FDR when the president came to Chicago to deliver his famed "Quarantine the Aggressors" speech on October 3, 1937.

Summarizes historian Kantowicz: "Though the Catholic Church was America's largest denomination as early as 1850, it lacked status and respect both in Rome and in the United States. The leadership of Cardinal Mundelein and his generation of big city bishops raised the status of American Catholics, giving them self-confidence and clout both at home and at the Vatican."

Beyond all these qualities, he was eager to dispense what the Church called the corporal and spiritual works of mercy. Mundelein reinvigorated and reorganized Catholic Charities, determined to move the Church in uniquely humane ways to serve the poor. Knowing his priests personally by name, he was always on the lookout for talent, finding those who could effectively do this work.

More than just a bricks-and-mortar authoritarian Mundelein was, in the words of latest successor and enthusiastic admirer, Francis Cardinal George, "a teacher of the faith." The misbegotten idea that he arrogated unto himself the role of corporation sole without precedent is wrong, Cardinal George has written in the archdiocesan newspaper *The Catholic New World*. "[It is] almost as if it were unique to Mundelein or Chicago to protect the assets of the Church by having the diocesan bishop be recognized, in civil law, as a corporation sole. In fact, over half the Ordinaries in the country are corporation sole, wherever the laws of the state admit that form of corporation."

In 1927, three years after having been named Cardinal, Mundelein published *Letters of a Bishop to His Flock*, explaining in the preface that he had been asked to write an autobiography but refused. There were, he said, "really no outstanding events in my life...and there is the ever present danger of taking too much to ourselves the credit for what has been accomplished through us by the Holy Spirit."

The letters are still fresh and vital today—nine emphasizing Catholic Charities, nine on catechetical instruction for Sunday sermons by priests at Mass, ten on the First World War and the postwar period, and three to the Eucharistic Congress held in Chicago. Still, cynicism in Chicago dies hard. Clerical opponents, afraid to speak against him while he lived, were heard to say after his death that his episcopal motto *Dominus adjutor meus* ("The Lord is my help") translated as "The Lord is my assistant."

This is an unkind jest, writes Cardinal George. Mundelein worked tirelessly for "orphans here in Cook, Will and Grundy Counties, and hungry children abroad, in Ireland, Poland, Germany, Austria and Mexico." He wrote about "refugees, the education of women, the generosity of religious Sisters and obligations of family men as well as their employers." Thus was Mundelein one of two leaders to take hold in Chicago in 1915.

* * *

With the second man to rise to citywide prominence in 1915, Mayor William Hale Thompson, things were far different. Acting as a buffoon, he was also a bombastic demagogue with an eye for appeal to a city where nearly a third of the voters were foreign born. In multiple though non-consecutive terms [1915–23; 1927–31], Thompson opened the doors to unparalleled greed, venality, and organized crime. Unlike most big city bosses, he was not a poor boy who scaled the mountain with grit and resolve. His family had been in America for six generations, since 1700. His father had added to an inherited fortune as a Boston broker, and then moved his family to brawling Chicago in 1868. Before he turned 15, young Bill Thompson, who showed no aptitude for school, had gone to Wyoming to be a cowboy. He managed a cattle ranch before returning to Chicago after his father's death. He ran the family's hugely successful real estate business. A sports enthusiast with the Chicago Athletic Association in an era where men's social clubs gained wide attention for their rivalry, Thompson entered the city council after accepting a $50 barroom wager that he couldn't be elected. Big, pompous—with a zest for life—he beat Democratic county clerk Robert Schweitzer whom he labeled the creature of boss Roger Sullivan, a key figure in the natural gas rate scandals of the 1890s.

At first Thompson played the role of reformer, keeping his pledge to shut down saloons on Sundays. Indeed, 7,150 drinking establishments were told to do so. But a flourishing industry of corruption arose when, for a price, police shrugged at closing hours. When Prohibition became legalized in 1920, Thompson winked at the law as mobsters formed an unsavory partnership with politicians to protect the bootleg industry through pay-offs to his machine by mobster front groups. And more help for corruption was underway.

In 1916, national elections had returned a Congress where "wet" members outnumbered "drys" by two-to-one. But the Prohibition movement was a long time brewing, since 1840, when businessman Neal Dow of Portland, Maine, made a study of the effects of alcohol in that city. His belief was that an overwhelming number of evils were spawned by it. He and his followers lobbied the State of Maine to ban all liquor sales. Militant women took up the cause, linking women's suffrage to it, and Maine became the first state to outlaw liquor in 1851.

Following the Civil War, feminists redoubled their energies, forming the Anti-Saloon League of America which held its first convention in 1895. Mobilizing Protestant church congregations, with the aspiration of women to vote, the League crusaded to prohibit saloons as a first step to prohibiting sales of liquor altogether. By 1916, 21 states had banned saloons.

In December 1917, with thousands of young men engaged in World War I—neglecting to vote—Congress yielded to "dry" pressure and submitted to the states the 18th Amendment, outlawing all liquor sales. By 1919, the amendment was ratified, changing the Constitution to ban "the manufacture, sale or transportation of intoxicating liquor." By the time of ratification, the Volstead Act, making the U.S. dry, had already been passed by Congress and the amendment took force in 1920.

While Prohibition spurred organized crime, much has been made of a myth that it increased drinking and spurred widespread gangland murders. Not so. U.S. health statistics show cirrhosis death rates for men dropped by two-thirds and alcohol consumption declined by up to 50 percent during Prohibition (although, assuredly, deaths occurred and health was impaired by drinking shoddily distilled moonshine), while homicide rates continued unchanged. John Burnham, professor of history at Ohio State University, and the acknowledged authority on Prohibition, attributes the amendment's "bad rap" to sensationalist journalists eager to sell stories about gangland slayings and undercover bars. In the end, Prohibition even was blamed, falsely, for causing the Great Depression. Anti-Prohibitionists promised that liquor taxes would bail out the nation financially.

*   *   *

In December of 1919, a sinister émigré came to Chicago. He was from Brooklyn, just 20, who came as an assistant to Johnny Torrio, a hired killer. In order to put the best possible face on his business, the young importer re-did a storefront, hauling in an old piano, three tables, a planter, a rocking chair, and an aquarium. He printed up cards:

Alfonse Capone, Dealer in Antiques, 2222 South Wabash.

Monsignor McDermott notes dryly, "He buried all his antiques." Capone was to succeed Torrio; Thompson was to ally secretly with Capone. By 1924, four years after the start of Prohibition, there were 15 breweries in the city—going full blast—and an estimated 20,000 speakeasy saloons.

* * *

In addition to housing Mundelein, Thompson, and Capone all at one time, Chicago rocked with excitement for other reasons. The year 1919 was the political debut of 25-year-old Jim McDermott. He had followed Uncle John Bradley's career into law and politics, under the tutelage of legendary South Side Judge John J. Sullivan, whom many saw as a masterly political strategist.

Sullivan [1880–1951] was Democratic committeeman of the old 30th ward (now the 14th) and a judge, serving for a time in both roles. This was then legally permissible. One of eight children, Sullivan, who had sold newspapers at Halsted and Archer, graduated from the old South Division high school and Chicago Normal School. He started as a teacher at James Shields public high school where he met his future wife. He went to night law school, receiving his law degree from Kent College of Law in 1905. Sullivan's prowess as a political organizer and Democratic strategist was legendary, and he rose swiftly in politics and the law, becoming a municipal judge at 31. He later served on the Superior Court and Circuit Court and, at his death, Judge Sullivan sat on the Illinois Appellate bench. His son, John J., was a Circuit Court judge; his grandson, the Reverend John J., an admirer of Jim McDermott and close friend of Monsignor McDermott, is pastor, at this writing, of St. John's Catholic Church in suburban Glenwood.

Judge Sullivan's career and working habits were extensively covered by Robert A. Slayton's *Back of the Yards: The Making of a Local Democracy.*

Monsignor McDermott is quoted by Slayton as saying that Sullivan "was one of the pioneer architects" of the 14th ward Democratic organization.

"Sullivan loved politics and was in it 'knee deep,'" Slayton wrote. "His younger brother was personal secretary to Edward Dunne, governor of Illinois from 1913 to 1917, and a close friend of Tom Nash of the prestigious political law firm of Nash and

Ahern. Throughout his career the judge refused to sit on a bench higher than the Appellate Court because it would have meant leaving politics. He also avoided any type of limelight and preferred working behind the scenes, which suited his position as a judge."

Writes Slayton:

> At that time, two politicians, Billy Lynch and William O'Toole fought for the alderman's position, draining each other's energies and permitting an occasional independent Democrat like streetcar conductor Joseph Mahoney to slip in. Sullivan persuaded Lynch and O'Toole to run in alternate years, thus keeping the organization firmly in control. According to the best account of the 1914 meeting, the judge told them, 'Now there's no use you two beating your brains out. One of you run this year and the other support him and the next year vice versa.' The two flipped a coin to see who would run first and O'Toole won and became the alderman. From then on, Sullivan was the undisputed arbitrator and boss of the ward. That very year he began to appoint precinct captains and establish a formal ward organization.

Judge Sullivan chose the ward's alderman as well as Democratic ward committeeman and dictated their actions in addition to his work on the bench.

Slayton writes:

> The people, as well as the local politicos, turned to Sullivan. He controlled all the city jobs in the ward and eventually many throughout Chicago. He was particularly efficient in arranging matters for prospective captains of police. The Democrats downtown recognized Sullivan's shrewdness, even-handedness, and most of all, his brilliance at slate-making. The judge was a master at setting up a winning ticket, knowing whom the voters would accept for which office. Jacob Arvey, chair of the Cook County Democratic party, claimed that five men ran the Democratic organization in the thirties and fifties and that Sullivan was one of them. These five men also made up the slates, often in Judge Sullivan's basement on Garfield Boulevard. He was asked to act as arbitrator in the highest political circles and he was the only man to sit on the Cook County Democratic party Central Committee without being elected to it. The observation that Sullivan 'helped found the whole Democratic

party that exists today' (i.e. the Democratic party machine) seemed accurate.

The job of ward leader was a taxing one and took long hours, sometimes seemingly without end. There were really two positions, ward committeeman and alderman. Committeeman was a party post and its incumbent was elected by the precinct captains. He handled requests for patronage jobs, chose candidates for the Illinois House of Representatives, Senate and judiciary, sat on the party's central committee; and ran the election campaigns in the ward. The alderman was the elected representative of the people and sat in the City Council. He handled complaints, dealt with its constituents and in general was the front man for the ward. In the 14th ward, the alderman and the ward committeeman was [sic] usually one and the same, ensuring a united organization.

The ward's residents turned to the organization for all manner of help—cleaning up dirty alleys, having garbage collected, getting out of jury duty, fixing broken curbs, obtaining food, finding medical help and gaining admission to Cook County Hospital, getting kids out of jail, obtaining financial assistance, appealing real estate tax assessments, having gutters and street lights put in, obtaining and getting jobs...Though the alderman met his public every day of the year, Tuesday night was always ward night, the appointed time for citizens to seek assistance. Always accompanied by their precinct captains, the voters filed in with petitions. The alderman and ward committeeman would sit in the back room and as the people would come in with their precinct captains, they would be handling job requests and services.

Favors were not automatically granted. If someone complained that an assessment was too high, the alderman went downtown and checked it out. If he could do nothing about it, he told the constituents that the assessment was fair. Usually the constituent needed another favor later and the score could be evened. The Democratic party's helping hand was always extended. Richard Daley...instructed his people, "Don't worry if they're Democrats or Republicans. Give them service and they'll become Democrats."

One of the 14th ward's great aldermen and the foremost protégé of John J. Sullivan was James McDermott. He served as alderman from 1933 to 1942 and as ward committeeman from 1932 to 1948.

McDermott's big chance came in 1933. From 1923 to 1931, the 14th ward's alderman was William O'Toole. His perennial opponent was Thomas O'Grady, a fiery person with ability and talent, and a good orator. In 1931, O'Grady ousted O'Toole so the judge [Sullivan] dumped O'Toole and chose McDermott to replace him. In 1933, McDermott, the new regular candidate, won; he remained alderman until 1942 and ward committeeman until 1948. Years later, when O'Grady died, McDermott took care of all his relatives and gave them jobs.

James McDermott was perfect for the role of alderman. He was tall—six feet three inches—and very handsome, with silver-gray hair. Nicknamed "Big Jim," he was a fiery speaker and cut a fine figure. Father Joseph Kelly described McDermott as "a great, beautiful...father, victory-triumphant figure...He had presence."

The Town of Lake Journal (now *Back of the Yards Journal*), an independent paper not tied to any political organization, spoke of the "brilliant, powerful, forceful Jim McDermott, known not only on the South Side but throughout the whole city." His precinct captains saluted him, and one described him as a "gentleman...you couldn't find better. At parties...he used to dance like heck when he had a few drinks and every Christmas he bought all the nuns a little something."

Judge Sullivan saw that Jim McDermott moved into politics and a berth with Chicago's most powerful law firm, Nash and Ahern. Jim McDermott's first major case was to defend shortstop and sometimes third baseman, George "Buck" Weaver in the celebrated "Black Sox" scandal. The White Sox won the World Series in 1917 and the pennant in 1919. The Sox went into the World Series of 1919 the heavy favorite against Cincinnati. But seven Sox players decided to lose (an eighth kept this knowledge to himself). A jury acquitted all eight players, including Weaver, of fraud. Newly appointed baseball commissioner Kenesaw Mountain Landis banned all eight from the game forever.

Judge Sullivan's grandson, Father John J. Sullivan, describes Jim McDermott with these words: "Tall, six feet three or so with a similarity to Father Ig of today. Both were there for the underdog, both were always there in times of need. Both men had the uncanny sensitivity with human beings of realizing when there was a need—when a need presented itself, but before the person in need asked for attention or asked for help. So both were rather unique, I think, in offering assistance when they saw the need rather than put the person through the embarrassment of having to ask and possibly being turned down. Always there to help people in any way possible. Great senses of humor. Both have and had short fuses."

Notwithstanding their many victories on the field, the White Sox were an unhappy team in 1919. A prime reason: while no club played better ball, few were paid so poorly. Writes one baseball historian: "Many knowledgeable observers believe that it was Comiskey's stinginess that is largely to blame for the Black Sox scandal; if Comiskey had not grossly underpaid his players and treated them so unfairly, they would never have agreed to throw the Series. Comiskey was able to get away with low salaries because of the 'reverse clause' in players' contracts. This clause prevented players from changing teams without the permission of the owners. Without a union, the players had no bargaining power."

Also, Comiskey was, reportedly, not a man of his word in dealing with the players. He once promised them a big bonus if they won the pennant. The bonus turned out to be a case of cheap champagne. Comiskey even charged players for laundering their uniforms. When in protest they wore dirty uniforms, Comiskey removed the uniforms from their lockers and fined the players.

In 1919 the first World Series championship after World War I, enthusiasm was so high that officials decided to make the Series the best of nine games rather than the traditional best of seven. (It had been nine games in 1903, went to seven from 1904 to 1918, to nine from 1919 to 1921, then reverted permanently to seven.)

Baseball historians disagree about the details. But Chick Gandil, the first baseman, is generally called the ringleader. A few weeks before the 1919 Series, Gandil approached a "fixer" and said that for $100,000 Gandil and several of his teammates would make sure the White Sox would lose.

Endowed with a marvelous memory for names and details, Monsignor McDermott can—without consulting the records—rattle off statistics and players in the Black Sox scandal as if it were current sports-page fare. "I remember my brother got out of law school preceding the Black Sox scandal. Their scandal broke a year later. It took a year for the scandal to break, and I think a guy by the name of Abe Attell—a professional gambler or something—I think he was the source of it."

Exactly right. Abe Attell, a former Sox player during the "hit-less wonder" years, contacted a group of alienated Sox players and initiated contact with Joseph "Sport" Sullivan—another White Sox alumnus—at Boston's Buckminster Hotel, on September 19, to discuss a "business proposition." They were front men for Arnold Rothstein, the "Big Bankroll" of New York, who had bet losing money on the Sox in 1917, and who was eager to even the score.

Sitting in his office at Haymarket Center, Monsignor McDermott, 80 years after the occurrence, said: "Buck Weaver was the third baseman of the White Sox and one of Nash and Ahern's clients. And then I think [Chick] Gandil, the first baseman. I remember Joe Jackson, who was a big star of the team, who came out of North Carolina; I remember what the papers were saying at the time—I was a kid, about 11. I asked my brother about it and remember him saying that Joe Jackson, the big star, couldn't read or write."

He knew about it, didn't he?

"They thought he knew about it, but they didn't know whether he could absorb it or not."

Did he take the money?

Yes, but "my brother thought he was innocent because of the fact that he couldn't comprehend it."

Looking at the Sox roster, who were clean?

"Buck Weaver was clean. He was the third baseman. Gandil was involved, the first baseman. [Eddie] Collins was Simon-pure. ['Swede'] Risberg was dirty. Ray Schalk was clean; he ran a bowling alley later on."

So the guys who were found to be "dirty" were—.

"Chick Gandil, the first baseman, Eddie Collins is two, Buck Weaver is three, Joe Jackson is four, Happy Felsch, the centerfielder, is five, Nemo Leibold is six, and did I say [Claude] Williams, the pitcher?—there were seven of them. [Dick] Kerr [another pitcher] was a diminutive type and he stayed clear of it."

People are still trying to get "Shoeless" Joe Jackson into the Baseball Hall of Fame—should they?

"Yes. And I hope they put him in there because I don't think he knew what he was doing. Besides, he was better than anybody else on the team."

* * *

Then in 1923, entered a species familiar to Chicago ever since: a clean, liberal Democrat vowing to reform the city. Many were found to be phonies, but this time voters elected an idealistic Democrat who was the real article. He dislodged Thompson but only for a single term. Ironically, he is forgotten today.

He was a true reformer, the first Catholic to become mayor, ex-judge William E. Dever [1862–1929]. He sought to remove politics from the schools, inspire a vision of dedicated service to municipal government, cut waste and run the gangsters out of town (Capone was forced to move to suburban Cicero).

With his friends, young Democrat Ignatius McDermott sang Dever's theme song, to the tune of "It's Three O'Clock in the Morning"—"*We will talk in the morning. We'll vote for William E. Dever. We promise that he will be fair and true. And on the first day of November, we will elect him mayor!*" Dever's clear reformism alienated those who benefited from corruption and, four years later, the "bad old days" with Bill Thompson came back.

As a youngster, a Sox fan, Ignatius held a variety of summer jobs—selling newspapers, working at ballparks, vendors' shops, and working at the Nash and Ahern law firm.

In 1924, the year reformer Dever upset "Big Bill" Thompson, Ignatius entered the former Sacred Heart Preparatory Seminary, designated as Quigley, awaiting completion of a new building. He was to receive a thorough education in the philosophy and theology of his Church, as prescribed by three great popes.

* * *

So-called "minor" (high school) and "major" (university) seminaries of Ignatius' time—and U.S. Catholicism during the first half of the 20th century—were influenced by three vivid popes. One was Leo XIII [reign: 1878–1903] who, within the framework of traditional teaching, sought to bring the Church to terms with the modern age. He stressed study of Thomas Aquinas, accompanied by denunciation of Kant and Hegel. His encyclical *Rerum Novarum* set him apart as an advanced social thinker.

"He had a tremendous pontificate," remarked Monsignor McDermott. "Didn't he die in his nineties?" Yes.

Leo wrote an eloquent description of the plight of the poor in industrial societies in which "a small number of very rich men have been able to lay upon the teeming masses of the laboring poor a yoke which is very little better than slavery itself." From this state of servitude comes socialism, which wrongly foments class hatred and denies private property. The rich have a duty to help the poor, declared Leo, in duties that go beyond charity. The state depends upon the rights of labor and in the healing of society; the state must play a part in support of regulations insuring a living wage that allows the worker to acquire property and a stake in society. He accepted the right to strike but insisted that the state should legislate to reform grievances that promote strikes. Leo caused a shift in emphasis to support a social mind, engaged with the problems of modern society, leading to solution of social problems apart from socialism. He was the fist pope to understand the international mission of the papacy in modern terms.

The second memorable pontiff was Pius X [reign: 1903–1914]. Later canonized, he was an opponent of "modernism," or relativism, within the Church. A strict conservative with the jolly mien of a country curate, he was a proponent of what he called "Catholic Action," the enlisting of lay folk in the work of the clergy, leading to the founding of charitable agencies and giving lasting stimulus to the spiritual life of Catholics. Pius reinvigorated Catholic worship by enjoining frequent Communion, lowering the age of the First Communion for children, easing of rules concerning Communion to the sick, and urging the laity not to simply observe the Mass but share in the sacrament.

The third was Pius XI [reign: 1922–1939], an intellectual who branded Nazism as anti-Christian with an encyclical (written largely by his secretary of state, Eugenio Pacelli, later Pius XII) that he ordered to be summarized from all pulpits. Pius XI not only reaffirmed but went beyond Leo XIII in stressing individual responsibility to the poor and opposing the arms race.

From their teachings came the stricture of clerical learning that took root at Mundelein seminary and others. The ironclad rules were written by Reverend John B. Hogan, a Sulpician priest whose book, *Clerical Studies,* prescribed how each subject in preparatory and major seminaries would be taught. These schools, wrote Hogan, should produce a priest who was an educated gentleman fitted for public life, physically sound, in sympathy with his environment, and filled with true missionary spirit. A young man was admitted to Quigley only if he exhibited a desire to become a priest for the archdiocese of Chicago. Students had to be proficient in Latin, Greek, and Hebrew. No classes were held on Thursdays (when meditation would be observed) and a strict demerit disciplinary system was enforced. There was a sports program but limited to intramural competition.

* * *

Ignatius spent part of the summer of 1927, when he was on summer leave from Quigley, in Benton Harbor, Michigan. There his father was "taking the waters," benefiting from the natural springs that supposedly healed arthritis and other ailments. One day while the 18-year-old seminarian was having a cup of coffee in a local restaurant and idling through a newspaper trying to find out how the White Sox were doing, a couple of burly, slab-faced men walked in with an air of sullen importance and asked the proprietor the location of the exits. After he told them where they were, one departed and returned with a short, sallow-complexioned man whose face was marked cruelly by a scar.

"It was Al Capone, who had a summer cottage at nearby Riverside, Michigan," says Monsignor McDermott.

Benton Harbor was also the home of Benjamin Purnell of the "House of David." Ignatius McDermott and his father attended a trial there of the sect leader, who resembled the fiery abolitionist, John Brown. Purnell founded the sect in 1903, which was purportedly based on the Book of Revelation promising the saving of a "righteous remnant" of humanity who would gather in one place to await the millennium. It was intended to be a celibate, communal society ruled by Purnell and his wife, "Queen Mary." This attracted more than 700 members who exchanged their worldly goods for the security of salvation. Members were vegetarians, gave their worldly possessions to a common treasury, which provided for the needs of all. Men wore long hair and beads and lived according to the apostolic plan. The "House of David" operated a famous summer resort, built entirely by the members. It also owned and operated a cold storage plant, a printing establishment, machine shops, greenhouses, and farms. But beyond everything else, there was a famous "House of David" baseball team. Monsignor McDermott and his family were well aware that the team played baseball well and was on the road constantly as a fund-raising exhibition.

"They were like the Harlem Globetrotters," he says. "They wore their long hair tucked up under their baseball caps. One specialty was an outfielder who would chase a fly ball, catch it expertly, and shake off his cap, whereupon a long flow of hair would escape, rolling down his back. The 'House of David' didn't believe in haircuts."

Benjamin Purnell was charged with the crime of rape in 1923 and was searched for by the police, the rumor being that he had fled the state, possibly even the country. However, on the night of November 16, 1926, he was apprehended in his residence, Diamond House. The state police smashed in the door, accompanied by photographers, "catching the dethroned leader in his slippers, shawl and nightgown with his women attendants scattering in all directions," wrote historian Robert S. Fogarty.

"During his confinement at Diamond House, Purnell had been cared for by a contingent of colony women—some old, some young—who ministered to his physical needs," Fogarty added. "Considering the nature of the offenses against him, there was considerable speculation about the nature of that care. Some expert testimony stated that his diabetic condition would have depressed his sexual activity, while others pointed to the presence of two attractive young women who were present on the second floor as his caretakers when the colony was raided."

In addition to the rape charge in the *State of Michigan v. Benjamin Purnell et al*, Purnell was accused of maintaining a fraudulent religious system and conspiring to obstruct justice. On November 7, 1927, the judge issued his decree mandating that the rape charge was inconclusive, but that Purnell should leave the colony and that the colony be placed in receivership to be appointed by the state. On December 16, Purnell, the messenger of the "House of David," died of tuberculosis. Loyal followers believed that he would undergo a resurrection as Christ did after three days—but when he did not, he was embalmed, and followers were told that he would rise at a later date. By 1936, the controversy died completely, but the baseball team continued to play for fund-raising events. Babe Ruth was offered $35,000 to play with them by Ray Doan, a former member, who said that the "Bambino" would not be required to raise a beard—but Ruth declined. The team continued to travel about the country until 1953.

*   *   *

Ignatius graduated from Quigley in June 1929. He worked that summer as a counselor at a boys' camp. That fall, he entered St. Mary of the Lake (informally known as "Mundelein") major seminary, which Cardinal Mundelein had placed under the tutelage of the Jesuits. As his close friend Father McLoraine recounted: "We were together through the first two years in what was the philosophy department. When we finished philosophy we moved into theology." Total training consisted of two years in philosophy and four years in theology taught by Jesuit priests at Cardinal Mundelein's insistence. Then would come ordination.

Life in the major seminary was rigorous, reflecting Mundelein's propensity for a military academy, which he nearly attended. Seminarians were to be in excellent physical shape. No matter how qualified a young man would be, if he was of illegitimate birth, he was barred.

Recalls Monsignor McDermott: "I had heard about whether [with Cardinal Mundelein] it would be the military life or the priesthood—the spiritual world or the military world—and I have a feeling that this was verified with the attire of the seminary. In those days, we all had to wear a cassock, a Roman cassock. A Roman cassock would be buttoned from your head to toe, with a collar, and there wouldn't be any tape on it. The Jesuits who taught us wore sort of a Jesuit cassock without buttons, and they had a black sash around it. We wore this *zimarra*. It was a coat that was reminiscent, practically a replica, of the uniforms worn by cadets at West Point. You see the cadets dressed in a coat that has a cape around the neck that goes down below the shoulders and it goes from head to toe. And that was the GI uniform with us when we were at Mundelein."

Seminarians at St. Mary of the Lake seemed to live in their cassocks. Monsignor McDermott recalls the schedule with the precision that has always been his characteristic: "We'd get up every morning at 5:25 a.m., would be in the chapel at 10 minutes to six and we'd have morning prayer. Then, after morning prayer, we had a meditation for half an hour. At 6:30 a.m., Mass would be offered which would be concluded at 7:00 a.m., and we would have thanksgiving after Mass for 15 minutes and then we would go to breakfast at 7:15 a.m.

"After breakfast we could recreate until 8 a.m. At 8 a.m., we'd retire to our room to study. Then, at 8:55 a.m. go to the lecture hall; 9:00 to 10:00 a.m. in class; 10:00 a.m. to 10:15 recess; 10:15 a.m. to 10:45 in our rooms; 11:00 a.m. to 11:45 class; 11:45 a.m. to noon in chapel for *particular examen*; noon to 12:15 p.m. a break; 12:15 p.m. lunch and a visit to chapel; 1:00 p.m. to 1:30 free time; 1:30 p.m. to 2:00 study in rooms; 2:00 p.m. to 3:55 class; 4:00 p.m. to 5:00 take off cassock, recreate or swim; 5:15 to 6:00 p.m. chapel; 6:00 p.m. dinner; 6:30 p.m. visit chapel; 6:45 to 7:15 p.m. free time; 7:15 p.m. study in room; 9:00 to 9:30 p.m. chapel; at 9:30 p.m. return to room. Lights out at 9:45 p.m."

The cardinal pioneered a seminary "that was the ultimate for the students, with each one having a private room and private bath. Prior to that time, I didn't know of any other seminary like it. Priests who preceded us years before were living two or three or four of them in a room or dormitory. Mundelein wanted to come up with the ultimate—which it was."

Restrictions at the seminary were heavy. Cigarettes were forbidden, but students could smoke pipes three times a day. "We were allowed to write and receive letters. We were not allowed to receive any packages, only at Christmas. We had Visiting Sundays. Since we returned to the seminary in September, right after Labor Day, there wasn't any Visiting Sunday in September. On the second Sunday of the month, the philosophers' parents would come out and on the third Sunday of the month, the parents of the theologians would come out." There were no student leaves for Christmas, the cardinal-archbishop stressing an apartness from family and the world for the seminarians.

"We never got home for Christmas," Monsignor McDermott says. "We would go home in January, around the 25th, and return about the 6th of February. Because we were home, we didn't have any Visiting Sunday in February, so we had a Visiting Sunday in March, April, and May. You went home again in June." Seminarians were only allowed to write letters to their parents and, if they chose, their pastors. All letters were inspected by the prefect of discipline before they were mailed.

What fun, if any, did the seminarians have in that era of rigid discipline? They found it in harmless ways. And the faculty had a tame way of instilling a scholarly excitement. On Epiphany Sunday, the cooks prepared three pound cakes containing one bean in each.

"Each seminarian who discovered the bean won a copy of the life of Saint Alphonsus Liguori," said Monsignor McDermott.

The seminary had rigid rules against newspapers on campus, hoping to isolate the students against secular influence. Ignatius resorted to his old role as newsboy, stealthily arranging with a vendor to drop a Sunday *Tribune* in a box on the baseball infield early Sunday morning. Then Ignatius would saunter by, pick up the paper, stuff it in a bag, and leave 15¢ for the paper, plus a small tip for the smuggler.

High times and excitement, circa 1930s, at the major seminary.

Was the world of Quigley and St. Mary of the Lake too strict? Were priesthood students stunted by lack of contact with women, as Dr. Eugene Kennedy, a former Maryknoll priest, would later complain?

"Did Eugene Kennedy have any sisters?" pointedly responds Monsignor McDermott. "I had two sisters; they had girlfriends coming in. We had mothers and aunts and nieces and cousins, so we had great exposure to the world of females. And you weren't welded in. You could leave any time you wanted. When you were at the seminary at Mundelein, if you felt this wasn't your cup of tea and you wanted to make your vocation married life and bring children into the world—maybe your son could be a priest and your daughter could be a nun, if you were thinking along those lines."

The rule of celibacy since the early days of the Church was clear, the words of St. Paul in Corinthians, ringing down through the centuries: "An unmarried man can devote himself to the Lord's affairs; all he need worry about is pleasing the Lord."

During the summer of his last year at St. Mary of the Lake, seminarian Ignatius McDermott worked at Arlington Park racetrack at concession stands for $7 a day. During those Prohibition days, he watched as patrons mixed booze with Coke. To get to Arlington Heights, a northwest Chicago suburb, he had to board a train at the Chicago & Northwestern station on Madison Street. "I'd walk from Halsted over to Canal, right through the heart of Skid Row. I noticed, in those days, the men were ranging in age from 45 to 75. I didn't see too many young fellas." He thought often of the down-and-outers who camped there and how he could help them as a priest.

But before that, there came an injury. In the words of his friend and classmate Father McLoraine: "It was in first theology that he was injured and he spent a great deal of time in the hospital." It was a football injury.

"I think his leg went underneath him. It wasn't a tackle. It was what they call touch football but they were allowed to block. Somebody blocked him and his leg went from under him and it was his knee that was damaged."

The injury delayed his ordination—indeed threatened it. Being sidelined in convalescence almost forfeited his priestly career. The story of how he overcame the rector's determination to eject him, which made him a rebel and youthful hero at Mundelein's seminary, follows in the next chapter.

As for the injury—with doughty courage he's limping today. For many years, it didn't show. He walked swiftly—so fast that often it was hard to keep up with him. Now, as a concession, he leans on a cane. Once, not long ago, he went to a doctor with a sore toe. When the physician examined the ravaged leg, he gasped, "Well! How did you do this—and when?"

"Forget that," said Monsignor McDermott, "I'm here for my toe!"

CHAPTER 5

On the DL—Then Back in the Game, 1931–1936

Sometimes the bad breaks end up to be the good breaks.

[about an attempted reconciliation between Al Smith and newly-elected President Franklin D. Roosevelt] *I remember reading that when Smith made his first visit to the Oval Office, maybe a year or two after election, the press said: "Governor, did you relish your visit with the president?" And he said, "Well, gentlemen, let me say: Did you ever nail a custard pie to a wall?"*

Well, gee, I really felt terrible. I figured I was going to kiss the White Sox goodbye.

To myself I said, "I'm not going to be Mickey the mope."

—Ignatius McDermott

Mundelein's seminary, run on military lines—the U.S. flag and the papal banner were hoisted when the Prince of the Church was in residence at the seminary—drilled men for the day they would receive the sacrament that Christ conferred on His apostles, known since the Council of Trent [1545] as "Holy Orders." Professors were Jesuits; the university was administered by an archdiocesan priest.

On ordination day, a bishop—always Mundelein himself—would pronounce the words "receive the Holy Spirit," before rows of young men lying prostrate before him to connote obedience. With the sacrament would come divine gifts—the power to consecrate bread and wine into the body and blood of Christ, and authority to absolve repentant sinners, which is now said in English, with these words: "God, the Father of Mercy, reconciled the world to Himself through the death and resurrection of His Son and gave the Holy Spirit in abundance for the forgiveness of sins. May He grant you pardon and peace through the ministry of the Church. And I absolve you from your sins, in the name of the Father, and of the Son and of the Holy Spirit."

Given their rigorous routine, the seminarians found it difficult to snatch even a few minutes for unprogrammed fun. Thursdays, they had free. In 1935, a few of them found a secret room under the theater orchestra pit where they would play Monopoly™ (the game was newly in vogue then), fortified by chicken à la king which they ordered from a nearby town via cab. The Monopoly™ sessions were organized by Roger Jones, later a prefect at Quigley. Ignatius McDermott joined the sessions attended by 12 leaders in the class. The clandestine meeting was interrupted one day when the door swung open to reveal the night watchman, Michael McDevitt. McDevitt was afflicted with a serious stutter which he sought to dislodge by stomping his foot and shouting, "Oooh, oooh!" He emitted two "oooh, ooohs" when the students calmed him down and prevailed upon him to keep their sessions secret, which he did.

As a relief from the rigorous academic drill, there was an intramural touch football league for philosophy and one for theology. The winner of theology would play the winner of philosophy in a "Rose Bowl" game on Thanksgiving Day. On October 22, 1931, Ignatius played his last game—one which would influence his priestly career forever.

"I was playing end on defense," he told author Bill Gleason (for a book, *The Liquid Cross of Skid Row*). "Here comes an end sweep, in my direction, with all available blockers in front of the ball carrier. A couple of those blockers moved me out of there, and I went down as the play went sweeping by me. My right knee popped out and, by the time the play was completed, I was in agony. But after they pulled my knee back in place, the leg immediately felt fine."

He hobbled to his room and lay on his bed and rested his leg while the other students were at evening church devotions. But when he got up from the bed, he knew he was in trouble. He told me, "I was holding my leg straight and as soon as it left the mattress it was out of place. It was a couple of hours before anybody returned from dinner. They brought me a tray from the dining room. I had passed out on the bed in extreme pain with my knee out of place. So they called a doctor from Libertyville [a neighboring suburb]. He was more of an obstetrics man. I went to Condell Memorial Hospital the next day and he put my knee in a cast."

This was the era of general practitioners, not specialists. The knee was in a cast "from October 22 until late November. He took the cast off and the leg was very straight." The treatment was a failure; there was no flexibility. Jim McDermott, now newly-elected Democratic committeeman of the 14th ward, and two law school associates, attorneys for the White Sox, contacted "a great bone man on the staff at Mercy Hospital who could treat athletic injuries. So I came in [to Chicago] on about the first of December and he put weights on my leg for a couple of weeks.

"In April of 1932, I went to see him again and he said that surgery was indicated. So I returned to Mercy Hospital and he performed surgery on the knee. I returned about four weeks later to the seminary, about the first week in May." Fifteen weeks of classwork had been lost.

Ignatius returned full-time to the seminary with crutches and a cane. "It was on a Sunday night, so I waited until the dining room had dispersed. I reported to the rector [Monsignor J. Gerald Kealy], a non-Jesuit. He said, 'The operation doesn't look too successful. You're on a cane.'" It was an ominous indication that Cardinal Mundelein's dictum that "only perfect physical specimens should be ordained" would be honored here.

"Well, I'm obviously not ready for the Olympics," Ignatius said—a remark the rector took as flip. From that time on, Kealy would argue that Ignatius was not fit for the rigor of the seminary and would concentrate on getting the wisecracking young rebel out.

Monsignor McDermott says, "So time marched on and we received minor orders. First order was tonsure." For centuries, up to 1972, a lock of hair was cut, varying in size, from the top of the head. This ceremony formally moved a layman to the clerical state.

"They clipped part of the hair. Then a year later in second theology you get first minors and second minors. So I went in to see the rector. He called everyone in singly."

The blow: "He said I would receive first minors and second minors, and then I could look for another seminary. I asked what would be the reason."

Kealy then spoke rather cryptically. "He said, 'You look into it.' I said, 'I can't look into anything if I have a negative report that is disturbing to you, which would make me ineligible for the priesthood.'

"'Well,' he said, 'I don't like how you walk.'"

When Ignatius heard that from Kealy, "I just figured I would be dismissed."

Disheartened, he did not pursue his studies, since he had no chance of ordination with his class.

A few weeks later, the seminarians lined up to see the prefect of studies, a Jesuit theologian from a famed Omaha family, Reverend John B. Furay, S.J., later to become president of Loyola University.

"He would ask how many hours we were devoting to each subject—how many hours to moral theology?"

When he asked this of Ignatius, the answer was: "No hours."

"How about dogmatic theology?"

"No hours."

"He said, 'Do you know what you're saying? We could expel you!'"

"I said, 'You're the second one who wants to do that.'"

Furay started. "He said, 'What did the rector say to you?'"

"The rector told me I'd be dismissed from the seminary in June."

But the Jesuits also had major say on who would come and go in Mundelein's seminary. Father Furay said quietly, "Ignatius, you go back and study."

Then a climactic faculty meeting between the rector, the prefect of studies and the spiritual directors took place.

"My spiritual director called me down—it was around the middle of May [1932]—and he said, 'There was a faculty meeting today and you are to keep this confidential: you'll be back next year.'"

What had happened to reverse things? "I figure the Jesuits had worked on Cardinal Mundelein that I should stay there." But did somebody work on the Jesuits or Mundelein himself? No one knows.

The only certain conclusion: Ignatius McDermott—named after St. Ignatius Loyola [1491–1556], the founder and patron saint of the Jesuits, a Spanish soldier who converted to Christ while convalescing from a serious battlefield injury to his leg—was saved for the priesthood by the Jesuits. Still, administrator Kealy was not to be so easily put off. Ignatius could not graduate with his class; he had to repeat the year. Monsignor McDermott reflects: "I just think Kealy had a personal animosity. I just didn't click with Kealy at all, so I had to repeat first theology, although I had passed the examinations. I was told I had missed too much time in 1931."

Nineteen thirty-two was a significant year for the McDermotts. Attorney Jim McDermott was now alderman as well as Democratic committeeman of the 14th ward, following in the footsteps of Uncle John Bradley and Judge Sullivan. And Ignatius McDermott? In September, having returned to the seminary, Ignatius was "sweeping the rugs (we were allowed two rugs in the room, one at our desk and one by our bed)." The prefect in theology hall came around looking for Mr. McDermott.

"I said, 'I'm here.' "

"He said, 'The rector would like to see you.' "

"I returned to my room, put on a cassock, and went over to the rector. It was late in September. He said, 'Mr. McDermott, where's the letter from the doctor stating that your surgery is all right and you are able to get along with that knee?' "

"I said, 'Well, I can't recall your ever telling me that I needed to have a letter.' "

"He said, 'That's another evidence of your misdemeanors. You get that letter in today.' "

"I said, 'May I go to see my doctor and get the letter?' "

"'No—' "

Ignatius said, "Well, that borders on the impossible."

Kealy said tersely, "Well, you look into it."

"He had the same expression he had when I asked him what was wrong with me and he replied he didn't like the way I walked."

It was a true catch-22. Ignatius couldn't leave the seminary to get the physician's letter and without it he couldn't continue as a priesthood student.

But Chicago-bred moxie—combined with Jesuit political skill— won the day. A priest friend, who was doing post-graduate work at the seminary, sped to Chicago that day. He went to see the physician, got from him a letter certifying to Ignatius' excellent general health, and brought it to Ignatius who presented it to Kealy.

He heard no more from Kealy on the subject.

Nearly being forced out of the seminary and graduation's postponement played a crucial role in his life.

In *The Liquid Cross of Skid Row*, Gleason relates the counseling Monsignor McDermott gives to a drunk who feels sorry for himself over a series of personal reverses. The drunk had been on West Madison Street's "Skid Row" for eight years. Bad breaks got him there.

> "Everybody has his own problems," the priest says. "That's something the men on the Street seldom remember. That's why some of them are there. Because they aren't worried about any problems other than their own."
>
> "And you?" the drunk asks angrily, "What problems have you had?"
>
> Monsignor McDermott's answer: "When you are going through Quigley you become convinced that you'll never become a priest because you see such wonderful kids falling by the wayside. You tell yourself that you're a .210 hitter compared to some of them, spiritually and mentally, and you wonder how you'll ever make it, if they can't. I managed to make it somehow and went up to Mundelein, but even then I didn't have it made. It was a hard blow and a little tough to swallow. It meant that after spending seven years with the same bunch, I'd be studying with a different group in the fall. I was afraid to play any sport because I knew that another injury to my knee could be an impediment to my kneeling and to my vocation. One thing a young priest should be able to do well is kneel.
>
> "I stayed a year behind but I never really adjusted to it. When my original class was graduated and the guys I had started with at Quigley left me at Mundelein, it looked like my cookie had crumbled. But over the long haul it has taught me the real meaning of 'Man proposes; God disposes.' The moral of the story is that nobody has it made. My whole life in the priesthood was altered by that knee injury."
>
> The injury reshaped his priesthood: "If I had been ordained on schedule with my original class, I would have been assigned to parish work. I think that's what every young priest wants and that certainly is what I had in mind. I wanted to follow in the footsteps of Father Tormey who had done a lot for me when I was a kid at Visitation."

(Bill Gleason was a Chicago sports columnist for 40 years before retiring in 2001. He was also a TV celebrity on the program, "The Sportswriters." He was born in 1922 and lived with his family on 22nd Street and Eggleston on the South Side. He started as a copy boy for the old *Chicago Sun*. He was drafted in World War II and received the Silver Star for "crawling through 50 yards of murderous [German] machine gun fire," after he and three buddies were pinned down, to dispense medical aid to a wounded man. He wrote sports for what was the *Southtown Economist* (now the *Daily Southtown*), moved to the *Chicago American* as a picture caption writer, then shifted to sports and started a column in 1961. He continued the column at the *Sun-Times* and, ultimately, went back to the *Southtown*.)

* * *

During the last summer of his seminary training, when he was a holdover because of his injury, Ignatius joined other members of his class for a few days at the archdiocesan summer camp at Clearwater Lake, Wisconsin. Every seminarian had a duty: Ignatius' was to head up a fund-raising committee that distributed modest amounts of prize money for winners of baseball, basketball hoop shooting, and swimming contests. George Cardinal Mundelein would come up on occasion to mingle with the students, knowing all of them by name.

Because of the injury, the imperious Mundelein may have had a soft spot in his heart for a young man who fought to stay in his seminary and won. The seminarian had to pay a visit to the cardinal at his cottage to get his token donation to the prize-money fund. When he was ushered in to see the prelate on a very hot summer day (there was no air conditioning in that era), he found the cardinal "in his screened-in porch in his clerical gown and his collar. He had a handkerchief around his neck. I walked in. He asked, 'How's the fund going?' I said, 'We're about $100 behind last year.' He said, 'Well, you won't be behind anymore.' And he gave me $100."

* * *

Ignatius was ordained as one of 56 in 1936—the largest group ever ordained in Chicago history.

"On the day of your ordination the cardinal would ask you, 'Do you promise to me and my successors obedience and reverence?' And you say, '*libentur*,' in Latin, which means 'freely.' Everybody knew what that meant." It meant, among other things, a kind of involuntary servitude as an assistant to tough, irascible pastors. It meant going where you were sent without a murmur.

"After the ordination was over, we gave our first blessing to our parents," Monsignor McDermott recalls. "Each one of our professors came over to receive our blessing. The first one to come over to receive a blessing from me was Father Furay [the prefect of studies who had sided with Ignatius over Kealy]. I thought that was rather significant."

Another blessing which, in time, Ignatius would realize: he had ties to two groups of graduates at the seminary—the class of 1935 and the class of 1936. Classmates always helped each other out in the priesthood in that era, and because of his accident, Ignatius had what classmate John McLoraine called "a double helping."

With ordination he was commanded to recite his Office from a breviary. It consisted of a one-hour Latin reading, one half-hour each morning (*Matins*) and one half-hour in the evening (*Lauds*). The breviary was divided into four parts, one for each season of the year. The mandatory reading of the Office was ended at Vatican II. But one practice he never ended was the voluntary saying of the rosary, a string of 50 beads divided into five sections. The rosary was devised in medieval days, when the Bible was so expensive it could not be readily available. Monks who could not remember the 150 Psalms made do by saying one *Our Father* and 10 *Hail Marys* per decade (10 beads). The complete rosary consists of three sets of "Mysteries"—Joyful, Sorrowful, and Glorious—representing periods in the life of Jesus Christ and the Church, five in each set, a total of 150 prayers in all. Many times Monsignor McDermott says all three sets of Mysteries at hospital bedsides.

* * *

Festivities surrounding a new priest's ordination in Chicago during those years seem lavish by today's standard. George Mundelein was caste-conscious. He would ordain the top academicians in each class on or near April 23, the feast of his namesake, St. George the Dragon-Slayer. The remainder of the seminarians would be ordained on or near September 21, the feast of St. Matthew, the date on which he was consecrated bishop. Ignatius' ordination date was April 18.

At the final banquet before leaving the seminary, Ignatius was the toastmaster. "Sitting on my right side was Father John Furay,

Jesuit, the prefect of studies." And on his left side: his old nemesis, one who (until recently) had served as rector and had returned for the banquet, Monsignor J. Gerald Kealy, non-Jesuit.

"When it came time to introduce J. Gerald Kealy, I had learned through the seminary that when he was a young fellow he loved baseball and was a catcher on the baseball team," says Monsignor McDermott.

"So I introduced him as follows: 'The next speaker will be Monsignor J. Gerald Kealy. I have learned that, in his younger days, Monsignor Kealy played catcher on our baseball team. This was most apropos because a catcher is supposed to have a good arm. If he hasn't got a good arm, he can't be a good catcher because the catcher has to be able to throw persons out when they're trying to steal a base.

"'I know about that because, as I was rounding home, Monsignor Kealy tried to pick me off!'" The dining hall roared with laughter at Kealy's failed attempt to tag McDermott out at home plate. Kealy was not amused. But before the banquet ended, Father Furay dropped a few words into Ignatius' ear: "You come back and visit with us. You're not going to be too far from me and from us." The meaning became clear later.

Says Monsignor McDermott: "At a later luncheon following ordination, of course His Eminence was there at the head table with the faculty, and seminarians who were below us in years were the waiters. We were all dressed in cassocks in those days. A seminarian-waiter came to me and said, 'The cardinal would like to see you.'

"To myself I said, 'I'm not going to be Mickey the mope. This guy may be pulling my leg.' So I looked around. The cardinal was sitting at the center of the head table. He smiled at me and sort of went like this—beckoning. So I went to the head table and bent over. He said, 'Well, Father, the mayor and the city council will be at your first Mass tomorrow.'"

How did that spectacular crowd assemble? "My brother was very close to [Joseph W.] McCarthy, who was the architect of the seminary. They were raised together and went to St. Gabriel's grammar school." Jim McDermott and Joe McCarthy collaborated to produce the special political-governmental attendance.

The next day, Father Ignatius McDermott took the North Shore train to Chicago, said his first Mass at Visitation at noon and—true to Mundelein's prediction—Mayor Edward J. Kelly and many, if not all, of the city council, were at Mass.

* * *

One attendee at the Mass—an usher—was a young man who, for the balance of his long life, would be associated with Ignatius McDermott—a young Jewish lawyer, five foot two and about 100 pounds, Abraham Lincoln Marovitz.

Marovitz was born August 10, 1905 in Oshkosh, Wisconsin. His father, Joseph, moved the family to the teeming Jewish ghetto around Maxwell Street on the West Side when Marovitz was five. He attended Jefferson elementary and Medill high school and became active in Boys Brotherhood Republic, a youth government. A speech he gave impressed Levy Mayer, a senior partner in the law firm of Mayer, Meyer, Austrian & Platt (now Mayer, Brown, Rowe & Maw). Mayer gave him his card and told young Marovitz to look him up. When he did, Marovitz found out that Mayer had died. He convinced Alfred S. Austrian to hire him to work in the law library.

All the while, he was fighting as a featherweight boxer at Kid Howard's gym on South Clark Street. He and a friend worked up a sparring act to perform at club dinners and parties. Two lawyers from the firm witnessed a beating he received from a steelworker and reported it to Austrian, who encouraged young Marovitz to go to law school. Austrian lent him the $60 semester tuition to attend Chicago-Kent College of Law. He was 16 years old and attended law school without a day of college.

He graduated in 1925, at age 19, and had to wait nearly two years until he took his bar exam, because Illinois law forbade anyone under age 21 from becoming a lawyer. He became an assistant Cook County States Attorney at age 22, the youngest to hold that position. Recalled Marovitz: "I met Father Iggy through his brother. Jim wasn't like Father Iggy. He'd get mad at me and call me a Jew so-and-so. [Jim] was with Nash and Ahern, a leading criminal law firm at that time" [Marovitz, the prosecutor, and McDermott, the criminal defense lawyer, were supposed to be "friendly rivals" but sometimes it got ugly]. McDermott would defend cases in the courtroom of Judge John J. Sullivan, who was his political boss. Sullivan was also the 14th ward committeeman, with clout over Jim McDermott. "They never could beat me in a case. One day he said something under his breath, but the jury could hear him and so could the judge, about a little Jew bastard. The judge called a sidebar and raised hell with him. I beat him in that case...but Iggy and I became very dear friends."

Fired in a change of administration in 1932, he met young Richard J. Daley, who was then a city council clerk. Marovitz teamed up with his brothers Sydney and Harold in private practice, representing labor leaders and a picturesque list of some of the most notorious gangsters of the day, including Gus Winkler, believed to be a machine-gunner in the St. Valentine's Day Massacre; North Side boss Ted Newberry; syndicate gunman Murray (The Camel) Humphreys; and confidence man Willie Bioff. At one trial, an FBI agent read a transcript from a telephone tape between Marovitz and a client where Marovitz began the conversation by saying, "Well, what bank did you hold up today?"

Marovitz became a close friend of West Side boss Jacob Arvey, who helped him get elected to the Illinois State Senate, the first Jew to be elected to that body. There he renewed his acquaintance with Richard J. Daley, who was also a senator. Marovitz left the State Senate in 1943 to join the Marines as a private, predicting in his farewell speech that Daley would be elected mayor of Chicago after the war. Though color-blind and 38 years old, he pulled strings to be sent overseas, and saw combat—taking part in the invasion of the Philippines. He was wounded but refused the Purple Heart saying, "I got a scratch and some guys were without limbs."

After he was released from military service, Marovitz became acquainted with Adlai Stevenson, introducing him to Arvey when the three were in New York for the World Series. Marovitz remained in the State Senate until 1950, when he was named a judge of the Cook County Superior Court. He was sworn in by Daley, then the new Cook County clerk. He served there until 1963, with a hiatus from 1958 to 1959 when he was chief justice of the Cook County Criminal Court. In 1963, President John Kennedy named him a federal judge, probably the last to be appointed without a college degree.

As federal judge he presided over trials of Jeff Fort, then head of the Black P-Stone Nation, later the El-Rukn gang. Then there was the corruption trial of Alderman Paul Wigoda. In sentencing Wigoda, Marovitz recalled when the two were in the service. Marovitz was a wounded Marine with shrapnel in his arm and Wigoda was a Navy medical corpsman. Wigoda removed the shrapnel. Said Marovitz: "It was painful for me that day, but I must confess that this is far more painful." Later Judge Marovitz even crossed Daley, his old friend. When the Daley administration balked at enforcing the Shakman decision, banning firing and hiring of public workers for political purposes, Marovitz said: "Tell your clients unless they want to take a vacation in Cook County jail, they better comply with this order."

He had close friends among Hollywood entertainers, notably Bob Hope, who Marovitz met when Hope was an unknown comedian. But his closest friend was Monsignor McDermott. Marovitz died on March 17, 2001, a day which found Monsignor McDermott riding in the city's St. Patrick's Day parade. On March 20, Marovitz was buried. Monsignor McDermott had this to say: "Brother Abe was your and my Hope Diamond friend. Abe was the Tiffany and the titan of thoughtfulness, and while Abe was performing his marathon of *mitzvahs* by stealth and writing them on ice cubes, his guardian angel was eternally etching them on that scoreboard in the sky. *Shalom*, my friend."

* * *

After the first Mass, the immediate family went over to the Visitation convent across the street. "In those days nuns were pretty well campused, so the family arranged to have a dinner for all the nuns of Visitation convent, including my sister [Martha, Mercy nun Sister Mary Jeanette] and my aunt [Catherine, Sister Mary Maurice]." The dinner was held "at the old Stevens Hotel which later became the Conrad Hilton. My brother had a room at the Stevens so, after breakfast, I went in and rested. Then we had a reception that night for all the people you couldn't invite to the dinner. Two days later we [the newly-ordained priests] returned to the seminary. We would stay there until May 30, when we would leave for three or four weeks' vacation, and await a letter from the chancery office as to where our first appointment would be."

All assignments were made by one totally familiar with each seminarian's qualifications—George Cardinal Mundelein.

* * *

Ignatius took a vacation at Jim's summer house in Long Beach, Indiana, on Lake Michigan. He brought a couple of classmates with him. The weather was warm "and we were down on the beach throwing a football back and forth." Then Jim's wife yelled that there was a phone call for Ignatius.

"She said there was a call from the chancery office. I was to go to the seminary in a day or two to meet Cardinal Mundelein." Again, Father Ignatius suspected it was a joke. Mundelein never met with newly-ordained priests for their first assignment; a letter they were to receive from the chancery would detail the assignment.

"I thought it was somebody pulling my leg, one of my classmates. So I called Reynold Hillenbrand, the new rector of the seminary, and said, 'I'm in Long Beach, Indiana, with a couple of classmates. My sister-in-law received a telephone call from the chancery office saying that I'm supposed to be at the seminary in a day or two to meet Cardinal Mundelein. Reynold, is this true or false?' He said, 'Iggy, you'd better be there.' So I knew it was for real."

When Father McDermott arrived at the seminary, a classmate was already there for an appointment with the cardinal—Father Edward Norkett.

Father Norkett recalls well their meeting with Mundelein. "I got a telephone call from the cardinal's residence—from Dan Ryan [the cardinal's secretary], who was the nephew of the Dan Ryan of the expressway out there [the late chairman of the Cook County Board of Commissioners, after whom the major expressway running to the South Side was named]. He said, 'The cardinal wants to see you.' Naturally, when you get a call like that you say, 'Nah, the cardinal doesn't want to see me.' So I was joking around. Anyway, Dan Ryan says 'Father, will you please hang up and call the chancery office?' So I thought: This is serious. Ryan added, 'You are to be at the seminary on such-and-such a date, like June 25, and the cardinal will talk to you and you will not be alone.'

"So I went out there on that day, at 9 a.m., wondering who else was going to be there and I see Ignatius McDermott. And I asked him, 'What are you doing here?' And he said, 'What are *you* doing here?' I said I was supposed to see the cardinal and he said so was he.

"So we went in to see the cardinal, just the two of us. We figured we were the first two to go off to one of those foreign missions, because nobody else had gone out yet. Before we were ordained, we had to sign a contract that we would be willing to be sent out of the diocese to any southern diocese or any American possession, like Puerto Rico, Hawaii, or Alaska, because they needed priests. We had more priests than we needed up here. The problem was that maybe they wouldn't need us up here because the parishes were having a tough time feeding the people, let alone trying to take on an extra priest and feed him and pay him $50 a month.

"We couldn't figure out whether we were going to be sent to Tuscaloosa, Alabama, or Texas or where we were going to go. And the cardinal knew we were wondering what would happen. We didn't care, actually, where we were going to go. We were priests and they could send us to China; we couldn't care less."

Ignatius McDermott did, however.

Mundelein's autocratic manner of making priestly appointments was awesome. A prime example that circulated through the archdiocesan clergy was how he had dealt with Father William O'Connor, a professor at Quigley who had caught the cardinal's attention.

"William O'Connor had been teaching at Quigley," recounted Monsignor McDermott. "It was October 10 or 11 and he was residing at Catalpa and Broadway, at St. Edith's. He received a call from the chancery office on a Thursday. I think that the next day was October 12, so Quigley would be off two days, Thursday and Friday, and he'd return to Quigley on Saturday.

"He went to see Cardinal Mundelein who said to Father O'Connor: 'I made arrangements for you to do social work in New York at St. Patrick's Cathedral. I've already been in contact with Cardinal Hayes [Patrick J. Hayes, Archbishop of New York]. You are to reside at St. Patrick's Cathedral, and you are to go to the New York School of Social Work. You will be there for two years to complete your degree. You will leave tomorrow on the Twentieth Century [the crack streamliner of the New York Central]."

In unquestioning obedience to a Prince of the Church, Father O'Connor packed immediately. The prefect at Quigley objected to the lavish expense of taking a streamliner. "That's what he said," O'Connor snapped, "so I'm riding the Twentieth Century."

Continues Monsignor McDermott: "So O'Connor left the next day for New York and stayed there a year. He came back for a brief stay in June, a couple of days before the Quigley graduation in 1936. Mundelein sent for O'Connor and the cardinal said, 'I'm appointing you superintendent of St. Mary's Training School in

Des Plaines and it goes into effect July 1.' O'Connor said, 'I left my trunk in New York. I completed only one year of social work school.' Mundelein said, 'Send for the trunk.'" Father O'Connor, brother of Len O'Connor, NBC-TV reporter, was eventually ordained bishop of Springfield, Illinois.

As Fathers McDermott and Norkett entered Mundelein's office, they had the O'Connor experience in mind.

After they kissed the episcopal ring (required in those days), the cardinal said ominously: "I'm going to make you two young priests missionaries."

Reflected Father McDermott: "Well, gee, I really felt terrible. I figured I was going to kiss the White Sox goodbye. Now that I've been ordained, I thought, I could go to see the White Sox, the Chicago Cardinals, and Chicago Bears. Not now."

Mundelein looked at them for a long moment, then said, "You won't have to board a giant ocean liner and you won't have to get in an airplane. You won't even have to take a ferryboat! In fact, you won't even have to cross the Chicago River. Right next door is St. Mary's Training School, a home for dependent children. You're going to assist Father William A. O'Connor."

Thus was the priesthood service of Ignatius McDermott dramatically changed. Of the 56 men who graduated from the seminary in 1936, 54 became parish priests. Ignatius was to be a missionary to the down-and-outs for most of his life.

* * *

Ignatius McDermott's acceptance of God's will is captured in Gleason's biographical novel, *The Liquid Cross of Skid Row.* The drunk shouts at Monsignor McDermott: "How does this apply to me? What does your life in the priesthood have to do with a bum on West Madison Street and his life?...[w]hat the hell does your experience in the seminary have to do with what I have to put up with down here?"

> "Forgive me," Father McDermott replied. "We're not on the same wavelength. What I'm trying to convey is that it could have been eight years for me...if I had let that lost year get me, if I had brooded about not being in parish work. I had to make a useful life for myself and the only way to do that was to forget about what might have been."

The injury changed the focus of Monsignor McDermott's career. It brought him to the personal attention of the cardinal who determined that, instead of parish work, the injured ex-athlete would be ideal as teacher and counselor to the young at St. Mary's Training School. Thus, the football injury ultimately brought great dividends to the fight against addiction. Why did Jesuit prefect of studies Furay come to the rescue? Years later, Furay told Father McDermott: "I saw how well-liked you were. Your classmates and the upper and lower students—that's why I liked you."

After he received his order from Mundelein to go to St. Mary's Training School, it was likely that, once away from the cardinal's residence, Father McDermott lit a cigarette, sucked in the smoke, and inhaled deeply. Because Mundelein hated cigarettes, in the seminary cigarette smoking had to be done guardedly. Father Ignatius was smoking three packs a day now, which would complicate another problem down the road.

CHAPTER 6

Assignments: St. Mary's Training School and Our Lady of Peace, 1936–1946

> *While an assistant at Our Lady of Peace, we would make a weekly visit to LaRabida sanatorium, a health facility for children. There we found an 8-year-old child, named Simon, who was crying. He was waiting for his parents to take him to Cook County Hospital, due to meningitis. One reason he didn't want to go was that he couldn't wear PJs, but a gown. Along with the toys on his bed was a Catechism. We picked it up and asked him: "What does this book do? Does it teach you to fly a kite in your backyard?" He looked at me with disgust and said, "No, it teaches me about God. I'm going to make my First Communion." We asked Simon, "Who is God? Why did God make you?" Finally—"Can God do everything?" Simon responded emphatically, "No." "What is there that God can't do?" His answer was: "God can't tell a lie." That was worthy of Aristotle. Some weeks later, we visited the apartment of Simon's parents. There was a funeral wreath on the door. And inside, there was Simon, attired in his First Communion suit. He had changed his hospital gown for the PJs of eternal life.*
>
> —Ignatius McDermott

St. Mary's Training School, to which Cardinal Mundelein sent Father McDermott, already had a rich and multi-textured history.

In 1882, Archbishop Patrick Feehan purchased a large farm 25 miles northwest of Chicago near Des Plaines, Illinois, and built an orphanage for dependent and neglected children. That year St. Mary's Training School (which in 1950 was renamed Maryville) was incorporated. Trustees bought 440 acres of land to offer an opportunity for "husky, active teenaged boys to learn and participate in agricultural pursuits." The following year, 41

Indian boys of the Sioux and Chippewa tribes were transferred, as a federal experiment, to the school from the Standing Rock (Oklahoma) Reservation (school records still list their names as Red Bull, Gray Bear, Walking White Buffalo) but, tragically, the experiment ended with the deaths of five youths from respiratory complications during the severe winter. They are buried in the small Maryville cemetery in a quiet, shaded corner of the school campus.

In 1893, Chicago's World Columbian Exposition featured a display of famous mansions, including a replica of Thomas Jefferson's famed home, Monticello. When the Exposition closed, the 35-room building was saved by a wealthy donor and moved to Des Plaines where it was renamed "The Villa." A disastrous fire in 1899 destroyed nearly all the central building complex except The Villa, the power house, and outer walls of the administration building. Archbishop Quigley slowly started the rebuilding. By 1928, under Cardinal Mundelein, renovation was in full speed, with design of much of the construction done by newly-ordained Father Vincent Cooke (later superintendent of Catholic Charities and Father McDermott's boss). Financial support for a gymnasium (cost: $175,000) with twin facilities—one for boys, one for girls—came from the family of former Chicago mayor John Hopkins, who had been a victim of the 1918 flu epidemic.

Christian Brothers from the former Bridgeport Industrial School had staffed the training school until 1906, when Archbishop Quigley transferred the responsibility to diocesan priests and the Sisters of Mercy. Now, in 1936, with the Great Depression ravaging the jobless and their families, Cardinal Mundelein was pushing hard just to keep the school open. Sisters of Charity of Providence replaced the Mercy sisters in 1936, Father O'Connor's first year as superintendent. Sources of income were failing; income-producing activities such as a printing shop, the greenhouses, and sale of agricultural products were coming to a standstill. Food was not scarce due to the farm and dairy animals, but money was hard to raise. Children came by foot, train, and bus with the anguished consent of impoverished families at the recommendation of over-committed public welfare agencies. Often children arrived carrying cardboard boxes marked "St. Mary's Training School." It was difficult for the school to find clothing and bedding. Fathers McDermott and Norkett were to spend five years there.

Recounting the era, Father Norkett says that St. Mary's "had 833 kids at the time. They had reached a capacity of 1,200 when things were really rough in Chicago and families just couldn't feed their kids." St. Mary's population contained "a mixture of everything. Some of their fathers were in jail; some fathers were in TB sanitariums; some fathers were not working and their mothers were sick and they just couldn't handle them. So Catholic Charities stepped in and took care of them."

"Most of them actually came through Catholic Charities and through Cook County. Cook County paid $15 a month for a boy and $20 a month for a girl. Nobody could figure out why the girls got more. Did it cost more to feed or clothe them? But it certainly was a minimum amount. In those days they got by and Catholic Charities made up the difference. That was my first close connection with Ignatius McDermott. We worked together. He got involved in sports right off the bat.

"It was a big place. It was a training school. The kids were supposed to go to school for half a day and be trained in some trade. We had a huge print shop out there. *The New World* [the archdiocesan newspaper] was printed there. We had a shoe shop; all the shoes were made there. We had a greenhouse, and all the kids were in different shops around there. That was one of my jobs, to take care of the employees as well as taking care of these kids."

Fathers McDermott and Norkett said Mass and taught the children the *Baltimore Catechism*. Father McDermott also taught history. The children were in the second, third, and fourth grades. Father Norkett says, "We didn't have the high school yet. They were boys and girls. The nuns taught reading, writing, and arithmetic. We taught them religion and the trades, like printing. And we were the disciplinarians—that was the big job, to try to hold those kids."

Neither priest knew much about industrial trades, yet they were to supervise the shops.

"We didn't know it when we started, but even those who were running the print shop were kids who had grown up out there, and the same way with the shoe shop. It was run by two or three fellows who were kids who grew up out there," says Father Norkett.

Monsignor McDermott says of the population, "They were all dependent children from the ages of pre-kindergarten through grammar school. Most were half-orphans. Some of the parents, perhaps, had emotional breakdowns. They were kids who had been passed over. After being passed over at St. Vincent's Infant Asylum, which was a crazy name in those days, they'd go out to St. Joseph's Home for Dependents at 35th and Park.

"At five years old they'd come out to Maryville. We had a kindergarten there. So the kids at Maryville—boys and girls—would range from five years old through high school. They could graduate from grammar school and stay on for high school if they wanted to. If they didn't want to, they could go to a foster home. The boys had it much better because if they didn't want to stay at St. Mary's Training School, they could go to 1140 West Jackson Boulevard, reside there, and go to St. Patrick's high school at Adams and Desplaines. The girls who graduated from St. Mary's could either go home at that time—or most went into a foster home."

He paused and added, "Here I'm 27 years old and on my first assignment, and here's 900 boys and girls running around St. Mary's Training School. I had taken my good fortune for granted through practically a quarter of a century. And sitting on a bench watching those kids run around, for the first time in my life I began to realize: Lord, how come you short-changed all these kids? And why was I given such a wonderful family and wonderful home?"

And there was something else—profoundly touching. "Visitors Sunday" was on the first and third Sundays of the month, when parents would come out to see their children. "The kids would have visitors between the hours of one and three," says Monsignor McDermott. "I saw more than a few fathers and a couple of mothers [who would be] pretty much 96-proof at the time, struggling across the yard to embrace their children. After the visiting hours were over, the kids would hold a post-mortem about their parents. They'd say, 'Was your old man funny! Falling over himself!'" And reflecting the touch of idiom that endears him to Chicagoans: "And the kid whose father or mother was alcoholic, who was in Tap City, you could see how beaten up and crestfallen he was. I'd talk to that kid at night."

It was even tougher talking to kids whose parents didn't show. "Where were they?" the kids would ask. *Where indeed?* wondered Father McDermott.

Father McDermott used to love to play newspaper editor with his young charges at St. Mary's Training School. Once, in a burst of whimsy, he wrote in the small St. Mary's newspaper, in official reporter fashion, that the school would be paid a visit by none other than James A. Farley, postmaster general and chairman of the Democratic National Committee, the top political aide to Franklin Roosevelt. No sooner was the article printed than the priest received a call from Fred Fulle, publisher of a suburban newspaper chain, asking when Farley would appear. "He will not appear," said Father McDermott, as the article was fictitious, which disappointed Fulle who thought he had a real scoop.

With Mundelein's help in fund-raising, Father O'Connor initiated a program that converted the children's sleeping quarters into smaller, more intimate living units, 20 in total, each accommodating 35 children or fewer. Each building had offices for supervisory staff, a large living room for relaxation and social activities, complete washroom facilities, and locker rooms.

* * *

In 1938, two years after joining the training school, Father McDermott came down with pneumonia. Respiratory illness seemed to be a family trait. A brother suffered from tuberculosis and was hospitalized for a time at the Chicago Municipal Tuberculosis Sanitarium. The McDermotts didn't want this to happen to Father Ignatius.

In the 1930s, pneumonia wasn't dismissed lightly; the belief was that it could turn into tuberculosis. Doctors recommended a dry climate, specifically Tucson, Arizona, for several months. "I had a classmate in Tucson, Arizona, who led me to St. Mary's Sanitarium, a hospital with a TB facility conducted by the Daughters of St. Joseph of Missouri," Monsignor McDermott says. He secured the permission of the bishop of Tucson to enter the facility. Convinced by his physician, he gave up cigarettes—also coffee. He has been drinking hot tea with lemon ever since.

As he was recuperating, Father McDermott came upon an opportunity for a unique work of mercy. It entailed a relationship with one Father Joseph Rooney that lasted on and off for many years, long after Father McDermott returned to Chicago and moved beyond St. Mary's Training School to other assignments. It illustrates the years of care that Father McDermott invested in a client who came to him, including many who skipped out, avoided treatment, and got into trouble.

"The sister superior and director of the hospital came to me and said there was a priest downstairs who was rather inebriated," says Monsignor McDermott. "He was seeking asylum there. It was against the bishop's orders for any padre to be accepted in the hospital unless the nuns received the green light from the bishop. And since the bishop was on the confirmational circuit, he was unavailable. Sister consulted me. Here I was out of the seminary only two years at the time.

"'Well,' I said, 'charity is the greatest of virtues. Why not accept him and get permission from the bishop upon his return to Tucson?'" The priest roomed next to Father McDermott. When the bishop returned, he met with Father Rooney. Father Rooney's credentials were the highest—a degree from the Sorbonne in Paris, plus studies in moral theology on the graduate level. The bishop had an assignment for Father Rooney: an assistant pastorate in a remote Arizona desert town. "I thought it was in snake-bite territory," says Monsignor McDermott, "out alone in the bush. He wouldn't thrive on being alone. He would be playing a return engagement with this dependency."

When Father Rooney spurned the assignment and asked that his treatment be continued, the bishop ordered Father McDermott to eject Father Rooney from the hospital. Father McDermott pondered what to do. Father Rooney was an alcoholic and had no money. Father McDermott had no money. As a young priest in the Mundelein era, he was forced to live on a small stipend. "I was equally economically deprived, receiving $50 a month at that time for my salary, which continued throughout my stay at Tucson. So I called my brother [Jim], who was the alderman of the 14th ward and a famous attorney in Chicago, and asked him for money for transportation to send Rooney to Chicago to find a job where he could also get treatment." The money came. He put Father Rooney on the Golden State Limited to Chicago and contacted a friend, who was secretary to Chicago Auxiliary Bishop Bernard J. Sheil, head of the Catholic Youth Organization. After a few months in Tucson, Father McDermott himself returned to Chicago to resume his work at St. Mary's Training School—but he stayed in touch with Rooney.

In Chicago, Father Rooney lived with a group of German priests who were learning English while he worked at a job Jim McDermott found for him. It was with the city Department of Streets and Sanitation, holding a "Men Working" flag and redirecting traffic where they were repairing a street. He worked there a short time but disappeared. Police found Rooney sleeping under the porch at St. Patrick's rectory at 718 West Adams. Monsignor McDermott recalls: "They brought him to me and I immediately recognized him. I made a temporary arrangement for him at Chicago State Hospital, a facility for male and female alcoholics in those days. They had a few beds there and I used to bring some lads up there from Skid Row. He was admitted and got a job in the reading room there, categorizing books.

"One day, he mentioned that his anniversary in the priesthood was approaching, and I said, 'Let's celebrate your anniversary.' I didn't get a green light from the staff at Chicago State Hospital. Joseph Rooney was about five feet four, very small, so I had him lie in the back of the car to keep him from the gendarmes. We went to St. Mary of the Lake Seminary in Mundelein, thinking it would be good for him to see that on his anniversary of the priesthood. He was thrilled, overcome with the beauty of the place. Then I said to Joe, 'Let's have dinner,' but I got a guarantee from him that he wouldn't order any drinks at the meal. We went to a restaurant and devoured a steak, and I returned him to Chicago State Hospital.

"Time marched on and Joseph went AWOL from the hospital. He reappeared, came to me again. He told me that he had been a resident at Via Coeli [Gate of Heaven] Sanitarium in New Mexico. So I called Father Gerald Fitzgerald, the superior, to explore a return engagement at Via Coeli while Joseph was sitting in my office. Gerald Fitzgerald said to me on the phone, 'He's a drunken bum.' As he said this, I was looking directly across the desk at Rooney." Father Rooney was put on a train shortly afterward, and Father Fitzgerald met him at the other end.

Still no luck. "I don't know whether he went AWOL or whether Gerald Fitzgerald told him to leave, but he came back to me in Chicago. He had worn out his welcome with the city job. So I knew a mortician in Evergreen Park and I talked, on Joseph's behalf, with him. The mortician was looking for somebody to respond to telephone calls at night and live at the mortuary. I didn't divulge that Joseph Rooney was a padre. Now Joseph Rooney was also a diabetic and had to treat himself with injections. The mortician found Rooney resorting to the needle. Right away he felt he was a needle jockey and he called me, raised hell, and told me to get him out of there and pick up Joseph Rooney and get rid of him.

"I couldn't convince the mortician that Rooney was a diabetic. So I then found a place at Jackson and Kedzie, a funeral home, on the same block as Our Lady of Sorrows. I got him a job there, but he wore out his welcome. I contacted Dr. Jim West [the physician with whom Monsignor McDermott would later be associated in the historic Haymarket venture], who told me there was an opening operating an elevator at Little Company of Mary Hospital. We were able to find him a job there.

"Of course the nuns who operated the hospital didn't know he was a padre. He was operating the elevator for some time when a group of nuns got on. One was in the throes of discouragement, was talking about her tense job with a lot of demands on her time, and she was doubting her vocation. Then the elevator operator said, with all the finesse of someone skilled in moral theology plus graduate work at the Sorbonne, 'Excuse me, Sister, have you made this the object of your personal *examen?*' It floored the nuns. They asked, 'Who is this guy?'"

After years of relapses, Father McDermott was on the phone again with Father Fitzgerald of Via Coeli. Father McDermott put Father Rooney on a plane for New Mexico. "Well, it all ended satisfactorily," says Monsignor McDermott. "Years later, Father Fitzgerald called me and said that Joseph had expired. Thank God he died in the environs of Via Coeli in, as they say, the 'odor of sanctity.'"

That one-on-one drama is a trademark of service extended by Ignatius McDermott to the afflicted—for more than 60 years.

*   *   *

On October 1, 1939, Cardinal Mundelein died suddenly at age 66.

Mundelein's death removed the nation's most socially progressive prelate. Under his guidance, the archdiocese of Chicago grew to 422 parishes, ministering to almost 1,600,000 Catholics, making it the largest diocese in the U.S. and almost the world. Crowds lined up for blocks adjoining Holy Name Cathedral to pay respects to the man known as the "Dutch Master," who had given a clear vision to the diocese, systemized and consolidated its offices, standardized the largest Catholic school system in the country, and created the first central bank in any diocese, funneling financial assistance to poor parishes from the affluent.

During Mundelein's tenure [1915–39], Chicago had become the U.S. center for the program initiated by the late Pius XI, known as "Catholic Action." Two key appointments had reflected the progressivism of the Mundelein era. *First* was that of his auxiliary bishop, Bernard J. Sheil [1886–1969], the founder of the Catholic Youth Organization (CYO), who exercised considerable influence on the cardinal. He was a spirited activist for those whom he described as "the working class"—predominantly white union members and the black poor. At Mundelein's order Bishop Sheil addressed a rally of Chicago packinghouse workers in support of their drive for improved working conditions. A *second* major appointment was that of a 30-year-old theologian intellectual, Reynold Hillenbrand [1904–1979]. As rector at St. Mary of the Lake Seminary, Hillenbrand presided over a generation of priests known as "Hilly's Men," prepared to speak out against injustice in both the secular and ecclesiastical world.

In U.S. politics, as in his church, Mundelein's influence had been enormous. He had become a friend and supporter of President Franklin D. Roosevelt; they met a dozen times in FDR's presidency, keeping in close contact through personal emissaries. The prelate's warm support for the New Deal defused accusations by Father Charles Coughlin and others that Roosevelt's administration was socialistic if not pro-Communist. Mundelein had hosted Roosevelt at his episcopal residence at 1555 N. State Parkway, on October 8, 1937, when the president gave his "quarantine the aggressors" foreign policy speech. While some criticized Mundelein's later years as "too political," decrying that he was too willing a supporter of Roosevelt, it was undeniable that the cardinal's leadership raised the status of Chicago Catholics, giving them self-confidence and great influence at home and in Rome. Indeed, the president's top political aide, Thomas Corcoran, was staying overnight at the cardinal's residence at St. Mary of the Lake Seminary the night Mundelein died. FDR was seeking the cardinal's advice about installing a diplomatic representative at the Vatican.

Mundelein had encouraged, reorganized, and expanded the work of Catholic Charities in Chicago. He named Father William A. O'Connor, Father McDermott's boss, superintendent of Catholic Charities, and Father Eugene Mulcahey as head of St. Mary's Training School.

"Mulcahey was our boss for three years," Monsignor McDermott later said. "He thought the kids would need a change of scenery because they were there 365 days a year and many of those kids had been out there through eight years of grammar and high school. He said he'd like to get a summer camp for the kids.

"He and I scouted around during the months of February and March [1941]. We contacted a priest, Father Morgan Flaherty, in Antioch near Fox Lake, who, with the help of real estate agents, identified several sites. I went up to open the camp and had some boys and girls up there at the camp. Later on we decided they would go up for 10 days so every kid could get an outing at the camp. We called it Maryville Camp."

Mundelein's successor, Samuel Cardinal Stritch, continued the military staff system—which meant that priests were not "lifers" in one category.

A new assignment for Father McDermott came with a telephone call to Maryville Camp. "I was there about a week and Father Mulcahey called me and said—it was the middle of June 1941—'I'm getting a new assistant, Father [Francis] Garrity. You'll be leaving here.' I was disappointed at leaving, but the system decreed that five years was enough for anybody to stay there—and we were ordained to become assistant pastors. This was a job out of the ordinary, working in an orphanage.

"I said, 'Is there a letter from the cardinal's office for me?' He said, 'Yes.' I said, 'Why don't you open it up and let me know where I will be going?' He did, and said: 'You are to report in 10 days from now to Our Lady of Peace parish at 79th and Jeffery.' Father Mulcahey drove me out to 7851 Jeffery—Our Lady of Peace parish."

Thirty-two-year-old Father Ignatius knew he needed some experience in a parish—and this South Shore parish built up of brick bungalows and spacious apartment buildings was a good opportunity to become a pastor—but this wasn't what he wanted. He wanted to focus his priesthood on social service.

* * *

On December 7, 1941, Father McDermott was at the Bears-Cardinals football game at Comiskey Park. The announcement that the Japanese had bombed Pearl Harbor came over the public address system at half-time. The crowd sighed audibly, then was hushed. Many left the game.

* * *

The parish, the first dedicated by Mundelein after World War I, was designated "Our Lady of Peace" to commemorate the Blessed Virgin's new title, bestowed by Pope Benedict XV. In August 1939, Father (later Monsignor) Henry M. Friel became pastor. Father McDermott was to replace an assistant who had left to become an Army chaplain.

"The pastor said he'd like me to be in charge of the grammar school," says Monsignor McDermott. "Athletics were rather dormant, so I started basketball." Noting that Catholics pay taxes as well as others, he encouraged his brother, Jim, alderman of the 14th ward, to get a city crew to install basketball hoops, which they were doing in public schools, in the gymnasium of Our Lady of Peace. He also made friends with his own alderman who was one of the few Republicans in the city council, Nicholas Bohling. The personal touch, the nuance for things that only a politically savvy observer would notice, is always evident in Monsignor McDermott's life.

"In those days, on First Friday you would bring Communion to the people who were not able to go to church," he says. "I used to bring Nick Bohling's mother Communion every First Friday."

Nicholas J. Bohling was the long-time alderman of the South Shore's 7th ward. While the post of alderman was non-party designated, a heavy majority of the council supported Democratic Mayor Edward J. Kelly (and Bohling usually went along with their wishes).

All the same, Monsignor McDermott notes, Bohling's rise in the Republican Party was a fascinating part of Chicago genre. Bohling had gone to Notre Dame, the Midwest's most active breeding-ground for young Irish Democrats. "When he was at the University of Notre Dame, in his senior year, he sent a letter to Saul Epton [a Republican] who later became a judge," says Monsignor McDermott. "He sent a letter to Saul and said that he was president of the Young Republican Club on the campus of Notre Dame. Epton sent a letter to Nick and said, 'Young man, when you come in on your Christmas vacation, come to see me.'

"So Nick came in to see him and Epton said to Nick, 'I'm really overcome that there's a Republican club at Notre Dame. How many students would be members of that club?' Nick said, 'You're looking at him!'"

Bohling may have disappointed Epton but his contact with the influential Republican was fortunate. As Monsignor McDermott relates years later, with a politician's eye for detail, "Jimmy Ryan was the [Democratic] ward committeeman. He was an old-time politician and had a sister in the Mercy order. Some of his relatives lived in Our Lady of Peace, and he made the mistake of fostering nepotism—he put up his brother, Bud Ryan, to run for alderman. Epton was smart enough to put up Nick Bohling, and the rebellious cried, 'Nepotism!' Nick Bohling submerged Ryan's brother and Nick became the alderman."

It was at Our Lady of Peace that Father Ignatius perfected his style of visiting sick parishioners at neighboring hospitals, which led to other contacts. He comforted the sick, whom he didn't personally know, at many hospitals, entering with a wave to the desk after hours, going to rooms where the sick were alone and needed comfort. Father Edward Norkett said, "That's his pasttime, his recreation—to visit hospitals, every hospital in the city. And it's usually 9, 10 or 11 o'clock before he gets to some of them."

How did he get in? And how does he today?

"That's a remarkable thing," said Father Norkett. "Of course, he always wears his collar so they know he's legitimate. I know when I've been in the hospital a couple of times he was there. I was in Columbus Hospital for a month about 20 years ago and he was there every blooming night. He usually goes because he knows somebody there, but he sees 20 other people before he gets out of there. And he goes every single week just to say hello. And if he's in a funeral parlor, he goes to one wake—but there's two others, so he'll go and say a prayer for the others also. It just makes people feel better, that a priest was here and then another priest was here to say a prayer. He has a very outgoing personality. He can talk to any Tom, Dick, or Harry he meets, that's for sure."

For a diligent priest, no matter where he ministers, at a South Shore parish or on Skid Row, opportunities often come. Monsignor McDermott remembers hearing confessions one night at Our Lady of Peace. Notice the precision with which he describes the conditions, down to the specific numeral address of a hospital he visited almost 60 years previous.

"A woman said to me, after I gave her the absolution, 'Will you pray for my brother? He's been away from the Church for years.' I said I would offer Mass for him, and I asked, 'Where is your brother?' And she said, 'He's over at South Shore Hospital,' which was at 8012 South Crandon. We were at 79th and Jeffery. So I went over to the hospital. It was a hot night—it was summertime—and there was a five-bed ward, and he was in the bed right inside the room. The fifth bed was by the window, further removed. I came in and I said, 'My name is Father Mac and I had the privilege of crossing paths with your sister. She shared your sickness, and I'd like to say a prayer with me.'

"And he said, 'Get out of this room!' I said, 'Can I give you a blessing?' He yelled, 'Get him out of this room!'

"So the fellow who was in the bed by the window said, 'Father, can I see you?' I said 'Sure,' and went over to see him. He said, 'I've been away from the faith for a long time. I'm going to surgery tomorrow, and I've been praying for a priest to come in here. Would you hear my confession?' I said 'Sure.' And when he was finished he asked, 'What's the penance?' I said, 'Let's just pray the *Memorare* together.'"

So together they said it: "Remember O most gracious Virgin Mary that never was it known that anyone who fled to your protection, implored your help, or sought your intercession was left unaided. Inspired by this confidence, we fly unto you, Virgin of Virgins, our Mother. To you we come, before you we stand, sinful and sorrowful. O Mother of the Word Incarnate, despise not our petitions, but in your mercy, hear and answer us. Amen."

"I offered up my prayer for this guy. Then I went by the first guy's bed. I get outside the threshold of the door and he calls out, 'Father, can I see you?' I said, 'You certainly can.' He said, 'I'm ready to unload.' So I said, 'Gee, that's wonderful' and heard his confession."

* * *

On April 12, 1945, the day Franklin Roosevelt died, Father McDermott was getting a haircut at the Spaulding Hotel in Michigan City, Indiana, along with his brother, Jim, then an alderman. "Jim did not worship at the shrine of Franklin Roosevelt," he says.

* * *

More than 50 years after his service at Our Lady of Peace, a group of ex-students gathered to reminisce, on October 21, 1999. William O'Toole remembered a little Chevrolet coupe Father Mac drove, "really only a two- or three-seater." He would "pack about eight kids in it. He'd take us to Jackson Park when we were altar boys. We would have a picnic up in Jackson Park about May of each year.

"He also would cart the kids in the neighborhood to the various basketball games—I must confess that Father Mac was one of the world's worst drivers. I have subsequently learned that he hasn't improved."

* * *

During World War II, while at Our Lady of Peace, Father McDermott was visited by a "Gray Lady"—a Red Cross staffer— who asked if he knew a family named Walsh. He said yes, that, in fact, he had personally visited the family to give the father Communion after he had a heart attack. The Gray Lady then said she had bad news—that a letter from the Secretary of War had informed them that a son was killed in the conflict. Father McDermott went immediately to the family to comfort them. Not long thereafter, the same Gray Lady came to the priest again and said that a second Walsh son had been killed in battle. Again, the priest made a visit to console the family.

When Father Mac came to the parish, the boys (all senior citizens now) were disconsolate because his predecessor, an athletic-loving priest, who had taught them to box, had been transferred. What would the new priest be like? The boys stood around the school's cinder yard, studying him.

They soon got their answer. The new young priest took a football, ignored them studiously, posed with it, and kicked it about 50 yards.

The boys nudged themselves. Gee, would the Bears ever love to have him, they said. Later, at Father Mac's behest, the basketball court was built—and in the rectory was the place where athletic gear was stored: basketballs, footballs, baseballs, and bats.

The best story, all the "survivors" of Our Lady of Peace agreed, was the chicken story. Donald Kruse was in the sixth grade and somehow was taken with the sight of baby chicks. He saw them in a store window, on sale for a nickel apiece. The pet store owner made a deal with the boy. If he would raise them to full-sized chickens, he would pay Kruse a quarter apiece for them. Somehow he scraped together enough money to buy a dozen chicks. He brought them home to his mother's three-bedroom apartment, "up above the drugstore at 79th and Jeffery, across from the rectory."

When young Donald arrived with the chicks, he was not popular with his mother. She wanted to get rid of them, but they were so tiny and fragile, she relented—but eventually, she said, the chickens were to be banished. Until then, Don Kruse was to supervise them carefully. He put them in a cardboard box in the basement of the apartment building and rigged up an electric light to keep them warm.

The first thing Kruse did was tell Father Mac. "So I had Father Mac come down and take a look at them. He thought they were great. He laughed! He thought this was the greatest thing in the world—I was raising chickens! But the janitor and the owner of the building got wind of it. They told my mother: 'We're kicking you out of the building unless you get rid of those chickens.' By now the chickens were about two weeks old, and they had grown quite a bit."

So Kruse took the box over to the rectory, set the box in front of the rectory, rang the bell "and ran like hell. The housekeeper took the chicks in. About 15 minutes later, I got a phone call. Father Mac says, 'We've got something that belongs to you over here at the rectory.' I said, 'They're going to kick my mother out.' He said, 'Come on over and we'll talk about it.' So I went over there. He had me pick up the box, go outside to his car, and said, 'Tell me where you got these chicks.' I said 'South Chicago.'" He drove to where Kruse directed him. Father Mac negotiated with the storeowner, dropped them off, and returned back to the car.

"'Now,' said Father Mac, 'listen to me: this is a no-lose deal. They're happy, the owner's happy, and your mother's happy.'" Says Kruse: "We didn't get kicked out of the apartment. I got rid of the chickens and that's it."

Good-natured "rough-house" was Father Mac's style with the boys. Don Kruse had a job on a newspaper delivery truck. "So I'd sit on the back of the truck, and I'd ride around, and they'd pick me up on Jeffery. I'd run in and drop off four papers and pick up one, also pick up 30¢, and drop off 20 papers—you know what I mean. I'm standing on the corner one day with Mike O'Keefe, and Father Mac ambles up. Along comes the *Herald American* truck driven by a guy named Toots. So Toots, he drives by and honks the horn and I go, 'Hi, Toots!' Father Mac thinks I'm talking to him. He gives me a shot in the head and says, 'I'll "Hi Toots" you!'" The "shot in the head" was a fatherly tap.

Joan O'Brien Furlong recalled that she and a group of other girls got in trouble by producing an underground, unofficial newspaper. Outraged, the sister superior herded them into her office and, "was about to get our parents in on the scene, when Father McDermott breezed past her door. He stuck his head in and said, 'Sister, what are all these fine girls doing in here?'" The nun explained heatedly that they were running an unofficial newspaper, expostulating it in terms of major dereliction.

Father McDermott listened, smiled and said, "Aw, Sister, they are having a little fun. Why don't *you*, too?"

Furlong described a scene when her father was dying of cancer at South Shore Hospital. The exhausted family had gone home for the evening, leaving the patient sound asleep. When they came back to visit him the next day, he said he awakened in the middle of the night, saw a black figure standing over him saying the rosary. The sick man decided that he had died and this was the after-life. Then the black figure bent over him and said, "Hi, Paul. How're you doing? It's Father Mac."

But it was not all sweetness and light. James Littleton was one of a group of boys to whom Father McDermott taught the *Baltimore Catechism*. With boys, the priest had an initially gruff tone which would dissolve into laughter, ultimately. Their assignment was to learn by rote the names of the seven Sacraments of the Catholic Church. There were five "Sacraments of the Living" (those to be received in the state of grace): Baptism, the Holy Eucharist, Confirmation, Matrimony, and Holy Orders. The other two were called the "Sacraments of the Dead": Penance, now Reconciliation, and Anointing of the Sick.

"All right," Father McDermott told the class of boys after he had lectured on these Sacraments, "tell me—what are the Sacraments of the Dead?"

"Penance and Matrimony—'cause when you get married you're dead!" a kid chorused, and the classroom broke up.

The priest said, "No joking around now. What are the Sacraments of the Living?" They named them.

"Now the Sacraments of the Dead."

They chorused the same jocular answer—Penance and Matrimony.

Says Littleton: "So Father Mac got really hot. He says, 'The next wise guy who comes up with this Matrimony, I'm going to put his head through the wall.'"

Silence. There was a seriousness to his tone that meant he wasn't kidding.

"One lad, a member of the Our Lady of Peace basketball team, was lost in thought, musing and dreaming, looking out the window," says Littleton. He was startled into attention when his name was called.

"My friend," said Father McDermott, "I have just vowed to do bodily harm to the next guy who gives me a flip answer. Quick, what are the Sacraments of the Dead?"

Confused, drawing on his memory of the last discussion, the boy said, "Confession—."

Father McDermott said, "Yes—? And?"

A pause, then a serious look came to the boy's face.

He struggled. Says Littleton: "He could tell that Father Mac is really getting hot. He says the first one is Confession. Yeah and what's the second one? The kid's thinking, he's *thinking*. The tension is rising in the room—and the kid sitting behind him, he whispered to the kid, 'Matrimony.'

"The kid says, 'Matrimony.' The whole class goes crazy. Even Father Mac had to bust out laughing—like 'What can he do?'"

Jack Harper recalled a Fourth of July when he and some youngsters from Our Lady of Peace were hanging around a drugstore at 79th and Jeffery. Someone had found two "torpedoes"— flares used by trainmen to signal oncoming railroad engineers to stop. They set a flare on the streetcar tracks. When the old red and yellow Chicago Surface Lines' streetcar came down the tracks, the flare went off, causing the motorman to grind the car to a halt and run out and look around to see what was happening.

"The police arrived on the scene," says Harper. The motorman identified the kids as the culprits and, quickly, 23 boys from Our Lady of Peace were taken to Grand Crossing police station at 75th and Cottage Grove.

Names were taken by the police and the kids were scared. When Father McDermott came, he didn't minimize the severity of their crime. With a private wink between the officers and the priest, the boys were released on the recognizance of Father McDermott.

"Another time," says Littleton, "a group of parish boys ended up at the police station where the desk sergeant seemed unwilling to sign the boys over to the priest's recognizance. There was a standoff, and the kids got nervous, thinking they would spend the night in the police station."

At last, Father McDermott said to the sergeant, "Your name is?"

"William."

"Listen," said the priest, "I happen to know your baptismal name is Aloysius. If you let these kids go, I won't tell anybody your name is Aloysius, okay?"

The cop grinned and the hostages were freed.

* * *

No mention of colorful mid-20th century priests who were Monsignor McDermott's contemporaries would be complete without reference to Father Patrick J. Molloy. He served as pastor of two parishes: Annunciation on the North Side, and St. Leo the Great on the South Side. Known as "Muggsy," he was famed far and wide for a fund-raising at Annunciation that featured bingo, carnivals, and dancing, including a picnic that was attended by more than 14,000 people. It is a record that still holds. Father Molloy was, at one time, banished from the archdiocese by Cardinal Mundelein because, in violation of rules, he sanctioned funeral services for Dion O'Banion, the mob boss who was gunned down in a flower shop across from Holy Name Cathedral. It wasn't that Father Molloy was himself involved in Capone-era crime, although he could play rough. Once, he made a flying tackle on a thief who was stealing his church's poor box. As a jocular, wisecracking priest, he knew the players. The rumor was that he was highly knowledgeable and, possibly, too tolerant of mob friends. Mundelein had ruled that O'Banion would not receive funeral services of the Church, because it would create scandal. Father Molloy transgressed that rule. Accordingly, he was sent to Panama in a penitential assignment wielded by Cardinal Mundelein.

But several years later, one of Mundelein's sisters made a visit to Panama and returned to tell her prelate brother that a charming priest made her stay very pleasant. So when his term of penance was up, Father Molloy was transferred back to Chicago. There, he became a favorite of some priests and earned the nickname "Muggsy." Stories of him were legend—as when a prominent parishioner of Holy Name had his car stolen. The theft was suspected to be of mob origin and someone told Father Molloy. He smiled, took down the description, and went to the phone. Not long after, the car appeared in the parishioner's driveway, immaculately washed and waxed.

Father Molloy was a good friend of Monsignor Henry Friel, pastor of Our Lady of Peace. One evening when the two priests were chatting on the back porch of the rectory, Father McDermott joined them. Father Molloy produced a pass, an admission, good, he said, for free entrance to all major league sports events. "What do you think of that, punk?" said Father Molloy.

Father McDermott looked at it casually and handed it back.

"Muggsy," he said, "this couldn't even get me in at Shewbridge Park"—a playground at 74th and Aberdeen where Leo high school football was played.

Father Molloy looked discomfited. He examined the pass and put it back in his wallet.

"A year or so later," says Monsignor McDermott, "I was walking down a street when I heard someone call my name and say, 'Hey, punk.' It was Father Molloy. He ran up, produced a pass and said, 'See, this will get you in free at Shewbridge Park!' My remark meant that much to him."

Father Molloy was designated Monsignor by Cardinal Stritch on the 40th anniversary of his ordination in 1957.

* * *

More than most people, Monsignor McDermott is drawn to newspaper reporters. Of prime interest was the late Warren Brown, sports editor of the old *Chicago American*, a Hearst paper.

"Brown worshipped at the shrine of Knute Rockne and, though a reporter, served as an unpaid publicitor for Notre Dame," he said. Taking a few months off from Our Lady of Peace in 1942 to do field social work in New York City for his master's degree, the priest got himself invited to the press box at Yankee Stadium when the visiting White Sox were playing the Yankees. He found himself sitting next to Brown.

Since, if Ignatius McDermott had not become a priest, he would have certainly been a sportswriter, he asked Brown: *"How did you get this job?"*

"Well, I graduated from the University of San Francisco with a degree in journalism," said the very literate man who became the dean of Chicago sports reporters. "After I graduated, I went to Hearst Square where the *San Francisco Examiner* was published and, without an appointment, went to the lady at the reception desk and asked for a job. I came on the right day, I guess, because she gave me a long look and said, 'Sit here and I'll return.' She was gone a long time. Then she came back, beckoned to me and said, 'Follow me.' She took me directly to the office of William Randolph Hearst. And there I was, presented in front of the massive desk where sat William Randolph Hearst himself! I presented my credentials. The first question he asked was, 'Young man, do you drink?'

"I said no, I never touch it. And he said, 'If you are telling me the truth, you are going to walk over a lot of bodies in the newspaper world because journalists are afflicted with excessive drink.' And so I was hired. And Hearst was proved right. Many good reporters were struggling to retain sobriety, and I rose through the ranks."

Did Brown tell Hearst the truth—that he didn't drink?

"Yes," said Brown, "but what I didn't tell him was that I had a strong attachment to the ponies."

Brown [1891–1978] was a San Francisco native who, for a time, was publicity man for then world heavyweight champion, Jack Dempsey, but the greater part of his career was in Chicago. A 1915 graduate of St. Ignatius College, then part of the University of San Francisco, Brown moved from Hearst's *San Francisco Examiner* to New York in the early 1920s. He was transferred to the old *Herald and Examiner* in Chicago and became one of the biggest names in the city's newspaperdom for nearly a half-century. His fans said he ranked with Ring Lardner, Westbrook Pegler, and Damon Runyon. In 1941, Brown became sports editor of the *Chicago Sun*. Five years later, he rejoined the Hearst organization at the *Chicago American*. He was still punching out guest columns at the age of 80 for *Chicago Today,* when it folded in 1974. He was elected to the Baseball Hall of Fame at Cooperstown, New York.

Another press box friend was a tall, urbane, aristocratic sports columnist for the *Daily News,* John Carmichael. Carmichael, a talented after-dinner speaker and raconteur, wrote the column "The Barber Shop" and was a czar of the sports pages, determining what team got the news play, what sport was featured more prominently. One day Colonel Frank Knox, owner of the *Daily News,* who rode with Teddy Roosevelt's Rough Riders up San Juan Hill, was a GOP vice presidential nominee in 1936, and FDR's Secretary of the Navy in 1941, said to Carmichael: "Why is it that you don't report on polo on our sports pages?"

Carmichael said, "Because I don't like polo and am not interested in it."

Colonel Knox said with some passion: "Well, I like polo and am very much interested in it."

Whereupon the suave Carmichael bowed low and said, "I have just developed an absorbing interest in polo. Good polo, bad polo, mediocre polo. And polo, sir, you shall have."

Carmichael [1903–1986], one of the most universally liked sportswriters in the nation, was born in Madison, Wisconsin, in the days when the barber shop was the focal point of sports discussions. When he grew up, he became a sportswriter and titled his column, "The Barber Shop." He attended Campion Preparatory and the University of Wisconsin, taking a night job as police reporter for the *Milwaukee Journal* and later as reporter and drama critic for the old *Milwaukee Leader*.

He came to Chicago in 1927 and ended up on the sports desk of the old *Herald and Examiner*. He joined the *Daily News* in 1932. Two years later, he began his "Barber Shop" column, which quickly became one of the best-known columns in the nation. When he became sports editor of the *Daily News* in 1934, the *News* told its readers: "Mr. Carmichael's new duties will not curtail his freedom to go anywhere in the nation that exciting sports news develops. The only change will be that he will be okaying his own expense accounts." At a White Sox training camp in Sarasota, Florida, he was once approached by Warren Brown. Brown had to absent himself and asked non-teetotaler Carmichael to wire his column to the *American*. Hours later, Brown returned and wanted to make sure Carmichael had wired in Brown's column. Carmichael said, "Hell, yes, I wired it in hours ago." Then, shoving his hand in his pocket and withdrawing a sheaf of papers, "You know what? I still have it here in my coat!"

Carmichael frequently scooped other reporters on fast breaking sports developments. One day, he even scooped himself. He promised to cover for writer Jim Gallagher of the *Chicago American* during an absence at the winter baseball meetings. As soon as Gallagher left, pitcher Thornton Lee was traded to the White Sox. Carmichael wrote 580 words, signed Gallagher's name to it, and wired it to the *American*, a keen rival of the *Daily News*. That's what friends are for, Carmichael believed. Later, he was chatting with friends about the trade when a hotel bellhop handed him a wire from his office: *American has a story, Sox to get Lee. What about it?* "It hit me like a bolt," said Carmichael. "I had forgotten to file my own story!"

In 1975, he was inducted into the Baseball Hall of Fame in Cooperstown, New York, and five years later, was one of the first writers named to the Chicago Press Club's Journalism Hall of Fame. Above all, he was an unashamed American League baseball fan. The low point of his career, he said, was the 1938 All-Star game won by the National League, 4 to 1, when his entire *Daily News* column consisted of a blank white space with a single comment at the bottom: "Mr. Carmichael has nothing to say to his constituents today."

*   *   *

Significant events between 1941 and 1946 coincided with Monsignor McDermott's work. Jim McDermott left the city council for the influential Cook County Board of Tax Appeals, while retaining his post as 14th ward Democratic committeeman and preparing a campaign for the Superior Court bench. In March 1941, the *Saturday Evening Post* published the first article to appear about an organization known as Alcoholics Anonymous. The story related the religious experience a "hopeless" New York City alcoholic named "Bill W." had in his hospital room in December 1934, and told the story thus far of AA. In May 1935, a dried-out Bill W. had sought out another alcoholic, "Dr. Bob," in Akron. They agreed that by helping themselves abstain from liquor "one day at a time," they could help others in a fast-growing network of self-therapy. By November 1937, they had counted 40 sober cases in Akron. John D. Rockefeller, Jr. had given the group its first grant in February 1938—$5,000—which Bill W. claimed "saved us from professionalism." Rockefeller said that a large bequest of money would destroy AA. The $5,000 was used to publish the first AA book.

In May 1938, Bill W. had begun writing his book *Alcoholics Anonymous*. In December of that year, in cooperation with Dr. Bob and others, he had composed AA's famous "Twelve Steps" to sobriety. The *Saturday Evening Post* article was the first major boost for AA. It won many thousands of adherents. In 1946, Bill W. published the *Twelve Steps and Twelve Traditions of Alcoholics Anonymous*.

The first version of the 12 Steps, which have helped millions to put into order their shattered lives, reads as follows:

(1)   Admitted we were powerless over alcohol—that our lives had become unmanageable.

(2)   Came to believe that a Power greater than ourselves could restore us to sanity.

(3)   Made a decision to turn our will and our lives over to the care and direction of God as we understood Him.

(4)   Made a searching and fearless moral inventory of ourselves.

(5) Admitted to God, to ourselves, and to another human being the exact nature of our wrongs.

(6) Were entirely willing that God remove all these defects of character.

(7) Humbly, on our knees, asked Him to remove our short-comings—holding nothing back.

(8) Made a list of all persons we had harmed, and became willing to make complete amends to them all.

(9) Made amends to such people whenever possible, except when to do so would injure them or others.

(10) Continued to take personal inventory and when we were wrong promptly admitted it.

(11) Sought through prayer and meditation to improve our contact with God, praying only for knowledge of His will for us and the power to carry that out.

(12) Having had a spiritual experience as the result of this course of action, we tried to carry this message to others, especially alcoholics, and to practice these principles in all our affairs.

Other variations in 12-step terminology have come along since.

Alcoholics Anonymous gained attention as an invaluable self-help program, principally within reach of the middle class. Bill W. had been a Wall Street stockbroker, and Dr. Bob, a well-known Akron physician and surgeon.

Monsignor McDermott embraced the doctrine of AA soon after its magazine announcement. It squared with his perception of addiction.

Monsignor McDermott's mission was to take the program, which was growing in acceptance by the middle class, to the true down-and-outs, the helpless poor of urban skid rows. He would found a Chicago institution to minister to those who, in the words of the late social activist, author, poet—and some say uncanonized saint—Dorothy Day, "are broken on the iron wheel of our time"— the poor, often homeless, addicted to illusory distractions from their agony: alcohol, drugs, sex, and gambling among them.

CHAPTER 7

Rebel with a Cause: Catholic Charities, 1946–1960

Skid Row is not a piece of real estate—it's a state of mind.

—Ignatius McDermott

Chicago's politics had changed drastically. The Democrats controlled the city starting in 1931 with the defeat of the last Republican mayor, Big Bill Thompson [1915–1923; 1927–1931]. A McDermott reminiscence tells it all:

"As a young assistant at Our Lady of Peace, I was attending a reception at the Conrad Hilton Hotel. A man drew me aside and said that at the adjoining Blackstone Hotel there was a faded political sight to be seen. He said, 'Father, do you know who's sitting in there in that lobby every day? He's the most lonely man in the world.' I said, 'Well, I wouldn't know. Would you share that with me?' He said, 'The former mayor of Chicago, William Hale Thompson.'

"So I walked in. We approached William Hale Thompson. He was sitting alone in the lobby and he had a newspaper in his lap. I'm sure it was the *Tribune*, run by his nemesis, Colonel McCormick. I said to him, 'Mr. Mayor, I recall you so well when I was a kid. In '24 and '25 [at Quigley] we used to be playing ball on the grass which is now the Outer Drive. It was noontime and after lunch we'd run over there to play baseball. I recall you going by in your big car, an open car. You'd be sitting in the back seat every noon and we'd say, 'There goes the mayor of Chicago.'"

The man who launched the Outer Drive and transformed a back street into Michigan Boulevard, the "Boul Mich" of urban fame, growled, "Father, I want you to know I did a hell of a lot of work before you saw me at noon."

Thompson's successor was Anton Cermak [1931–1933], a raw ethnic-coalition building genius, the prototype of all the successful Democratic bosses who were to take over urban centers in the nation. An anomaly as a Czech Protestant, Tony Cermak supported former New York Governor Alfred E. Smith for the Democratic presidential nomination at the party's 1932 convention in Chicago. Cermak's reason for being a Smith booster was to ingratiate himself with Chicago Catholics. After FDR's election, the mayor saw an urgent need to build a relationship with the incoming president. In a strange jumble of circumstances, Cermak came down with dysentery, contracted from sewage that had infiltrated the drinking water at the luxury hotel where he lived on South Michigan Avenue. Cermak went to Miami Beach to recover. He decided to take in a speech to be made by Roosevelt on February 15, 1933. As the mayor polished his relationship with Roosevelt at an open car, an Italian immigrant, Giuseppe Zangara, fired a revolver. Zangara got off five shots; four missed and one hit Cermak. Roosevelt was unhurt. Though not a mortal wound, it induced peritonitis, which claimed Cermak's life two weeks later. A longtime Chicago rumor has held that Cermak, not Roosevelt, was the intended target in an assassination engineered by Capone's successor Frank Nitti. Cermak's death, as his life, was to be forever analyzed for political implications.

A marvelous Chicago-style manipulation involved the unlikely choice of his successor. The scenario was orchestrated by Patrick Nash, 28th ward Democratic committeeman. He was soon to become chairman of the Cook County Democratic party, leader of the powerful Irish faction in the city council. Nash owned a sewer contracting firm that had been generously patronized by Sanitary District chief engineer Edward J. Kelly, also president of the South Park District, who transformed Grant Park from a trash heap to an urban scenic wonder. After Cermak's death, Nash prevailed upon the Democratic majority in the Illinois General Assembly to rush through a state law permitting the city council to go outside its membership in choosing an interim mayor. It was signed by Democratic Governor Henry Horner. Then, Nash pronounced his pick—Edward J. Kelly [1933–1947].

The two collaborated to build a political dynasty. Nash, a brilliant diplomat, soothed warring factions. Kelly became a nationally known political figure, a deep admirer of Franklin D. Roosevelt. Kelly helped orchestrate support for FDR's precedent-breaking third and fourth terms. But when Nash died in 1943, it was the beginning of the end. There came two serious miscalculations which, continuing uncorrected, eventually brought Kelly down. Chicago was paying the price for more than a decade of corrupt government that had been ignored during World War II.

Wrote Emmett Dedman, editorial director of the *Sun-Times*, "Kelly blithely ignored the dirty streets, loafing payrollers and open corruption of everyone from City Hall clerks to the police force. Chicagoans routinely carried five- or ten-dollar bills in their drivers' licenses, which would just as routinely be removed when a car was stopped for a traffic violation."

Author Len O'Connor estimated that the mob was laying out almost $20 million a year for protection for projects ranging from gambling dives to houses of prostitution, illegal slot machines, and the lucrative "numbers" racket favored by blacks on the South Side. It was corruption unseen since the era of Big Bill Thompson. Kelly and Jim McDermott were at odds, leading to Kelly's opposition to McDermott's reelection bid to the Cook County Board of Tax Appeals. As a result, Jim McDermott was defeated for the only time in his life.

Added to this was an open housing controversy. Liberals supported an ordinance that would outlaw housing discrimination by race. Not endorsed outright by Kelly, it was, nevertheless, seen as his private agenda through his fervent support of FDR's New Deal. Bitterness erupted as many South Side whites rebelled against what they saw as racial "block-busting." Returned World War II veteran Lieutenant Colonel Jacob (Jack) Arvey, 24th ward committeeman, became Cook County Democratic chairman and took a survey. The first poll taken in machine politics, it showed astounding results: Kelly was disliked by most of the constituencies that comprised the Democratic party, including white Catholics and Jews (only the blacks remained loyal to him). Arvey then spearheaded the dumping of Kelly in 1947, a move seconded by 14th Ward Alderman and Committeeman Clarence Wagner and his mentors, Judge John J. Sullivan and Judge Jim McDermott, Monsignor's brother.

Kelly was succeeded by a civic leader and businessman handpicked by Arvey who was as spotless as Kelly was seemingly corrupt—Martin H. Kennelly [1947–1955]. A millionaire who disdained any party post, Kennelly kept an arm's-length relationship with both the Democratic party and the city council. Initially, it was one of convenience, but one that brought dividends to both sides. On one hand, Kennelly's cleanliness brought the machine credibility; and the machine, headed by Arvey, would make the political decisions while the city council finance chairman, 14th Ward Alderman Clarence Wagner, would be the unofficial mayor of Chicago, leaving Kennelly free to cut ribbons and attend civic banquets. Joining Wagner in running the city government was a small coterie of aldermen known as the Grey Wolves, to which Jim McDermott, from his Circuit Court bench, was a key advisor.

The pressure on Kennelly to conform to the machine's wishes began to show early in his administration. The mayor was called "Snow White" behind his back. A bachelor and daily Mass-goer who lived with his widowed sister in a luxurious apartment, he was ill-fitted to be a politician. He was suited to be a civic leader. Also, he was a cold fish, one who seldom took a drink, was distant and polite rather than a backslapping politician. He had a distaste for governmental activism saying, "All I have is my reputation and I don't propose to have it dirtied up in politics." But he worried a lot about what conniving was being conducted by Wagner's Grey Wolves behind his back.

One day Kennelly's tension showed keenly to colorful Father John Ireland Gallery, pastor of St. Cecilia's parish at 45th and Wells. Gallery was the brother of several Navy veterans including Chicago-born hero Admiral Daniel Gallery, the first officer to capture an enemy vessel intact (a German submarine) since the War of 1812. Father Gallery arrived to visit with the mayor about plans to put the submarine on exhibit at the Museum of Science and Industry.

As Monsignor McDermott tells it: "So John Ireland arrived first at the mayor's office ahead of his brothers. The secretary said, 'Sit down and take it easy. The mayor is busy.' Then the mayor concluded an audience and she said, 'You can go in and visit with the mayor until your brothers come.' He said, 'No, I might as well sit here a little bit.' Then I guess she felt the mayor was becoming fidgety, so she said again, 'Why don't you join the mayor? He's in there alone.'

"So John went in and he told me the mayor had his hands behind his back and he was lost in sad thought, looking out the window. And John, who was never known as the keystone of diplomacy, says, 'Martin! Don't jump! Things aren't that bad!'" The mayor smiled only slightly.

The brokered marriage between Martin Kennelly and the machine first ran into trouble in 1950. That year Arvey picked a disastrous county ticket, losing the vital post of Cook County board president to the Republicans, and was sent into speedy retirement as chairman. Three years later, with ace-diplomat Judge John Sullivan dead, the cooperative deal between Kennelly, the party, and the city council went off the rails.

Kennelly's too-pure "good government" side was responsible, claimed the professional politicians. He was unresponsive to the needs of the machine by his attempt to dismantle the patronage apparatus on which the Democratic party depended. He also cracked down on the numbers games in the South Side African-American neighborhoods of powerful Congressman William Dawson. A struggle began for control of the Cook County Democratic party, which would be a prelude to pushing Kennelly aside to choose another mayor.

In 1953, "Who would be party chairman?" was the question. A small group of Southwest Side Irish politicians had a plan: Jim McDermott would resign as Superior Court judge and become chairman. Then, when the opportunity presented itself, either McDermott or Clarence Wagner of the 14th ward would be slated as mayor to oppose Kennelly. Another faction supported an ambitious aspirant for chairman, with a yen to be mayor, Cook County Clerk Richard J. Daley. A showdown was to come on July 8, 1953, at a closed-door session of the county committee at the old Morrison Hotel.

In this tong war, in which the Irish were divided, the team of Nash-Duffy-McDermott-Wagner was more conservative politically than the pro-Daley faction.

The players: **Thomas D. Nash**, managing partner of the most politically powerful law firm in Chicago, Nash and Ahern, which had provided legal counsel for Al Capone and Al's brother, Ralph. Nash had endeared himself to South Side Sox fans by winning an acquittal in court for the eight members of the 1919 White Sox who were accused of fixing the World Series. Tom Nash had run afoul of his late distant cousin Pat's latter-day supporters.

Chicago's unofficial mayor, Kennelly's floor leader in the council, Clarence Wagner, was a member of Nash and Ahern, as had been Jim McDermott, now Superior Court judge. Richard J. Daley had been affiliated with the firm for a short time but left. No one mentioned the reason for his abrupt and mysteriously sudden departure—and his sudden resignation has been unexplained to this day. "It was thought that Daley wasn't smart enough in the law," one secretary to the firm commented.

Nash's protégé, **John Duffy**, committeeman and former alderman of the 19th ward was the former chairman of the council finance committee. A native of the 14th ward, the politician operated a florist shop on Halsted Street, north of Garfield Boulevard. He was widely known throughout Chicago as a sponsor of semiprofessional and amateur sports teams. Duffy had given up his plum aldermanic seat with the council finance chairmanship and had lost his bid for Cook County board president because of, he believed, Arvey's miscues. Duffy couldn't decide if he wanted the mayoralty or would back Wagner but, for now, he wanted Kennelly to be gone and wished to exert control over Chicago's politics.

Clarence Wagner was the committeeman and alderman of the 14th ward. He had a German surname but his mother was Irish, Wagner never tired of explaining. He is described by O'Connor, as "a bright and audacious lawyer, with a sardonic sense of humor and a taste for strong drink." William Gleason characterizes him as "tall and bespectacled, witty and unusually sophisticated, for a product of Chicago's political school." There was a strain of mischief in his makeup, as when he slipped into a Republican convention at the old Coliseum, moved up to the rostrum and delightedly delivered a speech praising the Democratic party to the amazed audience and then departed in gales of laughter.

Jim McDermott was described by Len O'Connor as "standing tall with the rugged build of a football player," and by William Gleason in his book, *Daley of Chicago: The Man, the Mayor and the Limits of Conventional Politics*, as possessing "Gaelic features soft and fine, his hair white, himself tall and robust, [resembling] a matinee idol to whom nature had been generous." He was judge of the Superior Court, having been a member of the Nash and Ahern firm, committeeman of the 14th ward, alderman, a former member of the Cook County Board of Tax Appeals, and lower court judge. McDermott continued to maintain effective control of the 14th ward and Chicago policy making through his close friend and protégé, Clarence Wagner.

No Chicagoan had better qualities for political leadership than Jim McDermott, as incipient mayor, governor, and U.S. Senator, in the estimation of Father John J. Sullivan, the grandson of McDermott's original sponsor. A superb politician, a fastidious dresser, Jim McDermott, as most politicians, detested surprises.

"His widow, Helen, told me this story," says Father Sullivan. "She told me about a surprise birthday party she had lined up for him. When all the people who were hidden in the house for the surprise party jumped out and yelled 'Surprise!' he turned flaming red. He went upstairs and didn't come down because he had on a blue shirt and he thought he should have worn a white shirt." When a turn came for Democratic county chairman, McDermott was planning ahead.

Now, the Nash-Duffy-McDermott-Wagner combination faced the team of Arvey-Gill-Horan-Daley. Both groups wanted to force Kennelly into retirement by the election of a party chairman who would lie in waiting for 1955, when he would make his move for mayor.

Supporting Richard J. Daley were: **Colonel Jacob (Jack) Arvey**, who had been deposed as Cook County Democratic chairman. He was still remembered fondly for his picking a 1948 ticket that truly had national good consequences for the machine—Adlai Stevenson for governor and Paul Douglas for U.S. Senator. Arvey still possessed benign influence as the largely honorific Democratic National Committeeman.

Joseph Gill, retiring as Cook County chairman, had been a caretaker chairman since the resignation of Arvey. It had been expected that the elderly Gill would serve through the mayoral election of April 1955; but now that the party leadership had become disenchanted with Kennelly, he was ready to retire. Gill was also clerk of the municipal court, a post laden with heavy patronage.

Albert J. Horan, bailiff of the municipal court who did a lucrative insurance and bonding business with public agencies, held a public post that also was endowed with significant patronage.

Richard J. Daley, the only Democratic survivor of the ruinous 1950 year, was a party vice-chairman and Cook County clerk, having defeated Nicholas J. Bohling. Daley, too, was holder of a post rich with patronage and was primed to run for mayor.

As author O'Connor describes it:

> Duffy's defeat and Daley's victory had been eating away at members of the Nash group for more than three years when fifty Democratic ward committeemen and thirty township committeemen assembled at the Morrison Hotel on July 8, 1953. They had come to accept the resignation of the 68-year-old Joe Gill and to praise him fulsomely. They would elect a new county chairman who would revitalize the party for the national and state races in 1954 and for the

mayoral and aldermanic elections of 1955. Dick Daley was "in" according to all insiders.

Then Clarence Wagner arose and in his deceptively non-chalant manner moved that the committeemen postpone the election of the county chairman until July 21. Wagner's motion carried. Now the Nash faction had thirteen days in which to do something about Daley. Perhaps they could not stop him but they were willing to give it a try…

…For a change the battle lines were clearly drawn, as they rarely are in Chicago politics. This would not be guerrilla warfare. This was out in the open where the public could enjoy it. Everyone was aware that Nash and Wagner wanted the county chairmanship for one of Chicago's most dynamic and controversial figures. Their man was James J. McDermott, judge of the Superior Court. Jim had joined Nash and Ahern in 1920 soon after his graduation from DePaul University law school. He became committeeman of the 14th ward in 1932 and was elected alderman in 1933. During 10 years in the council…McDermott used charm, physical presence, bluff and vocal power to impose his will upon that pliable body.

It also was written that Big Jim's big voice had been stilled only once during a decade of thunderous and acrimonious debate. That was on October 6, 1937, the day that the bottom fell out of his chair. Even then his admirers and his enemies suspected that the crashing collapse of the chair had been arranged to illustrate a point. They thought it more than coincidence that McDermott, chairman of the City Council building code subcommittee, was listening to complaints from operators of small lumberyards when his chair fell apart.

Everyone was aware that if McDermott were to be county chairman, the party would be run with an iron hand and with an explosive temper. The master plan was that Wagner would step down as committeeman of the 14th. McDermott would be elected by the precinct captains thereby becoming eligible to be elected county chairman. After he ascended to that position, he would resign as judge. And in the spring of 1955 Wagner or Duffy would be the organization's candidate for mayor.

After the closed-door vote where he had been humiliated by being set unceremoniously on the shelf, Daley left the meeting in a state of shock, his eyes reddening. Daley reported to friends in a trembling voice, as recorded by eyewitness O'Connor in his book, *Clout: Mayor Daley and His City*, "Joe Gill is still 'acting.'"

What happened? Daley replied, choked up, "Clarence [Wagner] stopped it. Gill calls for a motion to nominate me and

Clarence gets up and says, "Now, wait a minute. Let's not be hasty." And there was a big argument and we didn't get to vote." Asked whom Wagner wanted for chairman, Daley responded: "Duffy wants it—for McDermott."

"But," O'Connor said, "McDermott can't be chairman, he's a judge." Daley said, "He'll quit as judge. Clarence will quit as committeeman of the 14th and Jim will take that. Then he'll be chairman." O'Connor asked: "And Duffy will run the show?" Daley nodded, with tears in his eyes. "That's their plan."

But death intervened, as it had so often with the fortunes of Richard J. Daley. Two days later, on July 10, 1953, at approximately 7 a.m., Wagner's city-owned Cadillac—rolling at 60 miles per hour—flew off a blacktop road near Nagurski's Corner in International Falls, Minnesota, on the way to a fishing camp in Lake of the Woods, Ontario, Canada. Bronko Nagurski, an old Bears fullback, was a symbol of power, courage and fearlessness. Admired even by all those who saw him play against their beloved Cardinals, he ran a filling station in his home town of International Falls. Wagner was killed, his skull crushed, in the crash in which five others survived.

The death turned Chicago politics upside-down—and the effects are with the city yet. Without the formidable Wagner, Nash-Duffy-McDermott couldn't prevail. The day before the county committee met, Judge McDermott announced: "In the interest of my party and to bring about unity and harmony, I have requested those committeemen who advanced my name to withdraw it."

Daley declared: "I think highly of the judge's magnanimous gesture." Arvey-Gill-Horan-Daley won. On television, chairman Richard J. Daley denied that he would seek the mayoralty.

"I would not run if the mayor [Kennelly] is interested in being a candidate," he said. But Kennelly's doom two years hence was certified.

Thus, it was Daley who would dominate Chicago politics from 1955, for more than 20 years, until his death in 1976 (starting a reign that, with some interruption, would be continued through his son into the 21st century). And where Judge McDermott, at age 58, had been inches away from being elected chairman of one of the most powerful party organizations in the nation, he was now relegated to staying on the bench—having gained an unforgiving enemy in Daley.

Years later, former Alderman Thomas Keane, a major power as chairman of the city council finance committee during the

Daley years, told *Sun-Times* political columnist Steve Neal that there was no question that, but for the Wagner death, Jim McDermott would have been elected Cook County Democratic chairman. For one thing, Chicago's powerful William Dawson, unrivaled leader of the South Side and U.S. Congressman, was for McDermott, said Keane.

Len O'Connor summarized:

> The political ambitions of Judge McDermott died when Clarence Wagner died; Jim McDermott knew that the Daley people would give him the treatment now. McDermott had one good round in the pistol, though, and he blasted his enemies with it before Wagner was placed in the ground. They had the sheer guts to come demanding something from McDermott before Wagner had been borne from his living room to his requiem mass in Visitation Church on Garfield Boulevard. And in return, McDermott pulled the trigger— hitting Wagner's erstwhile colleagues where it hurt—in their wallets.
>
> Judge McDermott, who had been friend and counselor of Clarence F. Wagner and was stipulated in the alderman's will as executor of his estate, had been on brief holiday at his summer home in Long Beach, Indiana when the news reached him that Wagner had been killed. As gently as he could he broke the news to Nora Wagner, Clarence's wife, and then drove to Chicago, a 90-minute trip from the Indiana Dunes, to see what had to be done.
>
> McDermott gave first priority to the matter of getting into Wagner's safe deposit boxes: one at the American National Bank, in the heart of downtown Chicago, and the other in the Colonial Savings and Loan Association, in his neighborhood.

Were there envelopes found in the boxes containing money as was rumored? Later, McDermott was visited by an alderman who claimed that Wagner had held money in an envelope for some council members for safekeeping.

"Were their names on the envelope?" asked McDermott.

No, but people in the council were expecting to receive it since Clarence was holding it for safekeeping.

To which (according to author O'Connor) Judge McDermott replied, "Well, in that case, I think the money—if there was any money—belongs to Nora and Clarence's children."

Not long thereafter, two famous council buddies, Aldermen Paddy Bauler and Charlie Weber, were discussing events with O'Connor in Bauler's saloon at 403 West North Avenue.

Bauler said: "Should I tell you how it was with Clarence as finance chairman? You could trust the guy. Only, we had this pot, see? And certain things that we got together on and voted for went into the pot, cuttin' it up at the end of the year—the guys who were in, that is. So Clarence has this envelope and then he gets kilt—."

How much money?

Bauler said, "A hundred grand."

Where did it come from?

O'Connor writes: "'I don't know,' Weber said. 'It was one of them franchise renewals, the phone company or the gas people or somebody. They wanted one of them exceptions to the ordinance or some [expletive] like that; so they pay and we give them what they want.'"

Not this time. Thanks to Judge McDermott, the money—if there was any—went to the bereaved family who put it to better use than a covey of aldermen on the take.

*   *   *

In 1946, Father McDermott received another marching order—to take up duties as an associate administrator at Catholic Charities. He would become executive director of the Dependent Child Commission and director of the Holy Cross Mission for Homeless Men. In addition, he was to spend three nights a week working toward a master's degree in social work at Loyola University, while living on the fifth floor of Catholic Charities, 126 North Desplaines, near teeming Skid Row. (He would be so busy with his work on the Street that he would not receive his master's from Loyola until 1970, when he was 61 years old.)

> Less than a mile from the Monroe Street police station, Father Mac was at work at his office on the second floor of the Charities' Building. He had come out of his corner so quickly this Monday morning it seemed that he intended to race the new week toward Saturday night instead of pummeling with it. The priest is convinced that every week has a major weakness. A week has no staying power. A week never lasts long enough to provide him with the time to do all the things he must do.
>
> This priest often gives the impression that he is wildly disorganized. The truth is that there is simply no orderly way for one man to direct a large department; to drive out to

the Kennedy School for Exceptional Children to counsel the retarded; to write dozens of notes, memos and reports; to interview volunteers for his program; to spend the early evening hours on Skid Row; to attend two or three wakes; to visit the sick at County Hospital; to return to Skid Row late at night; and to worry about the sports fortunes of the White Sox, the Bears, Notre Dame, Northwestern, Loyola, DePaul and innumerable high school teams. Father Mac does all these things; he does them at top speed and he seems to do them almost casually.

—William F. Gleason
The Liquid Cross of Skid Row

Father McDermott's 1946 assignment to Catholic Charities came from a man as different from Cardinal Mundelein as, seemingly, it was possible to be.

Nashville, Tennessee-born Samuel Cardinal Stritch [1887–1958], Mundelein's successor, was more conservative and less involved in social action. He was precociously bright, having finished grade school at age 10 and high school at 16. He was bookish and courtly. After completing his theological studies in Rome, he returned to Nashville as an assistant, then was a pastor in Memphis and, in quick succession, a bishop's secretary, chancellor and superintendent of schools, bishop of Toledo, and archbishop of Milwaukee.

When he was installed as archbishop of Chicago, on March 7, 1940, central casting would have placed him in the role of auditor come to inspect the books. But this was deceptive. As an administrator, he often skipped attention to detail and particularly loathed fund-raising, which had been a Mundelein forte. Samuel Stritch saw his work as primarily pastoral and thought it vital that he serve the spiritual needs of his people. He kept his Tennessee drawl, despite his years in the North, had rimless spectacles, was a cigarette chain-smoker in private and a man who enjoyed scholarly reflection.

Unlike Mundelein, he had a horror of memorable actions. He quietly transferred Monsignor Reynold Hillenbrand, the activist rector of St. Mary of the Lake Seminary, sharply scaled back the archdiocese's socially progressive involvements, and conducted Church business largely through two Mundelein holdovers, Monsignors George Casey and Edward Burke. This allowed him to ease up on the desk work he abhorred and appear more frequently at confirmations and church dedications.

Says Monsignor McDermott: "Mundelein majored in pragmatism. I think Sammy [the colloquial name priests used for Stritch] majored in spirituality. Like "The Music Man," Mundelein 'knew the territory.'" He tells a story that reflects Stritch's thoughtful self-absorption. Once, at a bishops' meeting in Washington, D.C., he got in a hotel elevator with two other prelates and barely noticed two other Chicago priests in it.

But Stritch was no wishy-washy prelate. In 1949 when he consecrated bishops (William O'Connor among them), he pressed the mitre (the tall peaked hat of authority) on their heads; Martin McNamara, a Chicago auxiliary, whispered, "It is hurting." "It'll always hurt," responded Stritch dryly. He had his own definite conservative views of church formalities, including art. He dedicated Mater Christi Church in North Riverside on June 28, 1953. The church was built in sharply modernistic style. As he said Mass his eyes darted up to a huge surrealistic crucifix high in the sanctuary.

"When he ascended the pulpit at post-Communion time," says Monsignor McDermott, "he said [imitating the flat twang of Stritch's Tennessee voice]: 'That cross is grotesque and tomorrow morning I'm going to contact Belli & Belli [the architect] and let 'em know my feelings!'"

Although he seemed to be a cold fish, nevertheless it was Cardinal Stritch who gave Father McDermott's career the push that sent him back to the work he loved.

"[Catholic Charities superintendent Father William] O'Connor wanted me," says Monsignor McDermott. "So he went to Stritch and asked for three priests—Father Gilbert Carroll, Father Joseph Holbrook, and myself. Stritch was pushing post-graduate training. He said, 'I'd like those priests to go to the Catholic University in Washington to pursue their degrees.' So O'Connor said, 'Well, Ignatius has more experience. He worked at St. Mary's Training School for five years, so he's five years ahead of them in a way. I'd like to put him in as head of the Dependent Child Commission. I'd want him to go to school, too, but I'd rather have him go as a part-time student, at Loyola School of Social Work, and he could still run the office.' Stritch said that'd be all right. So the others went off to Washington and I stayed and worked at the Dependent Child Commission all day and, at 4:15 p.m., I'd go to Loyola and take two or three classes."

Diagonally across the street from his apartment at Catholic Charities (where he would remain until 1991) was Haymarket

Square which, on May 4, 1886, witnessed a bloody struggle between demonstrators agitating for an eight-hour day and police seeking to break up the rally. An anarchist's bomb was tossed, triggering police retaliation. Eight policemen died, 59 were wounded; 10 civilians were killed and at least 30 were wounded. The struggle prompted an anti-immigrant Red Scare, leading to a trial that was termed by historians as a mockery of criminal justice: the bomb-tosser was never found, four anarchists were hanged, with one committing suicide in jail. Governor John Peter Altgeld, himself a German immigrant, pardoned the remaining three defendants, spurring a national protest that doomed his political career. The Charities' building, then a warehouse, served as a makeshift hospital and morgue on the night of the struggle.

"I came to the Catholic Charities in 1946, on June 22," said Monsignor McDermott. "The institutions in those days were excessively nationalistic. There was a home at Touhy and Harlem, St. Hedwig's, for children of Polish descent who were separated from their parents, or mothers necessitating their placement outside the home. There was an orphanage in Lisle, Illinois, for Bohemian children—St. Joseph's. The so-called Irish orphanage—I worked there from 1936 to 1941—was St. Mary's Training School in Des Plaines. Misericordia Home, which now caters to exceptional infants, was the German orphanage. Then they had the line of demarcation going in those days. There was a school for black girls, Illinois Technical School for Black Girls at 49th and Prairie. There was a place for girls who were experiencing disciplinary problems—the House of Good Shepherd, in the shadow of Wrigley Field, at 1126 West Grace Street.

"Then there was a home at 35th and Lake Park which had a terrible name—St. Joseph's Home for the Friendless. They harbored kids there between the ages of 6 and 18. Those were the kids who were adoptable, but they weren't adopted because they weren't Prince or Princess Charming. When the parents looked for an adoptable child, maybe they didn't have enough dimples or something. So these kids would leave St. Vincent's and go to St. Joseph's. When I arrived at Maryville in 1936, shortly after that, six boys came out to St. Mary's Training School who were adoptable but were not adopted because they lacked some charm."

There was also a school for mentally-retarded and emotionally-handicapped children in south suburban Palos Park. In 1953, it received a then-significant grant of money—$1.3 million—from the Joseph P. Kennedy family and the name was changed to "Lieutenant Joseph P. Kennedy, Jr. School for Exceptional Children." The grant was an expression of the family's devotion to their sister, Rosemary, born retarded, and housed at a Catholic convent in Jefferson, Wisconsin.

"The Dependent Child Commission," said Monsignor McDermott, "was an office where, if a man became a widower and he had kids of grammar school age, and he had to go to work and had nobody to take care of them, what would he do? The first thing he'd do is resort to his pastor. He would say to the pastor, 'You're well aware of my wife's death and the kids here, and I'm getting a week's vacation. What's going to happen to these kids 51 weeks a year? I don't get home from work until 5 or 6 p.m., and I'm quite concerned about their welfare.' The pastor would say, 'Go down to 506 South Wabash...there's an office there, and here's a letter...you talk to the people down there.'"

The Dependent Child Commission, originally called the Catholic Home Bureau, investigated and approved placements for children in orphanages and industrial schools.

In addition to his duties there, Father McDermott effectively became director of admissions to the Kennedy School as well as such institutions as Angel Guardian, St. Hedwig's, Maryville, Misericordia Hospital, Marillac House, St. Mary of Providence, St. Joseph's Home for the Friendless, St. Vincent DePaul Center, and St. Vincent's Infant Hospital.

*   *   *

It was at this time that Father McDermott met Francine Lamb. Trained as a social worker with a master's degree in the field, from Loyola, she joined Catholic Charities at the age of 22. A single woman, outwardly shy and self-effacing, but with a will of steel, she remained the priest's trusted assistant until her death in 1987 at age 62. Deeply religious, ultra-loyal, Fran Lamb served as his alter ego and gatekeeper (the latter function so zealously that critics claim that for too long Monsignor McDermott was shut off from attempts of help). Despite this, Lamb was, in the estimation of the woman who knew her best, Mary Ellen Flynn, her co-worker at Charities, "the great woman behind the great man."

Lamb, a tall, angular woman, six feet two inches in height, "worked for Father McDermott seven days a week," commented

Flynn. "The only time she ever took off was when he took off. If he was gone, then she took vacation time. She really handled everything for him. I mean *everything*. She did his Christmas shopping; she did every single thing for him. And she was always busy. She had a wonderful rapport with the men who came from Skid Row. They liked her. But she was, at times, hard to work for. She was very loyal to him, very focused. Sometimes, if something was laid out, you couldn't disagree."

Lamb's personal attention to individual human needs was legendary. She had a regular standing order for a cab each morning to take her from her apartment to Catholic Charities. Usually she got the same driver, a charming man named Freddy Gerard. One day he confessed to her that he had an alcohol problem. Lamb worked on him to join Alcoholics Anonymous, where he found sobriety.

Mary Ellen Flynn recalls the time when Lamb decorated the office with signs proclaiming "Father Mac—Our Hero!" because he and Father John Sullivan had interrupted a jack-rolling. "Father Sullivan and Father Mac were out to dinner," said Flynn, "when they saw a guy getting rolled. They cornered the guy and trapped him. They retrieved the wallet or whatever and turned everything in to the police and Fran decided to create posters that said Father Mac was a hero. She put the posters on the doors."

The McDermott function at Catholic Charities became her life, says Flynn—who insists that Lamb was and *is* a saint. "We always felt that when she got up to heaven, Haymarket would take off. It took off almost immediately following her death on October 4, 1987. She was the backup person. No one ever saw her. She never took credit for anything, but when she got up there [heaven] things took off."

Between Monsignor McDermott and Lamb there was gentle, ribbing rivalry about sports in the Charities' office from the beginning.

"She loved the Cubs and Father, of course, loves the Sox."

They would get posters from the ballparks and put them up. Each year the posters got larger. They were on the wall right outside the office. He put up the Sox and she put up the Cubs. Lamb also ran the most popular event at Charities, a betting pool for World Series games.

Lamb and Father McDermott had the same creative view of files and a careless regard for money, except what he could buy for the Charities' clients, Flynn said.

Cash went into envelopes and placed often, unaccountably, in file cabinets: "I think of it when I cash my paycheck and throw it into an envelope," Flynn recalled. "I'm immediately reminded of Fran and Father with all their envelopes and with cash. And a lot of times, one didn't tell the other one where it was—or tell us— and we'd be out there thinking we had nothing, and we had to pay this bill or something like that, when the money was in cash, in all these envelopes. Or you'd have files with four or five extra copies tucked in there. And you'd say, 'Why all these copies in one file?' They'd say, 'In case we lose one.' But they'd all be together! I would say, 'Suppose you lost the whole file? You'd lose all the copies.' But that wasn't supposed to happen. Later, what they did was create another file with more copies. His little office at Charities—there was stuff all over the floor, around his desk, filed there where he could get at them."

* * *

He occasionally commandeered classmate Father Edward Norkett to help him. Norkett had returned from military service as a chaplain and was stationed at a veterans' hospital. Father McDermott had Norkett play St. Nicholas at some institutions on the feast of St. Nicholas. Father Norkett particularly remembers his role-playing for the retarded children at the Kennedy School.

"Yes, I played the role of St. Nicholas," says Father Norkett. "That was quite a party every year from that. Father McDermott was out there quite a bit because he was working with the nuns day and night keeping the place going." It led Father McDermott to meet some of the Kennedy family and attend the wedding of Eunice to R. Sargent Shriver, in 1953 at St. Patrick's Cathedral in New York City. The wedding Mass was celebrated by Francis Cardinal Spellman, who had met the Kennedys when he was auxiliary bishop of Boston. At the wedding, Father McDermott met newly-elected Massachusetts senator, John, and younger brother Robert, then working as a staffer for the McCarthy investigating committee.

Shriver was a blueblood from a prestigious, but financially impoverished, Maryland family. He managed his father-in-law's Merchandise Mart and had been appointed president of the Chicago Board of Education. He asked Father McDermott to accompany him to a Bears game. When a policeman friend came by, the priest beckoned him over and said, "Meet Sargent Shriver." The cop said, "Glad to meetcha, Sarge. What station are you at?"

"No-no," Shriver stammered, "I'm not that kind of sergeant. That's my name!" The cop looked quizzically at Father McDermott. A guy named Sarge?

When he was the Democratic nominee for vice president, Shriver, with George McGovern, entered a workingman's bar in Back of the Yards and announced that he would pay for the drinks all around. As everybody in the blue-collar crowd was ordering shots and beer, the bartender asked Shriver, "And what'll you have, pal?" Shriver destroyed his rapport with the working class by his response: "A *Courvoisier*, please."

* * *

Yet another job for Father McDermott was running the Holy Cross Mission for Homeless Men, including a chapel where he would say daily Mass. The mission expanded into a true outreach vocation, which took up many of his nights. Catholic Charities was next to the Desplaines police station. The station's drunk tank was on a level with the parking lot of Charities. He would come out at night to get in his car and hear the drunks in their cells. Then he would go in and visit them.

He says, "The first floor was the police part of it and the second floor was the drunk part. Judges—municipal judges in those days—were assigned to the drunk part on the second floor. When I parked my car, I'd look down in the cells and talk to the fellows and throw them some cigarettes or candy bars. I saw quite a few of the people from Wheaton [evangelical Christians] coming in. They had a captive audience. They'd be talking to the fellas through the windows, saying, 'the wages of sin is death.' These guys had a gigantic, Grand Canyon-sized headache, were shaky and trying to get over it."

They reminded him of medieval galley slaves, jailed because of drunkenness when, in fact, as he felt even then, drunkenness was an illness, a condition worsened by a failure of will that required dependency on a Higher Power. So he took on a fourth job. His work now included: (1) management of the Dependent Child Commission; (2) management of the Holy Cross Mission for Homeless Men; (3) post-graduate study at both Loyola and DePaul Universities; and now, (4) figuring out what to do to help men on Skid Row who were fighting alcohol dependency.

This last job took him to nearby Skid Row at night to try to rescue the men before they could be arrested—to help them find some food and a "flop," a place where they could sleep without being "jack-rolled," i.e., beaten and robbed of meager possessions by roving, preying thugs. And he vowed that one day he would use his political skills to move state legislation that would take the public inebriate out of the penal system.

When did he sleep?

"You've got all eternity to sleep," he says. "The job at hand is to be a nine-inning player—be it in the sports world, or industry, or the clergy."

"Skid Row was two blocks away," he says, "and after hours, I'd go up and down Madison Street. I saw a preponderance—in those days—of kids who had served in World War II, including a lot of kids from the Bible Belt. They learned how to drink, and drink to excess, in the military, and they couldn't handle it. And they didn't want to go home and disgrace their parents."

He encouraged other priests to come and volunteer time on his staff. As he was performing four jobs and they were adding to their regular work, they were performing extra duties for which in Catholic theology there is a name, "supererogation," meaning diverse occupations typified by the credo of St. Benedict: *Ora et labora*.

Says Monsignor McDermott: "All this work was work of supererogation, as it were. Other priests were coming in on Charities' staff for years."

The Holy Cross chapel was visited by many—not just from West Madison Street but by others who were struggling with the problem of drink. It was at the chapel that Monsignor McDermott met a famous Chicago newspaperman—Clem Lane [1897–1958], city editor of the *Chicago Daily News*. He was born in Chicago, grew up on the South Side, and was educated at Campion Jesuit prep in Prairie du Chien, Wisconsin, and De La Salle Institute, Chicago. He served in the Army in World War I. He started his newspaper career as a reporter in Grand Rapids, Michigan, in 1921, and came to the *Daily News* shortly thereafter. There he rose from reporter to rewrite-man, assistant city editor and city editor. He gained citywide attention through a series of columns featuring a fictional West Madison Street character, Oxie O'Rourke, who commented on the news as a latter-day "Mr. Dooley."

Lane had problems with drink and found sobriety through Alcoholics Anonymous. As a result of his meetings, he met Dr. James West, a physician and surgeon at Cook County Hospital who, he said, was "operating on people Father McDermott was trying to save." Both met Father McDermott a few years after the conclusion of World War II. "Somewhere," says Dr. West, "around 1947 or 1948." It was a pioneering time in the history of AA, since barely two years earlier, in 1945, Dr. William D. Silkworth, the organization's first friend in medicine (who had pronounced Bill W. a hopeless alcoholic), had begun the first hospital treatment of alcoholics at New York's Knickerbocker Hospital.

Father McDermott asked Lane to establish a chapter of AA on West Madison Street, at Holy Cross Mission. At about the same time, he asked Dr. West for a recommendation of someone with AA experience who could work with the Mission. Dr. West recommended a skilled counselor named Jack O'Neill. It was the first time that Alcoholics Anonymous had moved directly to confront the problems on Chicago's Skid Row—or virtually on any Skid Row for that matter.

Evenings at Loyola were spent with sociologist professors immersed in theory but little practice who were teaching the young priest although he, not they, worked daily, full-time, grappling with problems of poverty, alcoholism, and homelessness. The professors lambasted the orphanages in stereotypical terms. This brought out the dormant rebel within Father McDermott—which had been lingering since seminary days. "I told them they were thinking of Little Orphan Annie," he said. Nearly 50 years in the future, some experts were advocating a return to the stable living some well-managed institutions provided, which was seen as preferential to repetitive placement of children in foster homes where abuses often occurred.

* * *

There was much frustration for a young activist priest working for Charities in those days. Catholic Charities had been formed in 1918 as a centralized fund-raising organization for agencies of the archdiocese, under Father Moses Kiley. From two professional staffers and three clerical workers that year, it ballooned as coordinator and recipient of federal and state funds generated during the Depression years and World War II. As with most bureaucracies, it took on a lethargic, detached, institutional character—and, sadly, often for Father McDermott, making an impact on it was like punching a soft pillow. But he deduced ways to get around obstacles. Few projects were more important than his ability to make common cause between Charities and an unusual group noted for its activism and disdain for bureaucracy: the Catholic Worker movement.

Lay activist Aristide Pierre (Peter) Maurin [1877–1949] was co-founder with Dorothy Day of the Catholic Worker. In these latter days of his life, he was in Chicago for a time, directing relief efforts and personally ladling out soup and distributing bread to the homeless (later, he was to undergo a series of strokes that would render him helpless and confused). With ex-journalist Day, he founded a network of Houses of Hospitality in major cities to house, clothe, and feed the poor. Maurin, a former Christian Brother, was a philosopher, writer, and critic of materialism and modern assembly-line civilization. His ragged corps of volunteers was being shunted by the police to and fro. Father McDermott stepped in.

"When Peter Maurin came to town, they were passing out soup and bread," says Monsignor McDermott. "I saw that operation, so I became affiliated with them. They were being moved from one locale to another in the area, so I said [to Monsignor Vincent Cooke, superintendent of Catholic Charities], 'They should come to the Catholic Charities and that's where they should pass out the soup and bread, and they won't be thrown out of here because it's our property.'"

They *did* come to the Charities—but there were objections to the soup line from businesses in the neighborhood. To these high-toned objectors, Ignatius McDermott had a curt response.

"I recall the police captain coming over to me and he said, 'Ignatius, this letter is going to hit the mayor's desk tomorrow and I want you to read it.' It was signed by five or six people who operated businesses in the neighborhood. They were talking about how this imperiled their workers trying to board a bus, and these nefarious characters, these Skid Row people, would be there and that wasn't good for the area."

"So I said to the police captain, 'Pick up the North Shore telephone book.' He said, 'What am I picking that up for?' I said, 'Let's look up the names of the people who signed this letter. They're probably milking Chicago for money and living in suburbia and not voting for either Republican or Democrat here. I think we should tell the mayor that.' So that's what he transmitted to the mayor's office."

Nothing was heard from the mayor—"so we kept operating the soup line." The name McDermott meant much in Chicago politics at that time.

* * *

A postscript to the Catholic Worker episode: during a three month internship in New York City for his long-postponed master's degree in social work, Father McDermott worked closely with Father Terence Cooke. Cooke, a young, self-effacing University of Chicago-trained social worker, was deeply influenced by Dorothy Day [1897–1980]. She was born in Chicago, the daughter of an itinerant sports reporter. Day became a gifted writer and political activist, a friend of playwright Eugene O'Neill and social critic Malcolm Cowley. She had a succession of lovers, had an abortion, and a child by an anarchist common-law husband. After she met Maurin, she radically transformed, turning her back on her past, including the man she loved very much.

Taking her daughter, Tamar, selling a screenplay in 1932 to Hollywood to sustain her, journalist Day covered protesters carrying signs calling for jobs, unemployment insurance, pensions, and relief for mothers and children. But they were Communists, a party at war not only with capitalism but religion. Torn between siding with their crusade and suspicion of the Communist ideology, Day went to the Shrine of the Immaculate Conception where she pleaded to end her torment: "I offered up a special prayer which came with tears and anguish, that some way would open up for me to use what talents I possessed for my fellow workers, for the poor." She pondered how she could serve the poor and yet not end up as a pawn of Communist demagoguery.

That answer came when she met Maurin. Together they advocated that the Sermon on the Mount be lived, not preached as an abstraction. She became a devout Catholic and had her daughter baptized.

"I wanted to believe," she wrote, "and I wanted her to believe, and if belonging to a church would give her so inestimable a grace as faith in God and the companionable love of the saints, then the thing to do was to have her baptized as a Catholic." But she didn't like everything about the Church. "It was often a scandal to me," she wrote. "But the Church was the cross upon which Christ was crucified. One could not separate Christ from His cross." Love it, hate its excesses, "one must live in a state of permanent dissatisfaction with the Church." But she believed deeply, implicitly in it.

After meeting Dorothy Day, Father Terry Cooke was touched. Later, as the seventh archbishop of New York, Terence Cardinal Cooke [1921–1983] put the formal cause of Dorothy Day up for

canonization. Monsignor McDermott, who never met Day but admired Cooke, says simply, "I can support that."

Three years after Day's death, Cooke died at sixty-two. It developed that he had secretly lived a life in great pain and suffering, having been treated for leukemia for 10 years without
anyone's knowledge. On St. Patrick's Day 1984, Bishop Theodore
McCarrick of Metuchen, New Jersey, now Cardinal-Archbishop of
Washington, D. C., wrote a letter to the incoming New York prelate, Archbishop John O'Connor. Both had worked closely with
Cooke and had witnessed what they believed was his self-effacing
sanctity. McCarrick urged a rare step: that canonization efforts be
undertaken for Cooke. Seeking to canonize an archbishop-prede-
cessor is unpopular with Rome (which fears a canonizing buddy-
system) but Cardinal O'Connor agreed. The job to advance the
case to the Vatican's Congregation for Causes of Saints was given
to Capuchin friar Father Benedict Groeschel, Cooke's confessor.

"Cooke did nothing extraordinary as an archbishop," acknowledges Father Groeschel, "except for one thing. He went far
beyond the call of duty. Cooke remained loyal and dedicated to
the Church in very difficult times. He is representative of a traditional Catholicism that is not going to go under. I think there will
be opposition to his cause. Many clerics and hierarchs will think of
him as too traditional and that is why I am supporting his cause.
He didn't lead progressive movements. He tried to keep the
Church on course when huge waves broke over it."

About Cooke's canonization, "Time will tell," says Father
Groeschel. But "every day we get reports from people, some of
them as far away as the Middle West, telling us of cures and favors
they've received after praying to Cardinal Cooke. Like the cause
of St. Thérèse of Lisieux, this case is going to go through on its
miracles."

A quiet attester to Cooke's sanctity, as one who knew him personally, is Monsignor Ignatius McDermott.

In that era, the Chicago archdiocese had many good priests—
and more than a few colorful characters.

Because Monsignor McDermott's sister, Sister Mary Jeanette,
was for a time superior of St. Paul of the Cross elementary school in
suburban Park Ridge, he met, on occasion, the pastor of St. Paul's,
Father Francis E. Smith. A devout but eccentric man, with a bad wig
which looked like it had been purchased at a fire sale, Smith was re-
sistant to abandoning the parish's original wooden church, which
was in poor shape and far too small for the growing parish. The

archdiocese pressured him to build a new church, but Father Smith declined to do so for many years. There was one major reason.

Why?

"It has been my experience," he said, "that whenever a pastor builds a new church, he dies right afterward. That isn't going to happen to me."

Father Smith, who was appointed pastor of St. Paul of the Cross in 1922, held out bravely until 1953, when Samuel Cardinal Stritch dedicated a new church built by Father Smith. Father Smith retired four years later and survived the new building for many years; the jinx he saw coming to him was broken. But Monsignor McDermott says, his prediction was right. He built a new church and ultimately he died.

*   *   *

Idiosyncratic proclivities of other pastors still flood Monsignor McDermott's memories. Once, while visiting at St. Pascal's, at Irving Park Road and Melvina in the Portage Park neighborhood, Father McDermott decided to put a half hour to good purpose by saying his office. He struggled to read his breviary by the weak light of a single bulb, supplied by the pastor, Father George Heimsath, who believed no dollar should go wasted.

"The good Lord believes waste not, want not," Father Heimsath commented acidly as Father McDermott squinted to read by the weak light.

"I know," said Father McDermott, "but He also doesn't want us to ruin our eyes when we are supposed to put them to good purpose."

One of the most brilliant, irascible, and fun-loving priests whom Father McDermott knew at this time was William A. Murphy, a former chaplain at Great Lakes Naval Training Center during World War I. He was uncle to William O'Connor, Bishop of Springfield, and TV journalist-commentator, Len O'Connor. Father Murphy, a droll Irishman who knew several languages and spoke impeccable Italian, had been named by George Cardinal Mundelein as pastor of St. Callistus parish in Chicago. There he presided over a largely Italian community for 10 years, before ill health forced his retirement. So popular was he that hundreds of Italian parishioners demonstrated at his retirement. So eloquent was he in Italian that the owner of the Como Inn, a favorite Chicago Italian dining spot, exclaimed to Father McDermott, "Hey, his Italian is better than mine!"

Father Murphy hated his imposed retirement. Then it ended. A seminary classmate of Cardinal Stritch, Father Murphy was appointed by Stritch to a pastorate at St. Mary's church in suburban Riverside, in 1948. Father McDermott drove him to his new assignment. He asked directions at a service station and was told to look for Longcommon Road.

"Is it not interesting," said Father Murphy as they rode along, "that the 'Prince of the West' [Mundelein, the first cardinal to serve west of the Alleghenies] first named me a pastor, and now his successor [Stritch] makes me pastor again after exile. Longcommon Road, you say? Is it not long comin' for me?"

*   *   *

His fellow priests were not the only colorful characters Father McDermott encountered. He met some of them as he tirelessly offered his presence as a priest to families, both in times of sorrow and in times of joy. If he was not on Skid Row or visiting the sick in hospitals, he was going to wakes where he would lead prayers for the deceased and the consolation of the survivors. He would start out visiting the homes or funeral parlors where friends and relatives would be laid out. Then he would extend the ministry to visit friends of those he had known and relatives of those whom he had once met. The circle of acquaintances was widened immeasurably. He would often go to one wake at a funeral home but be invited to lead prayers in another parlor of the place, when priests and ministers had not shown up. This is his prayer:

> Now may we say a prayer for our departed soul. Almighty and merciful God, look with pity upon Your friends on whom You have laid a heavy burden of sorrow. Take away from our hearts the spirit of rebellion and teach us to see Your good, gracious purpose in all the trials that You send to us.
>
> Grant that we may not languish in fruitless and unabating grief or sorrow. It's those who have no hope who through our tears look meekly up to You, the God of all consolation. O, God, while we lament the departure of [deceased] out of this life, we must bear in mind that we are most certainly to follow him. Give us grace to make ready for that last hour by the fountain of holy life. Protect us against a sudden and violent death. Teach us how to watch and pray that when Your summons comes, we may go forth to meet the Bridegroom and enter with Him into life everlasting. Amen.

May the soul of [deceased] and the souls of all our faithful departed through the mercy of God rest in peace. Amen.

* * *

It was about 1947 when the priest met Jim Mchugh (his name is spelled without the capital H). Mchugh was born in 1917 to a Visitation parish family that was on relief for five or six years, with no means for gas or lights. Mchugh, a stocky man who speaks "South Side Irish Chicago-ese" in short laconic phrases, never went to high school. He drove a beer truck for many years. He met Father Ignatius at a christening for a baby of a family named Doody (Mchugh was the godfather). Something about Mchugh intrigued Father Ignatius and they stayed in touch. Perhaps it was the following story of Mchugh's run-in with the IRS. Stories like Mchugh's always made for interesting listening.

"I was making $17.50 a week and I was like the breadwinner for a while. Two guys from Internal Revenue come to my house and my mother said, 'What happened to you?' I said, 'What do you mean, ma?' She said, 'There were two guys from Internal Revenue here and they said you got a penalty of $25.80.' I said, 'For what?' She said, 'James, I don't know what it's for.' I went down there and that's when they had sun visors [green eyeshades], remember? Marty O'Donnell went with me, I'll never forget.

"I walked in there and the woman told me to go up on the third floor. I went up there and this woman was sitting there and she said, 'See the woman with the white hair over there?' She said, "When that man gets up, you go over and sit there.' So I went over and sat there. She said, 'Young man, what kind of trouble are you in?' I said, 'I ain't in no trouble.' She said, 'If you're here, you're in trouble.'

"I said, 'All they told me was bring $25.80.' She said, 'Did you get a letter from us?' I said, 'No, ma'am.' She said, 'You can't tell them that. That don't go down here.' And I said, 'I'm telling you, I never got the letter.' So she said, 'See that woman over in the corner there?' I said yeah. She said, 'If she OKs this, you don't owe nothing.' So I sat there and she went over and talked to her and the woman turned around and was looking at me and she came back and said, 'Everything is okay. You don't owe nothing.' She said, 'The reason we do that, we had a fellow here the other day and he tried to bribe us with $2,000, but we had to have her hear what he said. We couldn't do it by ourselves.'

"So I went outside and Marty O'Donnell's out there, and Marty says, 'Why didn't you give her a fin for a box of candy?' So stupid me goes back. I put the fin on the table. And she goes, 'That'll be $25.80. These walls have eyes!' I said to Marty I ought to knock his block off."

Stories like these told in near-whispering, side-of-the-mouth South Side Irish dialect, were charming. One story—legend to those who have known Jim Mchugh for any length of time—involved how he became an extra in the film *Call Northside 777* starring James Stewart.

The film was shot in 1947. Presented in documentary style with local shots in Chicago, it was based on a true story but for notable artistic exceptions. *Call Northside 777* was a widely praised docudrama by 20th Century Fox. It was based on an unsolved murder of a policeman, the wrongful conviction of an innocent man, Joseph Majczek, and a mother's desperate plight to free her son from Stateville Penitentiary, with the help of a doggedly investigative reporter played by Stewart. Wrote Chicago crime expert Richard Lindberg: "Hollywood director Henry Hathaway and his 70-member film crew descended upon Chicago, September 22, 1947, to begin work...*Northside 777* is really a South Side story set in the Back of the Yards neighborhood. The murder of Officer [William] Lundy occurred not in a speakeasy as some writers mistakenly believe but inside a delicatessen, belonging to Mrs. Vera Walush, at 4312 South Ashland Avenue." The murder took place in the winter of 1932. Joseph Majczek lived in a two-story frame house at 2038 West 52nd Street.

The *Chicago Times* managing editor, Karin Walsh, noticed an ad offering $5,000 for the real killer of Lundy and sent reporter Jack McPhaul to check it out. McPhaul found that Majczek was arrested the day before a positive identification was made of him by a witness—evidence that the police were eager to find anyone who could satisfy the pressure put on them to "solve" the case. Majczek was released in August 1945, 13 years after his conviction, and lived until 1982.

Says Mchugh: "I was working at the Nectar brewery and Schaller's tavern was right next door, on 37th Street. [Richard J.] Daley's office for the 11th ward was right across the street. So we kept our trucks at 39th and Union in this garage. (The president gave all that property at 55th and Pulaski to the school. He had a daughter, a nun, see?) And we're pullin' out of the yard and a guy says to me 'You're going to be in the movies.' I says, 'You're nuts.' So I drove over to the garage. So when I got to the garage they says, 'You're wanted on the telephone.' It was the office and they says, 'Didn't the fella tell you that you're goin' to be in the movies?' I said 'No!' They said, 'Well, you better get back here.' So I went back there and there must have been 500 people out front, see?

"So I said, 'What kind of a movie is it?' Nobody knew what it was, see? So he said, 'See that fella over there? Go over there. He's the guy that was lookin' for you.' There was a bunch of people, you know, and he saw me comin' across the street and he said to the coppers: 'Move the people back so this guy—meanin' me—can get through.' So he said, 'You go in the tavern there.' So I went in there, and another guy, I can't think of his name, we're sittin' at the bar. And I says, 'What kind of a movie is it?' And he says, 'Jimmy Stewart's goin' to walk across the street, and he'll come in here and sit right alongside you, and he'll ask for a drink of scotch.' So they had put the bottle up in front of the three of us, the worst thing they could have done.

"So he started across the street and the streetcars were comin'. They had the tracks marked with X's. The camera starts, and Stewart starts walking, but a girl stuck her head out of our office window, and the guy hollered 'Cut!' He had to do it all over. The second time, he walked back again and he comes across the street. Then the camera's cover, a kind of sheep-lining on it, catches on fire. And Stewart stops and says, 'What's the matter now?' They says, 'The thing got on fire and we'll fix it in a minute.' So he goes back across the street. In the meantime we're hittin' the bottle, the three of us, you know. Well, when he comes in and sits down, the guy playin' the bartender picks up the bottle and it's empty! Again, the guy yells 'Cut!' Stewart says, 'I'm goin' to tell you right now, one more time and that's it,' Jimmy Stewart says to 'em, see? So he goes back across the street again. The director comes up with a fresh bottle. He says, 'Put the bottle under the bar. I'll tell you when to put it up there.' Just as he's comin' in the door he says, 'Put it up there.'

"So he comes right alongside of me and he sat down and he says, 'Give me a drink of scotch,' see? So the guy pours it out but he didn't drink it, though. The guy says, 'That's a take. Okay.' So I says to Stewart, 'I can see why half of you people are nuts.' Ho-ho, he started laughin'. I shook hands with him and he says, 'You see why we're all goofy with me walkin' back and forth across the street?' So I asked him for his autograph and he gave it to me on a picture. I think my sister's still got it. So they picked up their stuff and left."

Has he seen the picture? "Oh, yeah, my niece has got a thing of it. I weighed 280 pounds. I was drinkin' good then. Sure, just as he walks in the front door you can see me. I got a cap like Father Mac wears once in a while. I quit drinkin' after that. I hadda quit. I didn't have no underwear or nothin.' Everything went to booze, but I never missed a day's work though. No."

Many years later, Jim Mchugh, off the booze, became a resident of Haymarket and a kind of *ad hoc* personal assistant to Monsignor McDermott.

$$* \quad * \quad *$$

For the next several years, Father Mac continued to garner valuable on-the-job training. The experience he received helping others, whether in his office at Catholic Charities or on the streets of Skid Row, was the kind of education that cannot be duplicated in a classroom. Nevertheless, in 1957, Monsignor McDermott took some time off to attend Yale University's summer school of alcohol studies. While staying on campus, he felt the inward pressure of an Ivy League school focused on its own greatness—its hauteur was in full flower. A spectacular trophy case featured deflated footballs with inscriptions of the scores from games won by Yale. It occurred to him that there was an emptiness of traditional morals in favor of barren aesthetic thought. Then he discovered that some academics at the seminar were disparaging the work of AA, saying that it was conducted by amateurs who ignored specialists charged with perpetuating the medical inheritance.

"That's the trouble with you!" he scolded the professors. "You don't have time for the common people. You're the great experts! Don't you know that an alcoholic who wants sobriety is in many ways a better judge than you? Don't you know that AA has never rejected medical or professional science? Look at this trophy case. It says: Yale is perfect. The deflated footballs show the victories. But did Yale win all its games? I don't think so!"

It was vintage McDermott, putting in its place a bloated institution where average people's concerns were a fringe phenomenon.

* * *

One day in 1958, Father McDermott was at the Kennedy School in Palos Park, making recommendations for new arrivals, when a nun came to him. "The cardinal would like to see you," she said. He sighed. It meant driving back to Chicago to Cardinal Stritch's office, which was at his residence at 1555 North State Parkway.

When he arrived, a nun greeted him at the door with a soft smile and a twinkle in her eye. Father McDermott entered the cardinal's study and found the prelate reading a newspaper.

"Good afternoon, your Eminence," said Father McDermott, as he kissed the episcopal ring.

Stritch's memory was never very good. He looked absently at the priest, trying to recall why he sent for him. Then it came to him. "Good afternoon, Monsignor!" he said.

That signified the purpose of the session, the conferring of a papal honor that had been with the Church since 1377. Monsignor (technically *monseigneur*, meaning "my lord" in French) is a formal Catholic recognition for distinguished service by a priest to the Church. It was originally conferred on members of the papal household during the years of the pope's stay in Avignon, France.

But Stritch's days, both as Archbishop of Chicago and on earth, were numbered. In early 1958, while on a vacation in Florida, the 70-year-old Stritch was appointed proprefect of the Congregation for the Propagation of the Faith, in Rome. In Chicago, he had been an indifferent administrator and Rome wanted a younger, more efficient man in the post. Stritch tried to be excused from the appointment but could not convince Rome. Reluctantly, he departed Chicago in April and, while in Rome, fell seriously ill with an infection, which necessitated the amputation of his right arm. While recovering from the surgery, he suffered a stroke and died May 27, 1958.

* * *

The man who founded Alcoholics Anonymous on Skid Row—and who introduced Monsignor McDermott to Dr. James West—Clem Lane, city editor of the *Daily News*, died October 27, 1958 of a heart attack at age 61. A gifted writer, speaker, and humorist of the old Chicago school of newspapering, Lane never went to college. In the words of Edward J. Rooney, who worked for him as a reporter, "he could write circles around anyone else in the city room." A short, stocky man with a leonine head of white hair, Lane was "fierce but compassionate." He had a short fuse and a blowtorch temper; he would bawl out reporters one minute and extol them the next. Under his direction, the *Daily News* won a Pulitzer prize for local coverage.

Lane, leader of the 12-step program among the street people of Skid Row, was an outstanding Catholic layman. He was a leader of the Cana Conference ministry to engaged and married couples and the Christian Family Movement, which was devoted to strengthening the family unit. He was active in the Notre Dame Retreat League and founded the St. Gabriel League, an organization of Catholic newspaper reporters, television, radio, advertising, and public relations professionals. From it he received the St. Bonaventure Medal in 1947. He was appointed to a state commission on alcoholism and served on the Illinois Department of Welfare's newly formed division for care and rehabilitation of alcoholics. He was awarded an honorary doctor of law degree from Loyola University of Chicago, where he taught journalism part-time.

Rooney, who went to graduate school and received a doctorate in journalism, following his newspaper career, recalls that at Lane's wake when the dignitaries, ex-governors, and civic leaders moved away from the casket, a shabby denizen from Skid Row entered the room and stood by the casket, looking at Lane for a long time. "I'll never forget that scene," says Rooney.

In his sermon, Monsignor McDermott said, "The most powerful thing in the world is a good example and Clem gave that good example as a man, a Catholic, a husband and father. In his daily work where tons of ink were splashed extolling the good deeds and virtues of others, similar to an ad often carried in his paper, Clem also realized that the best ads were worn, not written. Clem truly lived the philosophy of Christ—that the best way of attaining happiness is to forget oneself and think of others. Often men go overboard in physical fitness programs. Clem's daily exercise was the practice of the world's great virtue—the virtue of charity.

"He was a kindly man, realizing that kindness is the only thing in the world the blind can see, the deaf can hear and the dumb can speak," said Monsignor McDermott.

For many years memorial Masses for Lane were offered by Monsignor McDermott at Holy Cross chapel.

*   *   *

On Monday, December 1, 1958, at 2:40 p.m., a blinding mass of flames, smoke, and gas roared out of Our Lady of the Angels School on the West Side. The fire began in a paper-littered waste barrel at the foot of a stairwell. It spread so quickly that within minutes, 1,200 students were running excitedly for the doors, many leaping from windows to escape the flames and smoke. Eighty-seven children and three nuns perished that day. During the following months, five more children died from the results of the fire. Monsignor McDermott worked throughout the night helping parents identify the dead.

"I was over at Holy Trinity rectory," he says. "The priests who were on staff at Maryville in Des Plaines through the years would meet annually around Christmas time. We'd have dinner and come up with some gifts for quite a few of the boys and girls who went in the religious life. That evening we were at Holy Trinity, in the shadows of Cook County Hospital. I arrived there from the Charities' office. I hadn't heard anything. I didn't have the radio on.

"When I arrived at the rectory they had their ears glued to the radio, which broadcasted this tragic fire at Our Lady of the Angels, and that they brought bodies over to the Cook County Hospital. So after dinner, I went over to Cook County Hospital. It was very garish. The basement was lighted by 30- or 40-watt bulbs embedded in the walls. The place was seething with humanity. Authorities had made a terrible mistake, I thought. They had the parents and grandparents and other intimate relatives there standing in line. I suppose it was very utilitarian at the time, but it seemed to be minus any kind of sentimentality or affection.

"The nuns were marking the names on pieces of paper and pinning them to the shirts and blouses of the little boys and girls. This was the only form of identification. The place was filled with intimate kin. They would call out the name of some little boy or girl and parents would approach, and the grandparents and the brothers and sisters. They would pull the sheet back—and the garishness of the place, with the green paint and the inadequate lighting system! The kids were on litters on the floor and relatives had to bend over and identify their son and daughter. Of course, the relatives were very emotional—and as soon as that sheet was thrown back and they looked at their little son and daughter, there was weeping, wailing and moaning, groaning and hysterical sobbing.

"I thought they needed a blotter of some kind, and I went to Barney's Market Club and talked to the owner, Harold Schwimmer. I said, 'There should be some coffee over in the morgue.' He said he'd prepare some coffee. Then I went out to a doughnut place. I think it was around 33rd and Wallace, and I talked to those people. Of course, the doughnuts were just coming out of the oven at that time. They were well aware of the tragedy. I had a driver with me. They gave me about 30 dozen doughnuts or so. I returned to Barney's Market Club, and Harold Schwimmer got the coffee, and we brought it to the basement.

"That night there were quite a few kids identified, the greater majority of them. There weren't many physical signs at all of flesh that burned. It seemed to be more smoke inhalation. They all looked very normal and natural. With some, though, the survivors were bringing in charts from the dentists, bills of sale from shoes, and so on, to identify some of the kids.

"There was one beautiful little girl there, about third or fourth grade, and there was an equally handsome couple just wandering around the place. They just couldn't find their child because there was a sheet over each body, and the name was pinned to their shirts and blouses. At the end of the day, they had squad cars bringing the parents back to their homes after they had identified their child. But this couple struck me. They went home, and I said to Walter McCarron [the Cook County coroner] that I looked at that little girl and the name doesn't coincide with those parents, except that there was a tremendous identification. I said, 'I think that girl looks very much like the mother.' So the parents were practically all the way home, and they [the authorities] called the squad station and intercepted them and brought the parents back—and that little girl *was* their daughter. I stayed there all that night and the next day."

* * *

All the while, after working long hours at Charities, his nightly excursions on Skid Row went on. On his rounds one day, he was passing Libby's Famous Ten on Desplaines Street, on the west side of the street just south of Madison.

"I was fascinated to see a woman come down the steps from the second floor," Monsignor McDermott says. "She had a baby with her and a collapsible baby buggy. She opened the baby buggy and put the child in it. I wondered who in the world would be living over Libby's? She looked up and said, brightly: 'Father Mac! How are you doing?'

"I looked at her and said, 'What are you doing here?'

"She said, 'I married one of the owners.'" She named him. Monsignor McDermott knew him. "She said, 'Yes, and we have an apartment upstairs.' She said they also had a steak house out on Irving Park across the street from the laughing academy [then known as Dunning State Hospital for the Insane]. I was in there several times because I used to bring men and women to the state hospital."

Not long after, Monsignor McDermott prevailed on her husband to allow another fleabag, the Capitol Hotel across from the Criminal Court building, to be used as an extension of Holy Cross Mission for the homeless on the North Side. Then he discovered the husband was a part owner of a sandwich shop. "So we talked to them about getting some tickets from them so when a man or woman came in and they were hungry, they could go over and get the blue plate special at this hot dog stand or get a burger or cheeseburger."

There was often a McDermott telephone call to Father Norkett. The former Army chaplain said: "When I came back from the service, I ended up at the Veterans' hospital, and he would call me and say, 'Hey, I got somebody here and I don't know whether he's a drunk or dying of a heart attack.' He'd put them in the car and bring them over, and I'd tell the doctors to get ready. I remember sometimes the doctors would say, 'Father, don't get so close. This guy is lousy. He's got cooties running all over him and they jump 15 inches, so keep your distance.' I know several times he had to have his car fumigated because it would get so filthy with all the little bugs running around. That's how Ignatius was. He didn't give a hoot about things like that.

"He always told me when we were down there, 'Don't ever give those guys a dime.' He said, 'They're going to run right to the bar and buy a glass of wine or some kind of cheap stuff.' He said, 'If they're really hungry, take them into one of the restaurants, pay the restaurant for some bacon and eggs and some coffee, but don't give money to them, because they'll never spend it on food even though they need it.'

"Ignatius never cared about money. He was not interested in money. To this day, I don't know if he even has a checking account. People send him Mass stipends, then he'll send me a cashier's check, from the bank right down at Halsted and Madison, for $30 or $40 and give me a list of Masses because he can't say them all.

"No, he was never interested in money."

* * *

While Father Mac was warring against alcoholism on Chicago's North and West Sides, sparks were beginning to fly on the South. At last, something to unite the warring South Side Irish factions— the Daleyites, who had taken control of government, and the Duffy/McDermott-ites, who were on the outside since 1953. It was the one soothing agent: the White Sox. The American League pennant race had been frenetic, right up to the end, between the "Go-Go White Sox" and the Cleveland Indians since opening day. Whenever he could go, Monsignor McDermott would cheer little Luis Aparicio, the Venezuelan shortstop; base-stealing demon, sassy little Nellie Fox at second base, his cheek bulging with a hefty tobacco chaw; Ted "Big Klu" Kluszewski at first; and the 39-year-old pitching workhorse with a name like something running in the first race, Gus "Early" Wynn.

By late July, around Monsignor McDermott's 50th birthday, the South Siders moved ahead but the Indians nipped at their heels. That is, they did until the climactic showdown, September 22, 1959, in Cleveland's Municipal Stadium. For a while it was scary.

In the bottom of the ninth, with the Sox holding a 4 to 2 lead, the Indians loaded the bases—with one out. In came reliefer Gerry Staley, who threw a single pitch—a low, outside sinker—to Cleveland's Vic Power. He slammed it to Aparicio's left, who expertly speared it, bolted to second, then fired it to Big Klu— double play—and the Sox won the pennant.

Immediately, Mayor Daley's fire commissioner Robert Quinn, a Bridgeport native, did what any South Sider with power to alert the entire city would do. He ordered a five-minute blast of all firehouse sirens. Unfortunately, some were out-of-the-loop; in this case, those non-baseball-oriented civilians, who feared that Nikita Khrushchev's Russians were coming, were filled with panic. Some families huddled in their basements saying *Hail*

Marys. Sadly, a later outpouring of fervently recited *Hail Marys* didn't produce a World Series victory. The Sox lost it to the Los Angeles Dodgers, 4 games to 2.

The number one fan of the Sox, Monsignor Ignatius McDermott, is eagerly waiting for the Sox to win another pennant and go all the way.

* * *

Monsignor McDermott's quality of bringing people down to earth is legend. One afternoon in the 1950s, he was dragged by a friend to inspect a showing of surrealistic paintings in the Chicago Art Institute. There he came upon Adlai Stevenson, the former Democratic presidential candidate, inspecting a work of art through lorgnette with admiration that can only be described as rapture. The work was a blotch of color with no design or cohesion apparent. When asked how it appeared to him, the priest said rather loudly, "Of course. It's Minnie Minoso sliding into third base!" Minoso was a famed White Sox left fielder. Father Mac then moved on under Stevenson's disapproving gaze.

* * *

Nineteen sixty was the departure year for the Chicago Cardinals. The Cardinals football team has become a glory team in nostalgia. Their names are legend in the estimation of South Siders. These included Paddy Driscoll, the most versatile of the early NFL stars, who was signed by the Racine Cardinals in 1920, and who helped make Chris O'Brien's team a contender in the American Professional Football Association; Ernie Nevers, who still holds the single game scoring record in the NFL; Phil Handler, a mainstay for the 1934 Cardinals, who later became head coach of the team; Charles Bidwell, whose ownership of the Cardinals coincided with the Great Depression; Jimmy Conzelman, who as coach was beloved by players, fans, and writers, who rebuilt the Cardinals, leading to the 1947 championship and another title in 1948, and who, shortly after the 1948 season, walked away from pro football, never to return. The team moved out of Chicago to become the St. Louis Cardinals and is now the Arizona Cardinals. There still remains among old Cardinals' fans a forlorn hope that the team will return to Chicago.

But for many, the spirit of the old Cardinals was typified by Elmer Angsman. A South Side native with poor eyesight, his determined will to succeed led him to romp through the NFL for seven seasons with the Cardinals. He still looms large in the team's all-time records, including the second longest run (80 yards), the most consecutive games with a touchdown (five), the third-best rushing average for a season (1948, 5.4 yards), and the fourth most career rushing touchdowns (27).

Jimmy Conzelman, the head coach, said: "I'll never forget Elmer getting ready for combat. He'd put in his contact lenses, take out his false teeth, put in a rubber mouthpiece, then get a shot in an ankle that was always bothering him." The former Notre Dame star broke two ribs and lost eight teeth playing with the College All Stars.

The Cards' departure left Ignatius McDermott with only one professional football team for whom to root—the Bears. Fortunately, that team has a lustrous history, whether it's in a winning season or not. It was organized by the man generally recognized to have invented the game of professional football, George Halas, referred to throughout his life as "Coach" Halas. It began as the Halas-coached Decatur Staleys. They were named after Decatur, Illinois corn products businessman A.E. Staley, who commissioned Halas to start an independent football club. The colorful Halas had held a bat before a pigskin, having played right field for the New York Yankees, until a hip injury ended his career (where he was replaced in right field by George Herman "Babe" Ruth), and he turned his attention to football.

Halas moved the Staleys to Chicago in 1921 and renamed the Staleys the *Bears*, capitalizing on the Cubs moniker. Bringing college football's most celebrated player, Harold "Red" Grange, to play with the Bears in Wrigley Field, in 1925, before 36,000 people, Halas took his team across the country on such a whirlwind tour that he infected Americans with pre-football fever.

Cardinal kicker Paddy Driscoll would use young Ignatius to return footballs he kicked. When the Bears fans waited for Red Grange to display his famous weaving run-backs, they were often disappointed. Driscoll would regularly kick the ball to the coffin corners of the field where they could not be run back.

George Halas was a one-man institution. He founded the American Professional Football League in 1922, the forerunner to the National Football League. Under his tutelage, the Bears were the first to introduce the "T formation" to the sport, in 1940. The Bears were the first professional team to practice daily, to take game movies to study their moves for strategy, to hire their own team band, to have their own team song, to broadcast their games over the radio, to have a team newspaper, to host a homecoming dinner for all ex-Bears, to issue player diplomas, to hold the longest wining streak without a defeat (30 games from 1932 to 1933), to be featured in the first coast-to-coast radio program of a game (the 1940 playoff against the Washington Redskins, which the Bears won 72 to 0), and to produce the first 1,000-yard runner in pro football history, Beattie Feathers, who ran 1,004 yards on 101 carries in 1934.

Among other achievements, Halas became the first coach to trade players on a first-round draft pick. He directed the team to the National Football League title in 1963, when the Bears beat the New York Giants 14 to 10 in a sub-zero, championship game at Wrigley Field. When TV brought the NFL to its peak, Halas was among the league owners who insisted that television pay for the right.

George Halas retired from coaching after 40 years and hired Mike Ditka, who on January 26, 1986 took the Bears to the Super Bowl and won—with Ignatius McDermott cheering them on. Unfortunately, Halas didn't live to see the victory (he died October 31, 1983, at age 88, the only person associated with the NFL throughout its first 50 years). He had won six titles and set a record mark of 324 coaching wins which stood for nearly three decades. He had played end for the Bears for 11 seasons. He was known as "Mr. Everything" in football. The team's ownership passed to Virginia McCaskey, his daughter. She and her husband, Ed, are generous contributors to Haymarket Center.

CHAPTER 8

A Fateful Partnership, 1960–1976

He was very understanding [about clerical alcoholism]. *Shakespeare said something about the good things some do is often interred in their bones, something to that effect. I thought that sentence applied to John Cardinal Cody.*

Today's world is over-saturated with a surplus of starters and a famine of finishers.

—Ignatius McDermott

Father McDermott's introduction to Dr. James West—arranged by Clem Lane in the late 1940s—was the first of what early Greek theologians called *kairos*, or a providential occurrence. The McDermott-West *kairos* opened a fresh chapter in the treatment of substance abuse, not just for Chicago but for medical history. The McDermott-West partnership has endured for more than a half-century.

Prior to this meeting, these beginning steps were recorded by Alcoholics Anonymous in the modern struggle against addiction: **December 1934**, the spiritual experience of Bill W. in Towns Hospital; **May 1935**, the meeting of Bill W. and Doctor Bob in Akron; **June 10, 1935**, the founding of Alcoholics Anonymous; **1939**, the total national membership list stood at 100; **September 1939**, the rapid growth of AA in Cleveland; **February 1940**, the first AA service office established in New York City; **March 1941**, publication of the *Saturday Evening Post* article that created national attention; **1942**, the first prison AA group meeting at San Quentin, California; and **1945**, the beginning of treatment by Dr. Silkworth at Knickerbocker Hospital, New York. These were essential beginnings. Yet the McDermott-West brotherhood (for that is what it became) made a clean sweep of the board—removing criminalization of the inebriate and reaffirming that in the darkness of alcoholism a flickering light was visible—that detox can be achieved safely (indeed more easily and satisfyingly) without medication. Because both men were used to challenging spurious prevailing "wisdom," they were ideally suited to each other.

James West was born in 1914 in Chicago. He was educated in Chicago, received his medical degree from Loyola University, and was engaged in the practice of surgery at Cook County Hospital. If he had done nothing else, he is famed for performing, with another surgeon, the world's first kidney transplant.

West courageously stood up to the then-prevailing prejudice against organ transplant—incredible by today's standards—which argued that it was somehow immoral.

He challenged "the idea of taking part of a dead person and putting it in a live person—and having it work—violated many of the so-called beliefs of society: the idea being that when a person dies, everything in him dies." The world's first kidney transplant, co-performed by Dr. West on June 17, 1950, transformed what had been known by science—and contradicted some cherished beliefs.

"To take a person who's already dead, whose heart has stopped, whose brain isn't working and whose organs are dead— to take that out, wash it out with a saline solution, which I did while another surgeon was taking the diseased kidney out of another person who's alive—and then the both of us putting the kidney from the dead woman into a live woman, so that it became alive again as we hooked it up to the blood supply of this woman" seemed to be voodoo stuff. Dr. West's patient lived for about five years. And it was a year and a half before any other surgical team attempted the same procedure.

"I became interested in addiction from a formal standpoint," Dr. West said, "due to my own being in recovery since 1945. I met Monsignor McDermott when he was a younger priest in the inner city of Chicago on Madison Street. I was a young surgeon at Cook County Hospital and wanted to know more about addiction, so I set an agenda for myself for taking some formal courses in psychiatry, to learn what psychiatrists knew that we in Alcoholics Anonymous didn't know. Eventually, because of publishing some things that had to do with substance abuse disorders, I became qualified as a member of the American Psychiatric Association—

but that was a parallel career to my surgery. Most of my time was spent as a surgeon."

Dr. West says, with quiet understatement, that at the historic first meeting between the physician and Monsignor McDermott, "Monsignor and I developed kind of a working system between us after we met—perhaps casually."

Whenever Monsignor McDermott felt someone needed serious medical care, Dr. West would put the Skid Row habitué in the hospital. "I was kind of on the medical end of what he was doing in the '50s and somewhere in the '60s. I was down here in County Hospital doing operations on the same kind of people he was seeing in the saloons."

Some of the people were priests who had hit rock bottom and were living on Skid Row.

Says Monsignor McDermott: "I recall there was a padre on West Madison Street by the name of Johnny Walker. He was called 'Red Label' at the time. I guess he saw that I was for real. We had a soup line going, and he was in the soup line from time to time. He was making a great recovery. I asked Jack O'Neill [the Holy Cross staffer Dr. West had recommended] what we could do for him. He took Father John Walker to his home and told his kids that he was a priest. It was tremendous dedication on the part of Jack O'Neill to take that priest into his house. Also, it was a great manifestation on the part of Jack and his wife to graphically bring home to their son and daughter, a man about whom they said, 'This is a priest who is recovering from alcohol.' That was a tremendous chapter in those days."

Dr. West added: "You see, alcoholics at that time were considered by about maybe 95 percent of the population as having some kind of moral disorder or deviation of some kind. Now only about 60 percent of the population of the United States thinks that way. We've been able to change a lot of that by affecting what happens in medical schools with regard to putting the disease [alcoholism] on the curriculum."

* * *

While the McDermott-West partnership prospered, Monsignor McDermott was pioneering rehabilitative programs at Catholic Charities. An early venture, in 1961, he designated— with a publicist's flair—as ACES (Addiction Consultation and Educational Services). Founded as a support for families of alcoholics, particularly children, it featured a program once a month called "Thirst Sunday," a free seminar where families could learn from professionals about various aspects of addiction. "Thirst Sunday" so named because it reflected the drinker's need for a drink and the thirst on the part of the families to understand alcoholism. At the same time, Monsignor McDermott began a counselor training program at DePaul University, the first of its kind.

Part of the ACES program was called Christmas Joy. Clients from addicted homes were identified by ACES counselors to receive gifts and food at Christmas. Weeks before Christmas, letters were sent out for funds to support Christmas Joy. Generally between $5,000–$6,000 was raised. Father Mac would often make up any difference in actual costs from personal checks he had received.

About 100–200 families were served. Each child in a family would receive two small and one large gift (in terms of monetary value). These were wrapped and delivered by volunteers. Mary Ellen Flynn and Ray Soucek, along with Soucek's daughter Jennifer and her friends, would invade the local Toys R Us store allowing the kids to pick out presents for the other children. Shopping carts (10 or better) filled with toys would be lined up for checkout. The astonished cashier would inquire about the volume of toys, to which Flynn and Soucek would reply, "The kids were very good this year."

At Christmas and Thanksgiving, the men of the Street were fed by the Holy Cross Mission. More than a thousand men would like up for a turkey dinner with all the trimmings. At Christmas, each person was given a bag with a cap, gloves and other winter necessities. The practice of feeding the poor continues today with carryouts to various churches that have volunteers to serve the meals. More than 25,000 meals were served in a recent year.

On one occasion, the feeding took place at Barney's Market Club on Halsted and Washington streets. That year, restaurant owner Harold Schwimmer informed Father Mac that while he wanted to help him, he could not afford it because the men would walk off with his silverware. The next year, a police officer was stationed at the exit deterring any would-be thieves.

Another program—in 1963—was the Central States Institute of Addiction. It was noted for development of a DUI (driving under the influence) program, working with the Circuit Court of Cook County to get such offenders into educational classes. It began with a chance meeting between Monsignor McDermott and a circuit judge after a wedding both had attended.

"I was at a wedding reception many years ago," Monsignor McDermott related. "There was a judge, Adam Stillo, and his wife sitting at a table with four other couples. He had been at the church service. So I joined them at the table. It was rather late because they were sitting at the table; the cocktail hour was over. People had consumed two, maybe three, cocktails. On the table were a Rhine wine and a rosé wine. As the meal was concluding, the master of ceremonies said, 'The orchestra is now here, dancing will begin and the bars are re-opened for your pleasure.'

"The judge said to me, 'Father, what would you do if you were a judge? Look at these people. They come from middle-class or semi-opulent families, and they may have imbibed too much. On the way home they could be stopped for driving under the influence and thrown in jail. Let's reverse our roles. You be the judge and I the priest. What can we do to make these people realize that they may have a drinking problem?'"

Monsignor McDermott considered it, suggested that they get together after a few days. When they did, the priest suggested that the judge begin sending some of the offenders to his office at 126 North Desplaines Street.

Beginning with a trickle of people served by the priest and one staffer, Central States Institute of Addiction has grown to become one of the largest providers of DUI services in the nation. (Later Monsignor McDermott went to Springfield, secured the support of then Governor Richard B. Ogilvie and the legislature for Central States Institute and received a state appropriation to help run it.)

He enlisted Sister Patricia Kilbane, of the Dominican Sisters of St. Catherine of Kentucky, to help him with the program. Sister Patricia had met him when she was a child. Her father and he were close friends; her sister, Estelle, also a nun, had been stationed at Our Lady of Peace where she and Father McDermott ran the altar boy project. After Vatican II, nuns of her order could decide freely what to do. Sister Patricia, with a master's in education and history, had been a teacher in Boston and New Jersey, an instructor at Creighton University, Omaha, and a high school teacher there. She was pondering her future, engaged in what her order called a "house of prayer" in Libertyville, a suburb of Chicago. She bumped into Monsignor McDermott at a memorial for a religious colleague, Sister Joanne Gill, who had died of leukemia. The latter had written a curriculum for children of alcoholics for the Catholic school system at Monsignor McDermott's request.

Sister Patricia says, "At the wake, Monsignor said he didn't know I was in town. I said, 'I'm really not in town. I'm making a house of prayer.' He said, 'What are you making a house of prayer for?'" She said that she was trying to determine her future. He indicated the shortness of life, citing the recently deceased nun—adding, "There's your sister in the casket. Come work for me." So she did, becoming what was virtually the principal of the DUI school.

His recruitment technique was a mixture of persuasion and good-natured, unremitting pressure, as was shown when he picked one who was to become a key force at ACES. Mary Ellen Flynn's father was an alcoholic. He played for the Cincinnati Reds in the '20s. She met Monsignor McDermott when she was 18, after she had helped start a group called "Alateen" [children of alcoholics] in Chicago. He convinced her to go on a road show he was taking to "parishes, schools, any place that would have us." That association led Flynn to a lifelong career in alcoholic treatment and care.

"He had a traveling minstrel show," recalled Flynn, "where he would take these people, all of whom had personal experience with alcohol. One was a priest who was recovering, and the other was a woman member of Alcoholics Anonymous. Another, the wife of an alcoholic, who was a member of "Al-Anon" [family member of an alcoholic], and me, the child of an alcoholic. He would try to get his foot in the door through the fathers' club or mothers' club. Usually, if we got in there once, we were asked back.

"I can probably say that he had a profound influence on my life, probably more than anyone else," Flynn added. "He started by asking me to help with Alateen at Catholic Charities. I kept saying no, I didn't want to come all the way downtown and he kept asking and asking. One of the men who worked in the basement [Holy Cross Mission of Catholic Charities, then in the building's basement, where men would come off the Street and try to stay sober], John Burke, said: 'You're going to work with Father Mac someday.' I said: 'No, I'm not.' He said: 'Yes, yes you are.'"

Burke was right. "I accepted the job with Father Mac and my life has never been the same," said Mary Ellen Flynn.

Withdrawal and a penchant for secrecy marked the middle-class alcoholic at that time. Also, "respectable" parishes tried to keep the McDermott road show out, but eventually he got in.

"Just being interested in a priest getting up there, or people getting up there and being honest enough to say what their problems were was important," continued Flynn. "Because this was unheard of—for a priest or anybody to get up in front of a group of people and say, 'This is my problem, and this is where I went for help.'"

Learning that a prominent banker was fighting alcoholism, Monsignor McDermott went to see him to offer assistance. The banker refused to acknowledge his drinking problem, declaring that he would vehemently deny the meeting ever took place if asked. The banker took the priest first to a small room then, circuitously, to a smaller one, finally sitting himself at a desk. The watchword was secrecy.

The priest reached over, pointed to a drawer and said, "Why don't you open it up and we'll both crawl in?" The banker melted, opening up a drawer to produce the Alcoholics Anonymous handbook that he had been secretly reading.

That same tough love was used as last-ditch therapy at night as he made his rounds on Skid Row. Author William Gleason portrays Monsignor McDermott shouting at one seemingly incorrigible drunk he was trying to save—a man who lied repeatedly about trying to come to AA meetings on Desplaines Street, but who never came: "Look, Tim, I'm not the least bit concerned about where you eat or if you eat! Nor am I concerned about where you sleep tonight or if you sleep! If you're ever going to find what you're searching for, for so long, go back up to the Street you love so well, and see if you can find it there!"

> The words hit like successive blows to the stomach and Tim reacted as though they had been. He vomited. The stomach, which had held no food for almost two days, rebelled against the mistreatment and rejected the last of the wine that had been poured into it. Tim tried to hold back the vomit but he could not. Horrified, he watched it cascade toward Father Mac.
>
> The priest stepped back, quickly but calmly. Refuse that had been expelled by the abused stomach of a man he loved splashed on the floor in front of him, spattering his shoes and the cuffs of his trousers.
>
> "Look at what that ignorant bastard done," somebody shouted. "We ought to throw him out of here on his ass." There were shouts of agreement.
>
> Father Mac held up his hands, shook his head from side to side and smiled, "Everybody relax now," he said. "Tim isn't the first guy who threw up around here."

"Let me wipe off that stuff," Art Dixon said as he moved forward with a clean handkerchief.
"Forget it," Father Mac said. "I'll run downstairs and clean up."

—William F. Gleason
The Liquid Cross of Skid Row

* * *

While he was a member of a civic committee on alcoholism, Monsignor McDermott met a fellow panelist, Merrill C. Meigs, after whom Meigs Field is named. A newspaper publisher for Hearst—and one who could call for a chauffeur-driven limousine—Meigs would nevertheless call the priest, who drove a Chevrolet, to hitch a ride to committee sessions. One day when they attended a funeral together, Meigs, an Episcopalian, exclaimed that, "The Catholic Church will rue the day that it let so many of its traditions go." A colorful man, standing 6' 4", Meigs was affectionately known to his friends as "Babe." He acquired the nickname while attending the University of Chicago.

Meigs was born in 1884 in Malcolm, Iowa, and worked on his parents' farm until he was 17, when he entered Iowa Business College. While in his teens, he became a salesman for J.I. Case Threshing Machine Company in Racine, Wisconsin. Because his trips took him to South America, he enrolled in the University of Chicago in 1905 to study Spanish. While at the university, he played guard in the famous 1905 football team under Amos Alonzo Stagg. The squad won the Western Conference championship by beating Michigan 2 to 0. He paid for his tuition by working as a correspondent for the Hearst *Herald and Examiner*. After returning to J.I. Case as advertising manager, he joined Lord & Thomas Advertising Agency in Chicago in 1914, and in 1917 moved to the *Chicago Evening American* where he served as advertising director until 1926. He was publisher of the *Chicago Herald and Examiner* from 1926 to 1929, publisher of the *Chicago American* from 1933 to 1936, and vice president of the Hearst Corporation in Chicago from 1942 to 1962.

As head of the Chicago Aeronautics Commission for many years, he advocated a lakefront airport. His dream was realized when one on Northerly Island was opened. It was renamed Meigs Field in 1948.

Meigs' interest in flying began after Charles Lindbergh flew a solo, nonstop flight from New York to Paris in May 1927. He started taking flying lessons immediately afterward. He was the first paying customer on a Chicago-San Francisco airmail plane in 1927. The newspaper executive was chief of the aircraft section of the War Production Board and senior consultant on aviation from 1942 to 1945.

Meigs claimed to have given Harry Truman two flying lessons—one when Truman was a senator and the second after he left the White House. A friend to many, including J. Edgar Hoover and William Randolph Hearst, Meigs once played 18 holes of golf with the Duke of Windsor, whom he called "a lousy putter." He also accepted a cigar from Winston Churchill, which he preserved, unsmoked. He flew his own plane until he was age 83. He died in 1968, at age 84, while on vacation in Palm Beach, Florida. He was married four times, divorced three times, and widowed once.

Frequently, Meigs had offbeat thoughts about religion.

"You know, Ignatius," he said, "what I can't understand is why Christ stood by and let his best friend be beheaded."

Says Monsignor McDermott: "He meant John the Baptist. I guess Merrill didn't understand that Christ didn't come down here to run the show but to atone for our sins. He didn't even spare Himself."

*   *   *

When, in 1961, Catholic Charities disposed of its orphanages, the man who ran the Dependent Child office was rewarded with the offer of a prominent parish. Says Father John Sullivan: "The parish they offered was not just any parish."

Monsignor McDermott could have become pastor of St. Thomas the Apostle, at 55th and Kimbark, a jewel of the archdiocese in the Hyde Park neighborhood, the section of the city where the prestigious University of Chicago is housed. Hyde Park is an attractive residential neighborhood with an excellent location along the lakefront. Its Hyde Park urban renewal project was attaining national renown.

The church and convent qualified for national historic landmark recognition. Its impressive brick edifice represented a significant departure from church architecture. Built without pillars, the edifice is almost as wide as it is long; therefore, worshippers are brought in close contact with the celebrant. The balustrades that decorate the church were designed by sculptor Alfono Iannelli, the Stations of the Cross and magnificent Pieta, by Alfeo Faggi.

Astoundingly to some of his priest colleagues—but not to those who knew him well—Monsignor McDermott turned down the assignment. He had found his parish—on Skid Row. He stayed with Charities, picking up yet another project—Sousa Shelter, located in the old John Philip Sousa School on Jackson Boulevard, an overnight residence for homeless men and women, funded by public funds, including some from the City of Chicago.

His new boss was Monsignor Vincent Cooke, the head of Catholic Charities. One of the more notable performances by Cooke was his annual performance as Santa Claus at every Charities installation. Never to be forgotten was the time Cooke hired a helicopter with pilot and, with Father McDermott in tow, flew throughout Chicagoland, dropping in to visit the orphans in the regalia of Old St. Nick. Cooke, a short, heavy man, sweated profusely in the cramped quarters of the cockpit. Moreover, he enjoyed cigars. So, as the copter flew, he doffed his wig and fake beard and inhaled deeply from a Corona-Corona. When the helicopter landed, the cigar was not yet finished so Cooke went on his rounds sans beard and with a cigar jutting out of his mouth.

"I tried to reason with him that this impression is not really Santa Claus," says Monsignor McDermott. "Cooke's answer was, 'What? Do you want me to set myself afire with that beard?'" For hundreds of orphans, a new visage of Santa was inculcated that day.

* * *

On November 22, 1963, the day John Kennedy was assassinated, Monsignor McDermott was working at Catholic Charities, 126 North Desplaines, when a female office worker came to him with the news. He recalled the day when, in 1947, young Congressman John Kennedy came to Chicago to speak at the Irish Fellowship banquet. A stirring photograph was taken of Kennedy, then age 30, with Judge Jim McDermott.

* * *

The late Cardinal Stritch had been succeeded by another prelate who had come from Milwaukee, Albert Cardinal Meyer [1903-1965]. He was known as a quiet, undemonstrative man, who was transformed by Vatican II, taking a keen interest in the document prepared by Father John Courtney Murray on religious liberty. Meyer became a forceful advocate for ecumenical amity, issuing a pastoral letter on interdenominational cooperation. Monsignor McDermott began a campaign to make Meyer aware of alcoholism in the priesthood.

Monsignor McDermott recalls Meyer exerting a gentle, understated yet firm admonition after a confirmation at St. Mary of Providence, 4242 North Austin, a school for retarded girls. The cardinal was flanked by Monsignor William E. McManus, superintendent of Catholic schools.

"When confirmation was over and they were serving cake and ice cream, Meyer was standing there conferring with the sisters," Monsignor McDermott recalls. "Two little retarded girls came up to the cardinal (I'm sure they were programmed by the sisters to approach the cardinal). McManus was standing right behind him and a little girl said to His Eminence, 'Cardinal, may we be off tomorrow? Can we have a free day?' And the cardinal looks at McManus and McManus says, 'You'll have to make it up some other day!' Meyer turned around and said quietly, 'Monsignor.' I thought that was the epitome of understatement."

The attempt of McManus to ingratiate himself with the prelate by cracking down on little retarded kids still rankles Monsignor McDermott.

The last time Monsignor McDermott saw Cardinal Meyer there was an unmistakable clue as to what could happen to the archbishop. "I remember the cardinal used to appear, in the octave of the Immaculate Conception, at the St. Vincent DePaul Society function at the Congress Hotel. So, being a football fan, before the doings I went to the Bears game with Monsignor [Vincent] Cooke [superintendent of Catholic Charities]. In the middle of the game, Cooke said, 'I have to leave because of the St. Vincent DePaul Society, and I want to meet the cardinal.' I said, 'Well, I'm watching the rest of the game and after the game is over, I'll see you at the Congress Hotel.'"

Cooke frowned and left. The McDermott independence of spirit flourished. Cooke stalked off, went to the Congress Hotel, but had trouble finding the holding room for the cardinal. After the game, Monsignor McDermott went to the hotel and found the holding room where he was alone with the cardinal.

"[After the game] I went to the Presidential Suite. I found Cardinal Meyer, in pain, rubbing his head. I said, 'Your Eminence, you seem to be in a lot of pain and anguish.' And he said, 'Gee, Monsignor, I have a very bad headache.' In the meantime, Cooke and the others were looking upon me, I suppose, as Dennis the Menace. I stayed to watch the football game, and they got lost on the elevators. They were supposed to escort the cardinal—and here's the culprit—and I'm standing in front of the door talking to the cardinal! That was between—December 8 is the feast day, and the octave would be seven days later. Albert Gregory Meyer entered Mercy Hospital and never came out of it."

In February 1965, Meyer was diagnosed with a malignant brain tumor, and although he submitted to surgery, he never recovered. He died in Chicago on April 11, 1965.

* * *

The campaign to rescue clergy from dependency on alcohol resumed in earnest with Meyer's successor. He was John Cardinal Cody [1907–1982], Chicago's most controversial, and some say under-appreciated, archbishop. A detail-conscious administrator, Cody had been archbishop of New Orleans, where he had taken a strong stand in favor of integration. He invoked a public excommunication of several Catholic politicians when they supported continued segregation in their political subdivisions. On June 2, 1965, Cody was named eleventh bishop, sixth archbishop of Chicago.

In 1967, Pope Paul VI made him a cardinal, the fourth in Chicago history. He served for 17 years. He was, Monsignor McDermott feels, unjustly criticized by a rising, angry coterie of priests who wished more freedom from the chancery office. One of their complaints was the lack of an archdiocesan health plan for clergy—"And," testified Monsignor McDermott, "I thought that was the keystone chapter in the life of John Cody."

"Some of the younger priests were on the malcontent side. They were operating in an *ens rationis* world, whereas John Cody operated in an *ens reali* world." To get a health plan for priests, nuns, and brothers, Cody met with a nun on the staff of Little Company of Mary Hospital.

"He talked with her about the problems. One of them was mental health and physical health. He showed her his program and she responded, 'You're missing the boat here. There's one thing you haven't touched upon. There should be something here about alcohol and chemical dependency. You realize that some of the sisters in the hospitals are living in fertile territory where they could become dependent on chemicals. Their days are long and they're seething with anxiety and apprehension.' She suggested adding a program on alcohol and chemical dependency. He said, 'Thank you for the suggestion. Would you have anybody whom I could confer with?'

"She said, 'Yes, there's Dr. James West on the staff here. He's majored in taking care of priests and nuns who have a dependency on alcohol and drug chemicals.' Cody called Dr. West over to 1555 North State Parkway [the cardinal's residence].

"So Jim West arrived there and the cardinal was occupied, I guess, with somebody else that day. Dr. West was waiting in another room and when the cardinal entered the room, Dr. West said, 'Am I the only one here?' The cardinal said, 'Should there be somebody else here?' And Dr. West said, 'Yes, I'm surprised that Ignatius McDermott isn't here. He and I have worked intimately through the years with priests who have been dependent on alcohol.' 'Well,' said the cardinal, 'by all means we'll get in touch with Ignatius McDermott.'"

Cardinal Cody named Dr. West and Monsignor McDermott to a commission to recommend ways to approach the problem of alcoholism in the clergy.

"Well," said Monsignor McDermott, "I don't go for big committees. I just go for small committees. I like to have only four members on the committee—people like Dr. Vincent Pisani, a psychologist, and Father Andrew McDonough, a psychologist teaching at the seminary on the college level."

"I found Cardinal Cody a most understanding person relative to priests who experienced a dependency on alcohol," said Monsignor McDermott.

With Cardinal Cody's strong support, priest members of Alcoholics Anonymous would speak at gatherings of clergy. Cody's achievements were substantial but unheralded, maintains Father John Sullivan. "I was at a First Mass a few years back, and a priest from Milwaukee was at my table who made a derogatory comment about Cardinal Cody. I started to list some of the things that Cardinal Cody had done. He originated and strengthened the commitment to inner city schools—worth about $15 million a year. About 45 schools went on subsidy at that time, which continues to this day. He secured health insurance for his priests so after retirement they would not be charity patients at Catholic hospitals. He gave us car insurance so that we could make our rounds. And, of course, it was Cody who, with Father Ig, started the first program of its kind in the country for alcoholic priests, for their being assisted physically, mentally, and spiritually in order to beat addiction." Priests with obvious dependency problems were visited by Monsignor McDermott and Dr. West and convinced to go to Guest House, a treatment center in Rochester, Minnesota. Bills for the treatment would be sent, not to the Chancery office where names could be leaked to gossips, but to Monsignor McDermott for hospitalization, Dr. Pisani for psychological treatment, and Dr. West for medical care.

How did the visits by McDermott and West go? Suppose the priest involved would deny he had a dependency problem.

"Well," said Monsignor McDermott, "the premise was if he did not succumb to our approach, then—'I'm sorry, you'll be hearing from Cardinal Cody.'" That solved the problem, but it rarely got that far.

"I remember one day we went to a rectory," says Monsignor McDermott, "and we walked up the stairs and the priest we're supposed to see said, 'I've got a sick call.' He was faking the sick call to get out of there because he knew. We sat down and we said, 'Let's stop kidding yourself. You're not going on any sick call.'" He agreed to treatment.

* * *

A singular case of recovery involved Father Daniel Joseph Mallette, who since the 1960s has had a national reputation as a civil rights priest. Born in 1931 on the South Side, Father Mallette, of French, Irish, German, and Polish extraction, fought alcoholism since he was a young priest. At the same time, he was gaining widespread attention for his rapport with the poor. "On my Irish side, it seemed like there were a lot of people getting shot in bars in the history of the family," he said. "The funny thing with me: my dad drank like a fish when I was a kid, would go into a saloon. He was in the slot machine business, ran all the slot machines at the Catholic carnivals. When I was 18 years old, and I was going to Mundelein [seminary], he quit drinking, quit smoking. He got out of the gambling business, went to Mass every day for the rest of his life, and worked for me at Visitation. So I used to say, 'Mallettes, we quit when we're 49 [laughing].' But I never made it."

His drinking (he thought) was hidden. By drinking vodka, his secret alcoholism didn't impede his rise through the Church. He was on a fast track: Quigley Preparatory Seminary, 1945-50; St. Mary of the Lake Seminary at Mundelein, 1950–57; first appointment, St. Agatha at 3147 West Douglas Boulevard. Active and widely quoted as a Chicago civil rights priest, he met and knew Martin Luther King, Jr. He marched with comedian and rights advocate Dick Gregory and CORE founder James Farmer. Father Mallette cut a wide swath in civil rights in the 1960s. He sought to put the Catholic Church in the forefront of the civil rights movement.

"I remember standing there in Hattiesburg, Mississippi," he recalled, "and seeing this Catholic Church that was half burnt down because there had been a voting rights drive there." He remembers a meeting in Jackson, Mississippi, as a member of the Student Non-Violent Coordinating Committee (SNCC), when he met Father Bernard Law, then a priest-secretary to a bishop, with whom he stayed friends through the years. Law became cardinal-archbishop of Boston.

While in Washington, D.C., for a civil rights march, when the capital city still had a southern orientation, Father Mallette was eating in a restaurant when he spied a portrait of Alabama Governor George Wallace on the wall. He removed the picture.

"The next thing you know, we were arrested. I was supposed to have slugged a policeman."

Did he? He can't remember. He was arrested, spent a night in jail, then pulled strings to hide the arrest out of fear his priesthood would be destroyed. His superiors in Chicago never heard of the fracas. Instead, the archdiocese seemed to support his efforts in behalf of civil rights.

Through many of those years, while he managed his priestly duties carefully and worked around the clock, Father Mallette drank heavily.

"Drinking was more and more of a problem in my life—it had always been," he said. "I went to my first AA meeting when I was 17 years old. It was 26 years later before I went to my next meeting. In between, drinking would often pop up as a problem with me."

John Patrick Cardinal Cody was alternately, as Father Mallette says, the bane of his life and one of the best people he ever met. A run-in with Cardinal Cody came when Father Mallette wanted to hold an inter-religious Christmas event at his church and had invited a black Baptist minister to co-convene it. Cardinal Cody did not grant permission. Father Mallette, who was drinking heavily, shouted, "Well, Merry Christmas to you!" and slammed down the phone. But Cardinal Cody, who recognized Father Mallette's value, took the abuse. He allowed Father Mallette to go to New York as a professor at the prestigious Jesuit college, Fordham, to teach about the urban poor [from March 1968 to mid-1971].

Once in New York, Father Mallette determined to learn the working life of the poor first-hand. He wanted to drive a cab.

"I was working at Fordham, and I wanted to learn Manhattan better," he said. "I loved New York, so I got a job driving for the Long Island City Cab Company. I used to drive Friday nights, Saturday nights, and Sunday nights in New York. I said Mass every morning at Lincoln Center, and I got myself an apartment in Hell's Kitchen. It was just six blocks from the chapel where I was saying Mass. I did that for about a year, and then some lawyer's kid wanted to emulate me. The kid's father flew in to see me, and I was busy driving the cab. I sent some friends of mine to meet the guy at the Plaza Hotel. He—the lawyer—took affront at that. And the next thing I knew, he reported me to the chancery in Chicago."

The chancery heatedly objected to Father Mallette's driving a cab.

Father Mallette retorted: "*Why not?* You let priests be lawyers, you let priests be psychiatrists. Why can't I be a cab driver? Every penny I make I spend for the kids in my program."

Then Cardinal Cody called, and Father Mallette flew back to Chicago for a crucial meeting.

"I'll never forget that. He was being picketed by the young priests' caucus [outside his residence]. It was Holy Week. I remember sitting there. I always had this fear of authority. I loved him, and I'm sitting there with him. Then he said, 'Father, can you imagine the embarrassment this would have caused me if, as a cab driver, you had been shot?'

"He said that to me! I had such love for him, and said, 'Sir, I could just picture the blood streaming down the back of my head and saying, 'Oh, poor Cardinal Cody!' That was what I liked about him, though. But he said, 'You can't do that anymore.'"

Later, Father Mallette was named pastor of Visitation parish, Monsignor McDermott's old home, where his alcoholism continued to worsen. Cardinal Cody asked him to fly to Rome to address a convocation on inner city ministry at the North American College, where Chicago seminarians lived. He flew over, bought a fifth of Cutty Sark to loosen himself up for the talk, drank it all, and didn't show up.

"You always think: I got this under control, and I can handle this and I can handle that," he explained. But then at Visitation, I'll always remember when they took me on a tour of the buildings and there was a wine cellar—the place was two square blocks of buildings and a high school and everything else—filled with ready-made Van Heublein martini and Manhattan mixes, even though the parish was poor at the time. I'll always remember: they opened the door to the wine cellar. I'd seen the bowling alley and all the buildings and I looked at that wine cellar. I said, 'My God, I'll never be able to drink all of this [laughing]!' And I think four years later there was one tiny bottle rolling around."

Monsignor McDermott got wind of the young priest's problem and alerted Cardinal Cody to the fact that Father Mallette needed treatment. Today, Father Mallette admits, "I was at death's door" with alcoholism. Monsignor McDermott would continually visit him.

"I always thought he came to me out of a vodka bottle. He would pop in—'How ya doin', Dan?' He'd talk about the Sox and what was going to happen. Then I was told that we had to have lunch. He would set it up. It's kind of foggy, because it was a foggy period in my life then. I was supposed to meet him and Dr. Jim West at the Beverly Country Club." It was an order. "I was more or less *told* I had to meet Ignatius and Dr. West at the Beverly Country Club."

The day of the meeting, Father Mallette got "bombed out of my mind." On the way to the club, he drove his car into a post on Halsted.

"I recall my poor dad picking me up, getting the tow truck," he said. The priest wasn't ticketed for drunken driving—priests tended to be absolved from embarrassment in those days in Chicago. He "pulled all kinds of strings" with the archdiocese. He said he wanted to go to Puerto Rico to learn Spanish (actually, to prove he wasn't an alcoholic). "So they made a deal when I flew off to Puerto Rico for a month learning Spanish," he continued. It was kind of a vacation from Visitation. Not that long a period; you're due a month's vacation."

He didn't drink in Puerto Rico. He came back. "Ignatius was, I just remember, he was always hovering around my life, and I liked him a whole lot." Father Mallette's dad died, "...and I remember his last words were: 'Dan is still drunk.'"

The problems of Visitation parish bothered Father Mallette. It was far different than when Ignatius lived there as a boy. The neighborhood had, in the ominous Chicago sense, "changed." Recalls Father Mallette: "There were so many tragedies. There were murders every time you turned around, and there would be a fire next door. I'd bring the whole family in, move them into the rectory. I'd have 35 people living in the rectory. It was complete chaos. Also, I had this high school. I didn't have money to pay the teachers. It was a huge girls school.

"On April 9, 1975, I had called a holy hour because I wanted to be able to pray, and I took one slug of wine to calm myself down, but apparently never went to the holy hour. The next thing I knew it was the morning, and I was at my mother's apartment out in Riverdale. The phone was ringing. I was ordered to go to the chancery office. They handed me a letter ordering me to go into treatment." The treatment center would be Guest House, a facility for alcoholic Catholic religious at Rochester, Minnesota. "I was such a nut that I went and got a lawyer to sue Cardinal Cody, to slap an injunction on him. This wonderful young Jewish friend of mine was saying, 'How are you going to keep this Catholic clientele if you start suing the cardinal?'

"Then I drove to Detroit instead of going where they wanted me to go." Father Mallette decided he'd go to a sanitarium in Detroit to spend a weekend there—still in denial about his alcoholism. But there was no room in the treatment center. He called Guest House in Rochester to say he wasn't coming. "I said I wasn't coming. I haven't got the time. I've got a big parish. I've got a sick mother. The director said, 'Well, Father, we won't be expecting you then. But listen to me: I'm a recovering alcoholic myself. Tell me before you hang up who takes care of your sick mother when you drink?' I almost ripped the phone off the wall I was so angry. But he had quite a point. I could see all the avenues of escape were closed. My cousin got me up in the morning and put me on a plane in the Detroit airport at about 5 a.m. I was going to go from Detroit to Chicago to Rochester. I remember my family begging me: 'Dan, don't get off at Chicago.'"

He arrived at Guest House on April 11, 1975.

"They picked me up," he continued. "I walked through the doors and they said, 'None arrive too early, none return too late.' I met a guy named Bill Walker who was my counselor. He shared stuff with me for the first time in my life. 'It seemed like people had tried to help me for so long,' I said. 'I can't understand it. I'm doing everything I don't want to do—I drink.' He said, 'Well, the call is cunning, baffling, and powerful.' He's my sponsor today, 25 years later. They took me to an AA meeting two nights later. I heard a guy say, 'Let go and let God'—that was the first thing I heard—and that stuck with me. I've had 25 beautiful years. It was a great joy."

Monsignor McDermott came up to Minnesota for Father Mallette's departure Mass. Father Mallette said, "So, I remember so well driving him to the airport—him and a psychologist, Dr. Vince Pisani. He's still the head of the health committee of the diocese. I spoke to him—I remember the date—on July 16, 1975. I had Ignatius McDermott and him in my rental car. I was driving back to Chicago. I thought I better say something nice to this guy, since he's got a lot to say in the archdiocese: 'Dr. Pisani, have you any advice for me?' And he got out of the car and said, 'Yeah, Mallette, save your own ass.' [Laughing.] And he slammed the door. Which has been the nicest thing I could have ever heard."

Since then, Father Mallette has been in regular contact with Monsignor McDermott.

"For the last 25 years, I brought him a couple hundred people, I bet. Any time of the day or night—I've got four guys there now. I asked a guy yesterday: Do you want help? We'll go see Monsignor McDermott. I started this morning, at 6 a.m. I talked to a guy who's there. I brought a guy in last night, a guy who's in trouble. Rich, poor, black, white—Ignatius takes them all in. He's an incredible man."

The much-reviled John Patrick Cardinal Cody was also a remarkable man, says Father Mallette. His inarticulation but good heart intrigued the intellectually-nuanced Father Mallette.

Taking all these indignities and administering strict justice caused Cardinal Cody to save Father Mallette's life, the priest believes. "Saved my life," the priest elaborated. "When I came out of treatment, he was there. He was behind you, and he trusted you. Then a year-and-a-half later, he made me administrator, briefly, of St. Norbert's in Northbrook. He made me pastor. There was something so good about him—no bullshit. I always remember— a great moment to me—when I was coming to make my amends to him I said, 'Your Eminence, I did a lot of harm. I'm in AA now. I'd like to make amends for any embarrassment I caused you, or insults.' He's...like, squirming there, and he said, 'Well, Father, when I was in Kansas City I had more insane asylums than any other bishop in the United States.' What did that have to do with it? I'm thinking, 'What the hell [laughing]?' Then I looked at him and I thought, 'I love this guy'—because he was nervous, too; didn't know what to say."

On March 1, 1977, Father Mallette was appointed pastor of St. Margaret's of Scotland on the South Side.

The ingenious thing about Monsignor McDermott, Father Mallette maintains, is that, "He hasn't been depersonalized. He's the same figure that you used to see walking along West Madison Street. I could pick up the phone now and reach him or get there to him and say, 'Give Steve a chance, please' and he would. I brought a woman down who is a 26-year-old mother. Eight kids living in abject poverty, five survivors, and this—the grandmother herself was a little girl, 40 years old—freezing to death in an apartment on the West Side, now in the throes of alcoholism, and all of a sudden we're right in Monsignor's office, and he's inspiring her to give it a shot this time and make it."

Why aren't there more priests today like Ignatius McDermott? One would think there would be, with Vatican II emphasizing closer ties between clergy and laity.

But these days, Father Dan Mallette feels the passion of Vatican II has been detoured by those who misinterpreted it. He regrets "people twisting it, saying we no longer wanted converts. When I was ordained a priest, I was on the teeming West Side. The kids were on triple shift in the public schools and we had 16 wonderful BVM [Blessed Virgin Mary] sisters. People were fighting to get into Catholic school. And we'd make all the parents come to instructions. Then 60 to 70 percent of them would become Catholic and would join the Church. We had something wonderful to offer."

"A change came in the '60s where people said that this was co-ercive and the young priests in the African-American work kind of lost that interest. The converts disappeared. I recently went to the funeral of a wonderful priest out in Orland Park [a far south suburb]. This guy taught at seminaries. But I looked around and I thought: 'There are thousands of people here and only a couple of blacks—two priests—and in our own way we've got a more seg-regated Church than they had in the days when the priests were considered racists.'

"I had an incident not too many months ago—a wonderful guy, but homeless, who had this terrible problem," Father Mallette continued. "He would drink and then he would beat up his wife and his girlfriend. I desperately wanted to get him help. We had him talk with Ignatius, and he'd walk away. He walked away from Haymarket several times. I just remember coming home one night when I was begging them to take him back. I think about holiness when I recall Ignatius and I talking with this guy, and Ignatius said, 'You can always come back.' Then Ignatius said, 'Let's end with the *Memorare*. There's a holiness to Ignatius— you know. There's a saintliness to him."

* * *

It was when he was making his rounds in his Skid Row "par-ish" that Monsignor McDermott discovered that many of the men were extolling a quiet benefactor—one who gave them money to tide them over for a flop, who staked them to soup and sand-wiches and even held their money for safe-keeping. Skid Row men were worried about being rolled or having their pockets picked as they slept. Someone they trusted greatly, a man called "Patsy the Barber," would put their money away and would give it to them on request. Patsy would give free haircuts; occasionally he would be able to talk men into going to detox. Curious as to this man, Monsignor McDermott sought him out.

"Patsy the Barber" is Pasquale Colemeni. He is a tiny man, im-peccably clean, who is proprietor of "Pat's Barber Shop" on the second floor of one of the last remaining single room occupancies in Chicago—the New Jackson, 768 West Jackson Boulevard, a seedy building that has stood at its location since 1878. It has 120 rooms, which in 1999 were going for about $21 a night.

Colemeni was born in Canfili, Italy, in 1912. He learned barbering in Italy, immigrating to Chicago in 1929, living with his parents. Patsy started work at 432 South Halsted. As the buildings he worked at were torn down, Patsy moved—to 1724 West Madison, across the street from the Chicago Stadium, then to 1604 West Madison. One day Father Mac walked in, introduced himself, and asked for a haircut. Patsy has been cutting his hair ever since. They talk about the men and the Street, changing times, and review the politicians and other celebrities they have met. On his wall Patsy has a newspaper photo of Clarence Darrow, showing the famed attorney shaking hands with the barber. Other pictures on the wall are of memorable Italians, including Al Capone, who allowed Patsy's late partner to shave him in Cicero, a suburb of Chicago. Frank Sinatra's picture occupies a prominent place, as does Dean Martin's.

"I shoulda went to school, but never went to school [in the United States]," Colemeni said. "So I just pick up a little bit from people, that's all." He is no philosopher but has definite opinions about how slum clearance has direly affected the men of Skid Row. "A lotta people on the Street they make homeless when they knocked down the small hotel," he says. "You get a flop for couple bucks a night, but these places are all going. So they [the men of Skid Row] come out to be homeless."

He rebukes the developers for building luxury apartments, which made the old Skid Row a choice residential area, but which dispossessed the poor.

"All at the expense of the poor man," he says. "They throw the poor people out. The system make 'em homeless. They don't build nothing for them, very, very little. They build the condos for $100,000 up."

Patsy says that war is particularly hard on the young. Skid Row became a home for dispossessed veterans of World War II, Korea, and Vietnam who couldn't shake loose from their experiences. "They're depressed people, very depressed," he sighs. "When you're depressed you gotta fight your own battle. Drinking is just temporary. Then they get into the habit and that's it— they don't stop. They wanna drink, that's it, couldn't stop, couldn't stop."

Could Patsy administer "tough love" to these men? He shakes his head.

"I know—but it's pretty hard to be tough, pretty tough," the barber answered. "Some, they won't listen. Then another thing, a lot of young people who come from the Vietnam War, they are all depressed people, they all take cocaine or whatever they drink. The war ruined these people."

Pasquale Colemeni lives in suburban Westchester and drives to work five days a week, preferring to work in an area where he can serve the men who live at the New Jackson Hotel—and cut Monsignor McDermott's hair.

*   *   *

Jim Mchugh, the movie extra in *Call Northside 777*, was driving a truck—an 18-wheeler that hauled grain from the silos out in Indiana Harbor—destined for breweries—when he suffered a heart attack the night of the Grant Park big mêlée with the Democratic National Convention in 1968. It was unrelated to the political excitement, but Mchugh determined to retire.

Mchugh knocked around a lot.

"You know them streetcar safety islands they used to have? I once stepped off a safety island at 64th and Stony. A car hit me, rolled me right up on the hood, where I broke the windshield. I was stinko, but not hurt. If I was sober, I'd be dead.

"Then I tended bar at a bowling alley and bar at 60th and Halsted. Didn't know what I was doing about bartending. Guy comes in and orders a sloe gin. I poured him a stiff one of gin. He says, 'This is not a sloe gin.' The boss says, 'Excuse him, I'm just breaking him in.' He pours a gin and takes a can of cherries and pours the juice from it in the drink. My eyes popped as he was doin' it. Guy says, 'Now that's terrific. Thanks.' The boss knew even less about bartending than me."

Now Jim Mchugh decided to become a full-time McDermott volunteer.

"I went down there to Catholic Charities to see him," Mchugh recalls. "Fran [the late Francine Lamb, Monsignor McDermott's secretary-executive assistant] was there and she told me Father would be with me in a few minutes. Mary Ellen Flynn came in...she brought me a cup of coffee and started talking to me. Father came and asked how I was doing. I said I was doing fine and asked how he was.

"He asked what I came down to see him for. And I told him I had a lot of time on my hands and I was looking for something to do. So he said he would get me a job in a tire store. I told him, 'No you don't. A friend of mine owns one and I've worked in there.' He asked if I knew much about engineering, because he said a guy was looking for a fellow who knew a little bit about it. I told him I didn't know anything about it. He told me if he ran into something he'd call me.

"It was about a week later I got a call, and he said he wanted to see me. So I went to see him, and he asked me if I knew anything about carpenter work." Mchugh said he could do "rough carpentry," not finished stuff. He has served as an unpaid handyman, jack-of-all-trades, ever since, living at Haymarket and proudly wearing a badge that attests he is "Liaison to Father."

"Then we had Sousa Shelter," Mchugh continues, "and I worked there. I was with Don McCready. Don is in a nursing home now, and we both worked together. He was making $4 an hour. We did everything over there. We did the plumbing and the electrical stuff, changed the boxes for fluorescent lights and all that. He'd go on a drunk. He'd be on a drunk for maybe two months. He was living over at the hotel at the time. So I'd take over, and I'd go there seven days a week. The toilets were blocked and we'd fix them. They'd break the toilets, and we'd go up on Milwaukee Avenue and buy a secondhand toilet. They wanted about $125, and we got it for $35 and cleaned it up and put it in. So that's the way the days went."

Bit by bit Jim Mchugh helped Monsignor McDermott dispense personal charity. He recalls a nun, Sister Joellen. "She's Back of the Yards. There was a Catholic school back there" in a ruined building the archdiocese sold to her for $1 "and they also gave her the convent for $1." Every Wednesday she fed 125 people. Mchugh would bring bread and doughnuts as a gift from Monsignor McDermott.

"Anyway, I would take the stuff over here to her," he said. "A fellow came with me, and we took it over there. She was really happy. We brought it in, opened it up, and put it in the big freezer. She said she hoped she had enough room. One day I came by and she said, 'I'm in trouble.' I said, 'What do you mean?' She said, 'They're [the archdiocese] taking the building from me.' I asked her how they could take it from her. 'They gave it to you for $1.' She said she got a letter from a lawyer, and the lawyer said they couldn't live here—they had to vacate. I told her somebody's crazy and asked if she went to the chancery office. She said she was going down there. But she said, 'Jim, pray hard. Pray as hard as you can.'

A couple of days later, I stopped back there and she said, 'Jim, our prayers have been answered.' The lawyers were stopped in their tracks. She said, 'There was a mistake on it.' "

But she was desperately hard up for money to keep the shelter going.

"Anyway," says Mchugh, "maybe a month or two went by, and I went to work, and I got the money and..."

From whom?

"I can't say who I got it from. Anyway, I went over there, and when I got there I saw her coming down the street with her head way down. She looked up and she said, 'Oh, Jim.' And I said, 'Boy, you're really in deep soil, ain't you?' She said, 'Jim, I got $20.00 here, and I'm trying to figure out how I can get enough chicken wings to feed these people today.' I said, 'You remember, Sister, a while back you said to me, 'Pray real hard'? We both prayed and got it. You look like you were prayin' real hard. She said, 'I was, Jim.' So I handed her the money."

How much?

"I don't want to say. She said, 'Jim, I don't believe it. Our prayers have been answered again.' I said 'Right!' She hugged me and I said, 'Aw, wait, people will think we're goin' together.' But that's the way she is."

* * *

During all this travail, one man was close to Monsignor McDermott, having moved from the Skid Row streets to the responsible position of Director of Facility Service. He is a tall, stocky black man named Luther Phillips, whose eyes scan Haymarket continually, a man with the appearance of command. He was rescued from the Street by Monsignor McDermott and is probably the closest person to him, in an emotional sense.

He was born in 1936 in Coldwater, Mississippi, the oldest of nine children, to Carrie and James Phillips, a family whose father (whom he greatly feared but also loved) made his career in the military. He was reared by his grandmother and stayed in the South until he was 14, when he came to Chicago. He was educated in the public schools with some time also spent in the Catholic parochial system.

By the time Luther Phillips was 15, he had lost his father from a heart attack. His mother never recovered from the sorrow. "I had to stand by her because she wasn't that strong," Phillips said.

His grandmother became the key to his life. When she died, Phillips said, "I died twice. It kind of had me confused." He was married, at age 16, to Annie Johnson, 15.

"I kind of got tied into marriage at a young age and put her in a spot where she got pregnant and had my first child," he said. "I wasn't proud of that but tried to do what a parent was expected to do back in those days."

They moved to Cabrini-Green, a giant public housing project on the North Side. He worked for a laundry, a manufacturing plant, a kosher sausage company, and a printing company. He was employed in a grocery store plucking chickens, as a waiter, for a bicycle rental where he became expert at repair. He discovered that, while he wasn't much on reading the manuals, he had a natural mechanical ability and could fix almost anything if he had the tools.

Phillips had inherited a warm feeling for church from his grandmother.

"I hooked up with a bunch of groups," he said. "Not just one denomination—all churches. I loved all of them. Wherever I went, that's where I hung my hat. That's because I think God goes everywhere."

He joined a choir and discovered he had a rich singing voice. His wife's father was a deacon, and Luther took naturally to singing spirituals with church groups.

Children were coming fast. He fathered nine with Annie. Luther Phillips organized a singing group called the Gospel Clouds. The group sang nightly, moving from church to church in Chicago, while days he worked at the laundry. The group became popular. The Gospel Clouds took to the road, traveling to southern states, then back to Chicago. He quit his laundry job. The group was making money. "A lot of money," he recalled. "We were blessed with a lot of money. People gave us money and paid us for coming to sing from place to place, Little Rock, Arkansas; Tupelo, Mississippi. We did almost all of the South, just running and singing. We traveled in a car. We bought one car, then bought another one.

"You made money," he said, "and you sent some home."

He moved his family to his uncle's house in Chicago. But absence ruined his family life. One day when he arrived home, he found that his wife wanted a divorce. He couldn't blame her.

"I think I loved the road more than I loved to stay at home, because I could make money, and I was the boss," he said. "I wasn't being pressured. It was one day after the other; people would just not leave me alone."

The divorce and his shattered family rocked him. He sang with the group on weekends, worked weekdays for a manufacturing company. Its owner, a German American, taught him precision repair work. After the death of his brother, Luther Phillips, depressed and alone, took another job with a distillery. He wasn't drinking much; he was in charge of an assembly line and still singing on weekends. But the uncertainty of it all and the bills that were piling up got to him. He took a couple of drinks one night, started to drive, bumped into another car, and got embroiled in a fight with the police. He spent four hours in jail. Then his ex-wife complained that his child support wasn't enough. He grew depressed.

"I'd get up every morning," he remembered. "I'd look for a job. I'd walk, try to find a job. I didn't find anything. But if I found it, it wasn't enough for me to pay the bills with. So you go to this labor pool."

Whenever he scrimped a little money, a judge would freeze it for alimony and child support. So why try?

He hit the skids, by his own admission. The men he sang with were all drinking and he did, too. Worse, he found he was losing his singing voice. Once, out on the road, he had to come back to Chicago since he couldn't sing. By his mid-30s he was on Skid Row, and was told that he probably wouldn't live to be 40. He had dropped out of sight. He kept up his appearances and would check into Holiday Inns and Quality Courts on the edge of the Row, getting to know the chambermaids and the house detectives. They would sneak him into recently vacated rooms, *gratis*. Every day he would come in wearing a suit and tie, dressed like he was going to work. When an executive would check out, a maid would give him the word and he would move in. Because he was adroit and on good terms with the staff, he would live and eat free. He would carry a briefcase with a bottle in it, and every day he would read the newspapers and drink.

One night he was passing a bar on West Madison Street, known as Irish Mike's. "There was a guy laying down on the sidewalk," he said. "He had been jack-rolled. They had grabbed him. Now I was up and down these streets every day because I knew where to walk to kill time. This guy's head was bleeding. I pulled him up and took my handkerchief to his head and he said, 'That's all right. Father Mac will be by here.' I pulled him back up to the curb. I didn't know who Father Mac was.

"After a while a guy pulls up in a black car. He had a white collar and he says to this guy, 'Hey, George, what's happened to you?' The guy says, 'Oh, Father!' This guy with the white priest's collar looks up at me and says, 'Give me a hand, we'll put him in the car and take him to the hospital.' After we get him in the car, Father Mac says, 'Do you want to take a ride with me?' I say, 'Okay, got nothing else to do.' I got a bottle in my back pocket. We get over to Cook County Hospital. He pulls in the back. He pulls right up to the side door."

Afterward, Monsignor McDermott kept in touch with Luther Phillips and hired him in 1974 at Holy Cross Mission as director of facilities, "which meant that I was the chief cook and bottle-washer, fixing things up."

What captivated Luther Phillips about Monsignor McDermott? The priest's activism plus his slangy way of talking appealed to anyone on the Street. He would say, "Keep on drinking like that, fella, and you'll end up with a wooden overcoat." "He's hitting the sauce." "He's 96-proof." One day he said to Luther, "Say, this guy needs a pair of shoes. Go get him a pair at Holy Cross Mission, will you?"

And, so, imbued with the 12 Steps, he became the first employee at Haymarket where, often, he worked side by side with Monsignor McDermott. Together they tackled what was the toughest case Luther Phillips ever saw. He called himself Billy Conn—not the old boxer who had fought Joe Louis but a man who appropriated the name.

"This guy had been on the Street for maybe 10 years," Phillips said. "He had never had a change of shorts. His beard was down to here. It stands out in my life more than all the others because he was the greatest challenge we had. There were a lot before, but he was the greatest. This man's hair was as long as my arm. It dropped down almost to his knees. His beard was just that long; his hair was that long, and it was filled with everything you could name. He had a cast they had put on his arm, on his elbow, and it had never been taken off. It was part of his bones. His pants were stuck to him, along with his shirt. There wasn't anything under there.

"We took him in. They brought him in the wagon to put him downstairs in the basement in that building. We had to shower him. Me, I couldn't much stand too much of the smell. I could stay there with him, but I couldn't stand the smell. He didn't want to touch the water. We finally got the scrub brushes and scrubbed him and got him out of there. Then we took some shears and cut his hair, cut it with the clippers, and cut his beard. He was fighting us all the way, but we wrestled with him.

"We got him shaved down, cut down, washed down, and Father took his clothes off. His cast—maggots were coming out of it. We sprayed it and tried to kill the lice as best we could. We gave him some clean shorts, tee shirts, and clean clothes. It was the most surprising thing I ever saw in my life and made me feel happier than anything else in the world—that he liked what he saw. He didn't look the same! We didn't take a picture of him but I wish we had. He turned around. He went upstairs. He stayed for five days. Every day he got up he wanted to go and shower. We entered him back into society. But we couldn't get him straightened out. He's just one of those guys who stands out in my life. To see them come in. Some made it. I knew them all—Old Man McCoy, Thomas Gates, Grover Williams, Billy Conn, Bruce Smith. There's a lot of them."

Monsignor McDermott not only rescued Luther Phillips; he edified Phillips with his missionary spirit to help others.

"Someone went and got me, why shouldn't I help them?" said Phillips.

Some years ago, they approached a derelict shivering in the cold. Suddenly, without warning, he lunged at Monsignor McDermott, striking out and nearly hitting the priest who then was in his 80s. Expertly dodging the flailing fist, Monsignor McDermott said calmly, "Luther, go get him a coat and hat. It's cold out."

Luther Phillips added: "To me, Monsignor's not one of those guys who sits up in his office and gives orders. Father does more than anybody I know. You can't beat him. He goes 24 hours a day. Sometimes he needs to slow down, but he never does. I wonder about him. He says, 'God keeps us. I've got a lot to do. I've got a lot of things I need to do.' His family has died, a lot of his friends are dead and gone, but Father keeps moving on. He's got that inner strength."

How long will Phillips keep on working? "Until the day he [Monsignor McDermott] leaves here, I'll be here," he answered. "I'm not going anywhere." Occasionally, he looks back at his life. A daughter whom he hadn't seen in years smiled at him not long ago and said, "Daddy, where've you been?" He doesn't try to answer, but his eyes fill with tears.

"I had a learning disability," he mused. "I think I still have it. Nobody diagnosed it, but I know I got it. I understand that I can't learn that fast. But there are things that I can do. I'm pretty good with tools. I can do things by teaching myself, tool by tool. With hard work you can excel.

"My grandmother taught me that first. Father re-taught me that."

* * *

Countless hours were spent on personal service by Monsignor McDermott and Dr. West—to the homeless on Skid Row, to families of alcoholics, and to clergy who were struggling with trying to stay sober. But the priest's greatest accomplishment was his defiant resiliency—it rescued alcoholics from being violators of the law. Thanks largely to Ignatius McDermott, the decriminalization of the inebriate was secured, then came substitution of state-financed treatment rather than imprisonment. With Dr. West, he won public support for the program over the opposition of much of the medical community. It is known as social setting detox, validation of which began with an experiment in Canada.

Decriminalization of the inebriate involved a long campaign of education by Monsignor McDermott, Dr. West, and others. It came as a confrontation to lawmakers who maintained that those who drank too much did so because they wanted to—and that inability to stay sober was due to moral weakness. Criminalization played into the hands of those who turned their backs on the alcoholics because they were degraded, believing that the state and public opinion was fully justified to practice a kind of sorcery by punishing them for their ill deeds. At bottom, they rejected alcoholism as a disease.

To this view Dr. West has replied, "Let's start with the basic definition of all disease, which assumes that it has a harmful effect on the body or mind or both. Each disease has a train of signs and symptoms, which we see as clinicians, that can differentiate one disease from another. Alcoholism possesses a unique profile: gradually progressive loss of control over alcohol use, a preoccupation with acquiring alcohol, a continued use in spite of adverse consequences, and a pattern of relapse to alcohol consumption."

Yes, some lawmakers countered, but why should we remove from the criminal code a condition which is behavioral?

"All these symptoms are behavioral," Dr. West replied, "but some may have a physiological basis, such as an initial increased tolerance to alcohol or an especially positive response to alcohol, that may be a function of the neurotransmitter system in the brain. Further indications that alcoholism is a disease are the conclusions of familial and genetic studies that traced twins separated at birth. It was observed that alcoholism is an inherited primary disorder and operates independently of other personality and psychiatric disorders. Evidence continues to surface pointing to the fact that the relationship between brain chemistry and behavior is more than likely genetic."

Dr. West supplied the medical analysis and Monsignor McDermott the persuasion and utilization of the political arts, which ultimately won the battle.

The campaign to win public support for decriminalization and use of public funds for treatment lasted five years. It tested Dr. West's medical and psychiatric expertise as well as Monsignor McDermott's inherited native political skill.

The revolution in care for the addicted—the decriminalization of the inebriate and resultant "social setting detoxification" (detoxification without medication)—began in the late 1960s when Dr. West came across an article in a medical journal that stressed (in his words) "the power of the social involvement of caring people with the person who's detoxifying."

"It works a heck of a lot better than medicines or a hospital room," he explained. "There was an example of what was going on in this area in Toronto. I decided I was going to go there. I talked to Monsignor about it and said, 'I'm thinking of going to Toronto.' He said, 'When are you going?' I said, 'I think tomorrow or the next day.' And he said, 'I'll go with you.' I showed him the article. We went to Canada to learn something, and we did learn something," said Dr. West.

It was a quick flight, leaving Chicago O'Hare at 6 a.m. and returning at 11 p.m. the same day. "We learned something we thought was taking place in an informal way in homes and basements and bathrooms and bedrooms all over the country," said Dr. West, "namely, people detoxing themselves—but this would be a safe way to do it." Once there, Monsignor McDermott met a man who used to be on Skid Row; he was now working as a counselor in Toronto.

"The setting was that there can be a place, a safe place," Dr. West explained, "where the detoxifying alcoholic could come to sober up, detoxify, in a protected place where he could be nourished with good food and also some care ensuring that, no matter what shape he was in, he would be welcomed here. That worked as psychotherapeutically and effectively as detoxifying medications. We brought that back and tried to convince, for about three years, the alcoholism committee in the state Department of Mental Health and Developmental Disabilities that this was a great idea."

The usual forces that opposed decriminalization since 1970—lobbyists for the state medical society and hospital associations—mobilized to work against the team of McDermott and West.

Medical traditionalists argued: Look, the police will have no other recourse but to bring drunks to hospital emergency rooms. McDermott and West countered: *No, the bill would enable the state to fund treatment centers.* Nonsense, went the rejoinder, treatment centers would inevitably draw upon the resources of private hospitals and physicians whose services the state would not be able to provide, and private hospitals would be drained to fill the need, since physicians should be in attendance during detox.

Not really, said McDermott-West. *There is a whole new concept of treatment for alcoholics called "social setting detox" which does not involve person-to-person attendance by physicians. Besides, is it not incongruous that the healing arts professions are lobbying for imprisonment where little or no medical treatment is supplied for the public inebriate?*

So-called "treatment" without medical attention is recklessness, a dangerous fallacy, argued the medical society and hospitals. On the side of McDermott-West were the alcoholism councils and the mental health community, including the state Department of Mental Health and Developmental Disabilities, insisting that the progressive view of treatment would necessitate little or no medical supervision.

Dr. West's immense medical prestige, linked with Monsignor McDermott's matchless reputation, convinced state governmental authorities; but what also helped was a change in political command. Governor Richard B. Ogilvie's Department of Mental Health and Developmental Disabilities had initially opposed, but gradually came around to supporting, social setting detox. However, Ogilvie was defeated in 1972. His successor, Democrat Dan Walker, strongly favored the initiative.

After five years of false starts and interruptions, in 1975 the legislative battle was joined. The medical society "came out with the idea that [social setting detox] is not a safe idea," says Dr. West. "I knew it was safe. They thought that to do this kind of work with seriously ill people outside of a hospital wasn't a good thing. They weren't thinking of the hundreds of people who were doing the same thing in the Monroe Street jail every night. In fact, there were a couple of people in the alcoholism treatment business who were not for it. From the medical standpoint, they thought that anybody who was going to detox needed medications to keep from going into convulsive seizures and *delirium tremens*, which has a high death rate of about 15 percent. They asked 'How are you going to take these people in without any medicine and try to get them through detoxification?'

"I said, 'The only thing you can do is let us do it because we've seen it happen in Toronto, and it makes sense to do it. Everybody who has had a seizure has probably detoxified at home 30 times before he comes to a hospital. And once we get a guy who's in *DTs* already, which is a serious thing, we are only five minutes away from Cook County Hospital—where we transport them, give them the medicine, and bring them back to our place.'"

Victory in the struggle marked a turning point in treatment of alcoholic addiction and launched state assistance for the effort. In the state Senate, the job of piloting the legislation was given to Senator Dawn Clark Netsch, Chicago Democrat, ranking minority member on the Senate Welfare Committee. She was aided by fresh liberal forces in Governor Dan Walker's state Department of Mental Health and Developmental Disabilities.

"No matter what you think of Dan Walker now," says Netsch of the man who, after his single gubernatorial term, was convicted in 1988 for misuse of funds from his savings and loan in suburban Oak Brook, "he had a darned good mental health program."

Senator Netsch was later state comptroller and the 1994 Democratic nominee for governor. Joining her in the legislative battle in the Democrat-dominated House was Representative Eugenia Chapman, Arlington Heights, chairman of the Human Resources Committee. She turned over the bill to Robert Downs, a freshman Democrat from Oak Park.

Interviewed 24 years after he introduced the legislation, now a private citizen and lawyer, Downs admits that the issue "was one in which I didn't have the slightest interest. It had no relevance to my district [an upper middle class, then Republican-leaning suburb]."

But as he held hearings on it throughout the state, he tangled with heated opposition from the medical societies, many private hospitals, and some local law enforcement agencies, which whetted his appetite for victory. On his side were, in addition to the team of McDermott and West, Catholic Charities—somewhat dubious as to whether or not it should be involved but rather timidly following Monsignor McDermott's lead—state and local mental health associations, the Illinois Alcoholism Council, and the state Department of Mental Health and Developmental Disabilities.

Much of the debate turned on humanitarianism—and the issue of the imprisonment of the public inebriate. Once it was reasoned that a lock-up was not solving the problem, the issue dealt with costs to the taxpayer. All sides agreed that society paid a severe cost in human carnage for mistreated and maltreated inebriates who went through the revolving doors of prisons. When it came to treatment, the question centered on: *What was more expensive for the taxpayer—medical treatment in hospital emergency rooms or in state-subsidized detox centers?* Dr. Sam Cardone, then a staffer in the mental health department's division of alcoholism, says that the average cost per patient per day in a state-subsidized social setting detox facility was $50 per client compared to the average cost per day of a client in a general hospital, which was from $500 to $600 per day—a telling argument.

Still, traditionalists weren't convinced. When they finally came around, "Monsignor McDermott is probably the reason," Dr. West explained.

The Senate—the toughest test—went first. Rallying as many Republicans to join her as she could, Senator Netsch carried the decriminalization bill by only two votes, 24 aye, 22 nay, and one voting present on June 26, 1975. Five months later it passed the House easily, 109 aye, 42 nay, 14 voting present. The legislation was entitled *The Alcoholism and Intoxication Treatment Act*, and its Section 1 gave this as its central theme: *"It is the policy of this State that alcoholics and intoxicated persons engaged in public drunkenness may not be subjected to criminal prosecution solely because of their consumption of alco-*

holic beverages but rather should be afforded a continuum of treatment in order that they may lead normal lives as productive members of society."

The Act (which at its passage dealt only with alcoholism, not drug abuse) established a division of alcoholism within the state mental health department to develop statewide, regional and local plans for prevention and treatment. Enacted in 1975, it received funding in 1976.

Promptly, even before state funding started, Monsignor McDermott moved to launch an institution to receive those addicted to alcohol. What to call it? Why not "Haymarket," in recognition of the 1886 struggle? Termed "radical," it was merely one to win an eight-hour working day that had been a struggle which, like sobriety, was won only after sacrifice, pain and suffering. The original Haymarket Riot spurred a revolution for workers' rights; this Haymarket would dramatize a very real revolution for treatment, not incarceration and opprobrium for the addicted. So "Haymarket House" it would be called.

Monsignor McDermott and Dr. West were confronted with a problem. Under then church-state "separation" views, state government could not fund a single religious entity and Haymarket, as conceived, would be the property of Catholic Charities. Monsignor McDermott found an answer through the "Chicago Clergy Association for the Homeless Person." It consisted of the Salvation Army, the Chicago Christian Industrial League, the Cathedral Shelter (an arm of the Episcopal church), and Catholic Charities.

The Clergy Association filed papers as a non-sectarian, non-denominational, not-for-profit agency. The state agreed it would be the recipient of the funds. Dr. Sam Cardone, a clinical psychologist with the state Department of Mental Health and Developmental Disabilities, contacted Monsignor McDermott and advised him that Haymarket would be one of four agencies to be funded on an experimental basis—at $80,000 each.

The big question was: *How would Haymarket be funded for six months until state funding arrived?* Overtures were made to private sources but, at first, drew negative responses. Then came a breakthrough on a day in late 1975 when Dr. West was teaching psychiatry at Rush-Presbyterian-St. Luke's Hospital.

"I was eating in the dining room with the doctors," he said, "when some kind of a person showed up and wanted to see me. He said, 'I'm here to talk to you about an idea that you and Monsignor McDermott have about social setting detoxification.' I didn't know who he was. I thought he was maybe a reporter or something. It turns out that he was from the Chicago Community Trust."

The Chicago Community Trust is the largest foundation in Chicago, a consortium of private giving. How did it learn about the experiment? Through news reports of the legislation—but no one really remembers applying for a grant there.

"I always thought an angel appeared," said Dr. West. "That's what I thought. I don't know how else to put it. God works through humans. I never heard about them before. So he thanked me, and the next thing, Monsignor McDermott called me and said, 'You know, the man we talked to is interested—and we're going to his office to talk to members of the board.' We did, and got the money to operate for six months."

The Community Trust money was sorely needed—not just by McDermott-West but by the police. Raymond Soucek, now president and chief executive officer of Haymarket Center, tells the story: "The police needed some place to take [the street people]. The only places that would take them were the emergency rooms of hospitals, which was not an appropriate setting." Haymarket House came just in time. "So social setting detox was a concept that the police gravitated to very quickly," says Soucek. "Paddy wagons and squads would continuously pick up the guys from the Street and drop them off at Haymarket."

And where was the first Haymarket? Initially there was a hope that it would be at 117 North Desplaines where an eccentric owner, who would occasionally grab a free lunch at the Charities' soup line, reportedly had $1 million to give to the project. On June 5, 1974 (according to an interior staff memo) it appeared almost *fait accompli*—but it didn't work out. So Haymarket began at 12 South Peoria Street, in the basement and first floor of a ramshackle building owned by the Chicago Christian Industrial League. Haymarket House opened on an auspicious day known to all alcoholic and non-alcoholic revelers—December 31, 1975, New Year's Eve.

"The guys would stay there, sober up," Soucek continued, "get a sandwich, leave the building and drift around and return maybe a few hours—or few days—later. So it was a revolving door concept but the results were that people did not, in fact, lose fingers and toes to frostbite, did not get sunstroke, were not invading the Cook County Hospital emergency room or other emergency rooms. Now there was a place that could treat these people.

"The program was highly monitored by Dr. West who came there every day. He would instruct his staff as to what's an emergency, what's not, what's critical." This was in addition to his heavy schedule of surgery ("I had two assistants on my staff who helped out," he says).

"The rule of thumb was, when in doubt, refer them to a hospital," explained Soucek. "Obviously, the program was under a looking glass. It was controversial because no medications were used. People were taking a very close look at it to see if it was working."

Dr. Cardone remembers how frightened the early Haymarket staff was of possible misuse of state funds.

"I got this frantic call from Ann Konar who was the first director of the program. She said, 'Sam, you've got to get over here!' I said, 'What's up?' She said, 'We have lice, badly.'" They wanted to be sure that the time and effort removing the lice was covered under the state appropriation. Dr. Cardone assured her it was.

He says, laughing, "I think they wanted my support. They wanted me to know they were not misusing the state's money. So I made lots of visits, and I tried to be encouraging and helpful and tried to be in the mix, in terms of trying to help them through what I knew was going to be a bumpy period. That was my job."

Dr. Cardone would canvass the regional police stations while Monsignor McDermott covered Skid Row, recruiting men who needed help to become clients of Haymarket House. Dr. Cardone tried to space out the clients with the available rooms and staff assistance.

"There were times when the police would drop off seven to ten people at a time so, on occasion, Haymarket was inundated with clients. The clients were also riddled with what are called 'wine sores.' They were very unkempt. They had many layers of clothing and layers of not being clean. They were in various levels of disarray and distress—so we had a process of showering the clients first thing and using a special soap called 'Quell,' which is a disinfectant."

Dr. Cardone says "we" because he became enlisted in the effort far more than as a fund administrator. He wanted the social setting detox of Haymarket to work.

"So we worked very closely together," he said. "At the time they had about three on the first shift, three on the second shift, and maybe one on the third shift. It was very difficult to get people to work with this population. I remember talking to the staff and they said, 'Hey, Dr. Cardone, I'm not going to touch these people! They're filthy, they're smelly, they're full of disease!' It was difficult once they started there to keep them on."

As 1976 ended, Monsignor McDermott was now 67, a time when most men contemplate retirement or at least throttling down. But he had only begun his apostolate to the addicted. The priest had a huge job ahead of him, as can be seen from research by James Mills, author of *The Panic in Needle Park*. Mills explains the change that had come to America from within and without.

"The inhabitants of the earth spend more money on illegal drugs than they spend on food," he wrote in his book, *The Underground Empire: Where Crime and Governments Embrace*, a survey of the drug traffic. "More than they spend on housing, clothes, education, medical care or any other product or service. The international narcotics industry is the largest growth industry in the world. Its annual revenues exceed half a trillion dollars—three times the value of all U.S. currency in circulation, more than the gross national product of all but a half dozen of the major industrialized nations."

The illegal drug industry, however, has been welcomed, in some quarters of the U.S., by a nihilistic culture that has responded to prosperity with decadence and increased drug use based on lack of philosophical certainty, points out Dr. William J. Bennett, former federal drug czar under President George H.W. Bush.

Dr. Myron Magnet, a widely quoted social psychologist agreed, describing the changing culture within the country in these terms in *The Dream and the Nightmare: The Sixties' Legacy to the Underclass.* "Key shapers of American thought and belief—especially since World War II, when student bodies became larger and more diverse—colleges and universities traditionally transmitted a legacy of Western secular culture that had assumed a particular importance in the 20th century. [Since Darwin theorized] an entirely different account of the origin of species and the descent of man from the scriptural account, the religious understanding of the world has inexorably crumbled and a secular one has taken its place. In our century, religious certitude about divine authority has ceased to be the principal foundation of our beliefs, values and morality."

Dr. Magnet says it would be bad enough if only the "Haves" would defect; but in his view, the "Haves" have infected the poor.

"The cultural revolution created a spiritual vacuum that greedy selfishness could invade and fill," he wrote, "which opens the gateways to alcohol abuse and illegal drug addiction."

To which journalist Ben Wattenberg added in his book, *Values Matter Most*, that illegal drug use is not victim-free since it multiplies crime.

Finally, Haymarket's own Dr. James West, in his *The Betty Ford Center Book of Answers*, has stated that "while in the sixties the hippies got a little high from smoking weed, today's young people and not-so-young people who are smoking marijuana are experiencing a much more intense and damaging high, leaving them more vulnerable to its addictive consequences. In general, the choice of drugs seems to come in waves, depending on availability and a search for a new and increasing high or escape. But it's clear that drugs continue to come in many forms, and that, often hidden from public view is unwitting dependence on a variety of potent and dangerous prescription drugs."

Thus, the role of Haymarket expanded to include treatment of the drug addicted, not just alcoholics.

*   *   *

Moreover, the task, as Ignatius McDermott saw it in the late '70s (the goal came to fruition in the late '80s), was to add women to the Haymarket clientele. Why weren't they there up to now? Dr. Sam Cardone, the clinical psychologist, said it has to do with a combination of factors. First, the nature of the woman alcoholic led her to avoid Skid Row. Of 140 Skid Row habitués he studied in those early formative days, only a handful were women. *Reason*: women alcoholics were being housed by men who would use them, and abuse them, but their condition would keep them from the Street.

Second, there were few women in the statistics because of the prevailing prejudice against women alcoholics in the 1960s and '70s. The view that they were promiscuous or had abandoned their children or were prostitutes pictured them as social outcasts who would not be welcome anywhere, so they stayed away—stayed away from the Skid Row bars and from the Street.

"They were not welcome in most hospital emergency rooms," Dr. Cardone said. "They were treated as though they were hysterical and over-emotional; they were regarded as if they were exaggerating their illnesses. An alcoholic woman managed to find a male who would abuse her, beat her, would do all kinds of negative things, but she would stay because she had a roof over her head. And she might well go from one man to another."

Absence of women in the statistics led governmental agencies to believe, mistakenly, that there was no problem. But Monsignor McDermott knew there *was* a problem, only it was hidden. As the drug culture expanded, he worried about the women. What could he do to get them as clients—and, further, to help pregnant women get off drugs and alcohol so that their children would be born addiction-free?

These thoughts consumed Ignatius McDermott as he neared age 70. He continued to push forward. God meant him to be a game finisher, not a relief starter.

"Today's world is over-saturated with a surplus of starters," he told his staff at Haymarket. "A surplus of starters and a famine of finishers."

The staff smiled gratefully. Their Father Mac was telling them that because he expected them to play all nine innings, he was in the game to the finish—for the long haul.

*   *   *

The countless corporal works of mercy continued. Known to many policemen and firemen, Monsignor Ignatius McDermott would continue to do what he does to this day—buy day-old rolls and biscuits and deliver them to his own agencies and to others serving the homeless.

CHAPTER 9

The Flowering of an Idea, 1976–1985

You know who I'd like to talk to in the Great Beyond? John XXIII. I'd ask him how Vatican II was so twisted that they destroyed so many great things in the Church.

With the coming of Joseph Cardinal Bernardin to Chicago, I received a letter one day thanking me for my sensitivity to priests who were hurting, and that's it. You wouldn't have to be an Aristotle to figure out that you were being sacked.

—Ignatius McDermott

While Monsignor McDermott was helping to win change in the care and treatment of the addicted, dramatic post-conciliar innovations stemming from Vatican II [1959–1965] had transformed the Catholic Church. Now, through what seems like instant change, not only was the Mass to be celebrated in the vernacular, rather than the Latin usage, but the format of the Tridentine Mass, codified by the Council of Trent [1545–1563], and even then in usage for a thousand years, was sharply revised.

An illustration of the sudden change: On Septuagesima Sunday, February 14, 1965, almost every church altar in the U.S. was turned around and, for the first time in a millennium, the priest said Mass facing the congregation and in the vernacular.

Even more significant, while the Council produced a decree, *Lumen Gentium* [Dogmatic Constitution of the Church], which contained the strongest possible reaffirmation of hierarchical authority, two generations of Catholics had now been educated to believe that, in effect, the Council abolished the hierarchical conception of the Church. Not so. But as Church scholar James Hitchcock has pointed out, "The disorders which have plagued the Church since the Council all stem from the fact that the conciliar decrees, very general in nature, were set forth without much regard for the cultural context of the times...with no suspicion that the entire Western world was about to be engulfed in a major cultural crisis, assaulting its most fundamental beliefs, and that in such a situation the conciliar decrees, perfectly orthodox in themselves, perfectly in harmony with tradition, would be given contentious interpretations."

Misinterpretations of the Council by radical theologians confused the role of priest for many (blurring the priestly vocation with that of secular political activist, resulting in the abandonment of the religious life by many). Disarray and arbitrary challenges to episcopal authority, in the words of Hitchcock, "tended to propel one of the most self-confident and enduring institutions in the history of the world into what seemed to be an identity crisis of significant proportions, a crisis that has not been resolved yet. Immediately after the Council, rectories, convents and monasteries were revealed to be filled with those who desired nothing so much as to lead ordinary lives as their culture understood the ordinary, who were weary of holding the world on their shoulders, who were shedding the burdens of specialness."

A cogent listing of wholesale, freelance liturgical changes in the Church—approved and unapproved—has come from Father Frederic Heuser, in the key Catholic publication, *Homiletic & Pastoral Review* [December 2000]. They include: an entirely new Mass in the vernacular with the priest facing the people; laypeople allowed to touch the Sacred Host and vessels; diminution of the Eucharistic fast; occasional receiving of Holy Communion under both species (as Protestants do); receiving Holy Communion standing instead of kneeling; removal of many Communion rails; proliferation of laypeople in the sanctuary as ministers of Holy Communion; allowing girls to be altar servers; the practical elimination of Friday abstinence and the Lenten fast; discarding of religious garb by many priests and sisters; loss of the Legion of Decency, which issued guides to films; neglect of the rosary and Virgin Mary; lack of insistence of children attending Catholic schools; allowing Catholic weddings in Protestant churches; wholesale annulments of marriages as constituting "divorce Catholic style"; lack of respect for bishops; many bishops acting more like politicians than shepherds; dropping Ember Days,

Rogation Days, and vigils of great Feast Days; complete revision of the Church calendar, including switching of Feast Days that had been stable for centuries; stark, modernist architecture for many new churches, with traditional art replaced by a barrenness identified with Calvinism; radical renovation of glorious old churches to accommodate the stark modernist style.

Illustrative of the challenges to Catholicism were to be found in the book *The People Are the Church*, by Eugene Kennedy, then a Chicago priest-psychologist. The book insisted that the Church "must cast aside the absurdity of rigid legalism if it is to provide man with a spiritual structure that reflects his nature and spirit." Kennedy added: "It is time to take a stand for man. The Church is for man and must meet his needs or it is operating from a basic misunderstanding of itself." The book underscored, for many, a revolution inside the Church. Unsurprisingly, because he was at odds with Church structure, Kennedy later resigned from the priesthood and married. He became a novelist and biographer, known for his memoir of Joseph Cardinal Bernardin.

Vatican II didn't cause the disarray. Far from being a summons to revolution and indiscriminate challenges to Church governance and liturgy, Vatican II, as famed theologian and now Cardinal Avery Dulles, S.J., has written, reaffirmed the classic Catholic doctrine of human life on earth as tension between the natural and supernatural, the eternal and temporal, the material and spiritual with allusion to Augustine's concept of two cities [*Gaudium et Spes: Pastoral Constitution on the Church in the Modern World*, 1965].

Nevertheless, clashes were prompted by erroneous, occasionally mischievous, misapplications of the Council by often radical theologians. Then, too, with the supposed "liberation" of the laity, often personal egos would get in the way. Case in point: *Humanae Vitae*, the encyclical issued by Paul VI, on July 25, 1968, reaffirmed the Church's condemnation of artificial contraception. Originally, John XXIII took the question out of the hands of the Council and appointed a special commission to study the matter.

The commission was to operate within the guidelines of *Casti Connubii* ["Chaste Marriage"], according to Redemptorist theologian Bernard Haering. A prominent Chicago couple, Patrick and Patty Crowley, founders of the Cana Conference and Christian Family Movement [CFM], served on the commission and started as advocates of traditionalism before both switched positions in favor of contraception. An address by Paul VI gave a misplaced hope to some Catholic liberals that there would be a change. Initially, a majority of the commission voted to endorse artificial contraception, but when Paul VI stuck with the traditionalists, there was an outcry of disunion. Church historian James Hitchcock reports, "Some of the roots of American dissent [came from] the Cana Conference and Christian Family Movement, both of which originated in the archdiocese of Chicago." Although at first composed of intensely loyal and devout laypeople, Hitchcock writes, "By 1959, members of both movements had already begun to show signs of restlessness and an arrogant determination to move in directions inconsistent with Catholic teaching. During the Council, this tendency was escalated by the movement's director, Father Walter Imbiorski, and the Crowleys used their positions as members of the official commission in Rome to lobby for a change in doctrine, on the grounds that most CFM members wanted it." (In the process, Imbiorski subsequently left the priesthood and married, tracing a pattern that would soon become common among dissenters—demanding freedom of expression for dissent even as he systematically excluded orthodox speakers from addressing CFM meetings. The highest ranking prelate to defect was James Shannon, former president of St. Thomas College, St. Paul, Minnesota, and auxiliary bishop of the diocese of St. Paul-Minneapolis.)

Reaction to *Humanae Vitae* by Catholic liberals was fierce. In the U.S., secular and even some Catholic media gave huge attention to theologians and priests and nuns who supported contraception, while the voices of those who supported the encyclical were muted. In Chicago, Father Andrew Greeley, a sociologist and newspaper columnist, later to become a best-selling novelist, seemed to lead the assault, along with ex-priests Eugene Kennedy and Robert McClory.

The rumblings of discontent with ecclesiastical authority spread into dioceses worldwide. In Chicago, criticism of the administrative style of John Cardinal Cody (a close friend of Paul VI) came to resemble a political *putsch*, with newspaper-floated rumors that the beleaguered cardinal had diverted archdiocesan insurance business to a relative. The rumors became so prevalent that the office of the United States Attorney for the Northern District of Illinois, in 1981, opened an investigation of his finances. Nearing his 75th year, Cody's health began to fail as he fended off his attackers. He died in his residence on April 23, 1982. The charges against him were never proven; indeed, the office concluded that it was entirely possible that the disbursements in question came from the cardinal's personal funds. Cardinal Cody's troubles were worsened by his seeming inability to communicate to suspicious critics within the Church and to the secular media outside it.

All the same, Vatican II's true perspective enabled Monsignor McDermott to harmonize his work as a priest loyal to the Church's teaching *magisterium* and as chairman of Haymarket Center, a secular institution.

In 1978, the death of Paul VI (a man detailed, meticulous, but who agonized over decisions) gave the Church, as pope, the former patriarch of Venice, whose parents had been active socialists and who, himself, had been accommodative with Italian communists, 66-year-old Albino Luciani, who took the name John Paul I. With his election, the College of Cardinals demonstrated that it wished a completely new style of pope without connections to the curial establishment. Indeed, the omen seemed bright when Luciani, impatient of pomp and papal trappings, insisted on foregoing the coronation ceremony in favor of being invested with the *palladium*, a blanket of lamb's wool, as token of his pastoral office. The first pope of working-class origins in centuries, he stunned the world by holding the first open papal press conference before a thousand highly impressed journalists. It was thought that he would be another precedent-shattering progressive.

Three weeks later, he was found dead of a heart attack. Rumors of foul play were fanned by lack of autopsy. It had been said that he was poisoned because he wished to clean up a financial scandal at the Vatican Bank, demote certain curial officials, and revise *Humanae Vitae*, but the evidence produced was a tissue of improbabilities. A previously undisclosed poor health record convinced even skeptical secular journalists that his death was a natural one. Even as vitriolic a critic of Catholicism as Britain's John Cardwell, an investigative journalist, discovered that the vitality of John Paul's public presence was illusory. Luciani had a long history of circulatory problems for which he had received no medical treatment since the papal election. Accepting his election as an act of obedience, he was soon overwhelmed by the enormity of his administrative duties for which, by some accounts, according to papal scholar George Weigel, "He was given little help from the permanent staff in adjusting to his new situation." His remark to the College of Cardinals on his election: "May God forgive you for what you have done"—an echo of St. Bernard of Clairvaux—was recalled later as a prophecy of what was to be a death warrant.

Luciani was succeeded by the first Slavic and the first non-Italian since Hadrian VI of Utrecht in 1522, Karol Wojtyla [born 1920], who chose as his name John Paul II. The new pope would be far different from either Paul or his immediate successor. Wojtyla was an intellectual, hardened by experience in Cold War Poland, where he studied theology clandestinely while he worked a laborer's job in a limestone quarry outside Krakow. He rose in the hierarchy as a politically astute but forceful adversary of the repressive communist system. In his third encyclical, *Laborem Exercens*, written while recovering from a gunshot wound from an assassination attempt in 1981, he called for a new economic order—not capitalist or Marxist—but based on the rights of workers and the dignity of labor. John Paul II's favorite, immediately successful method of communication was to make spectacular, skillfully organized journeys to countries near and far.

Few popes have had such wide-ranging intellectual impact as John Paul II, possessor of doctorates in philosophy and theology, who had trained in his youth as an actor. His approach to theology, ethics, and politics is conservative. As early as 1979, he summoned the Dutch professor Edward Schillebeecks to Rome to explain his heterodox views on Christology, and asked German bishops to withdraw the license of Hans Küng to teach theology. In 1980, in a letter to the world's bishops [*Dominicae Cenae*], he sought to apologize "in my own name and in the name of all of you, venerable and dear brothers in the episcopate, for everything which, for whatever reason, through whatever human weakness...may have caused scandal and disturbance" through misinterpretations of Vatican II. That same year, in Chicago, he confirmed the Church's traditional teaching on marriage, contraception, abortion, and homosexuality, which certified him as seeking to restore to the Church the sense of direction it seemed in danger of losing in the latter years of Paul VI's pontificate. The pope would strive, against sometimes radical opposition, to validate traditional Catholicism, seeking to reinstitute its continuity with prior generations and reinvigorate the Church with zeal for evangelization.

*   *   *

In the Chicago archdiocese, three weeks after the death of John Cardinal Cody in 1982, Rome had announced the appointment by Paul VI, believed to have been made tentatively during Cody's last illness, of Joseph Louis Bernardin as Chicago's archbishop. The archbishop of Cincinnati, Bernardin [1928-1996] was born in Columbia, South Carolina, was educated in public schools before attending the seminary, and was ordained for the diocese of Charleston. He served under four bishops in many capacities. In 1966, he was ordained auxiliary bishop of Atlanta where, as the youngest bishop in the U.S., he worked with Archbishop Paul Hallinan, his first important mentor.

In 1968, he was elected general secretary of the National Conference of Catholic Bishops, to which he later was elected chairman. He attained national attention with the secular media as a progressive, drafting a pastoral letter signed by all U.S. bishops, "The Challenge of Peace," which opposed a unilateral defense buildup. With Reverend J. Bryan Heheir, he later articulated for the bishops what he called "a consistent ethic of life," moved away from single opposition to abortion, tying to that position views which squared with reformist liberal constituencies by supporting nuclear disarmament and opposition to the death penalty.

As a result, he was cited often as the leading liberal Catholic churchman in America by proponents of an "American Catholic Church," distinct from an institution shaped by curial decrees. In Chicago, he launched a "Big Shoulders Fund" to support the inner-city parochial school system. The fund raised $62 million in 10 years and implemented what he called a "collaborative style of leadership" in which progressive priests and theologians were dominant. He was elevated to cardinal in 1983. Soon after Bernardin's appointment, Monsignor McDermott received a letter from His Eminence thanking the priest for his past work with clerics troubled by addiction. And there were additional changes to come.

"With the coming of Joseph Cardinal Bernardin to Chicago," says Monsignor McDermott, "I received a letter one day saying he thanked me for my sensitivity to priests who were hurting, and that's it. You wouldn't have to be an Aristotle to figure out that you were being sacked."

Initially, Charities de-linked him from direction of the Sousa Center and as director of Holy Cross Mission, moving, at first, without his knowledge. In trying to get homeless people placed, he would find greater than expected difficulty—yet his name, the most recognizable in the Charities, was still on the stationery when Catholic Charities made its annual request for funds. But while the unhorsing of Ignatius McDermott appeared a setback at first, it was ultimately another providential occurrence.

So, at an age when other men stepped down, he fought a rearguard action within Charities—intent on not only staying active with Charities, but in doing far more ambitious things than it would allow. To many, he should probably have been administrator of Catholic Charities and moved beyond that to a bishopric, but he was a heroic foe of the get-along, go-along Church bureaucracy.

"He had novel, fresh ideas," says a former archdiocesan official. "He was the true entrepreneur who could start businesses that paid. His businesses paid for themselves, didn't run in the red. He made money."

"His colleagues," says an executive close to Charities who insists on anonymity, "got all this money and invested in annuities and stuff, saving the money, preserving the principal. They always asked, 'McDermott, where's the money?' which meant: never innovate, never take risks."

Raymond Soucek, Haymarket president and CEO, who had worked for Monsignor McDermott at Charities, agrees. "He was a zero-base budget master. With Charities, the only way they would see a program through was to spend every dollar you earned, but they would not support it beyond that. In the case of drunken drivers and the DUI program, Father was able to work the deals with the courts to get the rooms and the phone services and, in exchange for that, he provided an arm for the court to sentence DUI offenders."

In his later years, Catholic Charities couldn't appreciate him. Why not?

"First off," says the observer, knowledgeable about the inner workings of the organization, "Charities didn't want to rock the boat. McDermott would come up with a new idea and they would give him 25 reasons why it wouldn't work. When he bought the Haymarket building, they listed that many reasons why he shouldn't have done it. All those people would tell you why it couldn't work. Then, when it worked, they thought they could take it over from him. They had good intentions. They were good people, but they weren't right. They didn't understand the whole thing.

"Charities was always afraid of him," says the observer familiar with the era. "Cooke [the late Monsignor Vincent Cooke, administrator of Charities] said McDermott was a poor businessman; he had developed a reputation of being a poor businessman."

To this charge, the former archdiocesan executive says with passion: "He's *not* a poor businessman. He's a great leader." Agreed, says the former Charities administrator. McDermott "was a genius with a bunch of slugs. The genius was tied hand and foot; he couldn't do anything."

A second former high-level administrator at the chancery, now retired, agrees. "McDermott was *too good* a businessman," he said. "Too good in the sense that he had ideas that were better than his bosses' and they never forgave him for it.

"Early on, Ignatius McDermott was focused on the issue of alcoholism and drug dependency—which could have been concentrated entirely in Catholic Charities, but they would have nothing to do with something new or fresh. There he was always put down, put down because he was alone. There was nobody else there with him."

* * *

Monsignor McDermott's gradual displacement reflected change that came to Catholic Charities nationally. A penetrating analysis by the prestigious Manhattan Institute, a leading national urban think tank, shows how philanthropy became a liberal—some say leftist—quasi-political entity. Writing in the organization's *City Journal* ["How Catholic Charities Lost Its Soul"] in January 2000, Brian Anderson describes the radical direction that became, for a time, the bureaucracy of Catholic Charities USA.

> As advanced social thinkers rediscover the power of faith-based institutions to rescue the down-and-out by transforming the dysfunctional worldview that often lies at the root of their difficulties, you would think that Catholic Charities USA would be a perfect model to emulate, getting the poor into the mainstream by emphasizing moral values

and ethical conduct. But no: rather than trying to promote traditional values and God-fearing behavior, Catholic Charities has become over the last three decades an arm of the welfare state, with 65 percent of its $2.3 billion annual budget now flowing from government sources and little that is explicitly religious, or even values-laden, about most of the services its 1,400 member agencies and 46,000 paid employees provide.

Far from being a model for reforming today's welfare state approach to helping the poor, Catholic Charities USA is one of the nation's most powerful advocates for outworn welfare state ideas, especially the idea that social and economic forces over which the individual has no control, rather than his own attitudes and behavior, are the reason for poverty.

He notes:

> Catholic Charities first announced its politicization in a wild-eyed manifesto that invokes such radical sixties icons as Malcolm X, Gloria Steinem, Herbert Marcuse and—above all—the Marxist-inspired Liberation Theology Movement that (to put it crudely) equates Jesus with Che Guevara. Ratified at Catholic Charities' annual meeting in 1972, the so-called Cadre Study totally abandoned any stress on personal responsibility in relation to poverty and other social ills. Instead, it painted America as an unjust, 'numb' country, whose oppressive society and closed economy cause people to turn to crime or drugs or prostitution. Moreover, the study asserts, individual acts of charity are useless. We must instead unearth 'the root causes of poverty and oppression' and radically reconstruct—'humanize and transform'—the social order to avert social upheaval.

Some argue that governmental funding corrupted Catholic Charities USA. But this Anderson denies:

> In fact, CC officially already sincerely believed that government entitlements are the best way to help the needy when they began accepting government funding.

Comments Father Richard John Neuhaus, an urban activist who marched with Martin Luther King, Jr., and founder of the Institute on Religion and Public Life: "It is up to religious institutions to preserve their religious integrity. Defenders of CC and similar, albeit smaller, organizations in the Protestant and Jewish communities will protest that they do a lot of good. That is quite true, and quite beside the point of Anderson's critique. They do great damage by helping to perpetuate the excesses of welfarism and, even more important, by severely compromising, if not betraying, the spiritual and moral commitment that brought them into being in the first place."

"By the early 1980s, Monsignor McDermott had a real network going," Soucek says. "He was, in fact, a one-man conglomerate with the role he held at Catholic Charities; with ACES (Addiction Consultation and Educational Services), working with families of alcoholics; Central States Institute of Addiction, providing education to DUI offenders; Holy Cross Mission; Haymarket (variously called Haymarket House and Haymarket Center), utilizing social setting detox; Cees Manor; Sousa Center's program for homeless men and women; and the Chicago Clergy Association for the Homeless Person.

That was the high point of the McDermott leadership at Charities. The bureaucratic opposition to his entrepreneurial style was growing. It began with Sousa Center. Jim Mchugh, the retired trucker and volunteer helper, tells the story about the residence for homeless men.

"One day Father said to me, 'Jim, I'm asking you. Catholic Charities said they can run Sousa Center cheaper than I'm running it. What do you think?' I said, 'Father, you must be kidding. How can they run it cheaper? Don McCready gets $4.00 [an hour]. I get nothing. Some days we're over there for hours, maybe cleaning out the rain gutters where the trees overhang. How's it possible that they can do it? They call a plumber in and see what he's going to charge you! We go around and we shop, like for the round things for the shower, the plastics were $7.50 just for that. What do you think they're going to charge you to put it in?' I said, 'No, Father, I'm with you 100 percent.' So I got hold of Deacon Pete [Deacon Peter Wasialek, an accountant at Donnelley Publishing, who would go to Holy Cross Mission in the morning, then go to work, then come back at 4:30 p.m. and run the soup lines], and we left to go to Haymarket on Peoria Street with him."

Slowly, inevitably, Ignatius McDermott was being eased out.

* * *

The first Haymarket (1975–78), at 12 South Peoria on the Near West Side of Chicago—a Catholic Charities haven for homeless men—was located in a building so dilapidated that it was slated to be torn down. While searching for another space, Monsignor McDermott contacted a number of realtors and met George Butler. Butler owned a building at 14 North Sangamon, which housed a tropical fish plant and warehouse. It would become the second Haymarket (1978–85). Catholic Charities declined to continue full support, so Monsignor McDermott was forced to improvise. Within the building would be launched an institution known as "Cees Manor" (a name he took from the first letters of the sponsors' names—the Chicago Christian Industrial League, Catholic Charities, and the Cathedral Shelter of the Episcopal diocese). It consisted of a residential program, halfway house, and "non-dry" hotel.

Non-dry hotel?

The concept of the "non-dry hotel" had been devised by Dr. Max Weisman of Baltimore. Raymond Soucek, president and CEO of Haymarket, describes the concept: "It maintained that just because a person is drinking doesn't mean that he should be ejected from his residence. A lot of programs which were into treatment of substance abusers and chemically dependent persons would, upon a person's relapse, kick him out of the program and send him back to the street."

Soucek continues: "So this program said instead of kicking them out, we'll detox them and put them back into their rooms and we'll continue with their program. So that's what they did. They opened a home for the guys who were on the Street and it, too, was somewhat of a revolving door, although slower. It would accept a male; he would stay there, and if he did get drunk, he would be put into detox where they would sober him up, and he would be put right back into his room at Cees Manor where they would continue the program." Again, those who wished to punish drunks for misconduct wanted to see them turned out if they didn't conform to sobriety; they accused Monsignor McDermott of excessive "permissiveness." But, he argued, punishment was no substitute for steady, one-day-at-a-time ministry that would lead the men, ultimately, to Alcoholics Anonymous.

* * *

Not long after the second Haymarket was organized, there was a community disruption about the location of a rehabilitation center for alcoholics in the Near West Side community. A number of business people felt that Haymarket's clients would hurt their enterprises, particularly the owner of a car wash whose whopping charges were attuned to a prosperous clientele. In fact, many thought the prices charged by the car wash were out of line for the neighborhood. A showdown came before the Chicago Zoning Board of Appeals, at which Monsignor McDermott testified. At a memorable meeting on May 19, 1981, the car wash owner criticized the Haymarket clientele.

"Some of them are panhandlers," he said. "You know what? They keep hitting people for $1.25. Why $1.25? Do you know, Monsignor?"

"I certainly do *not*," said Monsignor McDermott. "But we know it's not for a car wash, don't we?"

The neighborhood audience, familiar with car-wash gouging, burst into laughter.

The zoning board granted permission to Haymarket to operate in the neighborhood. The first thing Monsignor McDermott did was hire a 24-hour-a-day security force. By patrolling the neighborhood, the security force greatly improved its safety, and recovering clients became a farm system for small business employment. Soon the very same businessmen who had complained about Haymarket were loudly singing its praises and hiring the Center's graduates.

* * *

Ray Soucek worked closely with Monsignor McDermott twice—once at Catholic Charities, later at Haymarket. He signed up first as a counselor at Catholic Charities in 1976 and recalls a deeply personal involvement between the priest and an alcoholic.

A Chicago native, Soucek graduated from Loras College, Dubuque, Iowa. After receiving a master's degree in human services from Concordia College, River Forest, he began as a teacher and coach in the suburbs of River Forest and River Grove. He moved into the U.S. Department of Housing and Urban Development in Chicago, did procurement for it and, having embraced the 12-step program, wanted to move to the field of addiction counseling. But before he embarked on the program, he believed he could kick addiction by himself—without reliance on a power greater than his own.

"I was through Lutheran General [hospital] twice, and I was through Lake Shore Hospital. Both of them had good programs. I wasn't ready to listen. [Then] I finally hit bottom and was willing to do whatever it took. It's called having no reservations. That's the way you have to approach it, to say: whatever it takes.

"I believe that people sometimes get well too quick. I think I did. I think my initial treatment came together for me rather quickly. I was physically in very poor shape and going into the *DTs*. Thirty days later, everything was put back together and everything was fine. The rationale that I went through was something like: Well, what's the big deal? I put this thing all together and I don't need AA. I don't need all this fancy stuff. I've got the best counseling in the world, all these psychiatrists. I wasn't ready to listen to what they had to say and, therefore, I didn't get sober.

"When I finally went into Riveredge Hospital, I met the same caliber of people. That's when I found out that everything had disappeared. I was bankrupt—spiritually, mentally, physically. I had a counselor who was guiding me through the program—and my ears opened up and I listened to him and, as I said, if he had told me to dance on the table I would have danced on the table."

The most important thing Soucek realized was that he was powerless, but God is all-powerful. "I can't. God can. Let Him: 1, 2, 3. That's the way it works. My life was definitely unmanageable. I recognized the powerlessness, but that never stopped me. What I didn't do is turn my life and my will over to the care of God, because I didn't know how to do that. I didn't know what that all meant. Finally, I caught hold that God is doing for me what I can't do for myself. Sobriety is a gift, a very precious gift. It's one of those things that every day you say, 'Thank you, Lord, for this day,' and you say 'Thank you' at night."

Soucek's quest to get into addiction counseling came as result of Father John Fahey, pastor of St. Luke's Roman Catholic Church in River Forest, Illinois, a seminary classmate of Monsignor McDermott. Like many others, Soucek tried to call Monsignor McDermott at Catholic Charities, using Father Fahey's name, but never got a return call (his staff was being too protective again)—so he had to act presumptively. Was the failure to contact Monsignor McDermott an incentive to redouble efforts to get through to the priest? Soucek says it was.

Finally, the meeting was set up. "I showed up and met with Father on Desplaines Street," he said. "We talked for a while and a job offer came from that. I had been talking to my counselor at the hospital about how frustrated I was, sending out résumés and looking for work, with nothing really coming forth. He would talk to me about being patient.

"One of the things the counselor suggested was to have a heart-to-heart talk with God about the job situation—just say, 'What do You want me to do?' I did that one day in a car driving by myself, and I said, 'Lord, I'm doing what I need to do. If I'm not doing what You want me to do, let me know what You need for me to do next. But I'm really frustrated!' I was kind of shouting. That next week, I remember, I got a call from one of the family service agencies in the suburbs where I had applied, asking me if I was still interested in working there. And then I got a call from Catholic Charities. They asked me if I was interested in working with Father Mac.

"Father offered the job to me on a Friday at the Charities, 126 North Desplaines, and I was to report to work on the next Monday. After the job offer was made and I accepted it, I walked down to the chapel with him. There we met a man who was the nephew of a famous cartoonist. He was a guy who was on Skid Row. His head was pretty much a road map with plenty of scars. This day he was sober and he was asking for money. Father had an envelope with him. He opened the envelope and asked me to help him count the money, which was [from] a trust fund that his wealthy uncle had set up, and Father was holding it for him. He started counting with me. It went $100, $200, $300, ending up at about $800. Well, I looked at the money. I was pretty down and out at that time and that was a lot of money to me.

"Father tried to convince the guy not to take the money, saying he would drink it up, that he would lose it, get jack-rolled. But the guy was insistent and, of course, it was his money. So Father had me witness that he gave him the money. We signed off, Father and me and the guy, on the envelope. Well, the weekend passed. I came in on Monday morning, my first day at work, and at the door was this guy—drunk, belligerent, and intolerable. And so my first assignment was to take him over to the first Haymarket

House, 12 South Peoria. I didn't even know where it was, but I remember a driver got into the car with us and we took him over there. We put him in bed. He stuck around there for a while but ended up being one of the revolving door candidates. And that was my introduction to the first Haymarket, seeing Father's personal dedication and all."

Later, Soucek left Catholic Charities for a private sector alcohol-drug treatment position, but he would return. All the while, the struggle with Catholic Charities was going on.

Monsignor McDermott administered personal—not institutional—care. Even as an elderly man, whenever he could, he scoured the streets of Skid Row. He would patrol the dingy streets even after Mass on Sunday morning. It was still the era where, under city ordinance, taverns were closed until noon. His sharp eye would notice the entrepreneurs—hustlers who were playing the angles.

"They had baby buggies, and they would find some pints and half-pints from the night before," Monsignor McDermott said. "They would arrange some clothes in the carriages to cover them up. They would have a doll or something in the carriages, and underneath the phony baby were the half-pints and jugs. They would be going down the street and the guys who were dying for a drink would come up to them a buy a pint or half-pint from them."

He continued a close familiarity with Skid Row alumni. "There was a young fellow from South Holland [a Chicago suburb], a very good-looking kid named George. He was on the Street, hitting the sauce. Then he turned to sobriety, was recovering and working. He told me his sisters lived in Poland. So he was relishing his first Christmas with sobriety, and he told me, 'I want to do something real nice for my sisters,' because they had been real good. He asked me what should he do—send them money? I told him he should be more noble than that. I recommended that he buy them a nice gift certificate for $50 or $100.

"He went down to State Street, went into Marshall Field's and picked up the gift certificates. I guess he figured they could transfer them in Poland.

"Then he's walking down the street, and he's imbued with the Christmas spirit, the bells are playing "Silent Night" and "Rudolph the Red-Nosed Reindeer," and he's thanking the Lord for sobriety and serenity.

"He goes by one of the corners and there was a young mother there with a kid talking to Santa Claus. He's in rapture watching Santa Claus talking to the mother and kid and Santa Claus is promising this kid whatever he's asking for. George is watching it. When the mother and the little kid walk away, Santa lifts up his whiskers and says, 'George, I need a flop.'" [*Skid Row lingo for a room.*]

* * *

Ellis Brown started drinking seriously in the early 1970s. He was fired from his job and hit West Madison Street. How he got to Haymarket Center and became a valued employee is illustrative of the personal care, coupled with tough love, dispensed by Monsignor McDermott.

Brown, an African-American, was on the way up in Chicago ward politics. Born in 1932 in Lexington, Mississippi, he went into military service in the Korean War at age 18. The Army was good to him. He was in a medical battalion in the war, re-enlisted, and was sent to Germany with the 7th Division. He made his rank as a master sergeant and married a German girl. His family— mother, father, and nine siblings—had moved from Mississippi to Chicago, and when he was mustered out, Brown and his wife came to Chicago.

"When I came back to the states in 1959, I lived on the North Side," says Brown. Looking for a job, he was taken to the West Side's 20th ward and introduced to its alderman—a legend in the Richard J. Daley Democratic party—Vito Marzullo, who was a fixture in the city council and crown prince of political patronage.

"Alderman Marzullo asked me how long I stayed in service, if I was married," said Brown. "I said I got a wife, I got married in the service, and I got one little baby. He said, 'Where do you live?' I said I live with my mother and father on Larrabee Street. He said, 'You shouldn't be living with your mother and daddy. You need to own your own place.' He said, 'I'm going to move you on Oakley, that's on the West Side. I'll move you off the North Side and move you on the West Side.'" It was in Marzullo's 20th ward. Then Marzullo gave Brown a city job in the Sewer Department (where Marzullo's son, Bob, was deputy commissioner).

"He said, 'I want you to move over there and then, Monday morning, I want you to go down to Lake Street and go into this yard, and tell them I sent you.' I went down there. It was across from the Conservatory and Lucy Flower high school, that's where the yard was. I reported there and the man said, 'Where's your shovel? You also got to have steel-toed boots.' So I went back home. My father lent me some money, and I went to Montgomery Ward on Chicago Avenue, and I got 'em. You had to buy your own shovel and your own boots to start out with. And that's how I started in 1959.

"I started off as a laborer in a gang—one bricklayer and a group of people to dig a hole," Brown continued. "The bricklayer would lay the bricks and build it all the way back up, and we would put sand and dirt around it. Then we would make up our cement. I was getting paid $3.15 an hour, which we thought was good. The Sewer Department paid good."

Brown stayed with the Sewer Department until 1984. He was promoted to assistant superintendent in Marzullo's ward.

"It was a good job, a beautiful job," says Brown. He had to work politics, of course. "Well, that's the name of the game. You had to work, even after I came home at night. We would still have to go out and put up posters and signs. We had to do all the duties that you do. I worked with the precinct captain at the time, Mr. Sanatella. So I worked with him. Then I made precinct captain in his ward. Alderman Marzullo made me precinct captain of the 6th precinct."

Being precinct captain for Marzullo was very prestigious.

"Precinct captain was the top," said Brown. "That was the top. Then he brought me into the [ward] yard, and then I made maintenance. But I had to deliver. I had some 600 people in my precinct, and I was expected to deliver. If you didn't deliver, you weren't fired but you wouldn't have that good job. You'd be back digging holes."

Brown was drinking heavily, but the climax came in 1984 when his wife died. He says, "I met my wife in Germany. A little town called Ansbach, 30 miles south of Nuremberg. My wife died of cancer. At the time she was some 40 years old."

"It was a loss," he said wistfully. "Something I just couldn't handle because, I guess, we were so much in love. I was so young when I met her, and there was nobody else before that who fulfilled the joy that we had. It was just too much for me, and I started trying to find peace in a bottle, to find peace drinking.

When I started off, I drank Crown Royal bourbon, which was my favorite. I would drink that, and then I ended up drinking some of everything.

"In order to keep from firing me—the city is good to people—they tried to get me to help myself, but I didn't do it. They didn't fire me. They said, 'Resign. We don't want to fire you. Just resign. And then you can always come back one day if you ever get yourself together.' But I didn't want to hear none of that.

"To be honest with you, I wasn't even thinking about it. One day I was drinking so much at home, I was out of it. My sister, nobody could do nothing with me."

So he hit West Madison Street. He found he was accepted warmly there—and he thrilled to the brotherly love that bound men together as bottle buddies on Skid Row.

"I was just walking one day and everybody was so friendly down there on Madison, and they began to sit down on old chairs and benches and lawns, and they were so nice and everything. They were passing the bottles around. Everyone was drinking and laughing. And they didn't have to know you to be friendly to you at that time. And I'd just blend in with all the people on Madison Street."

Where did he stay?

"Wherever the guys would stay. Some nights we would stay under the bridge. Some nights we would stay in old trucks, like those old 40-foot trailers. They had an old parking lot by a place—Vogt's—that used to be an old wine house years ago, where you could go and get your drinks. There was an old, big parking lot with abandoned trucks on Peoria Street. Old junks would be parked there. People would make their homes there."

To mitigate the suffering, the men clustered together for self-protection, much as servicemen do in wartime. It reminded ex-Army sergeant Brown of a happier time when he was in the military.

"Right," he said. "Everybody was so nice. Sometimes you could go out to work as a day laborer and you came in with a little money, and put it together and buy lunch meat and bread, and then you'd come down to the South Water Market [a wholesale meat distribution center], and they would give you meat, and then you'd get your nice clean pail and wash it out and start boiling."

What happened in winter?

"Usually the buddies would have enough blankets and warm clothes. But they'd rather not go to a flophouse. They would like it better when they were all together, so they would be outside together. Flophouses had little chicken wire rooms and, if you had anything there, and you went to the washroom and came back, some of those people would steal everything you got. If you were with your buddies, they would look after you and they would not let nobody steal nothing from you. They would look after each other. We'd rather live together in an old truck or build us a tent or something."

Luther Phillips, who knew Brown when Phillips was at the Chicago Christian Industrial League, added: "Day labor paid something like $16.00 a day, enough to set one up at a tavern like Irish Mike's. If you turned up there and had scrip, like a check, they would give you your money. They would cash it and charge you a fee. You'd have to buy a drink once you got it, and you kept the rest of it. Yes, bottle buddies were a community thing. It was the type of thing that if you got out to work and you made up the day and the other guy didn't make it, you met him and you shared the drink with him and helped him pay for his flop. So it was kind of a community thing. It was a social club. If one got sick and the other one knew he was sick, and he needed a drink, the other one would kind of go out of his way to get some help for him or get him a drink, because he knew how he'd feel."

A unique kind of Christianity?

"It was love," says Phillips. "A love thing. There were no women. They came later on. This was just men down there. We'd eat at Helping Hands Mission. There was Holy Cross Mission, Father's place. Listen, you could get three hots and a cot every day."

Brown adds, "When I first met Luther, he was at CCIL, and I went to get something to eat. Luther was working, and I was in line that day and he was telling us, 'Okay, you guys, if you want to eat, you have to get in line.' That's when I first got to know Luther. But the best thing we used to do was get a good old can and get meat from the Market and some hot sauce, mustard, and bread and boil it and cook it and eat it ourselves."

Where would they cook it?

"Anywhere. You could make a fire. When you get cold you get a can or something and cut the can open and make a fire, and then you make it just like you were sitting at a barbecue. Then you set another bucket on top of that and you put the meat in. You would get the meat from the Market. The Market would give you all the meat you want. Not old meat. The meat was hanging up on hooks."

Phillips recalls, "Everything the men had was in their bags. They walked with it. If they ever laid it down, somebody would take it. What would happen is some guys would go out to work, and they would pick up on South Water Market some kosher hot dogs and what have you. They come out and give you half of those. So one guy would come back with hot dogs, and we'd have hot dogs that day. The next day you'd have neckbones. The next day you'd have beef. So I got to know them by passing through. When I was driving a truck for Rothschild Liquors, I got to know them. They were all sitting around right there, some guys on tree stumps."

What if somebody got sick?

Phillips answered, "Then somebody would go around and tell Father Mac, or somebody would try to get you over to Cook County Hospital. But it was kind of the best of times, where they enjoyed themselves most of all trying to find tranquility, sitting around passing the jug and telling stories."

"Those were the best times," Brown agreed.

Then Brown, as Phillips did before him, met Monsignor McDermott.

"I met Father Mac in the soup line at Holy Cross Mission," says Brown. "I was standing in line and Father Mac walked over and he said, 'I've seen you around. Where do you come from?' He could tell a new man. I talked a little bit to him, and Father Mac asked me where I was staying. I said I was staying on the Street. He said, 'Come over tomorrow and go to the basement and tell Deacon Pete to give you some clothes, because the ones you have stink.' After that I was supposed to talk to him. I didn't do it then. I went back on the Street, got drunk. That was 1974, something like that. Then I saw him again, and he walked up to me again. He told me I didn't do what he asked me. I said, 'Father, I ain't got time.' He said, 'What do you mean you ain't got time? You aren't doing anything.' Then he said, 'Where are you from?' I told him and said I worked for the city, and he knew the same people I did. He said, 'You're Commissioner Quigley's guy?' Quigley was head of the Sewer Department. I said, 'That's right. I worked for Quigley.' He said, 'Get your tail over there right now.' I went over there. Deacon Pete gave me clothes. I took a shower. Then he sent me over to 666 Madison to the hotel, and that's how I got to be in the Holy Cross Mission and got to know Father Mac. I started working in the kitchens at 126 North Desplaines— Catholic Charities."

At Catholic Charities they had AA meetings regularly. Brown got close to Monsignor McDermott.

"He would come downstairs, in the basement, and he would sit at the table and cross his legs," Brown says. "There were cooks there, but he would call me and say, 'Make me a cheese sandwich.' So I'd make him a grilled cheese sandwich and hot tea, with lemon. When he didn't come to the basement, his secretary, Miss Lamb, would call me and say, 'Ellis, take a cheese sandwich up to Father.' He lived on the 5th floor. So I would take it up to him, and he would be sitting in the dining room and say to me, 'Sit down. Don't worry about what they're doing downstairs.' And then he would strike up a conversation. He loved to talk. We would talk about the guys in the Sewer Department. We would name some of the guys. He knew them all, even the guys I had worked with. And we would sit there and we would talk. So I started fixing dinner for him. He would have me fix him chicken à la king over rice—that's what he used to love.

"So I got to be a person that he could trust, and I loved it. We started working together, and he gave me things to do. He'd say, 'Make sure this place is clean. Make sure those guys don't leave anything dirty down there.'

"One thing he would tell me all the time—all of us living together in the basement and big old rats were running around. He would say to all of us as he sat in the basement, 'One day I'm going to get a place for all of you with a lot of windows in it, and you'll also have a place to stay, and you're going to be somebody.' I said, 'Father, is somebody going to give you that?' He would say, 'I've been praying to St. Joseph for this for a long time. St. Joseph is a slow saint,' he'd say, 'but one day I'm going to have a place with windows in it, and you'll all have rooms with windows.' From time to time I would say, 'Father, you still praying to St. Joseph?' He would say, 'Yeah.' I would say, 'Father, let's get another saint, because we're still down here in this basement. We ain't going nowhere.'

"One day he came downstairs laughing. He said, 'Ellis, I want to show you something.' So I got in his car, in the back. Deacon Pete got in the front, and Father drove us over here at 932 West Washington and he took me next door. I said, 'Father, this is a garbage dump you're showing me!' There was a big hole in the wall all the way to the top and in the back yard was old pieces of cars and things. I said, 'Father, no wonder somebody gave you this.' He said, 'One day, Ellis, this place is going to be the best.' And he was right. Take a look at this place now. You should have seen this place before we ever touched it. I laughed at it. I said, 'Father, is this what St. Joseph gave you?' He laughed. He said, 'That's okay, we're going to beg for money, and we're going to fix this place up.'

The story's not over. Ellis Brown had a relapse and began drinking heavily. One day he fell out of a window at the flophouse at 666 West Madison.

"I fell three stories," he says. "I broke everything. I guess I was unconscious for nine days. I didn't know anything. When I woke up, I was in [Cook] County Hospital and Father Mac was there. All of the doctors were there. They put my arms in casts and did an exploratory operation to see if my intestines were damaged, which they were. When I woke up, Father would be standing there. Deacon Pete would be standing there. Father prayed for me. Once, Deacon Pete asked what happened to me. Father said, 'Don't ever ask him what happened. Don't even mention it to him. Don't come in here asking him what happened, because the man's not supposed to be alive.' The doctor said, 'This man's not supposed to be alive, but he's still living.' I fell on concrete.

"I lay there in the hospital with a torn intestine for about a month. The doctor wanted to give me reconstructive surgery for my stomach. He told Father he couldn't guarantee that I would live. Father said, 'Ellis, there's no guarantee that I'm going to live when I get out of this chair.' The doctor told Father I would never walk. Father said, 'You're going to walk out of this hospital. You're going to walk out with me. Go ahead and take the operation.'

"When they took me for the operation, Father walked all the way to the door of the operating room. They told Father he couldn't go any further. So he left. I don't remember anything else. I don't remember how many days I was out—in a coma. They had pronounced me dead, but Father told them I wasn't

Key board members of Haymarket Center.
Left to right: the late Richard Athey, an entre-
preneurial powerhouse who helped steer
Haymarket to success; chairman Father Mac;
Dr. James West, co-founder of the Center;
Mrs. Jean Athey, wife of Richard.

Two early staffers who helped guide
Haymarket through its formative years (shown
with chairman Father Mac): Rev. George
Borneman, board member, associated with the
Chicago Christian Industrial League; and Ann
Konar, Haymarket's first executive director.

Haymarket president and CEO, Raymond Soucek, outlines Haymarket programs to Mrs. Gerald Ford,
Mrs. George Ryan, and many others at a session at Haymarket's chapel-general convocation center.

Two women who served Haymarket in major capacities, and a benefactor. Left to right: Sister Patricia Kilbane, a Dominican nun, who heads Intervention Instruction, complete with Internet capabilities; Mrs. Kay Zlogar, who until her retirement in 2002 was Father Mac's secretary; and Mrs. Lura Lynn Ryan, wife of Illinois Governor George Ryan, who has a keen interest in addiction treatment.

A huddle of professionals skilled in addiction treatment, shown with chairman Father Mac. Left to right: physicians Michael Baldinger and Harry Hannig (who served as Haymarket's medical director); clinical psychologist Dr. Sam Cardone. Seated next to Father Mac, his partner in founding Haymarket, the legendary Dr. James West.

William Dooner (lower left) credits Father Mac with his rescue from alcoholism. In recovery, he became a wealthy entrepreneur and generous contributor to Haymarket. He's shown with Mrs. Dooner and their family. A bronze bust of Father Mac, contributed by Dooner, stands in the Haymarket library.

Owner of the Chicago Bears, Virginia McCaskey, and her husband, Edward, are faithful supporters of Father Mac and Haymarket Center.

When the Chicago City Council designated the 900 block of Washington Boulevard to Father Mac in 1991, the priest co-founder posed with his good friend, the late federal Judge, Abraham Lincoln Marovitz.

Jack Brickhouse, voice of the Cubs, also gave play-by-play of Bears games (with Irv Kupcinet). Father Mac was a daily visitor to Brickhouse's hospital room in 1998, and gave a eulogy when the Hall of Fame broadcaster died.

—Brace Photo

A familiar sight at many sports contests (he roots for the Chicago Bears and White Sox, and says he pays his penance by going to Wrigley Field), Father Mac frequently receives tributes and contributions from benefactors. This is "Father Mac" Day at Comiskey Park, September, 1990.

Father Mac greets Pope John
Paul II in St. Louis in 1998.

Francis Cardinal George
visiting Haymarket and its
Father Mac-named Wholly
Innocence Day Care Center.

Joseph Cardinal Bernardin met with Father
Mac at Catholic Charities as Fran Lamb
(with eye patch), renowned as Father Mac's
assistant (and a Cubs fan), stands by.

Father Mac and Senator
Dick Durbin (D-IL) greet
children at Wholly
Innocence Day Care Center.

Former Senator Carol
Moseley Braun (D-IL) was a
firm supporter of Haymarket
and friend of Father Mac as
is her successor...

...Senator Peter Fitzgerald
(R-IL), who visited Haymarket
and stays in touch with
developments there.

Judge Jim McDermott, Father's brother, gives some pointers to young Congressman John Kennedy, before JFK's address at the Chicago Irish Fellowship Dinner, *circa* 1947. A future president gets tips from a Democratic pro.

Former President Gerald Ford visited Haymarket and with wife, Betty, helped raise funds. Here he visits with chairman Father Mac and Mrs. Mike (Helen) Howlett, widow of the late Illinois Secretary of State.

Father Mac with Congressman Danny Davis (D-IL), a strong supporter of Haymarket.

Illinois secretary of state and later governor, George Ryan gives Haymarket chairman Father Mac a personalized license plate. Mrs. Ryan (Lura Lynn) and Judge Abraham Lincoln Marovitz smile appreciatively.

Former Illinois Governor Jim Edgar (second from left), with Haymarket chairman Father Mac, Haymarket president and CEO Raymond Soucek, and board member Thomas F. Roeser (far right).

Chicago Mayor Richard M. Daley cuts ribbon opening new detox center at Haymarket in 2000.

Father Mac and Mayor Daley greet State Senator Margaret Smith (D-Chicago) with board member Dan O'Brien at the unveiling of the Center's undomiciled mentally ill substance abuse program.

Father Mac and former State Senator Robert P. DiTuri (D-Chicago) when they saved a state appropriation for poor children. They handed the diapered infants to hard-bitten state lawmakers and asked if they could vote against the kids. (They couldn't.)

dead. I woke up and he was there. And every night the nurse would tell me that Father would come and stand over my bed. Every night—not just one night. Every night. Some nights I would wake up and see him and some nights, they said, while I was sleeping he would just stand there and pray and turn around and walk out. He did that every day I was there, and I still didn't think I would walk.

"When they got me up and took me to therapy to make me walk, my feeling started coming back. And the day came when I walked out of County Hospital with him, like he told me I would. I came back to the basement and to his office and Father said, 'Ellis, see what God did for you.' He said, 'I know you don't want the sauce, the liquor, anymore. Now what are you going to do for God?' I said, 'Father, I'm going to serve you.' He said, 'No, don't say you're going to do anything for me. I want you to do it for God. I'm just going to open a way for you to do all these things that you want to do for other people.'

"That's why I'm here—because of that man. I promised him, but he said don't promise him, promise God. So I promised God that I would work for Him through Father Mac. God took care of me through Father Mac. Without Father Mac's prayers, I wouldn't be here. On top of that, I got sick over a year ago. I had surgery again—16 hours on the operating table. I had a tumor right under my intestine growing too close to my colon. It wasn't cancer. And he prayed for me again. He was at the hospital for me."

Today, Ellis Brown is supervisor of Cooke's Manor, "C" Building. He lives at Haymarket. He says, "I've got a home. I've got a daughter. I could leave right now. I'm retired. I'm not rich, but I could live on my retirement. But I have a feeling I'm not finished in what God wants me to do yet. Father Mac is still working, and I'm still going to work, too."

* * *

Recalling the days when Skid Row was in its prime, Raymond Soucek identified some true characters who were on the Street. When Monsignor McDermott ran the Holy Cross Mission for the homeless, he also instituted a soup line. When Campbell Soup Company would donate soup in dented cans, the cooks would throw various concoctions in one vat and have it cook all day for the men who would come in at night. The meal would "consist of anything from tomato soup to bean or vegetable soup, which would be all mixed together in a recipe that could not be repeated or recalled." One guy, Stanley Bartkowski, worked as a cook in the late '60s and early '70s. "He and Deacon Pete would go out to buy the meat off the Market. A lot of times the meat was liver, because it was cheap, so many of the men would get liver served once or twice a week. Many times Stanley, who was an alcoholic, would have assistance from Jim Beam, who came in bottle form and was 86-proof."

There was a Jim Miller, six feet four inches tall. Says Soucek, "Because most of the clothing donations came from people under six feet two, Jim always came up short literally. It was not unusual to see him with a pants leg about four inches shorter than it should have been." Miller had been a cook in the Army who only knew how to cook for one hundred people. That made it difficult when there was fewer than that number.

"The Street had become a street of bottle buddies. Gangs of guys or pairs of guys would team up. One of the members would go out and do day labor; the others would be holed up and look out for each other. The one who was holed up might possibly have been under the influence of alcohol. The guys who were working day labor would earn $16, come back and rent a place to flop so they would secure themselves and consume alcohol that might be enough for one or two days. Then they would go out and do some day labor, and they would take care of each other. The camaraderie of the men was strong where they were always looking out for each other because the guy who had the job and money today was the one who was going to be broke and penniless on the Street and needing some alcohol to keep his nerves steady. So they looked out for each other, in that respect.

"Two of these guys were Richie and Paul. They hung around together and one would go out and then the other one would go out, and when they worked, they worked extremely hard. They would oftentimes, after they got enough bankrolled, go off on a toot and you wouldn't see them for a while and then they would show up back at Haymarket and be recycled again through the whole program. They looked out for one another, and Paul was a braggadocio who would create some pretty extreme stories. One of them actually came true when he joined the Maharishi and went off in one of these cults and ended up not being able to escape. Father got a call from Paul, in Oregon, who asked if he could get him out of the cult. The best that Father could do was send some money. Paul was able to get on a train and come back. Eventually he found himself, once again, being attracted to the magnetism of the Street, his bottle buddies, and was reunited with his friend, Richie.

"There was a guy who worked around Haymarket named Frankie. Frankie was a man who, when he worked, he worked, and when he drank, he drank. Phillips hired him as the cleanup guy and Luther would notice that every now and then, Frankie looked like he was imbibing. Luther would come in and he couldn't figure out exactly if and when he was getting drunk. Luther would see him in the building and Frankie seemed to be drinking after hours, but since Frankie lived in Cees Manor at Haymarket House, he wouldn't leave the building.

"Frankie would appear to be intoxicated or under the influence, and Luther would know that he didn't sneak out the window or back door or the front door, and he kept thinking there were probably bottles inside, but he couldn't find any bottles. It turns out that Haymarket was moving and during part of the move they were cleaning out storage areas. Luther forgot that some mouthwash, which had been donated and stored in these areas, had 20 percent alcohol in it. When Luther discovered the bottles, they were all empty. He concluded Frankie got buzzed on it and had sweet-smelling breath as a result.

"The Holy Cross Mission was a place where people would oftentimes donate not just food, but they would also donate articles of clothing, and the men on the Street would receive items as needed when they came through the soup line. Some of the things that were donated were rather unique and interesting. In terms of food, sometimes there would be political events and fundraisers. The fundraisers would have a type of hors d'oeuvres appetizer available and many times the food would go unfinished, so they would send the remainder to the Holy Cross Mission. On occasions, the men would have mulligan stew and the hors d'oeuvres. One interesting item that happened was that during the winter months of a particular year, a shoe company went out of business and they donated a lot of shoes that they had in storage to Holy Cross Mission. When the guys would be moving through the soup line with their worn and beat-up shoes with holes in them, they were invited to try on some of the different shoes and wear them if they fit properly. Many of the men took advantage of this, and one of the consequences of this was the shoes that they were given had 2" to 3" heels with slick bottoms.

"Walking around in the shoes and under the influence, the men would have a double dilemma in that they would not be able to keep their balance because of the alcohol, but now they had the added problem of having shoes that were not the best in negotiating the weather conditions at the time.

"Another incident that involved food was the time that a freight car got derailed in Chicago and it was carrying grapefruits, and so the Mission received a call to pick up some grapefruit. We sent the guys over to the freight yard—who unloaded the grapefruit—and for a few nights the men would receive a bowl of soup, some bread, and grapefruit as well.

"The Good Humor Company, in Elk Grove Village [Illinois], had loads of ice cream to be picked up; however, it was a whole bunch of ice cream that was in the melting stages because the refrigeration system had broken down. It was 90°+ weather and Leo Miller, one of the counselors, took a van without air conditioning to retrieve the ice cream. The journey back downtown from Elk Grove was about one-and-a-half hours long. By the time the van reached the Mission, the ice cream had melted, covering the entire back of the van."

* * *

In 1984, George Butler sold Haymarket at 14 North Sangamon to a man who had other plans for it. The new owner courteously, but firmly, told the priest that he had to get out—unless he wanted to buy the building. Ignatius McDermott, patron of homeless men, was himself homeless.

Monsignor McDermott solicited each of the Chicago Clergy Association members for $12,500 each for a Haymarket III. Catholic Charities balked. Charities appeared to be increasingly restive with the multi-faceted activities of their dynamic associate director. The bureaucracy, which had already refused to fund the innovative social setting detox concept, wondered how many other activities he would get involved with. Trying to borrow $12,500 for his share of the Clergy Association funds, he was turned down by the banks which felt that, at age 75, he was too old.

What has been seen by many as another *kairos*, or providential intervention, came to Monsignor McDermott when he joined forces with a man who was chief executive officer of R.A. Kerley Ink, Inc., in suburban Broadview, Illinois. He is John J. Whalen, Sr., whose superbly attuned business sense and thorough, first hand rational, and yet instinctive knowledge of building require- ments gave Haymarket and Monsignor McDermott's work natu- ral support. Jack Whalen's work is exceeded only by that of Monsignor McDermott and Dr. West, say many close observers of the Haymarket story.

Born in 1929, in the Austin neighborhood of Chicago, Jack Whalen—a sandy-haired, bespectacled Irishman to whom laugh- ter comes quickly—saw early, firsthand, the ravages of alcoholism with the fate of his own grandfather.

"One day he passed out in the cold, around 20th and State, and got pneumonia. They brought him home and he died. After that, my father and I would go by the Skid Row area on cold nights and see if there were any guys out there. We would pick them up and take them over to the police station so they wouldn't freeze."

Whalen went, for a while, to Quigley Preparatory Seminary. A typical Chicagoan with a wry, irreverent sense of humor, he dropped out of Quigley because, as he says drolly, tongue-in-cheek, "I went there for two years and got wise to the whole thing," a com- ment which belies his devout Catholicism. He transferred to St. Philip's high school, graduated, and went into the Army during the Korean War, where he served in the military police (MP). After he came out of the service, he went to DePaul University.

"I went to a dance—the first dance of the fall season at DePaul," Whalen said. "All the veterans were there; they were serving beer, and everybody was drinking. I didn't drink. I wanted Pepsi or a Coke or something. This was the first time I met my future wife, so I gave her a ride home. By the third dance, the third Friday, I was drinking—and I found a new friend. I was a new man. By spring- time I was getting home from school at 4 a.m., drunk, sneaking in the house. So I went right down the tube."

He married, took over a struggling ink company, and kept on drinking. "I just had to go for the 10-year ride. My wife was hardly talking to me. My brother, Jimmy, said, 'Don't go around my friends. I don't know how to explain you.' My wife said, 'If you're going to get killed, get killed soon.'"

The turn-around came in 1957, when he stopped in at a magazine store across from the suburban Hinsdale train station for some reading matter. "I saw this book, *How to Live Without Liquor,*" Whalen recounted. "I didn't think liquor was my problem. I had real problems. I was going broke and everything else, but I didn't think liquor was my problem. So I read this book. It described alcoholism, the prognosis for it, and all of that. I said, 'That's what I got.'"

He knew that the people around him loved him and were serious.

"I knew I was in trouble. I said, 'Go to AA.' The next morning I went out and joined AA. That was it. I didn't know what was wrong with me. When I found out what was wrong with me, I was happy that that was all it was. That I wasn't nuts. That it wasn't going to cost a fortune or anything else. I was grateful."

He turned the business around, developing a new ink that made his company a success. And after hours, he started helping drunks on Skid Row, picking them up and taking them to shelters.

"It wasn't so much like it is today. There was a Salvation Army, the Pacific Garden Mission, and a few other places. I would go out at night. I'd be around and see some guy. I was at St. Peter's [the Loop Catholic Church famed for services and confessions from early morning until night]. They were about to shut the church down and some poor guy, the coldest night of the year, he'd be sent out to the Street. You wonder what he's going to do." Whalen would rescue them from the Street.

Then: "I'd take them around to all those different places. I used to take them to the Salvation Army. I'd take them to the Pacific Garden Mission. They'd say, 'Is he saved?' I'd say, 'I don't know. He just wants a bed.'

"I was about 31 or 32 years old. I said to my sister, Mary, who was with United Way, 'I get these guys in the car, and I'd like to find a place to put them. If there's some guy who's got some beds, I'd be happy to make a contribution to this fellow so I could have some place to put them.' She said, 'The man you want to talk to is Monsignor Ignatius McDermott. They call him Father Mac. He's with Catholic Charities.' She gave me the phone number."

A fiercely over-protective staff around the priest blocked, for years, a personal meeting between Monsignor McDermott and Jack Whalen. It is incredible to imagine, but it did. After initial difficulties in making personal contact, the two started an occasional correspondence. As the years passed and good fortune happened at the now prosperous printing ink company, Whalen continued his own work with the denizens of Skid Row, occasionally exchanging notes with the priest. After many false starts, all changed in 1975, when he determined to break through the barriers to link up with Monsignor McDermott personally. He sent his corporate controller, Tom Powers, down to Haymarket House. Powers' visit coincided exactly with the need of Monsignor McDermott to find $12,500, which would be his personal contribution for the Chicago Clergy Association's Haymarket House project.

Whalen tells the story. "Powers could get anything done. Tom went down there, sees McDermott, and says I wanted to meet him because I wanted to give him some money. So I went down to meet him just before Thanksgiving. I was going to give him $10,000 because it was the end of the year for us, and I wanted to make these disbursements for taxes. I was going to give $2,500 to another place, but Powers comes up to me and says, 'I wouldn't give to those other people. They're not doing anything.'

"So I said, 'What do we do with this money?' He said, 'Give it to the priest.'" It totaled $12,500, the exact amount Monsignor McDermott needed for the Chicago Clergy Association.

"So I came up with the dough," says Whalen. "Just coincidentally the right amount, $12,500."

Was that one of those providential things?

"What else?" says Whalen.

After making a number of other contributions off and on, Whalen was invited by Monsignor McDermott to a seminar on alcoholism at Concordia College. He brought his wife Betty. It was 1984.

After the seminar, "Father approached me and told me that he had lost his lease at Haymarket House. He wondered if we could get some fellows together and co-sign on a note. He assured me we'd get paid. Then he sort of walked away—walked away because he's a shy fellow and doesn't like asking. So Betty [Mrs. Whalen] said to me, 'What's that all about?' I said, 'I don't know but I'll see.' I walked over to where he was and said, 'Father, will you be around tomorrow?' He said 'Yeah.' I said, 'I'll come over and see you.'"

Whalen assembled enough businessmen to buy the building, which would be Haymarket III, for $335,000. One of them was an old friend of Whalen's whose involvement has been regarded as a third providential intervention. "I'm going to try to enlist a guy for this project named Dick Athey," Whalen told Monsignor McDermott. Athey was a wealthy Container Corporation executive. The priest gasped, "Would that be Red Athey?" It was. "I remember him from St. Mary's Training School!" exclaimed Monsignor McDermott.

Richard Athey had met Father McDermott as a child at St. Mary's Training School, years earlier, where Athey had been sent by his father after his mother had died. After high school, Red Athey went to the Marines during World War II. While on board an aircraft carrier in the Pacific, he suffered a serious leg injury when a Japanese kamikaze pilot slammed his plane into the ship. When he came out of the service he went to DePaul University, graduating at the top of his class in business. He won a scholarship to the Harvard Business School where he got his MBA, once again graduating at the top of his class. He took a job at Container Corporation and rapidly rose to division manager. One day, as he was sitting with Whalen, Red Athey confided that he would be leaving Container.

Whalen ruminated about Athey's career change. "And I said, 'Red, we all thought you would be a priest.'"

They started to laugh. "You're right about that," he said. "I'm going to the seminary." He chose the Dominicans. Whalen said, "How come you won't go to the Jesuits?" Athey's response: "Too much like the Marines."

Nor was the story over then.

Several years later, Whalen and then Father Richard Athey, O.P., had lunch. Red Athey stunned him with another bit of news. Now he would be leaving the priesthood, would be laicized. There was a serious clash, a strong difference of opinion between him and his Dominican superior, a difference that could not be resolved. Athey felt that if he did not oppose it, it would lead to his own spiritual disintegration. He left the priesthood, was laicized with the approbation of the Church, married, and rejoined

Container Corporation, first in Philadelphia. Then he was transferred to Chicago and took a top post.

Now Whalen wanted Red Athey to serve on the business group (among them William Cowhey, an executive with Arthur Rubloff—a realtor and developer) that was preparing to buy the Haymarket building.

Sorry, said Athey. He was preparing to take disability because of severe arthritis, was moving to Philadelphia, and would be driving there shortly. Whalen was dejected; Athey's financial expertise was essential for this project.

On the way to Philadelphia, Athey's car broke down. Forced to abandon the move temporarily, Athey came back to Chicago, determined to hang around for a while, and joined the business group advising Monsignor McDermott on purchasing Haymarket III. This is what Jack Whalen calls another work of providence: a top business expert—who was leaving town—has car trouble, abruptly postpones his departure from Chicago and signs up for the project.

The team fanned out across Chicago in search of a third Haymarket but found nothing. Then, says Whalen, in February 1985, they located a building at 110 North Leavitt, two blocks east of Western.

"But it was a dump," says Whalen. "I was in the hospital getting a back operation. When Father came out to see me he said, 'I don't want that place.' I said I didn't either."

Once again, members of the *ad hoc* business advisory group scouted around for a building that they could afford. No luck. During lunch at the Chicago Athletic Club, Whalen then suggested they make an offer on the Sangamon Street building they were due to vacate.

"Suppose we offer them half a million dollars for the building," he suggested. Athey crunched the numbers and agreed. But when they offered it, the owner turned them down saying, "We turned down half a million dollars twice before." He did grant a year's extension on the lease, a stunning concession. It was the Itenberg family (the prime decision-maker, Steve) who came through.

"They were in the restaurant supply business, and they had already changed the phone book and insurance and made all kinds of arrangements for this building," says Whalen. "It cost them to give us that lease because they had made all those plans to move."

At the same time they were helping Monsignor McDermott with additional housing for alcoholics, new high-rises were going up on Skid Row and the alcoholics were being pushed out. Monsignor McDermott had a month-to-month lease on a building known as the Major Hotel, a 150-room hotel where he was putting people who were evicted from the other flophouses that were being demolished.

But the central problem remained how to find a permanent home for Haymarket III. The Skid Row area seemed foreclosed. Urban renewal and evacuation of the homeless precluded locating there. The finance committee was looking at other sites in Chicago, consulting with Richard Ward—another friend of Whalen's—who was a contractor. He rejected as inadequate an old casket factory on Washington Street. They were seeking a building of some 25,000 to 35,000 square feet and coming up empty—either too much money was required or no availabilities. As weeks went by, no one had a clue as to where Haymarket could go. Then the weeks turned into months, the deadline was fast approaching and no opportunities existed.

"One Thursday night I had dinner with Father, then I was going to an AA meeting," said Whalen. "Father was very low. He felt very bad because nothing was happening. So I stopped in at St. Edmund's in Oak Park, because I was a half-hour early for the meeting. I started praying and I thought: Well, these are God's people and Father was watching out for them. God would not desert these people or abandon them, so I figured we must be doing something wrong.

"So I went back to Father and—this is the significant thing—I asked him, 'Where do you want to be?' He said, 'I want to be where I am.' I said, 'What do you mean? Like within three or four blocks?' He said, 'Yes, that's what I mean.'"

Why did it take such a long time to ascertain where Monsignor McDermott wanted to be?

"You have to be Irish," said Whalen. "Because the Irish will never tell you what's on their mind. When Father said to me, 'I want to be where I am' that was the turning point. We saw this building—the Maguire. It's now called the Maguire Luxury Lofts on Madison and Carpenter, and that was the only building around that was available and was about the same size as Sangamon Street."

Whalen met again with contractor Dick Ward. He wasn't enthusiastic about the Maguire building.

Ward said, "What the hell are you looking at that building for?"

Whalen said, "It's the only place around."

Ward retorted: "That's no good, it doesn't have any windows."

Whalen said, "We could put windows in."

Ward shook his head. "No, the other place is better than this."

What other place?

Ward said, "The old casket factory at 932 West Washington."

Whalen said, "Ward, I asked you about that place a year ago, and you told me it was no good. What's so good about it now?"

Was Ward Irish too?

"Oh yeah," said Whalen. "So I asked him what was wrong with it." He said, 'Well, it's 150,000 square feet.' We were looking for about 25,000 to 35,000 to replace the old Haymarket House. We went over and looked at the place on Madison just because we had the appointment. Then we went over and looked at the casket factory on Washington. There were three buildings, A, B, and C, under one roof."

"It was in terrible shape. Whole bays of floors were cut out in some of its three buildings. It was vacant, empty, virtually abandoned. So we go over and take a look at it. It's a derelict, it's a dump." Whalen calculated that it would have to be almost entirely gutted and rebuilt. But, there was something about the building that intrigued him.

"But it had *something*. It had some appeal. We all caught that."

You and Monsignor McDermott caught its appeal?

"Yeah—and Ward," said Whalen. "Athey wasn't with us that day, so he came next time. We all thought this was what we were looking for. We were doing a lot of praying, and we felt this is where we were led. Ward had been a partner in it, but he had sold out his end of it nine months before we saw it. Father liked it because it had windows—lots of windows.

"There were three lawyers who owned the old casket factory on Washington and they were tough customers. We dealt with a fellow named John Carr. They wanted $1,050,000. Well, you figured they would take off the $50,000. No, it was $1,050,000 or nothing. So we put $375,000 down. We were to make three payments of $225,000 each, due every six months. Initially, we got the $375,000 down. We didn't have any other money."

How did they get the remainder of the money?

"Well, I gave. Athey gave. McDermott had stock he sold. Somebody else came in with $65,000. I'm not sure how, but we got the $375,000 for the down payment."

Did you ever get the contribution back?

"No. It was just a contribution to Father Mac. We made the down payment."

One source of funds was Monsignor McDermott's friend from the days of St. Mary of the Lake Seminary, the man who retired as an Army chaplain with the rank of Brigadier General, the late Father John McLoraine. He talked with the author shortly before he died.

"When he came up with the idea of Haymarket House—that's his baby—I told him I was with him all the way and any financial help I could give him, I'd do it. And I have given him some. You see, I have three sources of income: the military, the diocese, and Social Security. I'm told that the average Social Security among the priests in the diocese is somewhere around $25 to $300 a month. Mine is $1,009, so I'm able to help him. My two sisters were also able to help him." Contributions of stock were significant. "There is today a McDermott Center, but it could just as well be the McLoraine Center," said the ex-chaplain known to his family as "Johnny Mac."

Help from these sources was heartening but insufficient of themselves. So Monsignor McDermott, Whalen, Athey, and Sister Patricia Kilbane went to the Harris Bank. Initially, they didn't get a mortgage but a construction loan, which was later rolled into a mortgage on the building, in the name of the McDermott Foundation, which would own the building.

Recalling that time, Jack Whalen said: "When we purchased the building, the selling price was $1,050,000—$375,000 down and three payments of $225,000 each, every six months. The $375,000 took every nickel that all of us could raise for the down payment. After we took care of the down payment, we had to make hay. We had no money for an architect, no money for a contractor, so we had to start raising money, and we had this

$225,000 note due in six months. The McDermott Foundation signed the note, including Father and me. And if we lost the building, we were out."

And the condition of the massive, gutted building they had just acquired?

Monsignor McDermott says, "It came equipped with rats— and I mean big rats, with saddles on their backs!"

Thus a tremendous financial obligation was placed, if future fund-raising were to fail, on the shoulders of a priest who was then nearly 76 years old. Signing the note was, said Monsignor McDermott, the greatest act of faith he ever was to perform.

Did the heavy obligation scare him?

"No, it didn't," replied Whalen. "It honestly didn't. We looked at the building and we said, 'Gee, this is pretty big.' It was grandiose thinking. Alcoholics are often guilty of grandiose thinking. We needed 25,000 square feet to replace the old Haymarket House, which was 25,000 square feet. Well, this building was 150,000 square feet."

Perhaps this throwback to grandiose thinking helped. "Who do we think we are?" said Whalen. "I talked to Athey about it and he said, 'We'll see where it goes.' Well, we made the deal. Father, Dick Athey, Sister Pat, and myself went down to the Harris Bank and signed this deal. We got temporary zoning which was grandfathered in.

"So we got all this, and we had to go out and hustle for the money. We went to every event. We went to every wake; we went everywhere. We didn't want investors because investors would own the building. We were talking contributors. We went out and gave them our story and the money came.

"When it came time for the second note, it was the 11th hour. It was a Thursday night, I recall, and we didn't have any money. I prevailed on Father to write a letter. I ran copies on my copy machine at work and sent them out. One guy called Father and said, 'Father, I see you're in trouble. I'll send $100,000.' We got the money. They were people Father knew."

Then, good fortune came by the buckets.

After that, there was fund-raising momentum. "When you see a building like this, and you've been giving a hundred dollars, you're inclined to give more," Whalen said. "That's a truism in fund-raising. But was I worried? No. I know Father had some sleepless nights. But we were doing things to get the money. As I have said, it was an act of faith."

When another due date came, Monsignor McDermott didn't want to send out another letter. Whalen recalls: "So Dick Athey and I sent a letter out. We got a mild response—about $28,000."

Now came two bad breaks—or at least they appeared to be so at first consideration. First, Monsignor McDermott learned quite by chance, by leafing through the Catholic Charities directory, that he was now totally removed from management of the organization. The long push by Charities to dissociate with him was completed.

"We simply don't know," commented one ex-Charities source, "how many dollars went to Charities because donors had supposed Father Mac was still there."

Finally, the time came when Monsignor McDermott was the only person living in the Charities apartments at 126 North Desplaines. Unaccountably, one day the hot water was turned off. When his supporters complained, an official of the archdiocese said, mischievously, "serves him right." So, with the help of friends, he moved to a high-rise, Presidential Towers, near the old Skid Row, ironically, occupying land where the Starr Hotel had stood.

"McDermott's fought with everybody downtown," says a high-ranking official of the archdiocese. "Well, he's been a model for me. I hope I'll have the guts to continue the fight after he's gone."

The second mishap could have been fatal. While negotiations were being conducted with Catholic Charities vis-à-vis Haymarket III, Monsignor McDermott was due to fly to Sweden for an international conference on alcoholism. He left Haymarket in a car driven by a Haymarket staffer.

Jim Mchugh tells the story: "He went and got his medicine. James was driving him in an '84 Oldsmobile, and they were coming down Desplaines. James hit an abutment—that concrete thing. Father got a broken collarbone and four broken ribs. They pushed him out of the hospital too soon and he wound up with pneumonia." But in the hospital, Ignatius McDermott put the time to good use concentrating on future plans. Jack Whalen carried on the negotiations with Catholic Charities.

George Borneman, a Presbyterian minister who used to run the Chicago Christian Industrial League, found a rich woman who gave $50,000. Little by little the money came in, in time.

"So, we'd get the money," said Whalen. "It was really an act of faith. Father said that God would provide. And He did."

While Monsignor McDermott recovered in the hospital, the administrator of Catholic Charities, Father Edwin M. Conway, later an auxiliary bishop in Chicago, met with Whalen and others and talked about moving the facilities into the building.

"[Father Conway] said they'll want to take over the place," said Whalen. "We said, 'No, that's not what we're talking about.' We said, 'If you want, you can remodel the "C" building. We're going to buy the property. You'll have to pay for the remodeling yourself.' He said, 'I can commit $200,000 a year to it for the first couple of years.' So we made the deal. We remodeled the "B" and "C" buildings, which were Haymarket House and Catholic Charities, at one time. When we got done with that, we had about $5.5 million, with the purchase price, invested. Anyhow, we got the whole thing done. Father Conway contributed about $465,000 from Charities and they sent a grant for $365,000."

Later, Whalen says, the Charities money dried up. Times weren't good.

To keep the building afloat, Monsignor McDermott decided to do something he wouldn't have otherwise considered. An understated man at his core, he would throw a fund-raising party for himself to mark his 50 years in the priesthood.

An intimate party for hundreds of people at McCormick Place was planned.

CHAPTER 10

The Hand of God, 1985–1990

[about some figures in the archdiocesan curia] *Often times I felt like I was living in a leper colony.*

God's will, our willingness.

[to a substance abuser who rebelled against treatment] *Keep on talking like that, fella, and you'll end up in a wooden overcoat.*

One frigid January day on our weekly safari to the Kennedy School [for retarded children], *we found the campus barren except for a 10-year-old lad, Butchy. He greeted me as we slammed the car door and said, "Everybody around here has a cold." We went first to make a visit in the chapel. As he knelt down next to me he asked me: "Do you know what I'm asking God?" I said no. He answered: "I'm asking God if He has a cold." Wow. To Butchy, God is a person residing in this room at the chapel. Today too many of us are intent on the gold standard. But Butchy was given to the God standard.*

—Ignatius McDermott

Disengagement from Catholic Charities was among a flood of providential occurrences that came to Monsignor McDermott, sometimes disguised as mishaps, even catastrophes. Many bloomed into good fortune. Among the changes that would greatly affect the social service career of Ignatius McDermott, whose life was consecrated to the priesthood, were changes in the structure of his Church. The Catholic Church had begun to emphasize collegiality between bishop and priest.

Vatican II's legacy of collegiality, linked with the willingness of Catholic Charities to be freed of a pesky, entrepreneurial innovator, allowed Monsignor McDermott to do what he wanted— launch a mission to the addicted in a secular setting with a non-coercive, voluntary, spiritual approach.

However, chancery maneuverings continued. Cardinal Bernardin, after removing him from his role as advisor to the program of rehabilitation for priests suffering from alcohol and drug dependency, attended a meeting of the Haymarket board. The archbishop suffused Monsignor McDermott with praise, telling him that his name was foremost among priests of the archdiocese who deserved high honor.

The founder of Haymarket Center was noncommittal. Then the conversation moved to an apartment located at Haymarket Center, which would be shared with two priests, that the cardinal would order to be built for Monsignor McDermott—an understated allusion that his service would be ended and that the archdiocese would send another priest-executive to take over Haymarket. The suggestion was inappropriate. Haymarket Center was a public, not an archdiocesan institution, and its affiliation with Catholic Charities was weakened with Monsignor McDermott's retirement from that agency.

Cardinal Bernardin wanted to honor Monsignor McDermott at a dinner at Mundelein. Each year they would select a senior priest to be honored. Monsignor would be the first.

Quietly, but firmly, Monsignor McDermott declined the "honor" and the apartment. The cardinal gave up.

"Sure, it was a grab to take over Haymarket," a former high chancery official mused with a chuckle, "but it was just the latest in a string of goof-ups we made about McDermott. In the old days of the Church, pre-Vatican II, a priest was treated as a kind of orderly. You know what's funny? We figured Iggy would fall in step like the old days. But he proved to understand Vatican II better than we did! What we worried about was that Iggy had so many friends in the media that Bernardin would end up the heavy. And if he was astute about one thing, Bernardin was about the media."

* * *

In the midst of the struggle with Catholic Charities as it sought the retirement of Ignatius McDermott—as well as the obvious intention of Charities to assume control of Haymarket—came what was to be a tragedy for him: the death of Fran Lamb, who had worked selflessly for him for 40 years. She had begun as his assistant as a young woman of 22 in 1947.

Death at age 62 of the dedicated Lamb, who since young womanhood had sought nothing but to be useful to him, was a profound loss for Monsignor McDermott.

Her co-worker, Mary Ellen Flynn, tells the story: "For a long time she needed dental work but she was afraid of the dentist. After she had a cataract in her eye, she developed an infection. The eye became inflamed and she was shot through with terrible pain. Father got the best doctor he could find, one who had operated on some pope, but there was nothing they could do for the eye. So they removed it at a small hospital on the North Side. Matter of fact, it was an emergency. So they took her eye. It was, I think, very hard. And then, of course, she didn't want anything cosmetically done. She just put a patch on. It was hard on her because she had had cancer prior to this, in the '60s, breast cancer. She had both breasts removed in the 1960s. Then she had uterine cancer, but survived that."

But she kept her sense of humor. During the baseball season she would wear a Cubs logo on her patch; during football season she would stick on a Bears logo.

When Monsignor McDermott was overseas at an international conference, Lamb died—not of cancer, but of a heart attack.

"Father Conway [head of Catholic Charities] called to tell him," Mary Ellen Flynn recalled. "It was very hard for him. He did not think she had died. He kept hanging up on Father Conway. He said, 'It's one of my sisters. It's not Fran. Which one of my sisters? You won't tell me which one!' He thought it was one of his sisters, either Kathleen or Sister Mary Jeanette. And they kept telling him, 'No, it's Fran.' So I called him. I asked for the number and I called him and talked to him—sometime in the middle of the night—and I said, 'Father, it's *Fran*.' He was just so grief-stricken. He wept on the phone."

But consummate planner that she was, Francine Lamb had given instructions on everything (i.e., where things were, such as hidden keys to files and automobiles) to Mary Ellen Flynn. "Another Charities worker, Katherine Del Genio, had died at the end of August 1987," Flynn recalled. "I had taken Fran to see Katherine. Katherine had had cancer. Then we drove up for her funeral and when I brought Fran home and dropped her off,

Fran turned around and said, 'When something happens to me, I want you to follow what I'm going to leave you in an envelope.' I said, 'Fran, Fran.' And she walked away from the car, then she came back and said to me, 'Do you promise me you will do that?' I said, 'Yes.' Little did I realize it would be six weeks later."

After Fran Lamb's death, Monsignor McDermott turned to Mrs. Kay Zlogar. Mary Ellen Flynn says, "I can say this—if Kay had not taken the job, I knew who was next in line, me." She gave a smile that said: *Better Kay than me.*

After Mrs. Zlogar, who had worked with Monsignor McDermott since 1980, became his top personal assistant, her husband came down with Legionnaire's disease. Night after night, during her husband's hospitalization, Monsignor McDermott would visit him, a journey that involved many miles to and from a far-suburban hospital. As usual, time meant nothing to the priest. He frequently entered the hospital long after visiting hours had ended, gaining access because of his fame as spiritual comforter. As a result of Monsignor McDermott's attention to her husband, who died from the illness, Mrs. Zlogar became consumed—like Fran Lamb—with the vocation of assisting the priest.

"The first really important thing that Father asked me to work on was his 50th anniversary [in 1986]," Mrs. Zlogar recalled. "He asked if I would be interested and I, of course, said yes." It would be an initial fund-raiser for Haymarket. Mrs. Zlogar thought at first it would be an intimate party since "he said he would only invite his personal friends."

She learned how large that acquaintanceship was when she asked where he wanted to hold it. He said McCormick Place, the cavernous city exhibition hall comprising 2.2 million square feet on the lakefront—a dramatic black-steel designed building that was commissioned to make Chicago the nation's leading convention center. They sent out 10,000 invitations.

As they prepared for the 50th jubilee, Monsignor McDermott stunned Mrs. Zlogar by reviewing the names of the 10,000 invitees. "As we got these mailings ready," she says, "he would look through them to see, and he'd say, 'Mmmm, mmmm, they're divorced,' or 'We have the wrong zip code here.'" He would give her a name to add to the list "…say, Mary Jones. I would look for Mary Jones and I'd come back and say, 'Father, I don't think Mary Jones is in our Rolodex.' He'd say, 'Then check her married name which is such-and-such.'"

April 19, 1986 began with Mass at Holy Name Cathedral. Monsignor McDermott's homily, vintage South Side Catholic, brimmed with sports allusions:

> The word "jubilee" is derived from the Hebrew word "joben," which is a ram's horn. This instrument was to be blown for all the Jewish celebrations. We are all huddled here to blow the horn to thank God for all of His benedictions.
>
> Our "kickoff" should be an utterance of gratitude to our eternal Father for not only having allowed us to have lived at the same time in history, but more so in seeing to it that our paths would cross and recross, on the speaker's safari on the turnpike of Melchizedek.
>
> Today's Mass, and the reception that will follow at McCormick Place, is our maiden party. Our silver anniversary, and the induction into the rainbow division of monsignors of 1958, was not noted party-wise. The committee decreed: This party is a must.
>
> Our next party will be a retirement one; the locale of that party will be Kenny Brothers Funeral Home, 2700 West 95th Street.
>
> It is good to host an occasion such as this, to make our faithful more sensitive to the potential embracing of vocations to the sister-, brother-, and the priesthoods.
>
> As Monsignor Vincent Cooke, our head coach for not enough years, would say: "In the wake of the dearth of vocations, our novitiates, seminaries and monasteries resemble a tag-day in Glasgow, Scotland.
>
> The daughters of St. Dominic of Sinsinawa, Wisconsin— Sister Vivian, our 3rd and 5th grade teacher, and Sister Celestine, who taught us in 7th grade, coupled with their Dominican companions, gave us the "bread and butter" plays of Christianity. They were truly God's talent scouts. They had the conviction that some of us would be their teammates in His vineyard of tomorrow.
>
> In our youthful seminary years, we were apropos candidates for the 4-H Club. Now we are the charter members of the "4-B Club": bursitis, bifocals, baldness and bunions.
>
> Years ago, our department was the intake for the applicants to the Joseph Kennedy School for Exceptional Children. We would go there every Friday, bringing the applications, and also being the spiritual father of these lads, six to twelve years old.
>
> One cold, bleak winter day, I pulled up to the administration building. As I closed the car door, Butchy, a ten-year-old, greeted me and asked me if we could take a walk. He

wanted to go to the chapel. En route, he was relating the names of the nuns and his classmates who had a cold.

I opted for a pew in the middle of the chapel. Butchy asked, "Can't we get nearer to the Lord?" We knelt at the rail in silent prayer. In a minute or two, Butchy was tugging at my sleeve. "Father, do you know what I am asking the Lord?" "No," was my response. "I'm asking the Lord if He has a cold."

To Butchy, the Lord is a person. How sensitive Butchy was to God's presence in his life, and in His healing power. Our Divine Master just had to be proud of Butchy. Did not the Lord say: "Suffer the little children to come unto me"?

Michael McDermott's words of wisdom to his six sons and two daughters were to be ourselves.

"Iggy" translated this into: What we are is God's gift to us. What we do with this is our gift to God.

This world is an interesting place because each one of us possesses singular talents.

There is nothing tailor-made to the forgetting of self and the thinking of others.

What does distinguish one person from the rest is not our physical, intellectual, or emotional endowments, our talents, our charm, our personality, our idealism *or* pragmatism, but what each one of us will risk for another.

In this valley of tears, we must be prepared to be Spartans—not Athenians. Nobody in this world ever gets a pass. He never promised us a rose garden, or that He would not rain on our parade.

A graduate of West Madison Street who had found sobriety and serenity after a 20 years bout with "the grape," had the beautiful practice of a monthly Sunday visit to the corner of Madison and Desplaines Streets. Getting out of his car, he would kneel for a minute, thanking God for the gift of sobriety, uttering a "quiet time" prayer: "Thank you, Higher Power, for this street, for it led me to sobriety and to serenity."

On our travels along the road of life, we have found bearers of the liquid cross both in the flophouses and in penthouses. We have encountered both the spiritual and the material millionaires.

God gives each one of us only today. With our eternal Father, yesterday is history, and tomorrow is a mystery. I have learned the above philosophy only too well, due to sitting front row center, via 50 years with the precious persons of AA, GA, Al-Anon, GAMANON, and Alateen.

At our reception line, please do not resort to "20 Questions." Some of us haven't recrossed paths in many years. Couple this with a fading memory. So, please, introduce yourselves: I'm the Lone Ranger—We are Fibber McGee and Molly—Telly Savalas—Julia Child.

Hal Roach—the famous Irish comedian's trademark after delivering a joke is to say, "Write it down."

Every good deed, every kind word we utter, should be written on an ice cube. Why not? With this game plan, our guardian angels would constantly be running out of chalk registering them on the heavenly scoreboard.

So why not daily strive to letter in kindness, for kindness is the only language in the world that the blind can see, that the deaf can hear, and that the dumb can speak.

The prodigious McDermott memory has been a mainstay throughout his life. Mrs. Zlogar was fascinated at watching it work during the 10,000-person reception.

"We were gathered to help him with some of the names," she said, "but he started saying, 'Hello, Joe, how did your job turn out?' or 'Mary Jane, is your mother still in that nursing home?' He never missed a beat. Not one person was made to feel he didn't know who they were or why they were there."

Enough money was generated to give Haymarket a good start. The success of the jubilee was, to Mrs. Zlogar's mind, a work of providence. But even more so was the *ad hoc* way that seemingly a divine plan materialized to solve financial troubles.

"I need to tell you," said Mrs. Zlogar, "that when he first bought the building at 932 West Washington, it was in shambles. I wrote the checks. I was not a bookkeeper, but I wrote the checks and I knew that we had, let's say, enough to pay the electric bill but not the water bill. There was a meeting, sort of a board of directors meeting, and they were trying to decide how we would get ahead, and as we sat down at the table, Father would say, 'You know, if we had $100,000 we'd be all set today.'" Those at the table had varying degrees of optimism; Monsignor McDermott's seemed unquenchable.

And the optimism was usually justified.

"The meeting went on and somebody came to the front door and left some clothes as a donation and an envelope for Father," Mrs. Zlogar continued. "After the meeting someone gave these to Father and he said, 'Oh, wow!' He opened the envelope and it would be a check for $100,000. I don't think I've ever seen anything like that."

A key factor in success was the Haymarket working team. Working with Monsignor McDermott, in addition to Jack Whalen, was Ann Konar. She was the first executive director; George Borneman, who had worked for the Chicago Christian Industrial League, consulted with Whalen on the building, and had secured some funding. Borneman served as a temporary executive director. There was also Dick Lewis, scion of a wealthy family in the construction business who had given many millions to Catholic institutions and universities. Lewis, who had been a contractor, had an impressive working knowledge of buildings, and gave Jack Whalen early instruction. He advised on what to look for as workers virtually rebuilt the old hulk at 932 West Washington from the ground up. Lewis came by almost nightly to talk with Whalen about the building, how to renovate it, and how to deal with contractors. Kay Zlogar did the invaluable details surrounding Monsignor McDermott's busy life. Mrs. Zlogar retired in 2002.

There were battalions of immediate problems: how to encourage more referrals of clients to Haymarket, how to find good staff, and the continuing search for funds to keep the institution going. Whalen spoke to Ray Murray of the W. Clement Stone Foundation.

"Jack," said Murray, "you're going to need from $100,000 to $200,000 a month to keep it running, so these little things like chance books and raffles won't work. You can't do it on volume; you've got to get people who'll give you the money." Yet another concern was Dr. James West, who had volunteered so much time as Haymarket's medical director. This pioneer of "social setting detox," had accepted a position of medical director at the new Betty Ford Center in California, which was patterned after the lessons he taught at Haymarket.

Dr. West and Monsignor McDermott would remain personally close, and the physician continues to serve on Haymarket's board. But when Whalen and Monsignor McDermott tried personally to run the institution in addition to tackling fund-raising, they got bogged down in details. Just when they were ready to throw up their hands in despair, help—in the form of funds and/or top executives—would come dribbling in to keep them going. At a Haymarket open house, Whalen and Dick Athey were burdened with worry about unpaid bills. Then Athey spotted a man in the crowd and nudged Whalen.

"That's a guy who gives Father money," Athey said. "Maybe he can give some now."

Whalen replied, "Red, God will have to inspire us, because there's not much we can say right now except we need dough."

They targeted business entrepreneur Dietrich Gross. As he mentally prepared for a meeting with Gross, Whalen employed his AA-generated step three theology of faith, of relying on God to carry the day.

For example, in buying the building. Whalen said, "All for God's people. If this is where we were led—to serve God's people—God is the principal and we're the agents. Therefore, He's responsible for this. So you can't take any credit, but you don't have to take the blame, because it's God.

"With the third step in AA you have a new principal and you're the agent. You're just an employee. And He will show you what to do when the time comes. If you have faith in Him and believe He will, He will. That's what St. Paul said, 'I glory in my weakness.' If you're weak, God can help you. If you're strong, He can't help you."

Exuding this philosophy, Whalen confronted Gross. He came up with $10,000.

Another one brought in a priceless resource: not just money but a man with sophisticated experience in finance. It began when Monsignor McDermott told Whalen simply, "A man has called who wants to give money. I'd like you to talk to him." He was John Butler, a recently retired top financial officer with the Chicago Northwestern railroad.

Whalen visited with Butler, who had been donating $2,000 here and $5,000 there.

Butler was looking for a cause to give more money to. Whalen took him on a tour of the ravaged Haymarket House, pointing out what it could ultimately be. Butler had been married in New York by a priest named Father Mac (no relation). On meeting Chicago's Father Mac, he became deeply interested. "What do you want me to do, buy some blankets?" he asked Whalen. Whalen said, "Give to the general building fund. We've got to rebuild the building. There's plenty of money for programs and food and blankets, but you must have a building to do this in."

"My mother gave me some stock when she died," Whalen told Butler. "I didn't know anything about stock receipts. You have to keep all these papers and pay tax and all this stuff. I didn't like it. I never had stock. So when we wanted to make an offer on a building I said, 'I'll pay it. I'll put up the money, $10,000. I'll give stock.' I went to cash in the stock and it turns out to be $27,000.

Now Red Athey was very generous, considering his station and his earnings. So I said to Athey, 'I'm going to give Father this money. If he buys the building, I'll give him money toward the down payment, $127,000. I gave him the $27,000 and I gave him $100,000. When he heard that, Athey gave him about $60,000."

Eventually he would give much more.

Butler heard Whalen's story and said, dryly, "I think I'll give to the general fund."

He donated $200,000. More important than even that, Butler joined the board and became chief financial officer of Haymarket, volunteering his time and ruling on important financial decisions. Then the unique McDermott theory of organization took over. Simply stated: *Able people should hold sway (within reason) in their field of expertise.*

"Butler's borrowed zillions," said Whalen. "If we want to borrow some money, Butler will borrow the money. He'll go to the banks. And you defer to the person whose expertise is in that particular area, because his guess or his works will be better than yours, and we don't have any trouble."

These were all striking providential occurrences. When acting executive director George Borneman decided not to do the job permanently, there came another. It proved to be the exact man to administer Haymarket, one who had worked for Monsignor McDermott earlier at Catholic Charities. He turned down the job once, then reconsidered. He was Raymond F. Soucek, about 40 years old when he officially signed on in 1986.

After leaving Catholic Charities in 1979, Soucek accepted another job, at better pay, for a private addiction counseling center; but throughout the years kept one eye on the struggle that Monsignor McDermott was waging to fund successive Haymarket facilities as full-time treatment centers. He was earning a good salary a few years later, but was still drawn to the Haymarket project, which wasn't going very well. Soucek was sure he was needed, but at first he didn't want to go. The liabilities, he noted, were substantial.

First, Haymarket was started in 1975 when Monsignor McDermott was 66 years old, an age when other priests prepare for retirement.

"That's number one," recalled Soucek. "Number two—the state and Catholic Charities didn't want to back the program. There was no financial support for Haymarket. So, Father goes out and finds the financial support and he hooks up with Dr. West, a very reputable physician, also a senior citizen, and, by his own admission, is recovering. Dr. West's teaming up with Father is a very interesting development. Most doctors would have probably given Father the time of day and that's it, they don't show up. That's not the way it was with Dr. West."

Ticking off the providential occurrences, Soucek says: "Then Father finds the funding. He and Dr. West get together. Dr. West takes an interest in what Father is doing instead of just blowing Father off, saying 'Yeah, you've got a great program, but...' But Dr. West sticks. Father and Dr. West become, the way I look at it, like Bill Wilson and Dr. Bob, the founders of Alcoholics Anonymous. You've got a priest and a doctor in this case. You had a doctor and a stockbroker in the founding of AA who came together in a very unusual situation—and Father and Dr. West came together. They stick as a team and they're both influential, and Haymarket as we know it today starts building.

"Then consider the steps that led to the present building at 932 West Washington. They moved from one building and then they moved to another. That second building is sold out from under them. The new buyer changes his business address and telephone number and everything. He's ready to move in. They plead for an extension and the guy gives them a year's extension! *Unheard of!* That to me is a divine intervention simply because most businessmen would say: 'I need the place; I've got to make money.' This guy—I don't know how he did it, but he said: 'Yeah, you can have the lease for another year.' So they bought a year of time.

"Then Jack Whalen comes into the picture. He has a hard time reaching Father and figuring out how things fit together. Here's a guy who not only gives his financial support but gives his encouragement and his professional support to the program. A guy of Jack Whalen's caliber, normally, if somebody shuns him and doesn't return his calls, he says, 'Okay, fine, I'll find another cause.' And God knows, Jack could have picked up the phone and gotten involved with the Salvation Army, or one of the other religious organizations, and put his support that way. But he persists. He finally meets Father and they hook up.

"By this time Dr. West has moved to California and the search is on for a permanent building. They're circling this area, looking north, south, east and west, and all the time the best building is a half-block from where they were. Finally, they stumble into this building. They're looking for 35,000 square feet to house Haymarket, which would have been all right at the time but very inadequate for what they have now. And again, in my opinion, divine providence comes to the fore. God knows what we need. He says, 'You don't need 35,000 square feet, you need 150,000 square feet. There's the right building down the street.'

"They don't know how they're going to pay for it," Soucek concluded. "They don't know how they're going to come up with the payment. But they do it. And we have the structure and the programs we have today."

Another event was taking place that eventually led Soucek to quit his private sector counseling job and join Haymarket as executive director, returning to work for Monsignor McDermott as he had earlier at Catholic Charities.

But an early introduction to Haymarket didn't enthuse Soucek about its prospects. After dropping in one day to help out with a soup line event, which turned out to be a disaster, he determined not to get involved with the risky Haymarket project.

Monsignor McDermott had the vision that city celebrities, ex-politicians, ex-judges, retired athletes, bankers, and journalists would volunteer working a soup line for the homeless and indigent. The crowds that would come would be solicited to give money for individual items such as desks and chairs. Unfortunately, the day the celebrity soup line opened was the hottest day of the year. So worried was Soucek that the event wouldn't succeed, he remained all day.

"They had Haymarket going but it wasn't going very well," he recalled. "They weren't getting a lot of referrals, and they had this huge building. So they put on this party, whatever you want to call it, a soup line in the street. And on this particular day, the temperature reached about 103 or 104 degrees. There we were with hot soup and hot coffee in the street. I came down early to help set up and we're all sweating like pigs. The way it was supposed to work was that they would have these people come by and we'd say, 'Okay, we need a wastebasket. We need a desk. Will you contribute money toward that?' There were tours. That's the first time I really saw Haymarket, which was in very bad shape. The courtyard had all kinds of debris in it, and there were broken windows."

Not long after, Soucek heard that they were looking for a full-time executive director, but he wasn't interested.

"My name popped up," he said. "I had been involved in community relations and marketing for this company. It had its ups and downs, and at this time, it was on the upside, so I was feeling pretty good about it. I was making reasonable money and fairly comfortable in my job. One day I got a call from Father's secretary, Kay Zlogar, who asked if I'd like to have dinner. Periodically, Father and I would go to lunch. It was no big deal, a cordial lunch. So I agreed to have dinner with Father and I came down. But instead of meeting Father, I meet Jack Whalen, the first time I ever met him. He introduced himself to me and said, 'Come on, I'd like to show you Haymarket.' He took me around the building. The only part of Haymarket that was renovated at that time was the "B" Building, the first three floors.

"I thought I was there to meet Father for dinner. So Jack starts talking to me and we go out to meet Dr. Harry Hannig [the new medical director], and he joined us for dinner as well. It became apparent to me—at some point in the dinner conversation—that they were looking for an executive director, and they asked did I know of anyone. I said I would think about it and would let them know. Jack called me a few days later and said, 'We're really interested in you.' And I said I thought that was what was happening and I really wasn't interested.

"I had heard about Haymarket and the problems they were having and I thought: 'It's not going to happen.' And all of a sudden, they were asking me if I wanted to be the executive director. I turned them down. I said, 'No, I'm not interested in becoming the executive director.' And Jack said, 'Can we keep in touch with you?' I said sure, you can keep in touch with me."

Then things at Soucek's private sector job started to disintegrate.

"Things there started to go south," he noted. "The ownership sold out, and the next thing I know is that while I'm not being shipped out, different things are happening. And I'm not real happy. I'm voicing my opinion and the next thing I know they're reprimanding me. So I made a call to Jack and said, 'Is the offer still open?' He said, 'Yes, as far as I know; let me check with Father.' About ten minutes later I get a call from Jack and he said, 'The job's yours if you want it.' I didn't know it, but Jack did not check with Father because he couldn't get hold of him. Jack did that on his own. So I resigned—gave them a month's notice."

Whalen says he made the offer because he knew Monsignor McDermott wanted Soucek. So Soucek, who had been happy with his old job, found the job suddenly turning sour. It made him reach out to become executive director of Haymarket.

Soucek took the job, never having managed a big enterprise before. "My worry," he said, "was that we had this huge building, and what are we going to do with it? My worries were finding funding because Haymarket prided itself on having the least expensive treatment available, which meant that our salaries were way down and our budget was about $1.5 million annually. We prided ourselves on taking in everyone who couldn't receive treatment anywhere else. So trying to make ends meet was really a challenge."

Once again AA's famed third step, the placing of one's problems in the hands of a spiritual entity, took over. Faced with problems to which he didn't have ready answers, Soucek would pause during the day, would kneel down by his desk if he wasn't readily observed, and ask God for guidance. Haymarket is a secular institution but not non-Godly. "What God really wants, in my opinion, is for us to be dependent on Him. He wants us to say, 'I need you, Lord. I can't do it without You.' AA says the same thing. I need Your help. I need to depend on—not this booze—a power greater than myself."

*   *   *

Now Monsignor McDermott was asked to reach out to the next goal—treating drug-addicted women after they gave birth to, it was surmised, their drug-affected newborn babies. The call came in 1988, at a meeting with Father John P. Smyth, superintendent of Maryville. A compelling figure in his own right, in social service, Father Smyth was an All-American Notre Dame basketball player who had turned his back on professional athletics, declining a first-round draft choice of the NBA's St. Louis Hawks, for the priesthood. His first and only assignment in the priesthood was Maryville. When Father Smyth's brother had died suddenly while at Maryville, Father Smyth took up the vocation.

The state of Illinois would fund a program to treat addicted mothers only after they gave birth, believing, according to its

research, that once a woman was five-and-a-half months pregnant, nothing could be done to prevent her baby from being born
damaged, sometimes irretrievably, from its mother's addiction.

The social problems, confronted at high tide of inner-city addiction to cocaine and crack cocaine, were dramatic. Babies born
of such women would be in what psychologists call a "never-land,"
not being able to attain their full potential. Cocaine's potent effect
induces mood elevation, irrational optimism, and anti-fatigue but
has dire repercussions for blood pressure and heart rate. In the
1980s, cocaine and its free-base form, crack, had been used increasingly by lower- and lower-middle class adolescents and
young adults, raising the fear about the long-term effects of cocaine on thousands of children. Cocaine-exposed children would,
it was warned, be more likely to suffer from growth stuntedness,
stillbirth, and premature separation of the placenta.

So accepted was the research that the state determined not to
treat addicted pregnant women until they gave birth, seeking to
spare taxpayers the legal liability associated with children's disabilities. After birth, Father Smyth's Maryville would take custody
of the drug-affected babies, and Monsignor McDermott's
Haymarket Center would treat the mothers, with a rendezvous
between mothers and children later down the road.

"The idea was that hospitals, or doctors, would identify a
woman who gave birth as drug-affected," said Soucek. "Immediately, authorities would take the baby from the woman, put the infant in Maryville and then encourage the new mother to take the
program at Haymarket, with the idea of some kind of reunification down the line. There was money available from the state for
this purpose."

Monsignor McDermott listened to the proposal, thought for
a while, and asked what seemed to be an obvious but simple
question.

*Why not treat the addicted expectant mother before she delivers, in the
hope that her baby could dodge the bullet, could avoid being born with
drugs in its system?*

The state patiently re-explained its research. Preventing a baby
from being affected by such an addiction that has gone on for five
months is not possible, according to the latest research. It would be
risky to experiment along the lines of McDermott's suggestion. The
approved procedure would be to receive women just about ready

to deliver, await the birth of the baby, and treat one or both as addicts, prompting separation at first and reunification later.

The same independence that characterized his entire career—from Quigley to Mundelein to Skid Row ministry—persisted as Monsignor McDermott urged the state, "Let's see if we could help her deliver a drug-free baby. I have the space. If you can help me fill it up, we can open up a program."

The state reluctantly agreed to fund the program—but it was chancy. If the McDermott gamble did not pay off, the program would be judged a failure and officials might be disillusioned about the worth of any future Haymarket program.

So, embarked on the gamble, Haymarket became the site of the first state-supported program in Illinois for pregnant women who were chemically dependent, treating them with the expectation of delivering drug-free babies.

"We built up the sixth floor of the "B" building for the pre-natal program, which we called the MAC unit—a double meaning: Maternal Addiction Center and "MAC" as in Father Mac," Soucek recalled.

At first it appeared that Monsignor McDermott was wrong and the state was right. The first two babies who arrived were delivered stillborn, which seemed to invalidate Monsignor McDermott's premise.

"But after that," says Soucek, "suddenly, women who were being treated for addiction began to deliver their babies well, addiction-free, full-term, and with normal body weight. To date we're at 500 babies who have been born drug-free through the Haymarket MAC program. We have had women who are in their eighth month—close to their ninth—who, once off drugs, have delivered babies drug-free.

"What we found is that the problem wasn't just getting the expectant mother off drugs, it was getting her on good nutrition, getting good medical care. So Father's insistence led to new research that is three-fold: first, take the woman off drugs; second, give her good nutrition; and third, good medical care. We went against the prevailing wisdom and the so-called research, and Father won."

Following that experiment—and partially because of it—the number of female clients escalated at Haymarket. Now the population for the once all-male facility is slightly more than 50 percent women. And the state researcher who had produced the erroneous findings announced, brightly, that he had just discovered fresh data that disproved the old and supported Monsignor McDermott's original position—a superb governmental coincidence.

* * *

As the decade of the 1980s ended, Haymarket Center equaled, and in some cases topped, in terms of treatment excellence, the care given at the far more prestigious Betty Ford Center in Palm Springs, California. At Haymarket, the poor receive at least the same quality of care—that is in some cases superior—than the upper-middle class clients and entertainment industry mega-millionaires, according to Dr. Sam Cardone. A clinical psychologist, he had guided the first state grants at Haymarket. He left state employment for a private consulting practice that includes several hours a week for Haymarket.

Now proudly calling Haymarket "we," Dr. Cardone said, "I've been to Betty Ford—but I think the issue is this: when we have our full complement of staff (which sometimes we don't because of funding issues), there's no question that we provide the same level of care."

And in some cases better?

"Yes," answered Dr. Cardone, citing that, because Dr. West is on the Haymarket board and was medical director at Betty Ford, comparisons can easily be made. "There's lots of comparability of cross-programs. In fact, they've modeled some of their programs after us, such as women's programming. They're very far behind us in terms of women's programming, other than residential care. I met with the clinical director out there about three years ago to help her put together a halfway house. We used our model that we have here in terms of a recovery home."

Dr. Cardone smiled as he looked back on the days he and Monsignor McDermott strove to make Haymarket justify the state's trust.

"Father Mac," he recalled, "would find people on the streets and he would say, 'You need to come to our place. I'll take you there. I'll find someone to get you there.' That was his role. He was truly the activist in all this. I was simply grateful to be in his presence at that time. I would escort him sometimes, and be with him, but certainly he was the activist. He was the prime mover in this geographic area, without question."

* * *

One character who crossed Monsignor McDermott's radar screen was Walter Miller.

"Walter Miller was a creature of Skid Row who interested me very much," said Monsignor McDermott. "He was an advertising man and had the unique ability to look one day like he came out of a bandbox—bright, articulate, well-groomed—and the next day, when he was drinking, like the wrath of God. One day he called me up and said that in recognition of five years of sobriety he would like to host a party at the Atlantic Hotel in Chicago and would I be the toastmaster. I agreed.

"We arrived and the reserved dining room filled up with the friends of Walter Miller. To each and every one he gave a salute. It was a memorable meal—filet mignon and all the trimmings. A few days after it, I was opening the mail and I got the bill. It was stupendous. And Walter went back to the booze.

"One day I got a call from Walter to come to a flea-bag hotel to rescue him. When I got there and inquired about him at the desk, the night clerk said, 'You want to see that drunken bum?' Before I could respond, Walter Miller came weaving down the corridor and announced in stentorian tones, 'Sir, I heard that remark and I am going to institute a suit against you and this hotel for defamation of character!' He carried off his indignity with such aplomb that I was impressed. However, the night clerk was not."

Another name that came from the prodigious memory of Ignatius McDermott was Luigi Giambastani. He was the pastor of Assumption parish in Chicago.

"I was going into a hospital to make my rounds of visits when I met Father Giambastani. He said one patient was so ill he wouldn't make it through the night. Then he wrote to the friends of the patient and expressed sadness that he died. But the patient survived. And Father Luigi Giambastani had to rewrite all the friends and say that, thankfully, he was wrong."

By the decade's end, Haymarket was nearing some 20 programs with almost every level of care to treat the addicted, except on-site medical care. And having fought for and proved the value of social setting detox, Monsignor McDermott was reaching out to provide in-house medical care as well. Maintained Dr. Cardone:

"Father McDermott had a vision to match services for the publicly-funded client at the level that the private sector was providing at every level of care." The James West Medical Clinic is an example of an on-site program for clients at Haymarket Center.

As he moved into the 1990s, he reached out for another challenge. One day, it came with a phone call from Chicago's new mayor—another Daley, also named Richard, the son of Richard J. Daley. But now a long history of enmity—Irish style—separated the Daleys from the McDermotts, stemming from the abortive attempt of the late Jim McDermott to displace the late Richard J. Daley as Democratic chairman of Cook County almost 40 years earlier. It was a long time as urban politics goes but not long at all as Irish feuds are reckoned, especially with the winning faction, the Daleys. However, the young mayor needed help from Haymarket for the busiest airport in the world, O'Hare International.

CHAPTER 11

Extra Years Well Used, 1990–1997

[modern Catholic burial practices] *When did the casual thing start? I'm really knocked out of the box when I see some of them. We blew so many wonderful things. The Jews kept them. I'm very deeply impressed going to Jewish funerals, to their chapels, their burial services and I go to a lot of them.* [modern Catholic slovenliness at Mass] *I remember I went there at Holy Name [Cathedral] and it was a jubilee or something. And I was kneeling in the pew and it was a day like today, raining. I was noticing the people at Communion time. I saw better-dressed people from West Madison Street. These looked like escapees from a clothing drive. It was terrible.*

[discussing some of the all-but-discarded traditional parts of the Catholic liturgy] *They had Latin Mass, the Gregorian Mass, Forty Hours, the Stations of the Cross, and Benediction. At one time there had to be some movers within the Church who were, really, the tail wagging the dog.*

[women in Catholic religious life] *I had a sister in the Mercy Order. My mother's sister was in the Mercy Order, and they were on fire with love and with dedicating their lives to children in grammar and high school. I met a person my sister taught, and she was telling me what an impact my sister had upon the classes she taught. I don't think she had to be a priest to make that impact upon them. If we're following the Bible, I'm sure the Lord, who instituted the priesthood, if He felt that should be, He's the author of human nature. Why did he say that the priesthood should rest upon the males of the Church?*

—Ignatius McDermott

Much had happened in Chicago history since the day in 1953 when, after the death of Clarence Wagner, Jim McDermott abandoned his bid for Cook County Democratic party chairman in favor of the current mayor's father, then Cook County clerk, Richard J. Daley. It must now be told, because Chicago's history is filled with immensely colorful characters and no understanding of Monsignor McDermott can be complete without a panoramic view of the complex strands of city politics, from Kennelly to the second Daley.

Richard J. Daley's first step as chairman was to set the machinery in motion to get himself elected mayor in 1955, which formally wrote *finis* to Jim McDermott's political career.

At a county slate-making session on December 15, 1954, Daley brushed aside Democratic incumbent Martin Kennelly, the personally popular but somewhat ineffective mayor, for the party's endorsement, which led to charges of bossism. Kennelly vowed to challenge the "bosses" of his party. Daley's winning margin of 100,064 votes depended on almost 99,000 in 11 organization-controlled wards.

He then faced the Republican nominee, Robert Merriam, a youngish reform liberal, former Democratic alderman, son of a University of Chicago professor who had earlier crusaded as political scientist and candidate against Big Bill Thompson's corruption. In the general mayoralty election of April 5, 1955, Daley won with 55 percent. This represented a good showing in view of the fractures within the Democratic party. He carried heavily in working-class wards and particularly among the blacks.

Daley was not a national figure when he was elected mayor, but in the 20 years of his incumbency he was elected mayor six times. He directed a series of successful local, state, and national campaigns, placing Chicago as reliably in the Democratic column as any metropolitan center of the United States. By doing this, he won for himself a role of national power and importance. But he had his troubles: trouble with African-American discontent, a riotous 1968 Democratic convention, and an unsympathetic Republican national administration whose local prosecutor convicted some of the proudest names in the Democratic party.

On May 6, 1974, nine days before his 72nd birthday, Daley suffered a small stroke caused by blockage of a carotid artery, which supplies blood and oxygen to the brain. He underwent surgery. After the operation he retired to his Grand Beach, Indiana, home for three months, striving to regain his speech and motor capabilities. In April 1975, the voters returned him to office with more than 70 percent of the general election vote. Undetected by many was that in the earlier primary a liberal Democrat, Alderman William Singer, had received a third of the Democratic vote. Yet hope bloomed for a national administration more favorable to Daley and Chicago when Democrat Jimmy Carter won in November 1976. But Daley would not live to see it. On December 20, 1976, at 1:35 p.m., sensing something was wrong, the mayor walked into the office of his physician, Dr. Thomas Coogan. A half-hour later he was dead.

Often right, occasionally majestically wrong-headed, of this there is no doubt: Daley was an icon of Democratic urban power and had the courage to lead. For example, despite the protests of more traditional Democratic supporters, he picked a central location for the new campus of the University of Illinois-Chicago, a move that destroyed the old, inner-city community of the West Side. UIC was built near Haymarket Center's location—destroying the flophouses where so many of the Skid Row people could at least find a haven. The university's new campus was an "improvement" that Monsignor McDermott deplored. Nevertheless, Daley gained the support of the business community, the upper class, labor union presidents, and industrialists. A small-business woman named Florence Scala fought Daley and led a protest that almost succeeded in derailing the U of I complex.

Daley was succeeded by 11th Ward Alderman Michael Bilandic, a bland, 53-year-old Bridgeport bachelor who spoke, like Daley, with immobile lips in distinctive South Side accent. In the special election to complete Daley's unfulfilled term, Bilandic was opposed by Roman Pucinski, a former Congressman, who received— similar to Singer earlier—a third of the Democratic primary vote, an ominous but then largely overlooked occurrence. Also threatening was the vote received by State Senator Harold Washington, an African-American, who took five middle-class black South Side wards, winning 11 percent of the citywide vote.

Washington had told the congregation of a black church "There is a sleeping giant in Chicago. And if this sleeping giant, the potential black vote, ever woke up, we'd control the city."

Two years later, running for a full term in the February 1979 primary, Bilandic was assured of victory in the Democratic primary, which only an act of God would prevent. His only opponent was Jane Byrne, a former city consumer affairs commissioner who had been fired by Bilandic. But then the act of God happened. On New Year's Eve 1978, it began snowing. When the snow stopped on New Year's Day more than 22 inches had fallen. The next day the Chicago Transit Authority's buses and elevated trains faced problems, despite the mayor's protestations that things were working. Loop employees told of waiting two hours at bus stops. By the time public transportation riders forgot their anger, the snow fell again. Beginning on Friday, January 12, less than two weeks after the first snowfall, over a two-day period, more than 20 inches of snow fell on top of what had come down initially. Then came days of subzero weather.

An angered Chicago Democratic electorate, by a slender majority of 16,675 votes, nominated Byrne, a diminutive 5'3" woman. The general election the following April saw her beat her Republican opponent with the biggest majority in city history, winning 82 percent of the vote.

The story of Jane Byrne is unduplicated in Chicago history. In less time than it takes a neophyte politician to move from precinct captain to assistant ward committeeman, she—a former debutante from a wealthy family on the Northwest Side—touched the late Mayor Daley's heart as the young widow of a Navy pilot and received an administrative post in city government, to which she added the co-chairmanship of the Cook County Democratic party before winning the mayoralty.

Once in office in 1979, Mayor Byrne allowed regular Daley Democrats in the city council to assist her, apparently believing that her reformist ideas could not work in the face of a freshly discovered deterioration of the city's financial condition—a budget deficit of $102 million.

Wrote historian Melvin Holli: "Cities on the high-risk list had difficulty in selling their bonds, sometimes absorbing massive losses through deep discounts, and some bankers were even looking askance at short-term tax anticipation warrants, which all cities needed to tide them over until taxes were paid."

Despite the fact that she was the highest profiled first-term mayor in the U.S.—proposing gambling casinos and stock-car racing, moving into the Cabrini-Green housing project to dramatize the need for public safety improvements there, suggesting rehabilitation of Navy Pier, instituting Chicagofest, and the transitioning of an abandoned department store into a public library—Jane Byrne saw as her nemesis the late mayor Daley's eldest son, Richard M. Daley.

He had tried to pass his law exam three times (making it on the third try), and was dubbed by columnist Mike Royko as "a very small chip off the old block." However, in late 1979, young

Daley, who had been a state senator from Bridgeport, began a drive to family political restoration by winning as Cook County States Attorney. There was a fervent anti-Byrne quality to his supporters, who could barely disguise their emotional zeal in turning her out of City Hall. Some thought that the appearance of Congressman Harold Washington would siphon off black votes and not threaten Byrne, since his poorly financed 1977 effort in the mayoral primary netted him five wards and 11 percent of the vote. Then there was the matter of his having served a jail term in 1972 for having failed to file federal income tax returns in the amount of $508.05, which the court categorized not as a felony but a misdemeanor.

Predictably, the two white candidates, Byrne and Daley, divided the white vote in the 1983 mayoral primary. A massive increase in black voter registration, coupled with a higher than expected return in black, white, and Latino wards in other sections of the city, gave Harold Washington the numbers to triumph, receiving 36 percent to 34 percent for Byrne and 30 percent for Daley. In the general election, Washington faced Republican former State Representative Bernard Epton. A liberal who became, overnight, the refuge of status-quo supporters, Epton made a tremendous run for mayor, not because of his own attainments (although as a millionaire lawyer he had compiled a progressive record in the legislature representing a district that included Hyde Park) but, as the *Chicago Tribune* stated in its endorsement of Harold Washington, "because he is white and the Democratic nominee, Representative Harold Washington, is black."

The general election was a squeaker, decided for Washington only because he was a Democrat in a Democratic city, with Washington getting 51.8 percent of the vote, 40,000 ballots showing no choice whatsoever for mayor.

A good part of Washington's first term was mired in bickering in what became known as "Council Wars." As mayor he sought to cut down the Democratic party's traditional patronage system in favor of new appointments of minorities and women to city positions. He sought to help economic development for the city neighborhoods, not just the Loop. Unfortunately, most of his time was spent in fighting his council opposition. There were scandals, too, as a federally managed mole secured the conviction of two aldermen.

In late 1986, Washington declared he would seek a second term the following year. He was opposed in the Democratic primary by Jane Byrne. He defeated her handily, then faced three opponents in the general election—Cook County Assessor Tom Hynes and Alderman Edward Vrdolyak running as independents, and Democrat-turned-Republican Donald Haider, Byrne's budget chief who had been a Treasury Department official under President Jimmy Carter. Washington won re-election in April 1987, with 54 percent of the vote.

Then, on November 23, 1987, while sitting in his office in the morning talking to his press aide, he suddenly slumped over, his face resting on the desk top, dead of a massive heart attack. Chicago's first African-American mayor, with a cheerful exuberance, had surmounted his enemies and had certified that there would not be further opposition to a future black mayor.

The days following Washington's death rekindled "Council Wars." At long last, after a night-long session at which at least one alderman hopped on his desk to address the unruly gathering, the white aldermanic bloc chose Eugene Sawyer, a black alderman from the South Side, to take over as mayor until a special election in 1989. For the February 1989 special election, Hyde Park's Alderman Tim Evans led a schism in the black community, determining to run as a third-party candidate in the general election. Evans's action was meant to forestall criticism of splitting the black vote in the primary, leaving Sawyer to oppose Cook County States Attorney Richard M. Daley.

Daley ousted Sawyer in the primary and easily disposed of Evans and Democrat-turned-Republican Edward Vrdolyak in the general election five weeks later. It was the second time in city history that father and son had held the office; Carter Harrison and Carter Harrison II served a total of 22 years between 1879 and 1915.

* * *

Now, in a city where Irish politicians have long memories, Richard M. Daley called for help—and received it—from the brother of his father's old adversary. The mayor, just two years in office, said that he wanted to talk about Chicago's homeless problems at O'Hare International Airport. Monsignor McDermott gladly agreed to take up the problem.

The problem was a huge one for the man known as Richie Daley. It started as a few drops, then a trickle: people coming to

O'Hare and taking up residence. It was a knotty public relations problem for the city. Three hundred homeless were camping at O'Hare. They entered the airport via the subway—sleeping on the benches, begging money from the airline consumers and fast-food restaurants. The airport afforded them what they couldn't get outside: a guarantee of stable temperatures and relative safety. The problem confronting Daley's new administration was that the so-called "homeless groups" perpetuated the idea that moving irreconcilables would breach their freedom, heedless of the fact that often addiction and mental illness foreclosed their thinking of their own well-being. The question was how to remove them, get them to treatment without appearing heartless, incurring ACLU lawsuits and bad press, and still assuring that they would be treated humanely? Which is why he asked Monsignor McDermott and Haymarket Center for help.

So, determined not to retire but to keep on going, doing what he could do, Monsignor McDermott attended a gathering in 1990 at which the mayor was in attendance. The Daleys had never been close to Monsignor McDermott, since Jim's attempt to topple a Daley. But now came an historic moment: a meeting between a Daley and a McDermott—but a different Daley and a different McDermott. Not Richard J., but his son, Mayor Richard M. Not Jim, but Monsignor Ignatius.

Among those in charge at O'Hare was Mary Rose Loney, who first came to Chicago in November 1989, at age 37, to assume the day-to-day operations of the world's busiest airport, as first deputy commissioner of aviation. Born in Pittsburgh, she graduated from the University of Pittsburgh with a desire to teach philosophy ("I was fascinated by existentialism"). But she switched to public administration, getting a master's at the University of Nevada.

"My responsibilities were primarily to administer the day-to-day operations of the airport," she explained. "When I came here, we had two significant operational problems. First, we had a lapse in security. Second, we had a large number of homeless who were living in the terminal buildings. The second problem leads to how I ended up meeting Father Mac. We estimated, at the time, that there were from 300 to 325 people living in the terminal buildings at O'Hare. Many of them had been there for as long as ten years. They would sleep anywhere in the terminal buildings—on the chairs, on the baggage carousels. They bathed using the sinks. There was a significant hygiene problem associated with them living there. Business tenants, who were otherwise well-intentioned, were actually exacerbating the problem by continuing to make it easy for them to live there.

"But perhaps the biggest problem was that the CTA Blue Line, going to O'Hare, provided a convenient access for them to get on the CTA in the Loop and travel out to O'Hare for a place that was warm and lighted—and with a lot of places to hide. There's about 4-1/2 million square feet of space across the three terminal buildings at O'Hare. So the challenge that the mayor posed to me was: you need to address both these problems, the security problem as well as the homeless problem. And the homeless problem was contributing to our security difficulties. In the final days of 1989, one homeless person stabbed and critically wounded another in the baggage claim area, which is an untenable situation. We began to look at a number of alternatives as to how we could address it because we wanted to do it, obviously, in a humane manner that would achieve permanent, lasting results—not just chasing the homeless out and not really addressing the core of the problem.

"We looked at establishing some alternatives for the homeless. We looked at a shuttered hospital, St. Anne's, on the West Side, as a potential place that could serve as an alternative to O'Hare Airport for the homeless. We also looked at establishing some temporary, transitional housing. I actually sent a couple of my staff members to Ohio to look at some modular buildings that we might put on the grounds of O'Hare to accommodate the homeless until we were able to determine how we could address their problems permanently. Neither of these alternatives was particularly appealing. We then began to look at the resources within the city of Chicago. And that's when I first met Father Mac and Haymarket."

"Mayor Daley had approached Father in a meeting and wanted to talk about the homeless problem," Ray Soucek added. "He had asked several agencies for a plan, but they had not come forth with one. He was frustrated with the homeless problem. So Father said he would think about it.

"Shortly thereafter, I attended a meeting with the city Department of Human Services." The answer was, Soucek said, "...that you go where they are. That means you reach out to these people, establish relationships. First you have to build rapport, then you convince them to get into treatment. So I said what we'd do is set up an office at O'Hare. We would have a staff that would go where the homeless are. We would work with the vendors at O'Hare to give the homeless food. The vendors would send them to us to get food. We'd have sandwiches, coffee, juice, rolls, and things like that. So we were working with the vendors, the airport security, and the homeless.

"The Department of Human Services asked: 'Can you draft up a proposal and get it to us within four hours?' We said yes. A couple of weeks later we received word that they were interested and wanted us to start up our program at O'Hare."

The situation Haymarket discovered was as highly unusual as it was unpublicized.

"We found people at O'Hare who had lived there for years," Soucek said. "They had everything—carts and their own little place to sleep. They had everything except showers. We had a homeless guy out there who was a retired airline employee. He had access to tickets, so he could get on a plane as a stand-by free, and he would fly to cities that had showers available. He would get on a plane, get meals, and then come back to O'Hare and live there. We had a woman whose daughter would bring her rent checks from her apartment buildings, which she owned. She would endorse them at O'Hare and give them back to her daughter. We had a woman lawyer who lived there."

Mary Rose Loney added: "Father Mac was the one who taught me first and foremost that before you can solve the problem, you need to understand how these people got that way. And you can't do this just with a broad perspective because each one of them is different. You're going to have to assess each one. Each one has probably entered into homelessness for different reasons, whether it's alcoholism or drug abuse or mental illness or a combination of all those things.

"He then suggested that we needed to set up an assessment office at O'Hare so that you can have people there who can talk to them to determine the extent of their problem. He said that this wouldn't be easy, because many of these people were chronically homeless and not inclined to seek help."

Haymarket set up two offices at the airport. "We would send out workers strolling through the terminals," Soucek explains. "They would sit with the homeless, talk with them, and seek to intervene. Sometimes the homeless would refuse and say they're all right. 'Hey,' we'd say, 'we've got sandwiches, coffee, juice, and rolls. When you want to come, we'll be here.' We began to build a relationship with these people. At first it was controversial."

The Homeless Coalition, an activist movement, grew agitated, charging that Haymarket was trying to cooperate with the police to put the homeless in handcuffs and eject them.

"We said we would not have taken the program if that was the concept," responded Soucek. "Our concept was to develop a relationship, give us time, let us work with these people and, eventually, we will move them out of the airport to where they could get better treatment and care."

There was impatience on both sides. The airport authorities wanted the homeless moved out quickly; the Homeless Coalition said the airport was pushing vigilante tactics. The demand for Monsignor McDermott came from three sides: the airport wanted him to front for it and get the homeless out; the Homeless Coalition wanted him to stand up to the airport; and the news media, particularly TV, wanted him to center their news coverage.

"There would be times," Soucek said, "when the city would call up and say, 'We need Father out at O'Hare tonight because the Coalition is coming, and he's the guy who can make peace.' The Coalition likewise. And he was the guy. He walked down and it was like the parting of the Red Sea. Everything is love and wonderful. His presence would calm the situation. Nobody was going to challenge the Gray Ghost of Skid Row. Nobody was going to challenge him or charge that Father Mac was out to do them wrong. The city had made a great choice in Father."

"So," Loney added "we shaped the program that would involve establishing an assessment center at O'Hare to address each and every individual to determine the degree of their homelessness, and then to determine what alternatives might be out there to offer them to get them off the homelessness path. We then needed a transitional place for them to go so we could immediately say, 'We have a better alternative for you than sleeping in a terminal building.' Father Mac was to provide some physical space for transitional beds at Haymarket, but we needed other resources as well. That's when we decided to enter into a joint partnership between the two where the Chicago Christian Industrial League provided two floors of their facility. We actually remodeled the floors and converted them into sleeping modules.

"The next step was then: How are we going to fund the program? The way the airports are funded in Chicago, the airlines underwrite the operations and maintenance costs of the terminal buildings, along with contributions from other non-airline sources of income, such as car rentals, food and beverage, and advertising.

"The airlines viewed the funding as a significant problem. They felt it was a city problem. When I first presented the concept to them, their sense was, 'Fine, it sounds like a good way to approach the problem, and it also sounds like it has the potential for creating a permanent solution, but you need to find city dollars to fund it, because this is really a community problem, not an airline problem.' My response was that there isn't a city agency in Chicago that has the resources to fund the level of effort needed. This was, at the time, about an $800,000 investment for the first year of operation, including establishing the assessment center and providing beds at the Chicago Christian Industrial League. I said, 'You're kidding yourselves if you think there's any social welfare agency in Chicago that's going to come out to O'Hare to solve this problem for us. We have to do it.'

"They recognized that—but they were still reluctant to allocate that kind of funding for it. That's when I called on Father Mac to come out there and help persuade the airlines that this was the right solution."

Monsignor McDermott met with a group of airline executives, called the Airline Affairs Committee. He was then 81 years old.

"Father Mac," Loney said, "used his wonderful way of articulating his background—how he established Haymarket and why this program was going to work. He spoke in ways they were unaccustomed to. He spoke with street slang, yes, but also in metaphors. Whereas they're used to conducting a pretty staid business meeting, all based on a bottom line, he talked about real people and real solutions that he had seen in his lifetime in battling the problems of homelessness and his inspiration to do it at O'Hare. It was very inspiring. By the end of the meeting, there wasn't any airline executive in that room who was going to vote against it. They said, 'Okay, Mary Rose.' That was in 1990. I will never forget how moving it was. I almost got the feeling that they [the airline executives] were all looking at me like, you know, 'You pulled one over on us because you brought in someone whom we could never say no to, after such a beautiful presentation.' So they agreed to fund the program.

"We set out that summer of 1990 remodeling the two floors at CCIL, building the assessment center at O'Hare. Ray Soucek put the team in place."

"There was resistance," Loney pointed out. "They actually started the outreach efforts in August of 1990. We were really working against the clock because we wanted to try to have the problem solved before the first really cold weather set in. Father Mac would come out at night. We would walk the terminals along with Ray [Soucek] and the social workers, trying to find homeless individuals, to convince them. Many of them had had bad experiences in shelters, so they were reluctant to believe in him. What we really hadn't counted on was a group of radical homeless advocates that didn't agree with our approach. They began to demonstrate. They set up picket lines at the airport and demonstrated against the program. The media would come out every night, as we had the protests going on every night. The protesters tried to engage the mayor. One of their chants was, 'Open the door, Richard. Open the door, Richard, to the homeless.'

"Father Mac would come out, and I have to give him a lot of credit for things not to have escalated into a confrontational situation. We never forcibly made a homeless person leave. During that fall period, we presented to the city council an ordinance that restricted O'Hare's terminal buildings from midnight until 5:00 a.m. The council passed it. This was also contentious with the protesters. But we solved the problem with Father Mac's inspiration. The media would camp out there hoping to get a picture of a homeless person being forcibly removed by a police officer. They never got the opportunity. We used inspiration rather than brute force."

Loney went on to become one of the most effective airport managers—with responsibility for Midway as well as O'Hare—in the United States.

Slowly but effectively, as Monsignor McDermott envisioned it, human needs were met at O'Hare. The homeless, the Homeless Coalition, as well as the airport, were served well.

"Many of the homeless are either on cocaine or alcohol or both. The end result of what happened at O'Hare," Soucek said, "is that we intervened on the side of the homeless. O'Hare put a curfew in. You have to be a ticketed passenger if you're in after midnight or 1:00 a.m., due to a city ordinance. Nobody was kicked out; nobody was brutalized. Nobody was kicking and screaming, or handcuffed or taken out. Today, when a homeless person comes to O'Hare, the vendors know who to call, the airlines know who to call, security knows who to call. We are there."

Since that time, Haymarket has expanded its services at both city airports, O'Hare and Midway, not just to deal with the homeless but with stranded passengers.

"We deal with medical problems out there," explained Soucek. "Many times we get calls from people at O'Hare who say, 'There's a plane coming in with a guy on it who's drunk, can you meet him at the gate?' We've dealt with employees at O'Hare who have said, 'I've got a substance abuse problem. Can I talk to somebody?'"

Haymarket deals with, on average, 1,000 homeless or stranded clients at O'Hare each year. That's not counting the interventions and encounters at the airport with repeat visitors. There are between 4,500 and 5,000 interventions a year there.

An example of an intervention? Soucek explained: "First I'll go up to you and say: 'Can I help you?' You say 'yes' and I do. You get a sandwich and are directed to a shelter. Three weeks later when you're at O'Hare again, I come up and say, 'What's going on? You were here earlier. I put you in a shelter. What happened?' You say you didn't like the shelter. Okay, we'll put you in another one. That's an intervention. Another three weeks passes and you're back and say, 'Well, you know, I left that shelter. I thought I'd get a job, and then I've ended up back here at O'Hare.' Then I say, 'All right, where do you want to go from here?' We probably deal on a yearly basis with clients at O'Hare, plus stranded passengers and every other contingency, which adds up to these interventions. But it all goes smoothly and we provide service to clients without embarrassment to them or to anyone else.

"We had a young man at O'Hare who had been living there for about three days. We intervened on him, and he finally agreed to come into treatment at Haymarket. We put him up in Cooke's Manor [a residence hall at McDermott Center leased to Catholic Charities for $1 a year]. One day he comes to Father and says, 'Father, I need to tell you something. My mother works here. We haven't talked in over a year. She doesn't know I'm here. I spotted her and avoided her, but I just wanted to let you know.'"

Monsignor McDermott invited him to his office for lunch, then invited his mother. Their reunion was tear-filled, successful.

"So," Ray Soucek smiled, "a lot of good things happen out at O'Hare."

*   *   *

Then there was a political problem involving funding for state services. Illinois Governor Jim Edgar, a social liberal but fiscal conservative, took office in 1991 with the nation's economy weakened and Illinois having lived well beyond its means. Edgar was forced to undertake reductions in expenditures and reduce a stack of unpaid bills. Unfortunately, rather than cut deeper in non-essential services, such as subsidies to Illinois businesses, Edgar slashed the social services. In 1991–92 there was a cutback of $1.3 million from alcohol and drug treatment for women with children. The legislature restored the cuts, but Edgar vetoed them. The last try to reclaim the services came with the 1992 fall session, where two-thirds vote was required to overturn the veto.

"We determined to do what we could to restore the funds," Soucek said. "We were told it was a hopeless case—but after conferring with Father, we decided to fight for them anyhow."

A newly-appointed state senator who was a warm friend of Haymarket was key—Robert DiTuri, replacing John D'Arco, who had been convicted of corruption. DiTuri was an assistant to the owner of a number of Italian restaurants in Chicago. As a legislative fresh face with a *Mr. Smith Goes to Washington* enthusiasm, DiTuri resolved to restore the budget cuts, even though his more sophisticated colleagues told him any effort was hopeless.

DiTuri's interest in Haymarket began shortly before his swearing-in, on April 16, 1992, and with his secretary, Barbara Cripe, who had been D'Arco's assistant for many years. DiTuri told her that he wanted his office festooned with pictures of himself surrounded by children.

"So she said to me," DiTuri said, " 'Did you ever meet Father Mac?' I said no. She said 'Well, here's the address. You'll find him remarkable.' " Also, Haymarket was in DiTuri's district.

"So I called up and made an appointment to meet Father Mac," said DiTuri. After a tour of the premises, on April 28, the priest took the fledgling lawmaker to his office.

"Senator," DiTuri quoted Monsignor McDermott, "whatever help you can give, we've got a problem. The governor is going to veto the appropriations covering Haymarket, and I need someone to represent us to show how the money can help us."

DiTuri came up with a plan, which he outlined to Monsignor McDermott: Bring Haymarket women and their children to Springfield to lobby personally for restoration of the funds. Monsignor McDermott enthusiastically agreed.

"So," Soucek said, "Father determined that we would lead the charge. We filled a bus with our women and children. Father rode along with us. DiTuri got us into the House and Senate with our moms and kids. We got a two-thirds in the House—but that was easy. The Senate would be the test. So the vote was coming up. DiTuri had the women bring the children to the floor. I had gone to the gallery and sat right above the Senate president, Phil Rock, to watch the action. The tote board was to my right. I remember walking in and the guard told me, 'DiTuri's a great guy, but this thing ain't gonna pass.' I said, 'Well, it's not over yet. We'll see.'"

"So we got to the Senate floor and Father came down with the babies," DiTuri recalled. "He sat next to me, and I had two babies in my arms and I was speaking to the senators about how important it was to make these programs work. I told them I met a mother who was living in a dumpster and now she's already out of Haymarket and has a college degree. I'm explaining to [Republican minority leader] Pate Philip's side and the Democrat side how important it was to vote for this bill even though the governor was going to veto it. So when the vote was called up on the floor—with Father Mac sitting next to me—we won the vote, meaning the money was going to stay in the budget. The Republican senators voted for it and the Democrats voted for it. Then the governor vetoed it."

The next step was to re-pass the bill over Edgar's veto. Monsignor McDermott came down to Springfield again and won passage in the Democratic House. But the real test would come in the Senate, controlled narrowly by the Democrats.

DiTuri said, "So I'm going to every senator—Republican, Democrat—but the Republicans said, 'Bob, we can't go along with this. We gotta go with the governor on this.' Now I'm fighting DASA [the Department of Alcoholism and Substance Abuse] and they're lobbying everybody on the Senate floor. We bring the kids down again."

The battle on the Senate floor was furious. "The lobbyist from DASA who was working for the governor said he couldn't work against the kids," said DiTuri. "I'm not going to give his name. He said, 'Senator, I'm leaving the floor right now.'"

As Soucek watched, down on the Senate floor DiTuri took babies from their mothers and passed them up and down the rows for astonished lawmakers to hold as the vote came up. State Senator Margaret Smith grabbed a baby and took it to the rostrum, handing it to the Senate president.

Soucek continued: "Then she took the floor and started pleading the case for these children. As she talked, DiTuri would take a baby from a woman and give it to a senator. There was a great deal of bustle on the floor and it seemed to be working. Finally they took a vote. As I watched the board light up, I figured, 'We're not there yet, not yet.' But slowly the green lights for passage started picking up and the red lights began to diminish."

As the babies squealed and lawmakers squirmed, the greens began to take over, then dominate. Finally, it hit two-thirds approval. And then one vote over two-thirds, when a female senator from DuPage County [Senator Beverly Fawell] voted to override.

"When I walked out of the gallery, the dumbfounded guard said, 'Wow, we did it!'" Soucek added. "No doubt about it. It was absolutely amazing. It was fun." And without DiTuri's support— and Monsignor McDermott's legendary prowess—it wouldn't have happened.

DiTuri is back at his old stand in the restaurant business, having served out the balance of D'Arco's term. But even now, whenever Monsignor McDermott enters the restaurant, the priest gets a cheer from the enthusiastic restaurant manager with the exultant cry: "We did it!"

* * *

As the 1990s unfolded, Monsignor McDermott became the sole survivor of his generation of McDermotts. Sister Mary Jeanette, a veteran teacher and principal at St. Paul of the Cross elementary school, Park Ridge, died in a nursing home on March 23, 1993, at age 96. She had completed her teaching career at St. Monica's parish. His sister, Kathleen, who had married Joseph Stack, died July 30, 1993, at age 93.

As he approached his 82nd birthday in brimming good health—despite his old football injury now forcing him to use a cane, but nothing more serious—Monsignor Ignatius McDermott could be forgiven if he opted to retire from active ministry and continue his life as a priest to enjoy what he had accomplished. But retirement wasn't part of God's plan for the man whose rugged independence had derailed the efforts of the Mundelein rector to keep him from the priesthood.

He had converted a bureaucratic job at Charities to undertake a singular apostolate to the addicted; he walked the streets after hours to give personal service to the men on Skid Row, won passage of legislation decriminalizing the inebriate in the Illinois legislature, and acceptance of social setting detox. He, along with Dr. James West, had surmounted the frustrations at Catholic Charities to launch a new institution for the addicted and homeless, which received national acclaim for compassionate and effective care. He took a gamble with the state's funding mechanism and instituted a program that pioneered treatment of addicted pregnant women that enabled their children to be born drug-free. He brilliantly blocked a chancery effort to retire him and absorb Haymarket into the formless bureaucracy of Catholic Charities.

Haymarket had now become the most sophisticated treatment center for the addicted in the nation. Far more than offering emergency services, Monsignor McDermott had hired a staff that developed a wide range of programs. By 1991, clients served by the institution numbered in the thousands—73 percent African-American, 19 percent Caucasian, seven percent Latino, with 83 percent qualifying as poor, 78 percent unemployed, and 90 percent with educational attainments less than a high school diploma and receiving public assistance.

In addition to devising new programs for treating chemically dependent people, it specialized in programs for special populations such as pregnant and postpartum women, drug-impacted children, homeless men and women, those with HIV/AIDS, mentally ill substance abusers, non-violent criminal justice offenders, and the elderly. The largest addiction and substance abuse treatment facility for women in Illinois, Haymarket's women's programs received national recognition from the federal government's Center for Substance Abuse Treatment.

Born of Ignatius McDermott's wish to expand a state program that ignored the prospect of saving unborn children from addiction to one that would spare infant addicts, its Maternal Addiction Center (the MAC unit) was the first residential treatment program for chemically dependent women in Illinois. Haymarket now boasted a full range of services, including 12-step groups, case management services, individual counseling, safety planning and shelter for victims of domestic abuse and violence, prenatal education, health education, parenting classes, and pre- and post-test HIV counseling. Plans were underway for an on-site day care center for use by clients, which Monsignor McDermott planned to call "Wholly Innocence Day Care Center," an allusion to the Holy

Innocents, those infants suffering death at the hands of Herod's soldiers seeking to kill the child Jesus [Mt. 2:13–18].

Through his labors he had become the best-known priest of the Chicago archdiocese and even beyond—with awards piling up for his reputation as a national authority on care for the addicted. And, despite all these accomplishments, he had not become institutional or smugly elitist. He continued to love the Sox and Bears, the camaraderie of the addicted, and to read the political news and chuckle at the vagaries of the human spirit. He was, in the estimation of William Gleason, the sportswriter, "a Monsignor but unlike any other Monsignor. He wasn't chubby. He was tall. He wasn't grim. He was bright-eyed. He wasn't solemn. He was humorous. He had beautiful white hair. And he talked street talk without curse words or vulgarities." So why not retire, sip hot tea and lemon, sit on the sidelines and watch the dancers?

Among his family, in 1991 only two siblings survived: Martha, Sister Mary Jeanette, RSM (born 1897), and Kathleen, Mrs. Joseph Stack (born 1900). His brothers were gone: John, Frank, Michael, and Al.

The swirl of activity, almost volcanic laughter and argument of the family he remembered from his youth was all but silent now. He recalled how thin his family's ranks had become. Uncle John J. Bradley, who was alderman, realtor, friend of Governor Dunne, and federal marshal, died on October 27, 1929. Eight years later his mother, Nellie, on November 28, 1937; his father, Michael, on July 27, 1940.

On August 29, 1965, Judge Jim—who very nearly beat out Richard J. Daley for one of the most powerful political posts in the nation—conducted pre-trial hearings in the Law-Jury court, had attended an outing of the DuPage County Bar Association at a farm near Naperville, and completed the day dining with his sister, Mrs. Stack. Now brother and sister had mounted the steps to her second floor apartment. She turned to open her door and stepped inside. She looked back to see Jim McDermott collapsing. He died immediately, of a massive heart attack. Monsignor McDermott offered the Mass. Jim—tall, oracular, brilliant, with a flair for the dramatic, a love of the thrust and parry of political life—would be sorely missed.

Wasn't it time to retire, say the daily Mass, spend more time with people like Abe Marovitz, go to all the Sox games, and root for the Bears? Judge Marovitz, a close friend of Bob Hope, was in the habit of visiting the comedian and his wife in Palm Springs, California, and bringing Monsignor McDermott with him. Both enjoyed the Hope family's hospitality. Hope was as entertaining at private dinner as he was in films and on TV. Wouldn't it be good now to pull away?

But retirement never was a possibility for Ignatius McDermott. Precisely because of his longstanding experience, he determined to put it to the use of others to the fullest in his work. He was imbued with the belief that as long as he was given time to be on earth, he would be required to perform. And he was still making his nocturnal visits to the hospitals, bringing spiritual comfort to those who were alone. As he would say, "You can rest in eternity."

He told an interviewer, "I think one of the most powerful things is the power of example—and I think one of the treasures of the Catholic Church is the corporal and spiritual works of mercy." (The corporal works: feeding the hungry, giving drink to the thirsty, clothing the naked, visiting the imprisoned, sheltering the homeless, visiting the sick, and burying the dead. The spiritual works: admonishing the sinner [with humor], instructing the ignorant, counseling the doubtful, comforting the sorrowful, bearing wrongs patiently, forgiving injuries, and praying for the living and the dead.) A living exemplar is Ignatius McDermott.

"I remember I used to visit two priests at St. Bernard's Hospital and both of them were disabled. I used to run over and see them every week and, if they were in the mood, I'd take them out for a ride with their nurses, or some nurse from the floor, and have dinner." Swinging into his 1930s era Chicago-ese jargon: "I remember it was hotter than the hinges of hell one night. The elevator was out of order, and I went up the stairs—their room was on the fourth floor—when I saw a man and a woman outside a hospital room. They were polishing the rosary beads [praying the rosary] and looking very agitated.

"So I said to myself, 'After I visit those priests, I'm going to go to that room.' I returned, walking from the fifth floor to the fourth floor, and nobody was in front of that room. Those who were saying their rosaries were gone. I knocked and went into the room. There was a woman alongside the bed, looking sort of lost, with her arms folded. I approached the bed. A man was lying in it and I held his hand and said, 'I'm Father McDermott. I'm a

Catholic priest. I saw the members of your family, and I'm sure you can hear me. I would like you to say: O, my God, I believe in You, and I hope in You, and I love You, and I'm sorry for my sins.' Before I could finish this request the woman screamed, 'Who allowed you in this room? How did you get in here?'

"I said to the man in the bed, 'If you can hear me, squeeze my hand.' He squeezed my hand. I gave him absolution and the sacraments while she shouted. I left, found respite in the chapel and was kneeling there when Mother Mitchell came up behind me. I could hear her rosary beads clicking as she came in the door. She was the night person just coming on duty. She said to me, 'The people you saw were the brother and sister of the man who is in the bed. They were chased away by this woman who was with him, who vowed that over her dead body would a priest see him.' Then I wondered: Gee, here were those people polishing the beads. Why was the elevator not working that day? Why did I round the corner? Why did I stop and see him? And here this guy goes into eternity in good shape."

*   *   *

In the 1990s, efforts by Catholic progressives to drive the Rome-directed Church off what some called its ideological barricades centered about Chicago's highly diplomatic, negotiatively skilled Cardinal Joseph Bernardin. Despite his Italianate-style diplomacy, he was portrayed by the secular news media (some said quite against his own intentions but aided by some fervent supporters) as a dissenter to supposed old-style conservative Catholicism. He emerged as the key figure in an "American Catholic Church," opposed to Roman authoritarianism.

Bernardin supported progressive secular trends with his pastoral letters on the liturgy (1984), ministry (1985), and health care (1995). He did more than apologize for ancient Christian-Judeo tensions. On an historic trip to Jerusalem for an address at Hebrew University, on March 23, 1995, accompanied by Chicago rabbis, civic leaders, and media, he traced what he described as anti-Judaic interpretations in the New Testament which, he said, were additions made in the first centuries of Christian history. To some, even those who deplored historic anti-Semitism, this approach by Bernardin marred the laudable effort to redress grievance. It appeared to them that he apologized for Christ's words during confrontation in the Gospel of St. John as applying to all Jews, saying that later revisionists added their anti-Semitism to the Scripture. Not so, said authenticist scripturalists: Christ was plainly addressing a specific sub-set of Jews. By declaring that the Gospel was later twisted, the cardinal appeared to be doubting the inerrancy of the Gospel itself. But all disagreements subsided when the prelate successfully surmounted two grave personal challenges.

One was his calm response to charges of sexual misconduct made in November 1993 by Steven Cook, a young man with AIDS, who had been a seminarian in Cincinnati when Bernardin was archbishop there. The embarrassing charges broadcast throughout the world were withdrawn by Cook the following spring. In December 1994, the cardinal and his accuser were finally reconciled in Philadelphia.

The second challenge came in June 1995 when the cardinal's doctors discovered that he had pancreatic cancer. Surgery slowed but did not cure his illness. Throughout the remainder of his life, the cardinal performed as an exemplary role model for serenity in the face of death. His progressivism continued: in mid-August 1996, he established what he called a "Common Ground" project designed to engage Catholics with various topics of colloquy, including at least one that Rome had stated was non-negotiable— women priests. Two weeks later, he informed the archdiocese that his cancer had spread to his liver and was inoperable.

On September 9, 1996, he received the Medal of Freedom, the highest civilian honor, from the hands of President Bill Clinton at the White House. His last words unified all and gained him widespread praise. In a letter to the Supreme Court justices he declared, "There can be no such thing as a right to assisted suicide. No such right can exist because there can be no legal or moral order that tolerates the killing of innocent human life, even if the agent of death is self-administered." He concluded with great eloquence: "I am at the end of my earthly life. There is much more that I have contemplated these last few months of my illness, but as one who is dying I have especially come to appreciate the gift of life." The cardinal died November 14, 1996.

On April 8, 1996, Pope John Paul II appointed Bernardin's successor, Francis George, OMI, born in 1937, the first native Chicagoan to hold the archbishopric. He was installed at Holy Name Cathedral on May 7, 1997. Holding two doctorates, one in theology and another in American philosophy, George had been the

Rome vicar general of his religious order, the Oblates of Mary Immaculate, and then bishop of Yakima, Washington (1990), and archbishop of Portland, Oregon (1996). Not long after his elevation to the College of Cardinals, on January 18, 1998, Francis George toured Haymarket Center and lunched with Monsignor McDermott.

* * *

In 1997, former President Gerald Ford and his wife, Betty, were hosted by Monsignor McDermott at a private fund-raiser, proceeds of which supported the Betty Ford Center as well as Haymarket's Wholly Innocence Day Care Center. In a letter to Monsignor McDermott, the former First Lady wrote: "Our visit together at Haymarket House was truly a special time for me. Your program is no less than amazing and has made such an impact on me. I was touched by the women and young children who seem to finally have hope in their eyes again. I know you are proud, as you well should be, of the wonderful things happening at Haymarket."

Then Illinois secretary of state, now governor, George Ryan and Mrs. Ryan, warm friends of Monsignor McDermott, were on the host committee. More than any other public official, George Ryan has been cordially supportive. When Monsignor McDermott was raising funds for Haymarket Center in the mid-1980s, Ryan helped him find contributions by utilizing his media consultant to produce a documentary outlining McDermott's work.

In 1998, Ryan and his wife, Lura Lynn, co-chaired an effort, along with McDonald's senior chairman Fred Turner, to raise $250,000 for the Wholly Innocence Day Care Center. The fund-raising event honored Gerald and Betty Ford.

How did Ryan, known as a crusty politician, become so tenderhearted with Monsignor McDermott? The need to fight addiction is important—but there was another, more personal side.

Sun-Times columnist Steve Neal wrote: "Ryan said the most memorable moment of his association with Father Mac was in the midst of a terrible storm. Ryan's mother, Jeanette, had just died and the bad weather had discouraged some of Ryan's out-of-town friends from making the drive to Kankakee [Ryan's downstate home, 70 miles from Chicago]. When Father Mac showed up at the wake of Mrs. Ryan, it meant the world to her son."

Ryan became a controversial governor, stemming largely from a drivers' license scandal as secretary of state, but there is no doubt that he used his position to support wide-ranging programs to keep drunks off the highways, and gave extensive support to Haymarket, providing countless hours of dedicated help. He crusaded for passage of a law that reduced the legal intoxication limit from a blood alcohol content of .10 to .08, receiving major awards from the National Commission Against Drunk Driving and Mothers Against Drunk Driving. Lura Lynn Ryan involved herself in a number of Haymarket programs and became a warm supporter of the Wholly Innocence Day Care Center. Ryan later was elected as the 39th governor of Illinois.

As he celebrated his 60th jubilee as a priest, Monsignor McDermott looked back on a string of entrepreneurial services he had devised during his priesthood to serve the addicted. These included: Thirst Sunday; DUI programs; alcohol safety education; Summer Institute for Training Counselors; Central States Institute; Intervention Instruction; the Chicago Clergy Association for the Homeless Person; Cees Manor; Alternative to Incarceration; Maternal Addiction Center; comprehensive outpatient programs; and women's special outpatient programs. He had taken as his personal inspiration the statement of St. Vincent DePaul: "When you no longer burn with love, others will die of the cold."

* * *

Ever the loving but tough taskmaster, Ignatius McDermott runs a tight ship—proving to his longtime friend, Jim Mchugh, that he's no pushover.

"When he tells you something," Mchugh said, "it's law—you do it. You can't come up with an excuse; that doesn't work with him. Like out here last week, stuff was laying there and he said, 'What—are we back on Skid Row again? What's this, Skid Row?' He said, 'I want this stuff out of here and I want it out of here now.' I told him I couldn't take it out because I didn't have anywhere to put it. He told me to take it over to the Indian nuns on Oakley. It was all this Christmas stuff. We had a vanload. We gave it to the Indian nuns. They serve food to the street people, about 50 people in the morning and 50 in the evening. You have to watch your Ps and Qs over there, because you're in the alley there and the gang-bangers come up the alley. You just tell 'em to keep moving. Don't give 'em any lip because if you do, you're in trouble."

Although chairman of Haymarket, Monsignor McDermott continues to be the independent operator, not governed by any set routine. Mchugh frets over him like a mother hen. "He always gets a weakness to pneumonia," Mchugh explains. "Like last night, he's walking out of here and I asked Kay where his cap was. He thinks he's a kid. I said, 'We ought to get one of those things like your mother used to use to keep your gloves on.' He said his cap was in his pocket, but it wasn't."

* * *

Monsignor McDermott tells this story about the late Father John Ireland Gallery, the bluff greeter of Mayor Martin Kennelly, described earlier.

Stories about Father Gallery are legend, including this one when he was visited at his South Side parish by Samuel Cardinal Stritch: the prelate came to bestow the Sacrament of Confirmation. Stritch was vesting in the sacristy. Father Gallery gave him a benevolent nudge and said, "It's a cold day, your Eminence. Would you like a mouthful of bourbon?" Stritch's cold stare through his rimless spectacles could have turned the holy water in the fonts to ice, but it didn't daunt Gallery.

Ignatius McDermott still is tickled by this scene that happened many years ago.

CHAPTER 12

Good People Form a Good Team, 1997–2000

Your dreams will become your problems; we have problems, God has plans.

Your daily game plan and mine should be to letter in kindness—for kindness is the only language the blind can see, the deaf can hear, and the dumb can speak.

—Ignatius McDermott

Mary Jane Miller is director of managed care and women's services at Haymarket. Few employees are more dedicated than she. She works at her desk long after quitting time. To her, Haymarket is not just a place to work but a way of life. It saved her life. "I would not be alive today if it were not for Haymarket Center and Monsignor McDermott's philosophy," she said.

"I had a nice home in the suburbs, a car that was paid for; I had a college degree. I had friends. I had a strong family that was supportive of me, and I think how that played out for me was that I entered detox because I was spiritually bankrupt. I was suicidal. I wanted to kill myself because I didn't like who I had become. I had no hope, and I had tried to stop drinking so many times; that is where my hopelessness came from. Part of that is when you have support, I would tell myself, that with all the things I have I should be able to stop drinking. There should be no excuse for me not to stop drinking! I looked at my house, family and children, friends. No one else had a problem. I was the one with the problem. Why do I keep letting people down? Why can't I be the mother I want to be? My children, father, sister all deserve more. For me, with all of the support I had, it made me feel more hopeless. But I was not destitute.

"I had gone through at least five different treatment centers with my ex-husband, who had a very early onset of alcoholism. He went through the Schick Aversion Therapy Program on the West Coast; the Betty Ford program three times; Twin Town; and Hazelden residential programs. He also went through Little Company of Mary Hospital's intensive outpatient program. By the time my alcoholism became apparent, I had no belief that treatment worked. To me, it looked like it was a place where people went to take a rest and left other people at home to clean up their garbage. I also did not believe in the AA program because my ex-husband told me he was always working the AA program, and it did not seem to be doing any good for him, so I had no faith that it would ever help anyone. He was the only person I knew who went through AA, so I didn't see that there were any other options for me. That added to my hopelessness. After the birth of my third daughter, I had severe depression. Psychiatrists put me on a lot of medication and then admitted me to the hospital to get off of it. That is when they diagnosed me with alcoholism, and when I got out of treatment, I went back to drinking. I didn't take pills anymore or have a problem with pills. I just needed to go into the hospital to get off of them. I tried going to AA, and the people seemed way too happy for me. It seemed like their problems were not as severe as mine.

"Then one day, my sister and a friend came over to my house and did an intervention. I said that the only way I would go into treatment is if they could find a place that was free, because I was not going to borrow any money from anyone, and I didn't believe in treatment, and I was not going to go further in debt. They found Haymarket and Lila Miner, who was the supervisor of women's detox. She said, 'Bring her in and let her drink before she gets here.' I don't think I could have gone if she hadn't said that. I was admitted, and within 24 hours I had the spiritual awakening. God told me that as long as I did not drink and did as they instructed, everything would work out. I had no idea what that meant and I still don't, but when I got here they let me stay. I stayed in excess of 10 days in women's detox. They didn't have residential treatment at Haymarket back then. After my fifth day of detox, staff would go to Monsignor McDermott to get permission for my treatment to be extended. Monsignor McDermott allowed me to stay until I found a women's treatment program and was safe. I even started helping out up there in the unit. They let me stay, and I stayed until I had enough faith in myself and belief to get into Hazelden.

"While I was in Hazelden, all I really held on to was the faith that I acquired while I was in the women's detox unit at Haymarket Center. My counselor at Hazelden was Swedish and she didn't even understand the program. I just kept reading the first three chapters of the Big Book [*Alcoholics Anonymous*], which they told me to do at Haymarket, and do not drink, and keep my mouth shut."

At Haymarket she caught a glimpse of Monsignor McDermott. "I saw him tour the unit once and that was really it. And I knew that because I was here so long, detox is usually a three- to five-day stay, [so] they would have to call and see if I could get an extension for more time. I knew that was being approved by Monsignor. I was able to stay longer because of extensions on a day-to-day basis, and I stayed until there was a bed, and I went directly from here to Hazelden. So I was not discharged until they knew that I was going to a safe place and where I could continue working on my recovery.

"When I was here, one of the things that I was grateful for was what Haymarket Center did for me, and I had always told the staff how grateful I was. And the staff would say, 'Come back and do an AA meeting here.' So I held on to that while I was away in Minnesota [at Hazelden]. I didn't just go through the 28-day treatment program at Hazelden, I also stayed for four months in a recovery home so when I got back from there, I returned to thank the unit and start doing AA meetings. They offered me a position which was an incredible godsend, because I really didn't know if it would work out in Chicago. My support people in Minnesota said there was no way I could stay sober in Chicago, because I didn't have anyone or know anyone in recovery, or even have a job. My sober support system in Minnesota wanted me to stay in Minnesota, where I had connections and people could help me. But I couldn't take my children away from my parents. My parents are from Chicago, so I knew I had to go back, and I came back, and by coming here and being offered a job, it filled the need and provided me with a means to support my daughters. What added to the early onset of my alcoholism was that my ex-husband had abandoned us. I was the sole support of my three children, and it was an answer to a prayer to be offered a job helping women recover. I had insurance, a job, and I had a burning desire to share my recovery with other women."

She came back as a volunteer and has been at Haymarket ever since. "I started as an intake worker at the Maternal Addiction Center, and that is interesting because that position was created for me," she said. "I always hold on to that because they didn't have intake specialists, only addiction specialists. Addiction specialists would either have to work Tuesday through Saturday or Sunday through Thursday. And when I met with administration, I said that I could not do that because I had to be home with my daughters on the weekends. They said, 'Fine, we will develop a new position so that you can take care of your children and work here, too.' The reason why that is real important to me is because I have always felt that Haymarket Center has supported me and allowed for me to be the best mother that I could be, and I don't know that any organization would have done that for me.

"From intake specialist, I went to a position that was called intake counselor. I did complete intake assessment and treatment plans and psychosocials. From there, I went on to be the clinical liaison between Haymarket Maryville's three postpartum programs in the Maternal Addiction Center. Then I took the position with the mothers' and children's postpartum program at Maryville, and advanced to the coordinator of the three postpartum programs at Haymarket Maryville.

"Then I came back to our main site and worked briefly in helping to get the risk management program started, and then as coordinator of professional development. From there I became the coordinator of managed care, and now I am the director of managed care and women's detox services.

"I think it is a small world, and addiction keeps you so isolated you don't even see what resources are right in front of you. Although my family knew Monsignor McDermott, my family never considered that Haymarket Center or Monsignor McDermott would be able to help us, but he is the one who helped us. My father currently is volunteering at Haymarket Center as an act of gratitude. My father believes he owes his depth of faith in God and financial blessings to Father McDermott for getting his daughter back. What I think is important for people to know about addiction is that all the things I have in my life today are a result of going through Haymarket Center detox, and the hand being there, and the care and respect and dignity of Monsignor McDermott. Today, I have self-respect. I have the love of three beautiful, healthy children that don't need to fall into the cycle of family dysfunction. I am a productive member of society. When everything gets back on track and in balance, no longer do people have to pick up the pieces for you."

She says often that God is directing the course and He wrote the script.

"I can still feel the feeling when I was in women's detox and got the feeling and knew it was God saying to me, 'Don't worry. Everything will be fine as long as you don't drink,'" she said. "I remember thinking: What about the girls? What about this? What about that? God would say, 'I am not giving you any answers. I am just saying don't drink and everything will work out.' And the progress—the gains spiritually, materially, peace of mind that I have gained—during the last 12 years has been amazing. The fact that I finished my master's degree and I am a licensed clinical professional counselor, and that I am looking at going back to school to become a doctor, that is more than I could ever imagine. I wasn't sure if I would live a week. I have become someone my daughters can look up to and depend on. That is the same every day. I live my life like this. I have no idea where I am going to be tomorrow. All I am going to do is show up and hope that I follow the path that God wants me to follow. Up to this point, He has wanted me to stay at Haymarket Center and it has worked for me for the last 12 years. If it is not broken, don't fix it."

*   *   *

As Haymarket's founder continued with a heavy schedule of appearances at hospitals, funeral homes, and public gatherings, Jack Whalen, vice chairman of Haymarket, wanted to see him travel as comfortably as possible. So Whalen, a multimillionaire printing ink executive, who comes from a car dealer family, arranged on good terms a black Lincoln Town Car for Monsignor McDermott's use. The Haymarket security police who guard the facility found a driver for the priest who, they say with a smile, was good for Father Mac's own safety.

The Illinois license plate on his car has been the same for many years—SOX 4, a number conferred by the late Michael J.

Howlett, who was secretary of state, and ratified by his successors. Why wouldn't Chicago's number one Sox fan have SOX 1? Only a Sox trivia expert would understand. Number "4" belonged to Luke Appling, a major hero from the misty White Sox past. Appling, known as "Old Aches and Pains," was a Hall of Fame shortstop who, from 1930 to 1950, boasted a .310 lifetime batting average while collecting 2,749 hits, 1,116 RBIs, 1,319 runs scored, and 3,528 total bases. He put together the longest hitting streak in Sox history, 27 games in 1936. That year he became the first Sox player to win the American League batting crown. His 1936 average of .388 remains an all-time White Sox high.

Monsignor McDermott told the *Sun-Times'* Ray Coffey that Appling's number "4" is why his license plate is SOX 4. He then added, "The Sox usually end up in fourth place."

*   *   *

One of Monsignor McDermott's most tender cases of caring for the sick involved Jack Brickhouse, the Hall of Fame radio broadcaster. The voice of the Chicago Cubs for four decades, Brickhouse didn't know the Chicago priest very well when the broadcaster took ill on February 27, 1998. As he was preparing to go to the funeral of Harry Caray, who succeded Brickhouse as cubs broadcaster, Brickhouse fell ill. He was diagnosed with a nickel-sized tumor in his brain. From the time of his hospitalization, Monsignor McDermott visited the retired sportscaster almost daily. They discussed sports fully during those visits. On August 6, 1998, Brickhouse died of cardiac arrest at St. Joseph Hospital, Chicago. He was 82 years old. Monsignor McDermott was one of the eulogists at the funeral.

Their closeness was interesting since Brickhouse was identified almost solely with the Chicago Cubs (although he did cover the Sox for one season).

"The only time that Ignatius McDermott went to Wrigley Field," the priest said, "was when our confessor said, 'Ignatius, for your penance, go to Wrigley Field.' But it could have been much worse, if it had been a double-header."

Brickhouse covered sports for Chicago's WGN-TV and radio, starting with the television station's first telecast in 1948. He also did play-by-play of the Chicago Bears with Irv Kupcinet on WGN radio for 24 consecutive years and play-by-play for the Chicago

Cardinals in 1947, also covering the Cardinals championship victory over the Philadelphia Eagles. In August 1983, he was formally inducted into the media wing of the Baseball Hall of Fame.

"As we bid fond *adieu* to Jack, we should be pondering and meditating on what type of death God has in store for you and for me," Monsignor McDermott said in the eulogy. "Will it be similar to Jack's—successful surgery, a long, painful recovery, rehabilitation, then a fatal heart attack? Or will we encounter death on the Ryan, the Kennedy, the Stevenson [Chicago expressways], or the Outer Drive? Or will it be a misdirected bullet from a gang-banger? Or will we be a passenger on an ill-fated airliner? But it is only in death that we possess that monumental moment to practice the virtue of hope: our ultimate reunion with God, our Creator."

* * *

By February 1999, during an arctic blast of winter cold in Chicago, concern was raised for the future of homeless men who had long been living on lower Wacker Drive, a concrete two-tier boulevard in the Loop. They presented a very real problem for Mayor Richard M. Daley, who was sensitive to concerns that the rights of the homeless not be abrogated in their dislocation—but also aware that the men would freeze to death if allowed to remain untended. Once again, Daley called on Monsignor McDermott to help. Chicago's Commissioner of Human Resources, Daniel Alvarez, selected Haymarket Center as a refuge for these homeless men. Haymarket responded by providing shelter and an in-house treatment program for them, including a variety of health and consulting services. "Most of the homeless are homeless because of some problem in life," said Ray Soucek. "In most cases, abuse of or addiction to alcohol more often than not is responsible, along with the combination of use and abuse of drugs."

* * *

Also in February 1999, there was a meeting of two men who had much in common. Monsignor McDermott had never met John Paul II and, through the gracious intercession of Francis Cardinal George, archbishop of Chicago, he had the opportunity when the pope came to St. Louis, Missouri, for a youth rally. The meeting was important to Monsignor McDermott because he had been inculcated with a devotion to the papacy. To believing Catholics, the pope is not the CEO of the world's largest congregation; he is the living embodiment of Peter and his receivership of a trust from Christ, which was recorded in a memorable way.

On a mountain peak in the district of Caesarea Philippi, picture the apostles following Christ in single file. Jesus, in the lead, tossed over His shoulder the question to them: "Who do men say that the Son of Man is?" The response of some: John the Baptist, Elijah, Jeremiah, or one of the prophets. He persisted: "But who do you say I am?"

The answer came from a blunt-spoken fisherman: "You are the Christ, the Son of the living God."

Whereupon Christ turned and fastened upon him a riveting gaze. "Blessed are you, Simon Bar Jona! For flesh and blood has not revealed this to you, but my Father who is in heaven. And I tell you, you are Peter and on this rock I will build My church and the powers of death shall not prevail against it. I will give you the keys to the kingdom of heaven, and whatever you bind on earth shall be bound in heaven and whatever you loose on earth shall be loosed in heaven." [Mt. 16:13–20]

Roman Catholics say John Paul II is the successor-rock. That was the main reason Monsignor McDermott went to St. Louis. A second reason was a unique, every 500-year occurrence. Of the 265 successors to Peter there have been saints, mediocrities, laggards, and some crimson sinners. But through the Church's ups and downs, there has been a rough cycle that produced great popes in times of adversity at least every 500 years.

Five hundred years after the crucifixion of Peter, when it seemed that barbarians would sweep away all Christianity, there arose a former Roman senator who left a Benedictine monastery to ascend the papal throne as Gregory II. Under Gregory, the tide was turned back and the process begun by which the barbarians were converted to what became Christian Europe. Roughly 500 years later, with the Church engulfed in heavy scandal, another Benedictine monk, Gregory VII, inspired the birth of spiritual medieval civilization, which saved manuscripts that preserved Christianity for the future. A half-millennium later, a great Dominican, Pius V, applied the reforms of the Council of Trent, setting into place much of the formal doctrine that remains to this day. After the passage of another 500 years, John Paul II arose to offset much of the challenge of world Communism and to supply balance against what some historians say is an invasion of secularism in the Church.

The meeting between John Paul II and Monsignor McDermott in St. Louis was short but meaningful. Those who accompanied the Monsignor saw joy at the meeting of two elderly men, long past retirement age, speaking in the certain tones of those who believe in providential destiny with all their hearts.

* * *

On June 10, 1999, Illinois Governor George Ryan, Mayor Richard M. Daley of Chicago, and other dignitaries shared ribbon-cutting honors, along with Monsignor McDermott, as Haymarket Center dedicated a new residential detoxification unit for male clients. It was funded by the City of Chicago and the Coleman Foundation. At the ceremony, Monsignor McDermott said he had a quarrel with urban renewal that had demolished the SRO (single room occupancy) hotels where street people could find shelter for modest rental.

In his talk, he looked back at the time he raised funds to build Haymarket, a task he was often told was hopeless. Monsignor McDermott recalled St. Frances Cabrini, known to Chicagoans as Mother Cabrini. "Arriving in New York from Italy," he said, "she saved $5,000 to found a hospital in a ghetto. An Italian countess, whose husband was a New York art patron, added another $5,000 and accompanied Mother Cabrini to present her plans to the archbishop of New York. The archbishop laughed at her plans and said, 'My good woman, $10,000 would not last a month.' Mother Cabrini nodded humbly. But not so the countess, who said: 'Your Excellency, remember that when we pray, we ask for our daily bread. We do not ask for bread for a year.'"

* * *

If it were possible to sum up Monsignor McDermott's work, the opportunity came not long ago following announcement that Haymarket's help would be extended to the Internet. Sister Patricia Kilbane, head of Haymarket's Intervention Instruction, had put counseling on the Web where it could be reached at www.whatsdrivingyou.org. At the Web site announcement, Monsignor McDermott repeated to a reporter the story of Haymarket—

in short form. It is as good a summary of his life's work as he has ever given. The Haymarket Web site is www.hcenter.org.

"Prior to Haymarket House, you had different denominations which took an interest in helping the homeless man along Madison Street," Monsignor McDermott said. "The Presbyterians had the Dawes Industrial Center. The Episcopalians had Cathedral Shelter. The Salvation Army was there. The Baptists were catering to the homeless man. And Catholics had Catholic Charities at Randolph and Desplaines.

"Then I decided that we were all lettering in the three 'Ss'— soup, soap, and salvation. I talked about forming the Chicago Clergy Association for the Homeless. Then, when we wanted to start Haymarket House we went to Catholic Charities, but they said they didn't have any money. When we went to the state, they said we'd have to start it on our own but they'd help later on. They said it had to be a concerted effort. When I told them we'd already started a symphony of agencies, they couldn't deny us.

"We began in the basement of a Presbyterian building that was later condemned. Shortly after, we found a man who rented us space in a building. Later we had to move and, eventually, found the building on Washington Street—in the wake of my 50th anniversary in the priesthood. Instead of receiving gifts, I asked people to contribute to the McDermott Foundation and that's how we got here."

Asked how he helped to keep Haymarket alive during the dark days, Monsignor McDermott replied: "Well, I'm God's agent. God employs me. So the greatest thing is faith. I believe in God, and I believed that the thing we were trying to do was to take care of the people He created who have developed a dependency on alcohol and chemicals. So I just asked the Lord to turn up His hearing aid and come to our rescue. He heard our plea. What keeps me going? The cards God has dealt me. Why wasn't I a denizen of West Madison Street? We are here to help those who have life harder than we do."

Concluding the interview, the reporter asked: "When people look at your accomplishments, what do you hope they'll say about you?"

His answer: "I hope they say nothing about me and say a prayer for the people we're privileged to serve."

CHAPTER 13

Haymarket

Our current society finds too many of us addicted to the monsters of materialism, the sedatives of self-sympathy or compliance, or the daggers of discouragement, or to the darts of despair, or to the arrows of arrogance, or to the lances of laceration, or to the drowsy opiate of monotony. In our daily prayers, we should be asking God for what we need and not what we want, where the rage of our age is overstated pleasures and understated treasures.

Back it up! Back it up! That guy calls himself an undertaker? [Procedure at Catholic funerals is for the undertaker to wait with the coffin at the church door for the blessing of the Mass celebrant. The mortician in question didn't wait, but wheeled the cortege into the church and left it front and center, prompting this justified rebuke.]

Some of those guys could be linebackers for the Bears and haven't worked since Baptism. They'll be womb to tomb. And they'll be that way until Gabriel blows his trumpet unless we do something about it. [his belief that recovering alcoholics sorely need work as therapy]

They gotta know who's their Chinaman. [Staff people have to understand accountability. *Chinaman:* the old machine term for political sponsor]

—Ignatius McDermott

They call Yankee Stadium "the house that Ruth built." Is Haymarket Center truly the house McDermott and West built— with their character dominating the management team, distinguishing it from other treatment facilities?

"Yes," said Ray Soucek, CEO of Haymarket. He sat at a table in his office and said, "I think the distinguishing factor about us, from my point of view, is our leader. Father is a leader, an entrepreneur, likes to be on the cutting edge of things. The people who work here, by and large, reflect that individuality. He gives Haymarket its distinct flavor."

What is that flavor that engulfs Haymarket?

"He rejects the idea that dismisses the poor as occupying a level below us." Soucek continues, "Sometimes, in the outside world, the idea gets across that services for the poor and homeless that are merely so-so are 'good enough for them.' He's been told, 'Well, Father, what we have may not be a palace but considering what comes in through our doors, it's good enough for them.' No way. He rebels against that. He says 'No, they get the best. We're going to provide them hope, dignity, care, concern, professionalism—just what every other human being in the best hospital ever would be provided.'"

Is it as good as the Betty Ford Center?

"Different," Soucek replied, "and in some ways better. Not taking anything away from Betty Ford, but we have Father. With Father there's a connectedness and a relationship. He genuinely cares for these people. He's a man who can mix with the most sophisticated people and yet is not afraid to go and pick up somebody off the street who's filthy, soaked with urine, who's just got done throwing up, and he'll hold his head. I've seen him do that. That example carries through.

"I think the employees of Haymarket fall into this category. They take on Father's ideology and say, 'Okay, he cares about the people.' He founded this place when he could be retired in California or whatever. He could have gotten out of this ministry a long time ago and said, 'I'm folding up shop.' Instead, he's 90-plus and he's still involved and caring and takes a hands-on approach with it. So I think our employees follow that example."

While Monsignor McDermott has the vision for Haymarket Center, it is Jack Whalen who supplies the architectural plans. During the necessary chaos of formation, when funds were sorely needed—and liaison was carried on with Catholic Charities—Whalen, low-key and self-deprecating, produced the business sense, knowledge, discipline, willpower, determination, sacrifice, and edifying grace to make the dream a reality. The full extent of his contribution is difficult to measure because he is suffused with salutary, but confounding, excessive modesty. He neither gives speeches nor writes about the early days. But the fact remains that, in the estimation of those who were present at Haymarket's creation, next to Monsignor McDermott and Dr. James West, it was Whalen, who began as a foot soldier and rose to key strategist in the enterprise, who was invaluable.

It was Whalen who mobilized the army of McDermott supporters into a cohesive unit, he who successfully negotiated with Father Edwin Conway of Catholic Charities, he who convinced bankers to support an elderly priest in his dream. Moreover, it was Whalen who supervised rehabilitation of the Haymarket III building and who, as Haymarket vice-chairman, still advises on almost every detail of the physical plant. Ray Soucek calls Whalen's presence "a continuing example of God's providence."

To Soucek, the ability of Whalen to step in after Monsignor McDermott was hospitalized following the automobile accident in 1985, in which the priest suffered a broken collarbone and four broken ribs, was a stroke of good fortune. Whalen alone had to convince Father Conway that Haymarket could muster the financial resources to keep going.

"So Whalen conceived of a dinner dance that he said could raise a significant amount of money," said Soucek. "Father Conway was dubious. But they had the dinner dance and Jack got everything together, including paying for invitations and paying the band. They had between 600 and 700 people and raised $98,000 clear. That made an impression on Father Conway. A couple of years after that, he began to run his own ball and called it the St. Nicholas Ball, on the feast of St. Nicholas."

Over the years, Soucek and Whalen have conferred by phone every day, have dinner several times a week. Whalen comes to Haymarket throughout the week and every Saturday morning for a formal building committee session. He walks the premises with Soucek, noting details that have escaped others.

"The building, actually three buildings in one," said Soucek, "is Jack's baby—the 932 [W. Washington] "A" wing, where administrative offices and some treatment facilities are housed; the "B" building, connected to "A," at the 120 North Sangamon address, where initial programs are based; and the "C" building—known as Cooke's Manor—a transitional living facility for men just off the street. It is managed by Catholic Charities but leased from the McDermott Foundation for $1 a year.

The entire building, all three segments, is owned by the McDermott Foundation. Charities invested about $400,000 for renovations and maintenance (although the entire upkeep of the building is about $2.5 million).

"So," said Soucek, "it's a good bargain for Charities."

"This is what Jack has, a common vision with Father," Soucek said. "Jack has the skills to make Father's vision happen. He has connections in the business world. He knows how to make a business deal. He's been a salesman all of his life. He's overseen the construction of the three buildings and the remodeling of the three buildings. He's the head of the building committee.

"He probably knows more about this building than anybody else. He's learned from people in the construction business what to look for and how things should be done. We had the good fortune of having a guy named Dick Lewis, now deceased, who was a contractor. Jack learned a lot from Dick."

A health crisis affecting Jack Whalen in 1996 was a crisis of sorts for Haymarket, because his advice was so crucial.

"He had some problems with pockets in his colon," Soucek said. "He had an operation which was major, but many, many people come out of it and are okay. They apparently used some procedure in a fairly routine operation that didn't work. When he came out of it—and I didn't see him at that point—his head was swollen, his body was swollen and he was in a great deal of distress and heavily medicated. Then he went into a coma and it looked like he wouldn't make it. He had everything from irregular heartbeats to super-high blood pressure problems. Father and I were in the hospital with him almost every day.

At the hospital where surgery was performed, Whalen seemed to show no progress. After several days, his family placed a call to Dr. West who recommended they call West's son-in-law, Dr. Mitch Byrne. Dr. Byrne recommended an immediate transfer to Loyola Hospital. This took place just hours before a tremendous snowstorm hit Chicago. The storm would have prevented the transfer. That transfer, via God's help, probably saved Jack's life.

"Some people thought he wouldn't make it," Soucek recalled. "I remember I was exercising and praying about this whole thing. I was riding a stationary bike at home, praying and going through this, when all of a sudden I felt this unbelievably calm feeling and words which were saying, 'It's going to be all right. Everything will be fine.' From that point on, I just trusted that feeling. I kept going to the hospital, and he hadn't improved.

"Then, probably a week later, there was a sign of improvement and the doctors began to say he was better—all of a sudden.

I still can recall that he was still in the intensive care unit and his wife and son were visiting him. I walked in, and I've never seen a bigger smile on his face, and I said, 'Thank you, Lord.'"

Not long ago, Jack Whalen, fully recovered and vigorous, pronounced that Monsignor McDermott, in his 90s, "is just coming into his prime." Just coming into his prime at 90?

"Yes," Soucek said. "Jack is right because, with the founding of Haymarket and the expansion of Haymarket and the recognition it has received, the program is rightly attributed to Father's vision. People began to know Father. Father always had his constituency with the people he married and buried, with the families where he attended their wakes and baptisms. But now he is a national figure, having received a good many awards which would not have come to him earlier."

Jack Whalen never forgets that he is an alcoholic. At times he says, "Aw, I'm just a drunk." It's a way to make himself humble.

Discussing Whalen's involvement with Haymarket led to a conversation with Soucek about what makes an alcoholic or addict.

"Dr. West talks about alcoholics being people who have the seed for addiction: low self-worth, low self-esteem, people who don't think highly of themselves," reflected Soucek. "I tend to lean towards that. I call an alcoholic an egocentric maniac with an inferiority complex. When I say that, it means I want to tell you how wonderful and how great I am, and I'm hoping you'll believe it so that you'll convince me, because I don't believe it. The alcoholic is always trying to prove this, but inside he has the idea: I'm not worthy. I'm worthless. I have no self-worth or self-esteem."

Then alcoholism has no biological basis?

"No, I believe alcoholism has a biological basis." He continued, "But alcoholism—and drug addiction to some degree—combines biology, attitude, and environment. Let's take police officers, lawyers, doctors. You can ask them: Does the frequency of these jobs run in families? They will answer yes. So I ask: Is there a gene for doctors? They say no, there's no gene for doctors. There's a gene for intelligence. There's a gene that says, 'I have the capability of becoming a lot of things because I have a gene for intelligence.' So that genetic factor is there.

"Now, having established a gene for intelligence, I go to the environment. I'm in an environment, as a child, that includes seeing my physician dad going to a hospital, meeting other doctors, being exposed to medical books, having an office with a lot of medical equipment in it. Now I come to the point where I have this environment and maybe some attitudinal things. My dad lives a pretty good life; he cares for people, he has money. So now I have all these factors going on and, suddenly, I have to make a decision when I'm 17 years old, graduating from high school, to make the beginning decision about a career. Are my chances better than any other person out there that I'll be a doctor? I would say yes. So it's environment, it's genetic, and it's an attitudinal thing."

Is it a nationality thing, too? What about the old tag line about the Irish liking their booze?

He responded, nodding. "Countries such as Ireland, Poland and Russia have a higher rate of alcoholism than Mediterranean countries. When we look at these countries we find a low rate of alcoholism. Why? Because alcohol is not looked upon in the same way as we do in America. In America, alcohol is looked upon as something associated with John Wayne: shots and beer, rugged he-men who down their shots at the bar with a gulp, who prove themselves by getting drunk. Now when you look at the culture of the Mediterranean countries—the Greeks, the Italians, the Jews even—it's inculcated into their societies that alcohol is, in fact, a food. It's something to be taken at meals. A kid who's three or four years old in Italy, in Greece, may be given wine, which is acceptable. They don't see it the way we do as a passage to manhood. They see it as a normal process, as just a meal and having a glass of wine with the meal. Their rate of alcoholism is low."

"It's not an infallible rule of thumb," he said, "but a pretty important rule nevertheless. There's a kind of bondage-inheritance with some nationalities that are victimized by alcohol. Indians—or Native Americans, to use the politically correct word—have a tragic history of being lain waste by alcohol," Soucek says. "But that came within the last 200 years, introduced by the white man. Native Americans and Alaskan Eskimos have a very short history compared to other races.

"We have a sky-high rate of alcoholism in the black population. How did whites control the slaves? By getting them drunk on the weekend. They would work them to death all week long and then when the masters wanted to take the weekend off, how did they keep them powerless? Get 'em drunk. The same thing you see on the street outside, those bottle parties and everything—'here's your bottle.' And they'd all get drunk. They would take the bottles away on Sunday night, and the slaves would be recuperating. They wouldn't be able to go physically anywhere but back to the fields on Monday. Work your butt off until Friday, and here's your reward. Keep them under control."

He discussed how alcoholism can creep up on the unsuspecting. "No one sets out to be an alcoholic," he said. "He sits at a bar and orders a drink. He watches a ballgame, he has a second drink, he leaves the bar. Next day he will be down at the bar again, having a drink. This pattern goes on. The next thing you know he sits at the bar and instead of having two drinks as he always did, suddenly he finds himself having eight drinks. He may catch himself at that point and say, 'That's too much. I've got to watch it.' But then he will go back to the bar three weeks later and have another eight. He hadn't intended to have the same eight, because it made him feel bad, got him sick—but he had the same eight anyway.

"Then suddenly, this is the pattern that occurs and recurs: loss of control simply means that once I pick up a drink, I cannot predict the outcome. I don't know what's going to happen to me— I'm going to pick up a drink, and I'm going to go out there and get drunk. Or maybe I'll go home and be able to be sociable with my family or whatever.

"Then it comes to the point when, every time the outcome is the same, it's very predictable. I go to the bar, get drunk, come home drunk, beat the hell out of mom, scream at the kids, go to bed, and not remember it in the morning. I don't know what's happening to me. I know that something's wrong. I know I don't want to be this way. But when I go into that bar I suddenly find myself drinking, and I'm ordering a second, a third, a fourth, and I'm closing the joint at 2 a.m. I don't want to do that. I hate myself for doing that. And I swear off. I make deals and I do whatever I can. What's going on with me?

"I go and turn myself into treatment and I say, 'Okay.' The counselor says, 'You know what you've got? You've got a thing called alcoholism. It's a thing that a lot of people have. There's an answer. It's the most curable disease we know about. Here's the answer.' And he begins to tell me about the answer, and the answer is things like: You need to get dried out. Second, you need to learn a little bit about alcoholism. Third, you need to begin to develop a spiritual program of recovery, including belief in a Higher

Power. Then you begin to turn to that Higher Power. Some do it by prayer, meditation and going to self-help groups, and involvement in AA.

"Now I have a problem that I've been able to diagnose, and I understand that problem. I have a choice. My choice is whether I take my medicine or not. My medicine is the things I've just said: prayer and meditation, belief in a Higher Power, and going to self-help meetings, things like that."

Some alcoholics get sobriety on their first try. For others, Soucek believes, their real recovery begins after the alcoholic falls at least once, insisting that, since he now knows what's wrong, he can handle himself without the self-help. "I decide: Well, I'm not going to my AA meeting tonight. I'd rather watch the football game or fall asleep. Then I say the next night: Well, I made it last night, so I think I'm not going to go tonight, because I didn't need it last night. It's called rationalization and it's the thinking path that leads to relapse.

"Then it's been three nights now, and I usually don't go to a meeting on a Thursday night, so I'll wait until my next meeting on Saturday night. Well, Saturday comes around. Look, I made it all week without a meeting. I'm not feeling too bad. I don't have this craving. And I begin to rationalize. But I don't take a drink. I begin to do things in place of taking a drink. I get in a spat with my wife—and I don't take a drink over that. 'Well,' I say, 'you can handle that.' Then my boss reams me out. I can handle that. I get fired. See, I don't drink over that. A loved one in my family suddenly dies. I don't drink over that. Then I wake up in the morning and find that the car has a flat tire. Goddamnit, I'm going out! That's it! I've had it!"

As he talks, Soucek reaches for an unopened can of carbonated soda.

"I'm not afraid to open this can now, after a fight with my wife, after my boss reams me out." He slowly shakes the can. "I get fired. A loved one dies. The car has a flat." He's shaking the can vigorously now. "Now this can of pop is ready to explode. Now I walk in the door and my wife says, 'Hi, sweetheart. Guess what we're having for dinner tonight? Pork chops.'" Shaking the can dramatically. 'Pork chops! You know I hate pork chops! That's it! I'm going to get a drink!'

"This can of pop," he explained, "is ready to explode right now, after a steady build-up of tension. The value of going to self-help group meetings and counseling and staying in touch with people on the phone is that you can talk it out. What's mentionable is manageable. If I can tell you that my wife is driving me crazy, it's an outlet."

But don't we all need this—not just the alcoholic?

"Yes, we all need it, but the alcoholic keeps it inside," he continued. Pointing to the can again: "Outside this can of pop are all these things—family, car, job, wife, pork chops for dinner. Inside the can is pressure, anxiety, fear, frustration, anger. It's all there, ready to explode. This is why you read about a man sitting in front of his TV, reaching for the remote control, and his kid says, 'I don't want to watch that station, give me the remote!' 'No, you can't have it!' 'Yes, I want it!' Bang! He blows his head off. Over the remote control? No. The kid kills his father because his father wants pepperoni pizza and the kid wants sausage. It's not over the pizza. It's everything that has built up. Unfortunately, these are real stories and they are happening every day.

"Self-help groups take care of the build-up. They give you a place to go. Alcoholism is a disease of the feelings. Drug addiction is a disease of the feelings. That's what we've got going on here. And the way you deal with feelings is to let them out slowly, a little bit at a time, instead of waiting for the big explosion.

"The diabetic says, 'I know my condition is diabetes. I have to take insulin every day. If I choose not to take my insulin, I'm going to take the consequences.' In the alcoholic's case, 'I make a willful decision not to go to AA meetings. I make a willful decision not to associate with members of AA. I make a willful decision to buy my cigarettes at a local bar. I make a willful decision to go to a party where there's alcohol and drugs being served.' When I make these decisions, I put myself in a position where I probably will tempt myself—we call it mental masturbation. I sit there with my Coke on the bar, and I'm watching guys drink, and we're watching the ballgame together. They're drinking and I'm not, and I begin to mentally masturbate myself saying, 'Maybe one won't be too bad. I can handle one.' And I probably could. I probably can handle one, but the thought is there, it's festering in my mind: See, I handled one and nothing happened.

"So I go back to that bar, and I sit with those guys. Now maybe I've made another willful decision. Now I'm going to handle two. And before you know it, I'm back up to 16 and I'm out of will. Will has no longer taken over. I've got to drink, because I made a decision not to take my medicine. Self-will is not an answer to self will, just as not drinking is not an answer to not drinking. If it were, we'd have a lot more people sober."

He turned to the papers on his desk, studying them. "When AA was founded, it was not with the Big Book [*Alcoholics Anonymous*] I gave you to read. It was founded with people gathering together in a room to try to help themselves. They began to look at information they gleaned, which supported recovery. It was logical that they turned to the best self-help of all, the Bible, particularly the New Testament.

"Through sin we miss the target. Christ wants to have a relationship with us. Because by our sinful nature as human beings, we don't want to have a relationship with Him. We fight it. Our flesh fights it. The world fights it. The nature of alcoholism is disconnectedness, a lack of a relationship. I believe it's spiritual. Bill Wilson, the co-founder of AA, said AA is a spiritual kindergarten. Once people are in AA they will often say, 'I'm sober now. I want more. I want to define that power better.' So they go back to church. They become more spiritual, maybe more religious. Spirituality is a connectedness, a relationship with yourself, others, and a God of your understanding."

But does one have to be religious to be AA?

"No, there are atheist AA groups. But they have to subscribe to a Higher Power. What's that Higher Power to them? They say, 'My Higher Power is you guys, the guys in my group, my fellow atheists. You can help me.' But there has to be a Higher Power. It's a prescription of AA that we totally support, the premise that people cannot recover on their own. They need the help of others and they need the help of a Higher Power."

Can alcoholism be cured?

"Not as far as we know. There's a story that illustrates alcoholism to me," elaborated Soucek. "It's the story of the pickle. Where does a pickle come from? Cucumbers. You put a cucumber into some saline solution. Eventually that cucumber becomes a pickle. When? Is it the first time it's put into that solution? Is it after ten hours? 15 hours? You can't tell. It's the same thing with the alcoholic. When does that person saturate himself with alcohol to the point that involves crossing the line? Once you have a pickle, can it return to being a cucumber? No. Once an alcoholic, you're not

going to become a non-alcoholic. You may become a recovering
alcoholic, but you're not going to be a cured alcoholic."

It appears that spirituality, however you define it—power of
God, or a Higher Power, or the power of the group—is key. What
about the role of government as a secular force in dispensing
treatment? Is the money spent by government effective? To get
the answer, go to Anthony Cole, vice president of Haymarket.

* * *

Anthony Cole, born in Chicago in 1950, was reared in a
middle-class African-American neighborhood, the son of a railway
porter and his wife. He matriculated in Chicago public schools
when they were far better than they are now (Lindbloom High,
for example, was regularly cited as high in academic scoring). He
received a bachelor's degree in criminal justice from Jackson State
University, Jackson, Mississippi, along with a master's degree in
alcoholic studies. Cole never had a drinking or addiction problem
but was motivated by the experience of his uncle and others in his
family.

"I had an uncle who was an alcoholic, who was very bright,"
he says. "He got into college at age 16 or 17. He read volumes
and volumes of books, articles, and what have you. He was very
bright but he would drink. He did okay if he wasn't working but if
he got a job—as soon as he got his paycheck he would go out and
get drunk. He was never able to keep employment. He stayed
with my extended family. We had a building with my extended
family, with three apartments in it. We lived on the first floor; my
grandma lived on the third floor. He lived with my grandmother.

"I saw many people affected, other members of my family as
well as the community, by drugs and alcohol—particularly drugs.
I wanted to do something to help them. That was probably my
motivation, plus they had a little stipend at the time for graduate
school. So I said, 'Well, I'll pick up this degree. If I can get a degree and get paid for it, why not?'"

After graduation, he worked in an eastern Arkansas regional
mental health center from 1978 to 1982, putting about 30,000
miles a year on his car. Then he came to Chicago to work at a
community mental health center on the South Side.

"I got acquainted with a fairly famous psychiatrist here, Dr. Carl Bell," he continues. "He really gave me a good orientation on the relationship of addiction with mental illness." At the mental health center Cole was what he describes as a "one-substance abuse expert. I would take over anyone who came in and was diagnosed with this problem. I worked on intake. I would do the assessment and would get up the treatment plans for these clients and put them in groups where they would be helped."

Moving up the ladder in the addiction treatment profession, he transferred to the Englewood Community Health Organization, another South Side group. There he was promoted to manager and then deputy director for their substance abuse division. Skilled in writing proposals for funding for the organization, in all-important site meetings with state authorities, he became an articulate advocate. But there came a time in working for government grants when a bureaucrat asked if Cole knew how much support he had from a representative.

Cole asked, "Who?"

The bureaucrat named a state representative.

"Amazingly," says Anthony Cole, "I was concentrating on the governmental need of these programs without seeing the political need. He said, 'Don't you realize this is a government agency? That the money you're trying to get access to is funded by way of political bodies, such as the legislature?' He said, 'You need to talk to the representative in your district. You need to talk to your rep and ask him to support your efforts.'"

Anthony Cole's focus broadened with that conversation. He found that state representatives and state senators were not all good or all evil but intensely human, responding as all do to personal motivations, to criticism which might jeopardize their reelection, or to praise that might support them in their drive to move on and up.

"So I started going to Springfield," says Cole. He discovered that he enjoyed phrasing his agenda in words and ideas that caught the imagination of politicians. The fun, the wit, the irreverence of politicians who congregated after hours intrigued Cole, an intensely sociable man himself, gifted with superb manners, which enabled lawmakers to feel better about themselves as they worked with him for his agency. And in Springfield, he met more than lawmakers and their staffs.

"I ran into the famous Raymond Soucek. Sometimes he and I would walk down the halls together in a common quest, seeking to educate legislators about issues that concerned us. He was representing Haymarket, and Ray and I saw a lot of things the same way."

Cole then inquired about Haymarket and gathered information from his colleagues.

"I recall I went to the state, one of the deputy directors of the Department of Alcoholism and Substance Abuse—and made inquiries," he said. "I wanted to know who had the best programs. The state was always going to these centers and evaluating them. The deputy director said the best program could be found at Haymarket."

So Cole sought out Haymarket. He happened to fit Soucek's needs. Trips to Springfield and Washington, D.C. were taking time away from management (despite the invention of the cell phone). When Cole was hired, Soucek told him that he had to be the "outside man"—the one who was to be the face and spokesman for Haymarket, the negotiator with the legislature and Congress—a major government relations task that was indispensable for Haymarket's success.

And Cole became a fan of Ignatius McDermott. There is a legend at Haymarket: if you're there any length of time at all, you run into an emission of fiery temper from the venerable Haymarket founder. When displeased with a turn of events, he can kick cabinets, punch file drawers, and slam doors. He can fire people and has fired echelons, but everybody knows however, smilingly, that they will be rehired. In fact, their being rehired is not even mentioned; it's taken for granted. Anthony Cole, with the sweetest disposition any lobbyist for public policy has ever exhibited, has never been "fired" by Monsignor McDermott.

"So in that way," says Ray Soucek, poker-faced, "Anthony is unique from all of us. We've all been 'fired.' Not he. He hasn't even been put in the 'penalty box.'"

Cole uses the cliché that, however hackneyed, is utilized by many.

"Father Mac," he said, "is a legend in his own time. He's—well, I won't say how old. I don't want him to beat me up! But, at any rate, he is well into his—no, I won't say it. And he still comes to work seven days a week. He's an inspiration to see. He still has that level of commitment, that energy, that enthusiasm to help people suffering from addiction. If I take a day off or so, he accuses me of playing hooky.

"One of the first things you notice right away about Father is that he's extremely sharp, has an enormous memory, can recall dates, facts, names, and places in detail. He's also very charming. He meets people where they are. He calmly approaches people. One of his first questions is, 'Where did you go to school?' then, 'What were your parents like?' and, 'What kind of work do they do?'"

When does the fiery spirit come?

"We've heard from time to time that perhaps the state was making cutbacks on treatment funding. He's been very fiery about that, saying that's one of the last places they should be cutting, that these people need help, and they're not getting enough help as it is."

Where is he most compassionate?

"Probably with the women and children. In his ministry he started out with children, and he still frequently finds the time to visit the programs and units where the children are located. He sits down with the women and talks with them about their trials and tribulations and how they're progressing in their recovery."

Is he detail-oriented?

"He's a *doer*. He's an inspirational leader. He's not going to tell you to keep the place clean. He picks up paper off the floor when he sees it. He's not going to tell you to treat the people well. He does by example. He says we're privileged to serve—that's his phrasing. But he's not just going to tell you that; he's going to show you by how he comports himself in the company of clients."

About Soucek, the Haymarket CEO, Cole says simply, "One of my definitions of the word 'leader' is this: someone who you would follow to places you would not go by yourself. And Ray is a person I have followed, and I've done things under his guidance that I would not have been willing to do otherwise."

* * *

Bettie Foley is associate director of Haymarket Center. She directs its outpatient program at the Haymarket West facility in Schaumburg, Illinois, and in addition oversees administratively the court programs within Haymarket including: the alternative to incarceration, work release, rehabilitative confinement, Haymarket Institute (an educational training program), court outpatient, and those serving clients of Illinois' Department of Children and Family Services.

"I was born into the field of addiction," she said. "Both my mother and father were alcoholics. My mother was also a prescription drug addict."

Professionally, she began as a registered nurse, then turned to teaching where she taught substance abuse prevention. After teaching high school for almost a decade, she received a master's degree in human services, with a specialty in addiction counseling.

She worked with Soucek at a private facility, Addiction Recovery of Chicago. After he went to Haymarket she followed, in February 1990. Earlier, Monsignor McDermott and Father John Smyth opened up the postpartum program.

"They knew a law was going into effect," Foley stated, "on January 1, 1990, that said any woman who gave birth to a baby testing positive for drugs could lose custody to the [Illinois] Department of Children and Family Services. At that time, the state asked Monsignor McDermott if he would consider setting up a postpartum program. He certainly would, and wanted to see if he could focus treatment on pregnant women to prevent their babies being born drug positive."

The so-called "smart money" was betting that he could not prevent babies of addicted mothers from being born free of the influence of drugs.

"So the state gave Father permission, and Haymarket's prenatal program, the Maternal Addiction Center (MAC), opened in March 1990," Foley continued.

"We opened up the postpartum program at Haymarket Maryville, on the North Side of Chicago, on July 1, 1991." She took the job as director of the MAC program, with the title of clinical director. She took on the alternative to incarceration program, including the one where those convicted of DUIs wear red shirts for identification. By 2001, this program had provided services for almost 4,000 offenders with compliance close to 99 percent. Bettie Foley is active in a number of groups, including a state committee for women in substance abuse treatment. She is also actively involved with the state office of alcoholism and substance abuse, co-chairing a major subcommittee. In addition to supplying professional testimony to legislative and congressional committees, she received an award from a major substance treatment advisory board for her work on developing programs in alternatives to incarceration and special services to women.

"One story comes to mind [of] a woman who slept on the streets," said Foley. "She was the daughter of a prostitute. She had given birth to 14 children, had never slept in a bed, and never parented her children."

She was in and out of treatment many times. When she became pregnant again, she was determined to parent this latest child. When she found out that she was going into early labor, she panicked and used cocaine again.

"We continued to work with her," Foley continued. "Unfortunately, the state doesn't always see the situation the same as the treatment provider does. They gave her back two of her children when she wasn't ready. She showed up at the door of the postpartum program and asked for help. We brought her back in, and she thought she could make it but didn't think she could be a parent. We tried to encourage her, and the success of all this was that she could not remain in treatment, but we were able to walk her hand in hand, carrying her children, as she signed them all over for adoption. This is a success story because those children—all 14 of them—are in other homes today. The mother continues to contact us, and some day may find recovery herself."

Foley pointed out that many "graduates" of the pregnant women's program came back for its tenth year anniversary, bringing their children with them.

"Most of them are financially independent," she said, "and have made successful and safe homes for themselves and for their children, and have also been able to pass their recovery on."

Reflecting on her career, Foley expresses satisfaction in her ability, through Haymarket, to serve the court program and other services of the agency. She noted the program's ability to provide bi-lingual services in Spanish, Polish, and sign language. All in all, a thoroughly satisfying program in substance abuse, with particular emphasis in rescuing convicted offenders, pregnant women and their children, from the slavery of substance abuse.

She says, "Our clients do come back and tell us of their successes. They are willing to come in on a volunteer basis with the current clients and let them know what struggles they have been through. It is worth it in the long run. We also have had some of those who have gone on to get an education in the field because they have realized what all of this has meant to them. They come to seek employment at Haymarket or elsewhere."

* * *

Haymarket Center is a secular institution, despite its founder being a Catholic priest. Its aid comes chiefly from governmental sources, thus there is no attempt to force either religion or spirituality on its staff or clients. But there are ample spiritual resources, if one were to seek them. These include a meditation room which is set aside for quiet reflection, and a chapel used by Monsignor McDermott for Mass. The chapel is also available for other religious exercises and, once the altar is put away, serves as an assembly room.

Aside from Monsignor McDermott, the only staffer who has as his mandate the job of providing pastoral care is a powerfully influential member of Haymarket, a Protestant minister with a master's in theology and a doctorate in pastoral care, Reverend William E. Miller.

Bill Miller, director of pastoral services and special programs, was born in Chicago in 1943, an only child whose mother was alcoholic. His father, a general supervisor at the main post office, was "an obsessive individual, who just made you crazy, and a tremendously controlling individual." Miller was, in his own words, "a pagan." Hating his parents, Miller graduated from Lane Technical high school, then went to the University of Illinois-Chicago when it was located at Navy Pier, a murky finger jutting into Lake Michigan.

The university conducted classes in makeshift quarters. After two years, Miller transferred to Bradley University, in Peoria, and graduated with a bachelor's degree in building construction technology.

He joined the Marine reserve as a college student, spending his summers at camp, aiming for an officer's commission after graduation. He chose the Marines because, he says simply, he hated people, wanted to kill them, and the Marines were reportedly the best in that business. Also, the Marines were less authoritarian than the intensive discipline his father had meted out at home.

He found that he loved the Marines. Hatred of the world, the desire to kill, passed. Now, since he was engaged to be married, he switched from reserve officer's school to regular reserve. He married, went to Camp Lejeune, North Carolina for combat training, and then settled down in the Marine reserve in Gary, Indiana, where he was a construction engineer.

Miller married a woman, also an only child, who was as self-obsessed as he was. "And, of course, this was a real disaster," he said, "because we never had to share anything. 'Let's not talk.' Anyway, what happened to me is that I was married to this poor lady for five years, and I was a terrible husband. I was in the construction business then, and I worked seven days a week. I was a workaholic. I learned very early in life the fallacy that you're only worth what you do. I was still a pagan. I worked for a couple of architectural firms, then for a structural steel company as a detailer and estimator, then for a company building houses. While I was with that company, my life fell apart. My wife had had enough of my craziness. I don't blame her."

At that time, "We had the Nixon recession," he continued. "I'm in the home-building business and I'm at the front end, purchasing all the materials they supplied. Well, you know what happens when the economy does a turndown. The very first business to be affected is the home-building business. We had all those houses strung out that we were building—building 500 houses a year in Buffalo Grove [a Chicago suburb]. And what happens is like we just stepped off the edge—nothing. Therefore, what I have to do is nothing. Day by day I'm just sitting there reading books, because I have nothing to do. We've established all the pricing, we have all the orders for everything we purchased, but we weren't selling homes. The economy went 'pffft.'

"I'm still a pagan at that time. My wife left. She said, 'I can't take this any more. I'm history.'"

At that point he had a secretary who was a Christian.

"I was now in the main office near O'Hare. We didn't have much to do. We would have lunch, and she's telling me that I need to get my life together, and I'm telling her she's crazy. So we would sit and talk for long periods of time about God, about life, about what was important. She was real sneaky. She prayed that God would get me and, ultimately, He did. What faith requires is information, and I didn't have any information. She would keep dropping information on me. The result was that I kept getting more and more information and, finally, I ended up going to church with her."

This sounds like the beginning of a possible romance, but it wasn't. Miller, the single-minded workaholic, now became obsessed with finding a spiritual mooring. He started attending a small Bible-reading congregation in Arlington Heights [a suburb of Chicago].

"A guy named Harry Williams spoke one week," Miller recalls. "He spoke about what it meant to believe. I thought: I can't believe it; this guy is talking exactly my issue. Literally, I got in the car. I'm driving home from Arlington Heights (I lived in Chicago at the time), and this little conversation is going on in my head and it's like this: 'Well, Bill, what's your excuse now? Gee, I don't know. You know now that belief is not kiss your brains goodbye. Belief is deciding in favor of some information. You got plenty of information now, so what's keeping you back from making the decision to trust Jesus as your Savior?' Well, my decision was a logical one: to turn to Christ and allow Him to control my life, because I've done a lousy job."

Bill Miller took one more job in construction after his divorce became final. But he soon moved into church-related activities. One was a prison ministry, another a Bible summer camp, where he met his current wife.

His decision to enter the seminary came when an uncle died in the mid-1970s, leaving him $20,000. "Even though we had two children, and my wife, a nurse, wasn't working in a hospital at the time," he said, "it was enough to give her the faith that, 'yeah, we could do this thing.'

"I went to the seminary, Trinity Divinity School," he continued, "and treated it like a full-time job. I left working at the prison ministry, and I went to school. I would go there at 8 a.m. and leave at 5 p.m. like it was a regular job. People usually finished in five years; I took three."

Armed with the divinity degree, he took up counseling at a private addiction treatment company where he met Ray Soucek. Soucek came to Haymarket in January 1989, and Miller joined Soucek at Haymarket in February 1989.

Miller acknowledges that alcoholism is a disease but disputes some modern theorists who move it out of the area of moral responsibility.

"I feel that the moral responsibility for the beginning of all this goes back to the point when individuals were faced with problems, difficulties," Miller said. "They made decisions to use mood-altering chemicals to do whatever they needed done in their life in order to maintain control. The problem," he elaborated, "is that addicts try to be God by being committed to maintaining as much as we possibly can an absolute control over our lives, so we can feel good. That's the essence of all this. When you think about it, you're functioning under a job description that, in a loose way, is God's job description. God controls things."

Miller leaned forward at his desk and further explained the diagnosis.

"We're trying to be God. And the result of our trying to be God gets us into all kinds of trouble. Therefore, in that process, what we've done is that we've allowed lower powers full control over our lives. The chemicals have acted as a lower power in our lives, and they've controlled us. So we need to have someone or something that is greater than our lives come in and control those powers."

He says the most difficult thing for pagans—and some believers as well—is to understand a basic truth. It is "the fact that Christ has paid for all of our sins. Christ has paid it all. Therefore, we have the opportunity to enter into a relationship with God—and God is not sitting there judging us. In fact, I like to take this as a picture. What we have is that we are like little children. When your children are young and they're learning to walk, what happens is they get up and you say, 'Come on, come on!' They take two steps and they flop. Our response is not, 'Let's order a wheelchair, the kid will never walk.' What we say is, 'Wonderful! Great!' Are they walking well? No. They have failed in the process, but our goal is to see them walk more effectively and, therefore, we encourage them. What happens is: Jesus has paid for all our sins. We flop, using the expression I applied to toddlers, when we act independently of Him."

Miller approached the theological argument, initiated by Martin Luther, that salvation comes from faith alone rather than good works.

Miller continued, "What it [Luther's faith argument] amounts to is that it's your motive and your method. If my motive is to gain points with God, I'm operating under a performance-based acceptance. But the fact is that the reason I do good works is not because I'm trying to build 'Brownie points' with God. I'm doing good works because first, that's what God has created me for and, second, it's a fun thing; it is really enjoyable.

"For example, in my lectures, I do three lectures on spirituality. I take the steps of AA. I can take the steps of AA, and I can tell you what they mean Biblically. I don't tell the clients I'm doing that. For example, take the third step: '[We] made a decision to turn our will and our lives over to the care of God as we understand Him.' That's what AA says."

There's the core theology of belief in this, Miller says.

When a client comes to Haymarket, it takes normally from three to five days to drain alcohol out of his system. One exception is the person who may have been drinking heavily for 20 to 30 years on a daily basis. One client didn't come out of the fog for three weeks. In the old days of incarceration, the sobered-up offender would leave—to become drunk again.

"What we try to do," explained Miller, "is try to encourage them to stay for treatment. We try to evaluate their motivation to change. Sometimes a person is here only because he wants the pain to stop. Okay, pain stops and I'm out of here. But we know theologically that human beings have a free will that is inviolable. Even God will not overrule a human's free will. That's the reason we do all kinds of stupid, crazy, self-destructive things. Does God want me to do that? Absolutely not. But He has given man a free will. And the beauty of a free will is that when we choose to love Him it is not a phony, fallacious thing. It's genuinely a decision of *ours* not His. He has not programmed us in this way. He has programmed us to be in need, to be searching for love. But the truth is He's the only one who can meet our love's needs. That's because He loves us so unconditionally, and no human being can love us unconditionally, completely."

Miller has strong beliefs on why some treatments of addiction fail. "The reason often is," he said, "because nobody ever tells the client about his need for a relationship with God and what the [12] steps really mean. Therefore, the client continues to fail and no one understands why."

A national problem, Miller feels, is that, increasingly, individualism allied with antiseptic secularism has raised impossible expectations.

"We expect people to act godly without God," he proposed. "Well, that's crazy. And that's what we have. We have all these people running around who are supposedly open to all kinds of thought. But they're not open to anything. They're open to everything except God's truth. And they refuse to listen to this. You can be an American Indian believing in Shamanism, or someone who believes in all other religions of the world. But if you come in and say you believe in Jesus Christ, you're immediately a bigot, a squirrel, a crazy. You're a religious fanatic, and you need to be exorcised."

Discussing the spirituality of fighting addiction, Miller said, "What happens frequently is that the Church has turned Christianity into a burden. But that's what Jesus zapped the Pharisees about. The Pharisees had made life with God an awful, miserable mess. They had all these rules and regulations and made people's lives horrid. And Jesus was out there with the Uzi blasting them. If you read the gospels, that's what's really going on. And what God really wants is, He just—Tom, you know what?—God loves you. He loves me. And all He wants us to do is hold Him by the hand and walk along and have a good time. Whatever needs to be done, He'll do through us. Therefore, the good works that Ephesians 2 talks about—that He has created us before the foundations of the world—are the works that He will do through us if we just stay vitally connected to Him."

Propelled by his ideas, he walks over to the window. "What about our moral imperfections? What does God want of me? God has got us in a training program. It is a boot camp for eternity, and what He's trying to train us to do is to stop functioning independent of Him and depend on Him.

"For example, in Revelation [Chapters] 1 and 3, Jesus has given to the apostle John, essentially, messages to seven churches. And to the last church, Laodicea, He says, 'To him who overcomes, I will.' Huh? What is He talking about? It's real hard to figure out. But here He makes a very interesting statement. This is Jesus speaking now. 'To him who overcomes, I will give the right to sit on my throne, just as I have overcome and sat down on my Father's throne.' [Rev. 3:21] Bingo! What's He talking about here?

"When you leave out all the throne-sitting stuff, He says, 'To him who overcomes as I have overcome.' That's Jesus speaking now. What did He overcome? Well, when you go back to the gos-

pels you have the temptations of Christ, the crucifixion stories—
particularly the scene in the garden of Gethsemane. If you take a
look at these things, what did Jesus overcome? Well, in each instance—Matthew [Chapter] 4, Luke [Chapter] 4—the temptation
is to act independent of the Father. When Satan tempts Him to
turn stones into bread, what's wrong with that? What's wrong
with turning stones into bread? Ah, there's one problem. Who's
calling the shot? Satan! Jesus responds, 'Man shall not live by
bread alone, but by every word that comes out of the mouth of
God,' quoting Deuteronomy [Chapter] 8:3.

"What's really happening is that Jesus says this: 'There are
those who are able to overcome the temptation to act independent of the Father, just as I have overcome the temptation to act
independent of the Father.' Therefore, the training program is to
get us to be able to learn how to trust God and to act dependent
on Him—exactly the flip side of what the world says.

"The world says 'Be your own person, be independent, act independent.' God wants us to become more dependent not more
independent. And that if you want a definition of sin, here it is:
acting independent of the Father. Jesus never acted independent of
the Father because He never sinned. And that's what God wants
us to learn how to do." That's gospel evangelism with a modern
application: a contrast from the hierarchical church of Ignatius
McDermott, but one that proclaims the rich diversity of the team
he built.

The idea of "putting a net around the United States" and
waging "a war on drugs" by blocking the interdiction of drugs is,
to Miller's way of thinking, a gigantic waste of money. "What we
ought to be doing is putting all our efforts into drying up the demand for drugs. By convincing people that there's a better way to
live, which AA and Narcotics Anonymous have always been about.
It's the idea that what we do is help people come to realize the
fact that drugs are not going to solve any problems—and then
help those who are caught in this thing to get treatment."

* * *

Providing that treatment is what Haymarket is all about. Susan Basile McKnight is the top staffer who deals with all
Haymarket programs that are non-clinical in nature. These include central intake (which takes admissions and makes assess-

ments), supervising case management, medical services, the day care center, utilization review, research, clinical records, quality assurance and licensing.

The alcoholic or addict enters Haymarket through the detox process. "There you'd sleep it off," said Basile McKnight briskly. "They would give you meals. They would take care of you to see if you had any physical problems. If there were, and you needed medical care, we'd send you to the hospital—Mount Sinai or Cook County or Presbyterian-St. Luke's. Of course, if there's an emergency we'd send you out by 911."

Barring the medical emergency, the client comes in, sleeps it off, and gets some food.

"Then," Basile McKnight said, "if you decide you're going to stay and want treatment, we assess you. The assessment department determines what level of care you need, meaning this: would you need outpatient, intensive outpatient, or residential recovery? What would you need specifically? Depending on whether or not there is a slot immediately available for you, you'd either go into that program or you'd go to a wait list.

"Usually, in cold weather there is a longer wait list than in warm weather," Basile McKnight explained. "Sometimes it depends on funding sources. If our public funding is running out, which it has a tendency to do at the end of the fiscal year, there's a longer wait list to get in for non-funded beds."

Residential treatment runs between 20 to 28 days. So people on the wait list are not just, according to Basile McKnight, "hanging around. Clients can come to Haymarket for a free meal and can get group services. But it wouldn't be actual treatment services. More of an intervention. We try to base everyone's stay here on an individual need. But if while you're here we realize: this guy's got a lot more problems than we thought, we discuss that with you. On the other hand, if you're really progressing well with your treatment, we can say: 'You know what? We think this guy might be able to make it in intensive outpatient.' Then we'll change the level of care."

Basile McKnight, 40-ish, has a master's in public health from the University of Illinois School of Medicine and School of Public Health as well as a bachelor's in elementary education. She has been in the field of addiction services for more than 22 years, has worked in about six or seven different places—mostly private-sector posts dependent on public funding. She is avidly concerned that there is too little money for research. If there were money, it could be used to track Haymarket drop-ins and follow Haymarket graduates. Her interest in alcoholism is personal—and her personal experience deeply influences the care that she imparts as she performs her job.

With an Italian mother and English father, she took Italian as her dominant character. As such, in a family to which alcohol was a festive part of life, she started drinking wine at age 3.

"They had no problem with the drinking," she said. "My mother used to keep the Mogen David up on the second shelf in the pantry, where she thought I couldn't get it. But what I would do is pull out the shelves of the cabinet, use them as steps, reach over and grab the Mogen David and drink it. I would know enough not to drink too much where she would catch me. If it was near the end of the bottle, I wouldn't touch it."

There was always a lot of tension in her family and she felt the wine gave her "the feeling of calmness."

The alcohol-induced calm was welcomed.

"In the household—in the same apartment—were my grandmother, my mother, father, sister, my mother's brother—who hated my father—and my mother's sister, who hated my father," she continued. "All together, in the same apartment, not the same building—the same apartment. Plus my mother's sister's daughter. Eight in a seven-room apartment in the Ravenswood-Uptown section of Chicago. And then my mother's other sister, who couldn't stand my father either, was married and lived around the corner from us. She and her husband would come over every night for dinner. We kids weren't allowed to say anything at the dinner table. And upstairs lived a bunch of my cousins. My uncle owned the building, and he lived on the first floor.

"So there was always this tension growing up, so I knew that the wine would make me feel calmer. As I got older, I wasn't drinking until I got into college. For the most part, I always felt like I had to be a real good kid at home."

Basile McKnight's father was an alcoholic and her mother was a seriously depressed, diagnosed psychotic. Experience with AA led Basile McKnight to appreciate "a Higher Power that would, could, and did save me and want what's best for me."

Is religion requisite for those suffering from addiction or depression?

"I don't know if it's so much a religion as it is a spiritual belief and belief in a Higher Power," Basile McKnight replied to that question. "Not only just a Higher Power. I've always believed in

God. I didn't know if I was crazy like my mom or alcoholic like my dad. I didn't want to be either. I never doubted that a Higher Power could restore me to sanity, but I always doubted that He would because I didn't see myself as being worthy enough for Him to do that."

Basile McKnight sees Catholicism as a system whereby one is able to "buy favors and buy your way into heaven"—something most Catholic theologians would seriously dispute—but to her it was "very harmful. But I think everyone in life needs to have that belief—certainly not just anybody who is suffering from any kind of mental illness or from any kind of addiction but every human being needs a Higher Power."

Sometimes she talks to her staff as friend-to-friend about this. "They'll say to me, 'I just don't know if I should accept this new position or not.' I'll say to them, 'Do you believe in God?' Yes. 'Do you believe in a Power that's greater?' Yes. 'Do you pray?' Yes. 'Why don't you go home and pray on it?'"

While Basile McKnight doesn't deal directly with clients, and her staff does not seek to convert or bring to their cases any particular religious beliefs, affiliation with a Higher Power is indispensable to the treatment, she says. Belief in Jesus—although she passionately holds it—is not necessary to do a good job in one's work at Haymarket. But belief in a Higher Power is. However, for Basile McKnight, belief that Jesus Christ "is my personal savior" is primary for herself.

Can she remember the day and date that she accepted Christ?

"I can't name the day and date, but I know what the circumstances were," she responded. "I was going through my second divorce. I was in turmoil—whether or not I should be doing this. What was I going to be putting the kids through? So I went to see Bill Miller. For a long time—years—I kept thinking: I want to know more about Jesus."

In a further response to a question about the success rate at Haymarket: "First of all, there's no money to provide research because we'd have to be calling people at home, seeing whether or not they are still clean. Second, it's really a skewed vision of defining success that way. For instance, when you take a look at [people with addictions] you have to take into account the whole person. The drinking is something you can point a finger at, but you should also take a look at how much they've been involved in illegal activities as a result of their drinking. How much have they been in debt? How much in terms of gambling? How much in terms of domestic disputes and violence, including spousal and child abuse? Have they been able to hold a job? Has their health declined considerably because of their use?"

It is this research that Basile McKnight would love to do.

"All we know about is people who come back," she explained. "This is a real tricky subject for people in the field. People not in the field think we're skirting the issue—it's like, oh yeah, quit pussyfooting around this whole thing. But it's true. We've had people who have gone through treatment. We don't know if they're going to drink in five years. If they do, can we say it wasn't a success? They stayed sober for five years, but do we say, 'No, that treatment was not successful'?

"At what period of time do we say it's a successful treatment? What we take a look at is the number of negatives, what we call the 'negative discharges' in the agency—which means leaving against staff advice. People who get angry and just say, 'I'm leaving.' The counselors will say, 'We really believe that you need to go into this other level of care.' They say, 'Forget it' and they're gone. But that person could walk out this door and have the seed planted of AA and of some kind of help, go to an AA meeting and never take another drink."

Perhaps when treatment receives more funds for more than just stopgap remedial efforts, Susan Basile McKnight, or someone like her, will be able to pursue this research. Her thinking on a Higher Power, looser, less Biblical perhaps than Miller's, far less formalistic than Ignatius McDermott's Catholicism, ensures a wide range of support for those in treatment. And considering that every Haymarket staffer brings his or her own philosophy of Higher Power to bear (some attesting solely to the Higher Power of the committed individual, sans God), clients receive a potpourri of intellectual-spiritual guidance in the house McDermott built.

* * *

When Monsignor Ignatius McDermott is down with a cold in his apartment and is confined there until it blows over, more often than not he has a small dinner with Mchugh. "I'll be 83 in February," said Mchugh, interviewed in January 2000. "He [Father Mac] says to me, 'When I was a kid, I used to wish I was old. My mother said, 'Don't do that. When you get old, you'll wish you were young.' He says to me, 'How true it was when my mother said that to me. I didn't believe it when she said it, but I do now. When I was 70 years old, the way they talked I was going to wind up in a rocking chair.' 'What did they tell you?' I asked. He said, 'They just said when you get old you'll just sit down or go to a nursing home.' 'Well it wasn't that way,' I said. 'Being around here keeps you going, keeps you young.' He says, 'That's what keeps me going here, Jim, I always got something to do.'"

On occasion, he gets a heavy cold in the winter. Jim Mchugh comes over. When he's very sick, Mchugh will sit in a chair listening to him breathe. "Then I make sure he has something to eat in the morning. He'll say, 'I don't need you tomorrow.' I say, 'Never mind what you don't need.'"

On Saturday and Sunday mornings, Mchugh is sacristan to Monsignor McDermott. He furbishes the altar at Haymarket—in a room used variously as community center and interdenominational chapel—for Monsignor McDermott's Mass. (Sunday Mass at 9:00 a.m. sharp is well attended by Center clients and an occasional journalist or two.) One morning, Mchugh washed the altar pieces including the paten and placed the big, unconsecrated host on it.

"I went out front and sat down. After Mass, I go back there and he comes in. 'Well,' he says, 'I'll tell you, you did it up good.' I thought that was a nice compliment, you know? Then I think it over as he's washing up at the sink, and I decide it's not a compliment. He says, 'I don't know how you got it on there, but you got it on there.' I looked up and I thought: Dear God, I forgot to dry the plate [paten] and the host stuck to the plate. So when he got ready to elevate it, it stuck. He had a tough time. So that's the last time I was an altar boy. But he looks up and smiles and everything's fine."

"Yes, when he's got something to say, he'll say it," Mchugh added. "He pulls no punches. We had a funeral in here one day of an old client who died of old age in here. You know how the priest comes down from the altar and goes to the front door of the church to greet the coffin? On that day the undertaker brings the coffin up to the altar.

"He stands there and says, 'Back it up! Back it up!' I wondered what the heck is the matter with him. He says, 'Back up! Back up!' They backed it all the way to the door. Afterwards he said, 'That guy calls himself an undertaker?' When the guy backed it up, Father said, 'Now you can proceed up to the altar. Come on, Jim.' So we walked back with it."

And always Monsignor McDermott goes out with car and driver to nocturnal visits at the hospitals, breezing past the reception desks to attend to the sick. Ed McCaskey, board chairman emeritus of the Chicago Bears, has had Monsignor McDermott as a friend for more than 35 years. "Father Mac is there even when you're not aware of it," he told the guests at the Haymarket Autumn Dinner Dance in 1999. "I still carry a note I found on my pillow in a hospital bed years ago. It reads, 'I was here at 3 a.m. You were asleep. God is good.'"

* * *

As a devoted sports follower, Monsignor McDermott has made it a point to get acquainted with baseball's big leaguers—including, on occasion, a member or two of the Sox's North Side rivals, the Chicago Cubs. One was Lewis Robert "Hack" Wilson, the Cubs' power-slugging centerfielder from 1926 to 1931, who, during his career, hit 244 home runs, averaging .307, totaling 1,461 hits with 1,063 RBIs.

Wilson, known for his prodigious drinking in his prime, told the priest, "You know, there were times when I'd wake up in the morning and have to get the newspaper to find out what I did in the game the day before"—the wonder being that the home-run hitter could have performed at all, befogged by alcohol.

Another time, Monsignor McDermott was introduced to Ted Williams, the famed Boston Red Sox superstar. "I've always hated you from afar," he joshingly told the startled Hall of Famer, "because of the times the Sox were on the way to winning only to be toppled by you."

Monsignor McDermott found Joe DiMaggio, the world-famous "Yankee Clipper," low-key, shy, and quite modest. "In life and sports, a winner has no need to brag," he explains.

CHAPTER 14

The Present and Future: A Reflection

We're so aware of a Max Factor, a Helena Rubenstein, and countless cosmeticians following in their footsteps who have erased the wrinkles of one's skin. But you and I know what is far more important is to erase the wrinkles in our souls.

—Ignatius McDermott

The life of Ignatius McDermott thus far has covered America for almost a century. The influence of the Teddy Roosevelt era has continued to this day. With it began the unique desire, which has continued through the 1900s, to put order into a frightening universe. There followed World War I, the Depression, the thrust of the New Deal, World War II, the Cold War, welfarism at home and abroad. But unparalleled progress brought with it spiritual illness and a loss of innocence which took root over these years. Restoring virtue—to make a great society also a good society— and reclaiming innocence is a promise to keep.

Along with widespread drug use that led many to addiction, it was the '60s and '70s that brought America to the pit of disillusionment and malaise, say a number of social scientists, reflected in popular idiom by David Frum.

While it is a mistake to categorize decades rigidly, the journalist-commentator maintained, it is clear that the 1960s gave birth to the aspiration for instant gratification in civil rights and world peace.

The 1970s saw this dream fall apart. The death of Reverend Martin Luther King, Jr., two years before the decade's start, had spawned nihilism and meaningless attempts at self-empowerment. The bloody Vietnam War turned into a quagmire. Violence came to the streets, masquerading as "peace." Watergate destroyed confidence in the electoral process. While Richard Nixon deserved impeachment in the estimation of legal expert David Schippers, the fact remains that he was forced to resign by a media *putsch* (his vice president having been forced to resign earlier, supplanted by the first appointed successor in U.S. history). Usurpation by the judiciary produced a Supreme Court ruling, seven to two, that abortion was a constitutional "right," precluding all state laws that had determined otherwise—a decision based on fallacious reasoning that even some abortion-rights advocates deplored. The oil embargo seemed to verify that the U.S. was a pitiful, helpless giant. The idealism of youth seemed to atrophy in the bleakness of Woodstock. Urban crime not only rose but seemed unprecedented in swinishness.

Sadly, the greatest change to come to the United States since the morose 1960s-1970s has been the death of a national innocence, if not faith. America is still a good country but most of us are acquainted, either first- or second-hand, with violent crime, divorce, suicide, abortion, welfare abuse, drug abuse, AIDS, and government scandal. Perhaps goodness will return as we struggle to fight terrorism at home and abroad.

This book, which began describing the era of Theodore Roosevelt, should near completion with the following citation from his *Letters*, written in 1909 (the year of Ignatius McDermott's birth): "The nation is in a bad way," wrote the president, "if there is no real home, if the family is not of the right kind, if the man is not a good husband and father, if he is brutal or cowardly or selfish, if the woman has lost her sense of duty, if she is sunk in vapid self-indulgence or has let her nature be twisted so that she prefers sterile pseudo-intellectuality to that great and beautiful development of character which comes only to those whose lives know the fullness of duty done, or effort made and self-sacrifice undergone."

The lessons of his innocent age need to be relearned by this one.

The shirking of personal responsibility has given young Americans unprecedentedly high rates of sexually transmitted diseases when compared to youth in other developed countries. The U.S. has the highest percentage of unmarried teenage mothers in the industrialized world. A higher percentage of American students, ages 15 to 16, use illegal drugs than in any other industrialized country.

Few have critiqued the current era more eloquently in mid-2000 than Dr. David C. Stolinsky, retired professor of medicine at the University of California, San Francisco, and the University of Southern California, in an article in *New Oxford Review*. Dr. Stolinsky, an observant Jew, views some of the excesses of our society as a surgeon dealing with an untoward hemorrhage.

"We remove the Ten Commandments from schoolrooms," he wrote, "then wonder why kids become amoral egotists. We give kids no source of transcendent meaning, then are baffled when they seek it in cults, careers, or violence. We discard the rituals of religion and patriotism, then are bewildered when kids search for meaning in the rituals of Satanism or Nazism. We no longer teach kids to identify themselves as Christians and Americans, then are depressed when they seek identity in black trench coats, gang colors, tattoos, or body piercing. We teach kids self-esteem instead of self-control, then we're perplexed when they develop a colossal feeling of entitlement.

"We give kids things instead of love, then are sad when they become unloving materialists. We try to be pals instead of parents, then are distressed to find that we are afraid of our own kids. We dose our kids with antidepressants and stimulants, then are appalled if they turn to drugs whenever they experience problems. We prevent smoke from entering their lungs, while allowing sewage to enter their eyes and ears, then are baffled when kids have healthy lungs but damaged souls. We disdain courage as too macho then are aghast when boys do not think it cowardly and dishonorable to shoot unarmed people. We no longer observe Washington's and Lincoln's birthdays, then profess surprise when boys observe Hitler's birthday. We start with euthanasia for the dying, then go on to the fatally ill, then the chronically ill, then the disabled, then the economically unproductive, then the depressed, then the annoying. The end result will be the total collapse of 'You must not murder' and the sinking of civilization."

If Dr. Stolinksy's review of the age is devastating, the judgment of social commentator George Gilder is more upbeat and an enduring validation of our needs. He says the task for the U.S. in the current century is clear: to redirect personal responsibility and sacrifice beginning with individuals and extending to institutions to build "the virtuous society." This has always been the goal of Ignatius McDermott.

What manner of man is he, has he been? A decade ago a newspaper columnist characterized him in blunt, Chicago-ese style.

"Except for our mothers, genuine article saints are something we don't run into very often around Chicago," wrote Raymond F. Coffey in the *Chicago Sun-Times*. "And again, except for our mothers, these advertised saints we do chance upon tend to be hard to take. They seem generally to be self-canonized, discomfortingly self-righteous and, well, a little too holier-than-thou. They are not often the kind of company you'd want at a ball game or dinner.

"We do have with us, though, one guy who is none of the above, who is no doubt going to be embarrassed by my going public here, but who is also—in my reckoning—the real McCoy when it comes to saintliness. He knows what he's talking about. Just 'warehousing humanity' in overnight shelters and putting people out the next morning only sets them up for 'playing a return engagement,' he says. 'People need discipline and guidance and to be treated always with dignity.'"

Coffey concluded by saying that Ignatius McDermott "is a good man."

"Yes, he is," he added, "and more than a good man."

What is the special essence of goodness and greatness of Ignatius McDermott, the apostle and friend to the addicted? He seems ever young, ever the macro thinker, ever the optimist.

His impatience with urban conditions was captured with rhetorical paradox by a homilist in 1931, five years before Ignatius' ordination.

"America, it is said, is suffering from intolerance," said Fulton Sheen. "It is not. It is suffering from tolerance of right and wrong, truth and error, virtue and evil, Christ and chaos. In the face of this broadmindedness, what the world needs is intolerance."

By that reckoning, Ignatius McDermott has been brilliantly intolerant of heartlessness, cruelty, coldness and selfishness. He rapidly demonstrated an intolerance with widely accepted conditions on Skid Row as he ministered one-on-one to those America wanted to ignore, intolerance with the law, which enabled him to press for the decriminalization of the inebriate, intolerance with unfeeling bureaucracy, which enabled him to shake the rafters at staid Catholic Charities, intolerance with his own well-being leading him to refuse a comfortable pastorate in the Hyde Park/University of Chicago area in favor of a rude pastorate of the Streets, ultimately creating for Chicago, at the age when some men retire, the enduring institution of Haymarket Center.

His intolerance was simple, rudimentary, utterly personal, broad-gauged, deeply impregnated with the true spirit of the Gospels. All the while some critics inside his Church were writing him off as a Lone Ranger. "Sometimes I thought I lived in a leper colony," he says of the earliest years.

When others of his generation opted only for governmental or political solutions, only he seemed to look clearly at the world, which was dismembered by its obsessions and factions—each faction claiming to be on the side of the angels and calling everyone else a devil. Spurred by media and false sociologists, they clung with mad hope to fanatical statist "solutions" whose only function was to foment violence, hatred and division. He alone seemed to be saying: will we never begin to understand the differences between such factions, which are often so superficial as to be illusory, that all of them are equally stupid? Only he seemed to believe the words of Thomas Merton, "For the world to be changed, man himself must begin to change it, must take the initiative, must step forth and make a new kind of history."

Such is what he did, through personal example and with Dr. West, when he created Haymarket. Honors have come in flurries.

Thus, as a promise to keep, Monsignor McDermott and his helpers at Haymarket vow that his intolerance and anger against injustice will continue. By becoming apostles to the addicted, many are joining the work to enable all of us to fight along with Ignatius McDermott for the good and virtuous society.

Glossary

ALLIGATOR [*n.*] A jibe at the late Mayor Richard J. Daley for his famous malapropism at a news conference: "They make allegations that aren't true. Always the allegations. What we gotta do is pin down these alligators and make 'em prove 'em." Those who make baseless political charges.

ARM [*n., v.*] As in "Put the arm on the guy"—either clamp down or force a special favor.

BEHEADED [*v.*] Anyone who was removed for political reasons.

BIG ONE [*n.*] Short form for $1,000, as in "Give me a couple big ones and we can talk."

CHINAMAN [*n.*] Patron of a city worker, from whose influence the worker got his job, as in "Who's your Chinaman? You know you gotta pony up for his golf outing, don'tcha?"

CHOP SHOP [*n.*] A hidden garage where stolen cars are taken, disassembled, and sold for parts.

CLOUT [*n.*] Political pull. Also a person with political connections, as in "He's my clout so keep away from me."

COLDER THAN A LANDLORD'S HEART [*McDermott phrase*] A frosty, uncharitable condition or attitude.

DEATH—THE MOST NATURAL THING WE DO IN LIFE IS DIE [*McDermott phrase*].

DOUBLE *A* PROGRAM [*McDermott phrase*] Alcoholics Anonymous.

DOUBLE CHIN PRODUCERS [*McDermott phrase*] Desserts, fattening food.

DOWNFIELD BLOCKER [*McDermott phrase*] As in "Who's his downfield blocker?" referring to a specific ally who aided a person to gain power or celebrity.

ELEVENTH & STATE [*n.*] Historic location of Chicago Police headquarters, as in "The word is he's hot at 11th & State." (Headquarters are now at 3510 S. Michigan Ave.)

ELEVENTH WARD [*n.*] Location of the Bridgeport neighborhood, but more specifically the home of prior mayors Kelly, Kennelly, Bilandic, and the Daleys. Although Richard M. Daley moved to a more posh location, he is still identified with the 11th Ward.

FIFTH FLOOR [*n.*] Location of the Mayor's Office in City Hall, as in "They really wanna get this done on the 5th floor."

FLOP [*n.*] A place to sleep and/or spend a night. As in "Hey, buddy, you got a flop for tonight?"

GOO-GOOS [*n.*] Reformers who want to punish machine corruption.

GOT OFF THE MAYFLOWER [*McDermott phrase*] Reference to his own advanced age status.

HEAVY [*n., adj.*] Indication that somebody has strong political influence, as in "He's very heavy."

HIT THE LONG BALL [*McDermott phrase*] To star in one's particular work.

HOOD [*n.*] Short for hoodlum.

HOTTER THAN THE HINGES OF HELL [*McDermott phrase*] Reference to heat—either summer weather or stifling rooms devoid of air conditioning.

HULA-HOOP CLUB [*McDermott phrase*] People who are out of date. Also, people who order rich, fattening desserts.

JUICE [*n.*] Originally gangland usury where instant loans come with a hugely inflated rate of interest. Now reference to person of clout as in "He's my juice."

"L" [*n.*] Short form for the elevated train, as in "I take the 'L' to work every day."

LAUGHING FACTORY [*n.*] Colloquial reference to any institution for the mentally deficient. Specifically, applied to Dunning State Hospital at Irving Park Road and Narragansett Avenue.

MAY THIS DAY BE THE WORST DAY OF YOUR MARRIED LIFE [*McDermott phrase*] Startling introduction to a blessing of bride and groom, which means that every following day will be even happier.

MILKING THE CLOCK [*McDermott phrase*] Stalling, dragging one's feet, or time's running out (aging).

MOXIE [*n.*] Skill and shrewdness in handling the problems of the secular world.

MUTUELS [*n.*] The facts unadorned by public relations or posturing, as in "I gave him the mutuels on Rooney."

NEVER GIVE UP ON ANYONE UNTIL KENNY BROTHERS SLAM THE LID SHUT [*McDermott phrase*] Admonition to keep on working until the undertaker closes the coffin lid. (Kenny Brothers is a famed South Side/Evergreen Park funeral director company.)

NINE-INNING PITCHER [*McDermott phrase*] One with staying power in his particular work.

NINETY-SIX PROOF [*McDermott phrase*] Description of a heavy drinker, as in "He came into my place 96-proof."

OLD SPARKY [*n., obsolete*] Colloquial description of the electric chair, as in "He's headed for Old Sparky."

PEARL DIVER [*n.*] A dishwasher at a restaurant—usually on the old Skid Row.

PINCH-HITTER [*n.*] Usually, a McDermott designation of a fine intellect, as in "He could be a pinch-hitter for Augustine or Aquinas."

PRESIDENT OF THE BAG-HOLDERS UNION [*McDermott phrase*] A gullible person left holding the bag.

SALT IT WITH GOOD CONVERSATION AND PEPPER IT WITH HUMOR [*McDermott phrase*] Admonition following Grace before meals, to make the dinner discussion lively.

SKID ROW [*n.*] Old designation of down-and-out section where drunks habituated and cheap saloons and flophouses were located. Traditional Skid Row in Chicago began at Madison Street just west of the Chicago River and ran west for about a half mile.

SLAVE MARKET [*n.*] Day-labor market where Skid Row denizens hired out as day laborers.

SOUP, SOAP, AND SALVATION [*McDermott phrase*] Referring to over-enthusiastic missionaries on Skid Row.

SQUEEZE [*n., v.*] To pressure. Also, the person who pressures.

STIFF [*n., v.*] A dead body; also avoidance of payment, as in "Do you think he'll stiff me for the drinks?"

SWINGING THE INCENSE [*McDermott phrase*] Adulation by those who idealize someone.

TAG DAY IN GLASGOW [*McDermott phrase*] Description of scruffy people, including those who attend Mass in leisure attire.

TAKE TWO AND HIT TO THE RIGHT [*McDermott phrase*] Baseball parlance meaning "take your time and act shrewdly."

TAP CITY [*McDermott phrase*] Reference to drunkenness; also, out of financial resources, as in "He was in Tap City."

TWENTY-FOUR KARAT OUTHOUSE [*McDermott phrase*] A garishly festooned facility that is not worth all its expensive furnishings.

TWENTY-SIXTH & CALIFORNIA [*n.*] Location of Criminal Court, as in "They're out to get this guy at 26th & California."

WORSHIPS AT THE SHRINE OF [*McDermott phrase*] Reference to enthusiastic followers, e.g., "He worshipped at the shrine of Knute Rockne."

YOU'VE GOT AN ETERNITY TO REST [*McDermott phrase*] His rejoinder to those who urge him to "take it easy."

Bibliography

Archival documents: Newberry Library Biographical Service; Peggy Tuck Sinko, Research Assistant.

Related manuscripts: Chicago Historical Society.

Interviews

Basile McKnight, Susan: 8/4/98.

Brown, Ellis: 1/2/01; with Luther Phillips.

Cardone, Samuel, Ph.D.: 10/4/99.

Cole, Anthony: 3/10/98; with Ray Soucek and John Whalen, Sr.: 6/4/98; with Ray Soucek: 12/2/99, 7/29/00.

Colemeni, Pasquale (aka Patsy the Barber): 11/19/99.

DiTuri, Robert P. (former state Senator): 12/28/00.

Downs, Robert (former state Representative): 8/20/99.

Flynn, Mary Ellen: 8/12/98; with Ray Soucek: 6/8/00.

Foley, Bettie: 5/16/01 interviewed by Ray Soucek; with Ray Soucek: 6/13/01.

Frum, David: 2/19/00.

Grannan, Thomas P.: 12/21/99.

Green, Paul: 6/24/98 with Monsignor McDermott, Ray Soucek, and John Whalen, Sr.

Kilbane, Sister Patricia: 8/18/98.

Loney, Mary Rose: 1/2/01.

Mallette, Reverend Daniel J.: 12/22/99.

Marovitz, Abraham Lincoln: 3/3/98.

McDermott, Monsignor Ignatius D.: 2/29/98, 4/7/98, 8/5/98, 8/13/98, 7/20/99, 12/7/99 (as well as unrecorded dinner conversations with him averaging twice monthly since 1997).

Mchugh, James P.: 1/4/00, 4/8/00.

McLoraine, Reverend John: 3/30/98.

Miller, Mary Jane: 2/2/01 interviewed by Ray Soucek.

Miller, Reverend William E.: 1/29/98.

Norkett, Reverend Edward: 3/30/98.

Our Lady of Peace class members (1941-46): Joan Furlong; Jack and Patricia Harper; Donald and Pat Kruse; James Littleton; Sister Honora [Gerri] McNicholas; William O'Toole; Bobbie [Mrs. Charles "Swede"] Peterson: 10/21/99.

Phillips, Luther: 11/13/98; 1/2/01 with Ellis Brown.

Smyth, Reverend John P.: 10/2/00.

Soucek, Raymond F.: 1/30/98, 5/27/98, 12/29/98, 12/7/99, 5/3/00, 7/29/00 (as well as unrecorded dinner conversations with him once weekly since 1997).

Sullivan, Reverend John J.: 1/31/00.

West, James, M.D.: 2/2/98 with Monsignor Ignatius McDermott.

Whalen, John J., Sr.: 6/4/98 with Ray Soucek and Anthony Cole; 4/8/00 (as well as unrecorded dinner conversations with Whalen and Cole once weekly since 1997).

Zlogar, Kay: 8/5/98.

Books and Secondary Sources

Ahlstrom, Sydney. *A Religious History of the American People, Vols. 1 and 2*. Image Books by special arrangement with Yale University Press, 1973.

Alcoholics Anonymous. Blue, 1939.

Alcoholics Anonymous: The Story of How Many Thousands of Men and Women Have Recovered from Alcoholism. Alcoholics Anonymous World Services, Inc., Staff, Third World Edition, New York, 1976.

Alcoholics Anonymous: "Pass it On"—The Story of Bill Wilson and How the AA Message Reached the World. Alcoholics Anonymous World Services, Inc., Staff, New York, 1984.

Alcoholics Anonymous Comes of Age: A Brief History of AA. Alcoholics Anonymous World Services, Inc., Staff, New York, 1997.

Alschuler, Albert W. *Law Without Values: The Life, Work, and Legacy of Justice Holmes*. University of Chicago Press, 2000.

Anderson, Brian G. "How Catholic Charities Lost Its Soul." *City Journal*, Winter 2000. Publication of The Manhattan Institute.

Barzun, Jacques. *Begin Here: The Forgotten Conditions of Teaching and Learning*, ed. Morris Philipson. University of Chicago Press, 1991.

————. *From Dawn to Decadence: 500 Years of Western Cultural Life—1500 to the Present*. HarperCollins Publishers, New York, 2000.

Bennett, William J. *The Index of Leading Cultural Indicators: American Society at the End of the Twentieth Century*. Broadway Books, New York, 1999.

Bloom, Allan. "The Democratization of the University," *Giants and Dwarfs: Essays 1960-1990*. Simon and Schuster, New York, 1990.

Bukowski, Douglas. *Big Bill Thompson, Chicago and the Politics of Image*. University of Illinois Press, 1998.

Carroll, James. *An American Requiem: God, My Father, and the War That Came Between Us*. Houghton Mifflin, 1996.

Carroll, Warren H. *The Cleaving of Christendom: A History of Christendom*, vol. 4. Christendom Press, Front Royal, VA, 2000.

Carson, Clarence B. *A Basic History of the United States*. American Textbook Committee, Wadley, AL, 1987.

Catechism of Christian Doctrine, A: Prepared and Enjoined by Order of the Third Plenary Council of Baltimore Together with Word Definitions, Prayer at Mass and Hymns. No. 2 Clear Type Edition. The Ecclesiastical Goods Co., Chicago, 1927.

Catechism of the Catholic Church, The. Liberia Editrice Vaticana, 1992.

Cheetham, Nicholas. *Keeper of the Keys: A History of the Popes from Peter to John Paul II*. Charles Scribner's Sons, New York, 1982.

Ciccone, F. Richard. *Richard J. Daley: Power and Presidential Politics*. Contemporary Books, 1996.

————. *Chicago and the American Century: The 100 Most Significant Chicagoans of the 20th Century*. Contemporary Books, 1999.

Cohen, Adam, and Taylor, Elizabeth. *American Pharaoh: Mayor Richard J. Daley—His Battle for Chicago and the Nation*. Little, Brown and Company, Boston, 2000.

Collier, Peter, and Horowitz, David. *The Kennedys*. Summit Books, New York, 1984.

Culler, Jonathan. *On Deconstruction: Theory and Criticism after Structuralism.* Cornell University Press, 1982.

Day, Dorothy. *The Long Loneliness: An Autobiography.* Harper & Row, 1952.

Dedman, Emmett. *Fabulous Chicago: A Great City's History and People.* Atheneum, New York, 1981.

D'Souza, Dinesh. *Illiberal Education: The Politics of Race and Sex on Campus.* Free Press, New York, 1995.

Duffy, Eamon. *Saints & Sinners: A History of the Popes.* Yale University Press, 1997.

Ellsberg, Robert. *Dorothy Day, Selected Writings.* Orbis, New York, 1972.

Flannery, Austin, O. P., gen. ed. *Vatican Council II, Vatican Collection of Documents, Vols. I and II.* The Liturgical Press, Collegeville, MN, 1982.

Fogarty, Robert S. *The Righteous Remnant: The House of David.* The Kent State University Press, 1981.

Fremon, David K. *Chicago Politics, Ward by Ward.* Indiana University Press, 1988.

Frum, David. *How We Got Here, The '70s: The Decade That Brought You Modern Life (for Better or Worse).* Basic Books, New York, 2000.

Gaffey, James P. *Francis Clement Kelley and the American Dream.* The Heritage Foundation, Bensenville, IL, 1980.

George, Francis Cardinal. "The Cardinal I Never Knew: George Mundelein." *The Catholic New World*, March 5–11, 2000.

Gilder, George F. *Sexual Suicide.* Quadrangle/The New York Times Book Company, 1973.

Glazier and Shelley. *The Encyclopedia of American Catholic History.* The Liturgical Press, Collegeville, MN, 1997.

Gleason, William F. *The Liquid Cross of Skid Row.* The Bruce Publishing Company, Milwaukee, 1966.

_____. *Daley of Chicago: The Man, the Mayor and the Limits of Conventional Politics.* Simon & Schuster, 1975.

Goddard, Connie, and Hatton, Bruce. *The Great Chicago Trivia Fact Book.* Cumberland House, 1996.

Gove, Samuel K., and Masotti, Louis H., eds. *After Daley: Chicago Politics in Transition.* University of Illinois Press, 1982.

Granger, Bill, and Granger, Lori. *Fighting Jane: Mayor Byrne and the Chicago Machine.* The Dial Press, New York, 1980.

_____. *Lords of the Last Machine: The Story of Politics in Chicago.* Random House, New York, 1987.

Green, Paul M., and Holli, Melvin G. *The Mayors: The Chicago Political Tradition.* Southern Illinois University Press, 1987.

_____. *Restoration 1989: Chicago Elects a New Daley.* Lyceum Books, 1989.

Gross, Paul, and Levitt, Norman. *Higher Superstition: The Academic Left and Its Quarrels with Science.* Johns Hopkins University Press, 1994.

Hardon, Reverend John A., S.J. *The Catechism of the Catholic Church.* Doubleday, New York, 1980.

Haymarket Center Papers. Presented at the 38th International Congress on Alcohol, Drug and Other Dependencies. Vienna, Austria, 1999.

Hayner, Don, and McNamee, Tom. *Streetwise Chicago: A History of Chicago Street Names.* Loyola University Press, 1988.

Heise, Kenan, and Frazel, Mark. *Hands on Chicago: Getting Hold of the City.* Bonus Books, 1987.

Hitchcock, James. *Catholicism and Modernity: Confrontation or Capitulation?* Seabury Press, 1979.

_____. "The Significance of the Papal Birth-Control Commission." *In Keeping Faith: Monsignor George A. Kelley's Battle for the Church-A Colloquy,* ed. Patrick G.D. Riley. Christendom Press, 2000.

Hogan, Reverend John B. *Clerical Studies.* Marlier, 1898.

Holli, Melvin G., and Green, Paul M., eds. *The Making of the Mayor of Chicago 1983.* William B. Eerdmans Publishing Company, Grand Rapids, MI, 1984.

Holli, Melvin G., and Green, Paul M. *Bashing Chicago Traditions: Harold Washington's Last Campaign, 1987.* William B. Eerdmans Publishing Company, Grand Rapids, MI, 1987.

Holt, Glen E., and Pacyga, Dominic A. *Chicago: A Historical Guide to the Neighborhoods, the Loop and the South.* Chicago Historical Society, 1979.

Jennings, Peter, and Brewster, Todd. *The Century.* Doubleday, 1998.

Johnson, Paul. *Modern Times: From the Twenties to the Nineties.* HarperCollins Publishers, New York, 1991.

_____. *A History of the American People.* HarperCollins Publishers, New York, 1997.

Kantowicz, Edward R. *Corporation Soul: Mundelein and Chicago Catholicism.* University of Notre Dame Press, 1983.

Kelley, J. N. D. *The Oxford Dictionary of Popes.* Oxford University Press, 1986.

Kennedy, Eugene C. *The People Are the Church*. Image Books, New York, 1971.

———. *Himself! The Life and Times of Mayor Richard J. Daley*. Contemporary Books, 1996.

———. *Bernardin: Life to the Full*. Bonus Books, 1997.

———. *My Brother Joseph: The Spirit of a Cardinal and the Story of a Friendship*. St. Martin's Press, New York, 1997.

Kilian, Michael; Fletcher, Connie; Ciccone, F. Richard. *Who Runs Chicago?* St. Martin's Press, New York, 1979.

Kimball, Roger. *Tenured Radicals: How Politics Has Corrupted Our Higher Education*. Elephant Paperbacks, Ivan R. Dee Publishers, Chicago, 1991, revised 1998.

———. *The Long March: How the Cultural Revolution of the 1960s Changed America*. Encounter Books, New York, 2000.

Kinkead, Reverend Thomas L. *Explanation of the Baltimore Catechism of Christian Doctrine for the Use of Sunday-School Teachers and Advanced Classes, An*. Baltimore Catechism No. 4. TAN Books and Publishers, Rockford, IL, 1988, based on copyright 1891, 1921, Benzinger Brothers.

Kobler, John. *Capone: The Life and World of Al Capone*. G. P. Putnam & Sons, New York, 1971.

Koenig, Reverend Harry. *A History of the Parishes of the Archdiocese of Chicago*, 2 vol. The New World Publishing Company, 1980.

———. *A History of the Institutions of the Archdiocese of Chicago*, 2 volumes. The New World Publishing Company, 1981.

Kwitny, Jonathan. *Man of the Century: The Life and Times of John Paul II*. Henry Holt & Company, 1997.

Lindberg, Richard. *To Serve and Collect: Chicago Politics and Police Corruption from the Lager Beer Riot to the Summerdale Scandal, 1855-1960*. Southern Illinois University Press, 1991.

———. *Ethnic Chicago: A Complete Guide to the Many Faces and Cultures of Chicago*. Passport Books, IL, 1997.

———. *The White Sox Encyclopedia*. Temple University Press, Philadelphia, 1999.

Levinsohn, Florence. *Harold Washington, A Political Biography*. Chicago Review Press, 1983.

Long, Dolores A. *The Chicago Trivia Book*. Contemporary Books, Chicago, 1982.

Magagnotti, Paolo. *The Word of Cardinal Bernardin*. Center for Migration Studies, New York, 1996.

Martin, Malachi. *The Final Conclave*. Stein & Day, New York, 1978.

Maxwell-Stuart, P.G. *Chronicle of the Popes: The Reign-by-Reign Record of the Papacy from St. Peter to the Present*. Thames & Hudson, 1997.

McBrien, Richard F. *Catholicism*, vols. I and II. Winston Press, 1980.

McCaffrey, Lawrence J.; Skerrett, Ellen; Funchion, Michael F.; Fanning, Charles. *The Irish in Chicago*. University of Illinois Press, 1987.

McInerny, Ralph. *What Went Wrong with Vatican II: The Catholic Crisis Explained*. Sophia Institute Press, 1998.

———. *The Red Hat: A Novel*. Ignatius Press, San Francisco, 1999.

Miller, Alton. *Harold Washington: The Mayor, The Man*. Bonus Books, 1989.

Miller, Donald L. *City of the Century: The Epic of Chicago and the Making of America*. Simon and Schuster, New York, 1996.

Morison, Samuel Eliot. *The Oxford History of the United States 1783-1917*, vols. 1 and 2. Oxford University Press, New York, 1965.

Morris, Charles R. *American Catholic: The Saints and Sinners Who Built America's Most Powerful Church*. Times Books, 1997.

Mundelein, George Cardinal. *Letters of a Bishop to His Flock*. Benzinger Brothers, New York, 1927.

Neal, Steve. *Rolling on the River: The Best of Steve Neal*. Southern Illinois University Press, 1999.

O'Brien, Reverend Thomas J. *Advanced Catechism of Catholic Faith and Practice, Based Upon the Third Plenary Council Catechism for Use in the Higher Grades of Catholic Schools*. The Oink Company, Chicago, 1929.

O'Connor, Edwin. *The Last Hurrah*. Little, Brown & Company, Boston, 1956.

O'Connor, Len. *Clout: Mayor Daley and His City*. Henry Regnery & Company, Chicago, 1975.

Our Sunday Visitor's The Catholic Almanac. Our Sunday Visitor Press, Huntington, IN, 1998.

Pallasch, Abdon M. "Courting Support, Illinois Style." *Illinois Issues*, March 2002. Publication of the University of Illinois at Springfield.

Rakove, Milton. *Don't Make No Waves...Don't Back No Losers: An Insider's Analysis of the Daley Machine*. Indiana University Press, 1975.

_____. *We Don't Want Nobody Nobody Sent: An Oral History of the Daley Years*. Indiana University Press, 1979.

Ratzinger, Joseph Cardinal with Messori, Vittorio. *The Ratzinger Report: An Exclusive Interview on the State of the Church*. Ignatius Press, San Francisco, 1985.

Reilly, Bill. *Big Al's Official Guide to Chicagoese: Translated into English for the First Time*. Contemporary Books, Chicago, 1982.

Rice, Charles E. *Beyond Abortion: The Theory and Practice of the Secular State*. Franciscan Herald Press, Chicago, 1979.

Roosevelt, Theodore. *Letters to His Children*. Charles Scribner's Sons, New York, 1909.

Royko, Mike. *Boss: Richard J. Daley of Chicago*. E. P. Dutton, New York, 1971.

Sautter, R. Craig, and Burke, Edward M. *Inside the Wigwam: Chicago Presidential Conventions 1860-1996*. Wild Onion Books, an imprint of Loyola Press, Chicago, 1996.

Sawyers, June Skinner. *Chicago Portraits: Biographies of 250 Famous Chicagoans*. Loyola University Press, 1991.

Schmidt, John R. *The Mayor Who Cleaned Up Chicago: A Political Biography of William E. Dever*. Northern Illinois University Press, 1989.

Schoenberg, Robert J. *Mr. Capone: The Real and Complete Story of Al Capone*. William Morrow & Company, New York, 1982.

Sizer, Theodore R.; Gustafson, James M.; Sizer, Nancy F. *Moral Education*. Harvard University Press, 1970.

Skerrett, Ellen; Kantowicz, Edward R.; Avella, Steven M. *Catholicism, Chicago Style*. Loyola University Press, 1993.

Slayton, Robert A. *Back of the Yards: The Making of a Local Democracy*. University of Chicago Press, 1986.

Stolinsky, David C., M.D. "Our Titanic Nonjudgmentalism." *New Oxford Review*, April, 2000.

Sullivan, Frank. *Legend: The Only Inside Story of Mayor Richard J. Daley*. Point West, Carol Stream, IL, 1989.

Sutton, Robert, ed. *The Prairie State: A Documentary History of Illinois—Civil War to the Present*. William B. Eerdmans Publishing Company, Grand Rapids, MI, 1976.

Swanson, Stevenson. *Chicago Days: 150 Defining Moments in the Life of a Great City*. Cantigny First Division, Wheaton, IL, 1997.

Teaching of Christ, The: The Catholic Catechism. Our Sunday Visitor Press, Huntington, IN, 1983.

Wattenberg, Ben J. *Values Matter Most: How Republicans or Democrats or a Third Party Can Win and Renew the American Way of Life.* The Free Press, New York, 1995.

Weigel, George. *Witness to Hope: The Biography of Pope John Paul II.* HarperCollins Publishers, New York, 1999.

West, James, M.D. *The Betty Ford Center Book of Answers.* Pocket Books, 1997.

Whittingham, Richard. *White Sox: The Illustrated Story.* Quality Sports Publication, 1997.

Woodward, Kenneth L. *Making Saints: How the Catholic Church Determines Who Becomes a Saint, Who Doesn't and Why.* Simon and Schuster, New York, 1990.

Ziemba, Joe. *When Football Was Football: The Chicago Cardinals and the Birth of the NFL.* Triumph Books, 1999.

INDEX